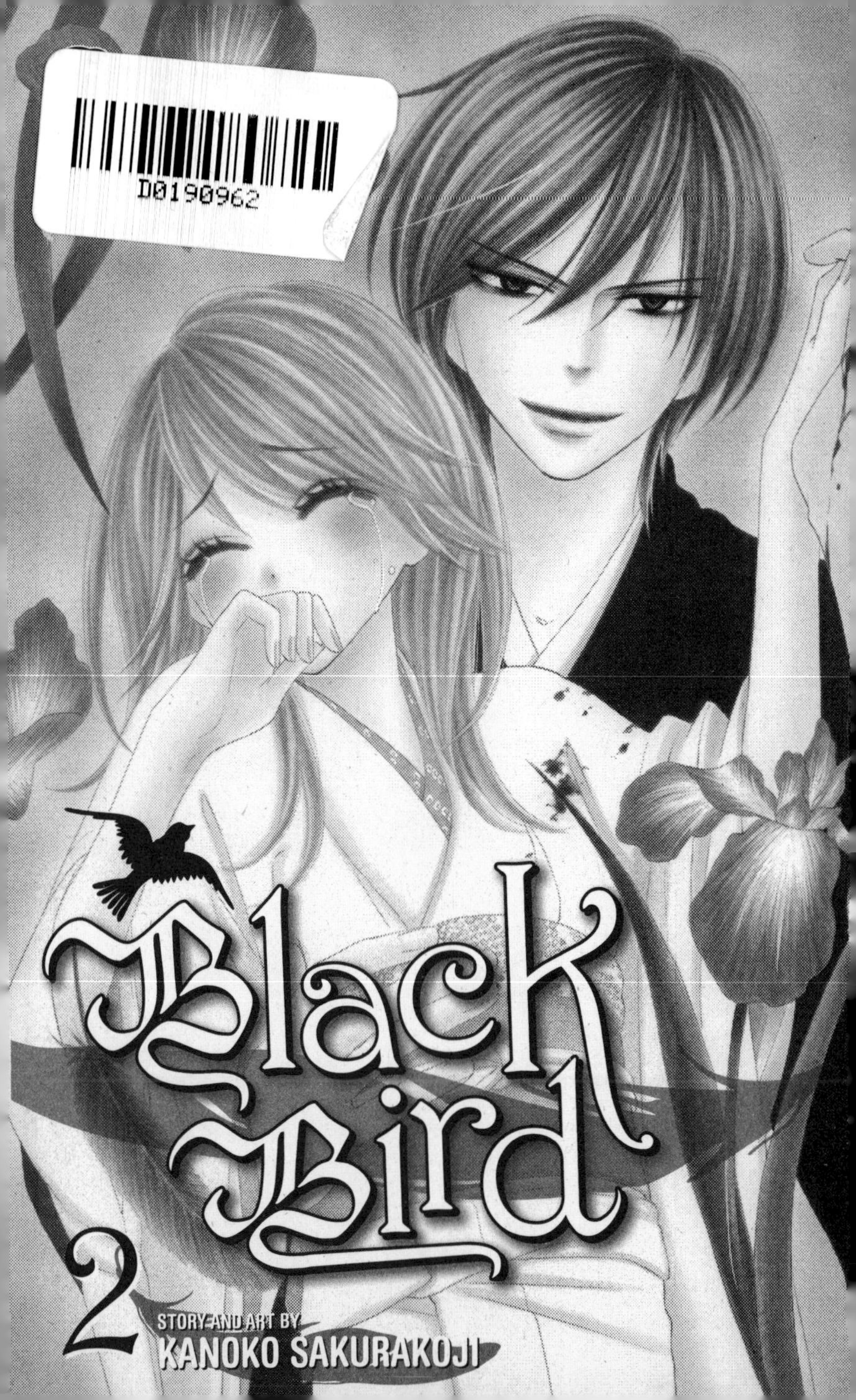
Black Bird
2
STORY AND ART BY
KANOKO SAKURAKOJI

Black Bird

CONTENTS

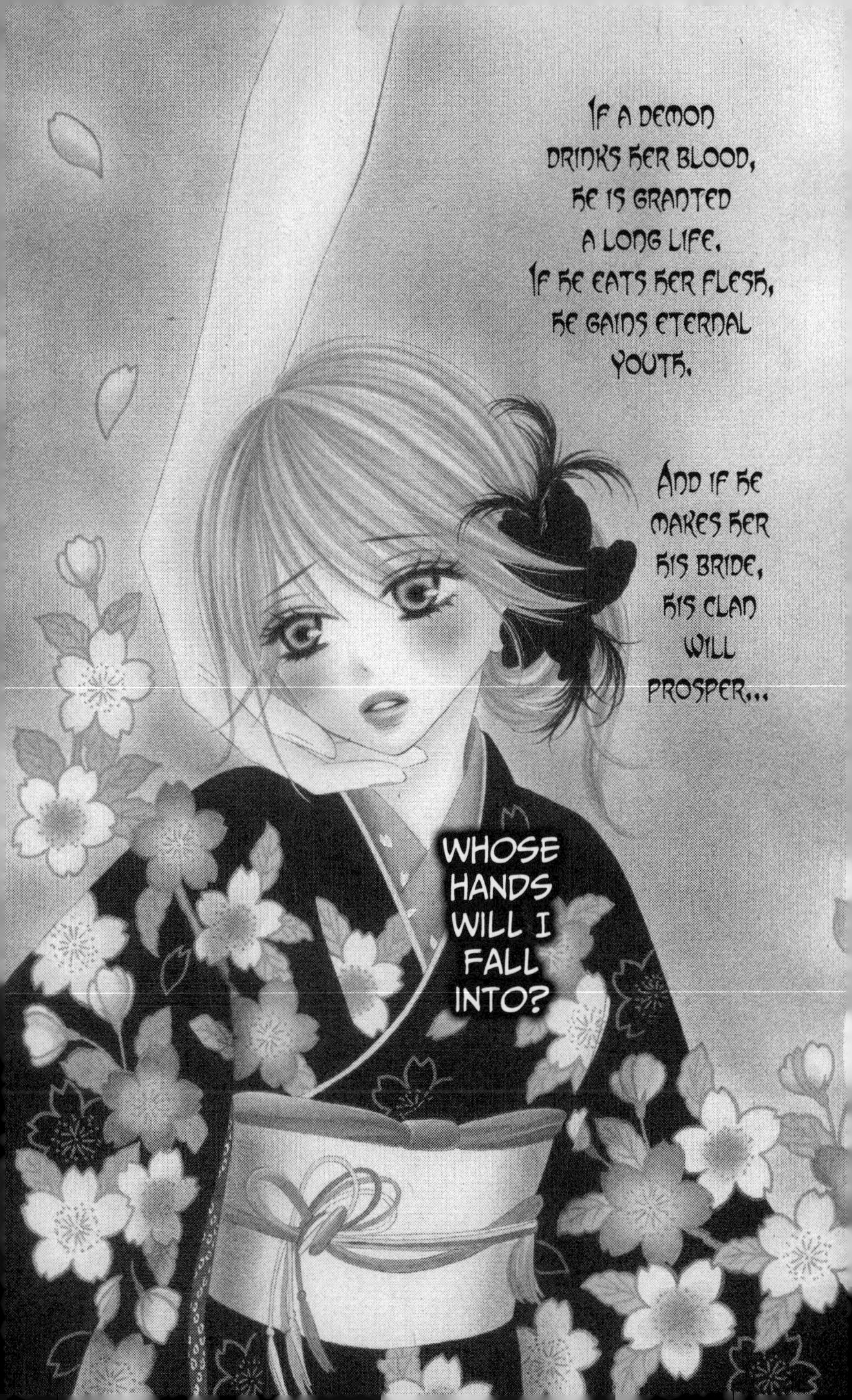
IF A DEMON DRINKS HER BLOOD, HE IS GRANTED A LONG LIFE. IF HE EATS HER FLESH, HE GAINS ETERNAL YOUTH.
AND IF HE MAKES HER HIS BRIDE, HIS CLAN WILL PROSPER...
WHOSE HANDS WILL I FALL INTO?

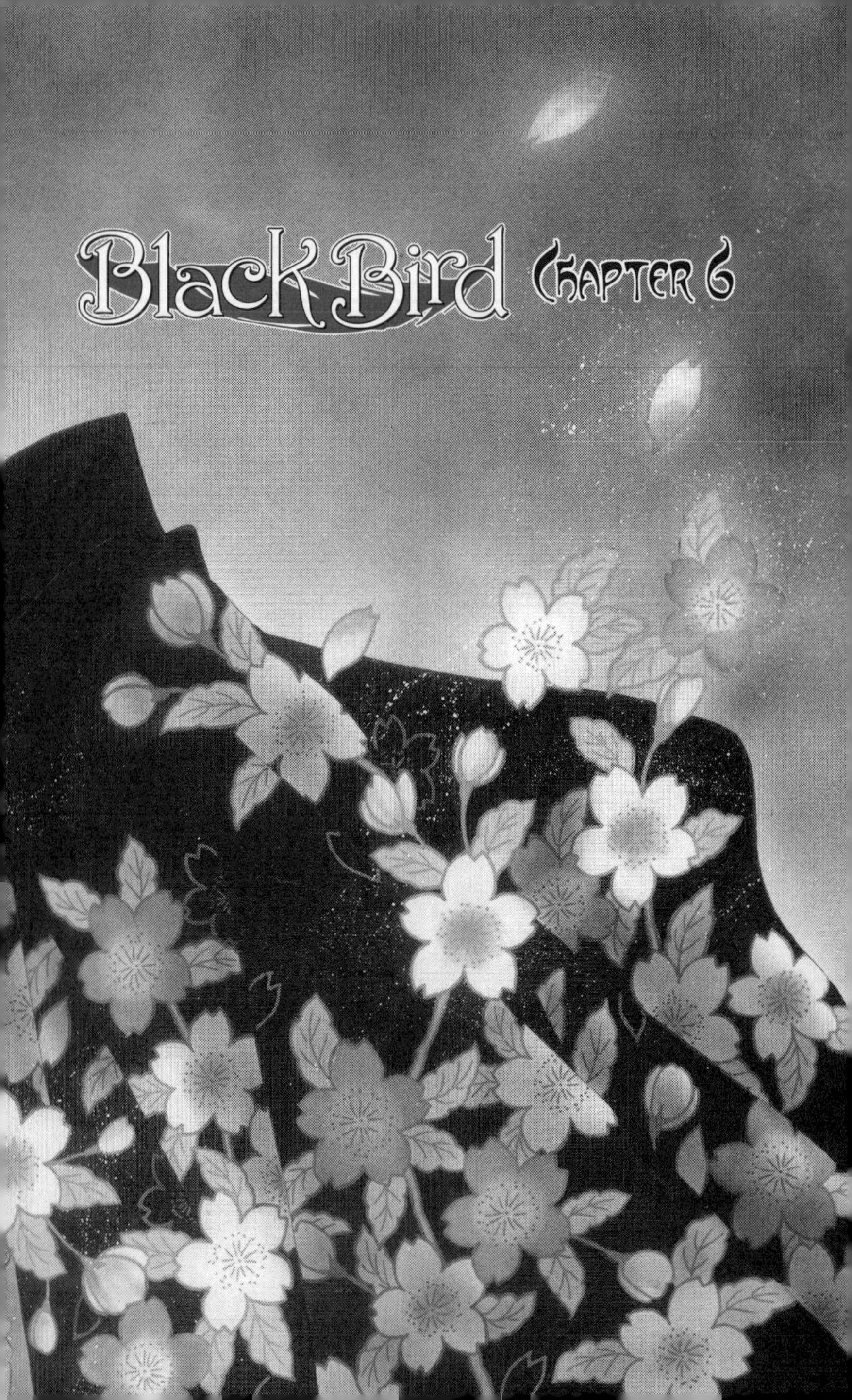
Black Bird
Chapter 6

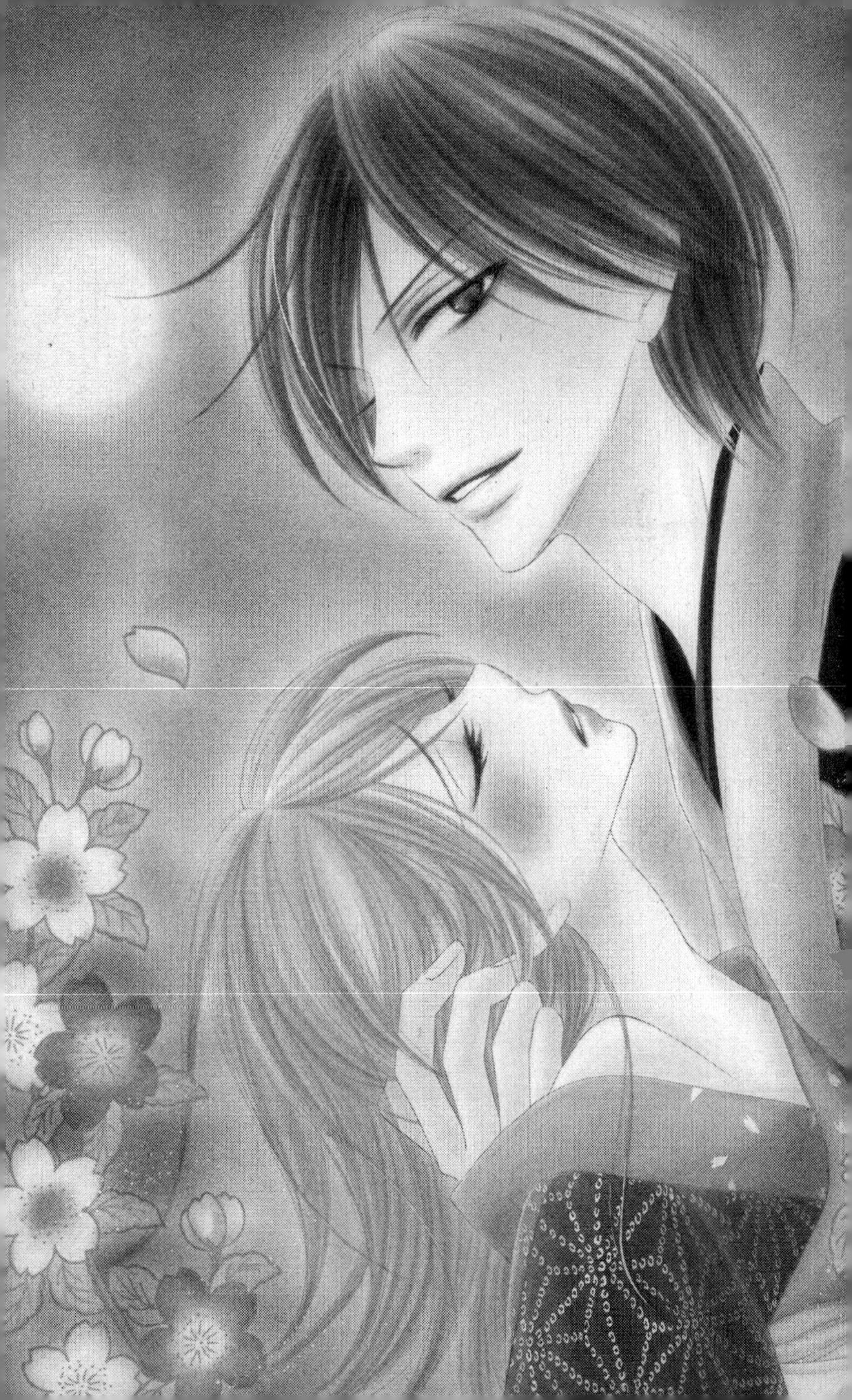

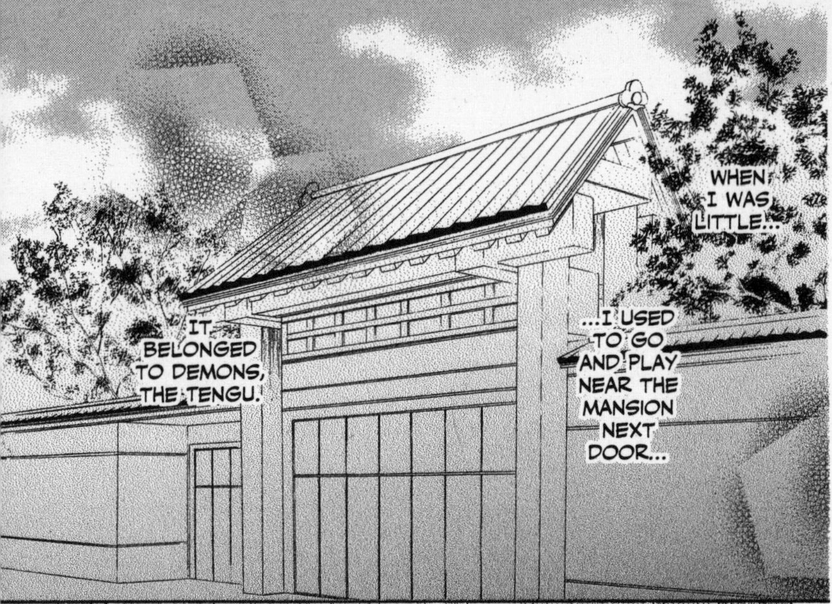
WHEN I WAS LITTLE...
...I USED TO GO AND PLAY NEAR THE MANSION NEXT DOOR...
IT BELONGED TO DEMONS, THE TENGU.

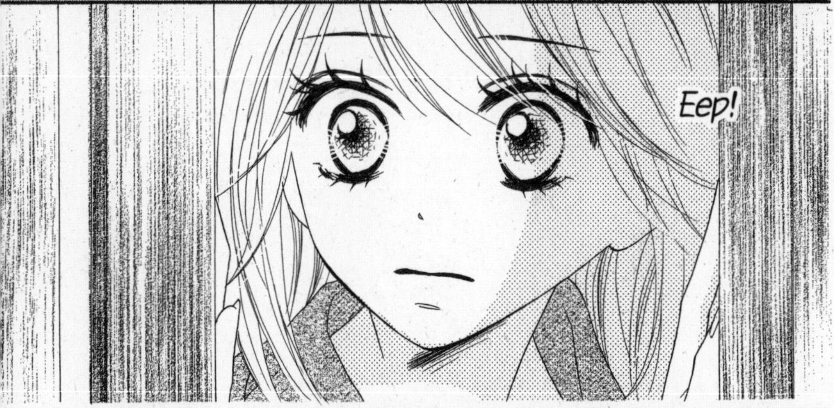
Eep!

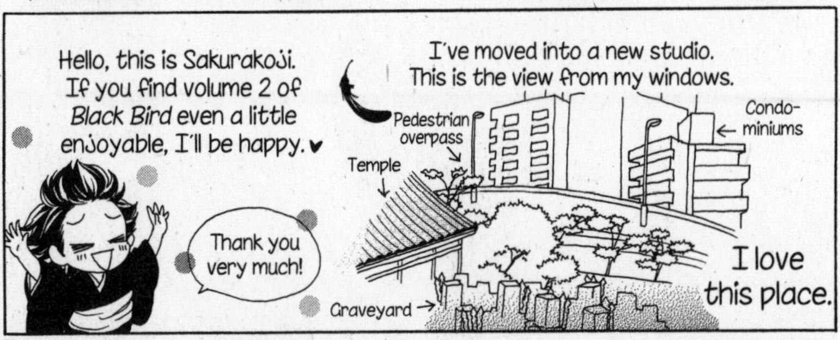
Hello, this is Sakurakoji. If you find volume 2 of *Black Bird* even a little enjoyable, I'll be happy.
Thank you very much!
I've moved into a new studio. This is the view from my windows.
Condo-miniums
Pedestrian overpass
Temple
Graveyard
I love this place.

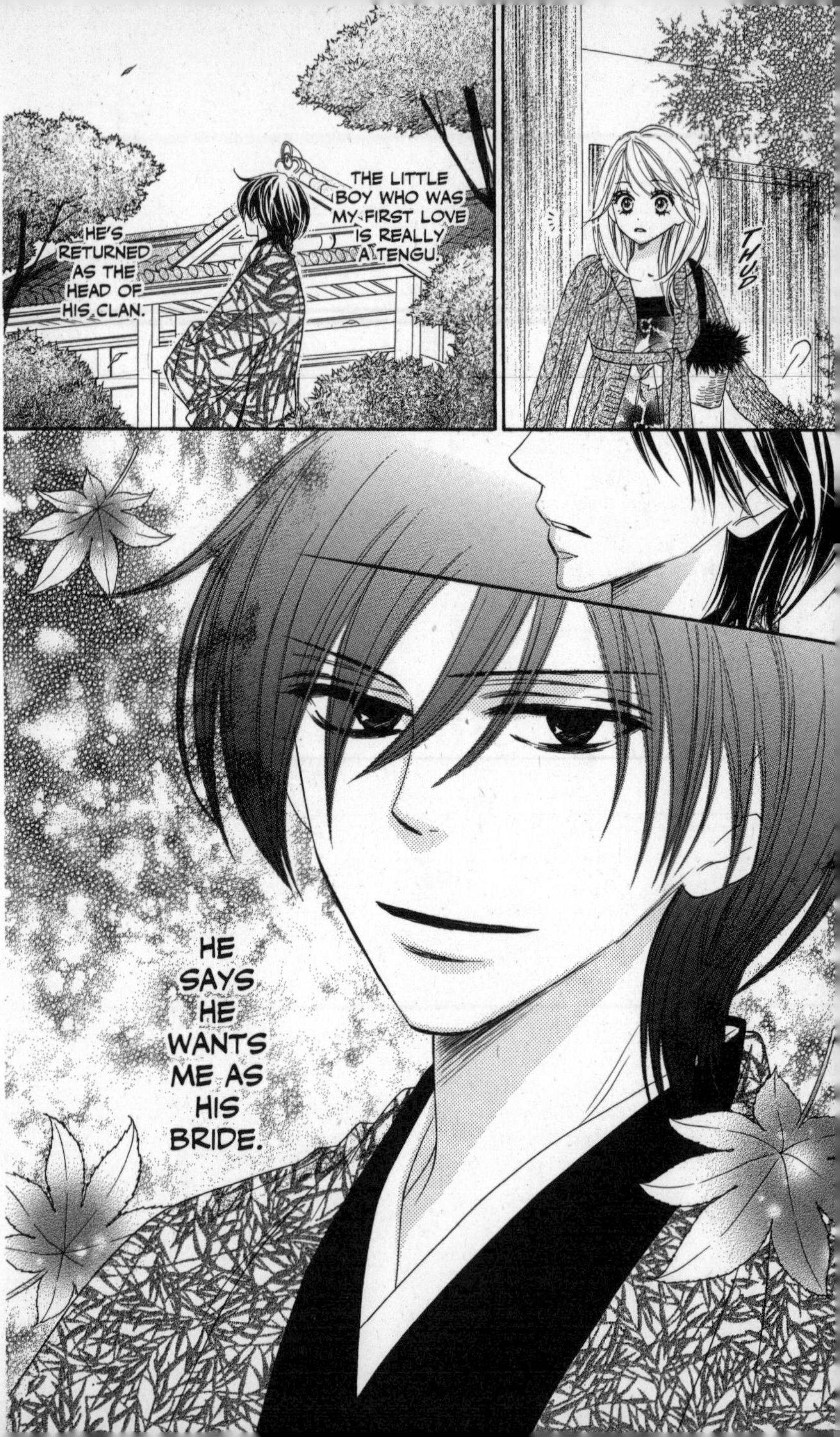
THUD
THE LITTLE BOY WHO WAS MY FIRST LOVE IS REALLY A TENGU.
HE'S RETURNED AS THE HEAD OF HIS CLAN.
HE SAYS HE WANTS ME AS HIS BRIDE.

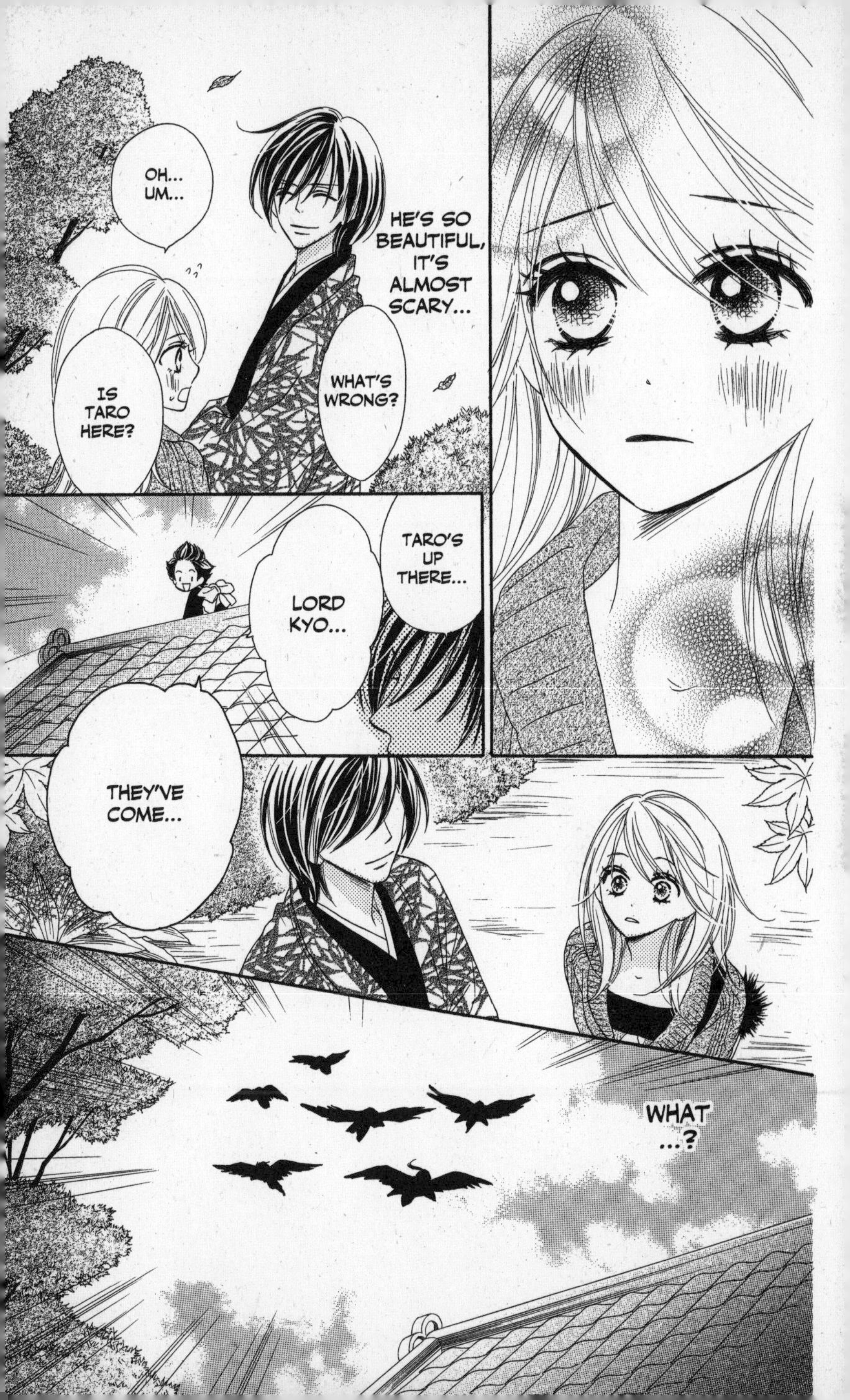
HE'S SO BEAUTIFUL, IT'S ALMOST SCARY...
WHAT'S WRONG?
OH... UM...
IS TARO HERE?
TARO'S UP THERE...
LORD KYO...
THEY'VE COME...
WHAT ...?

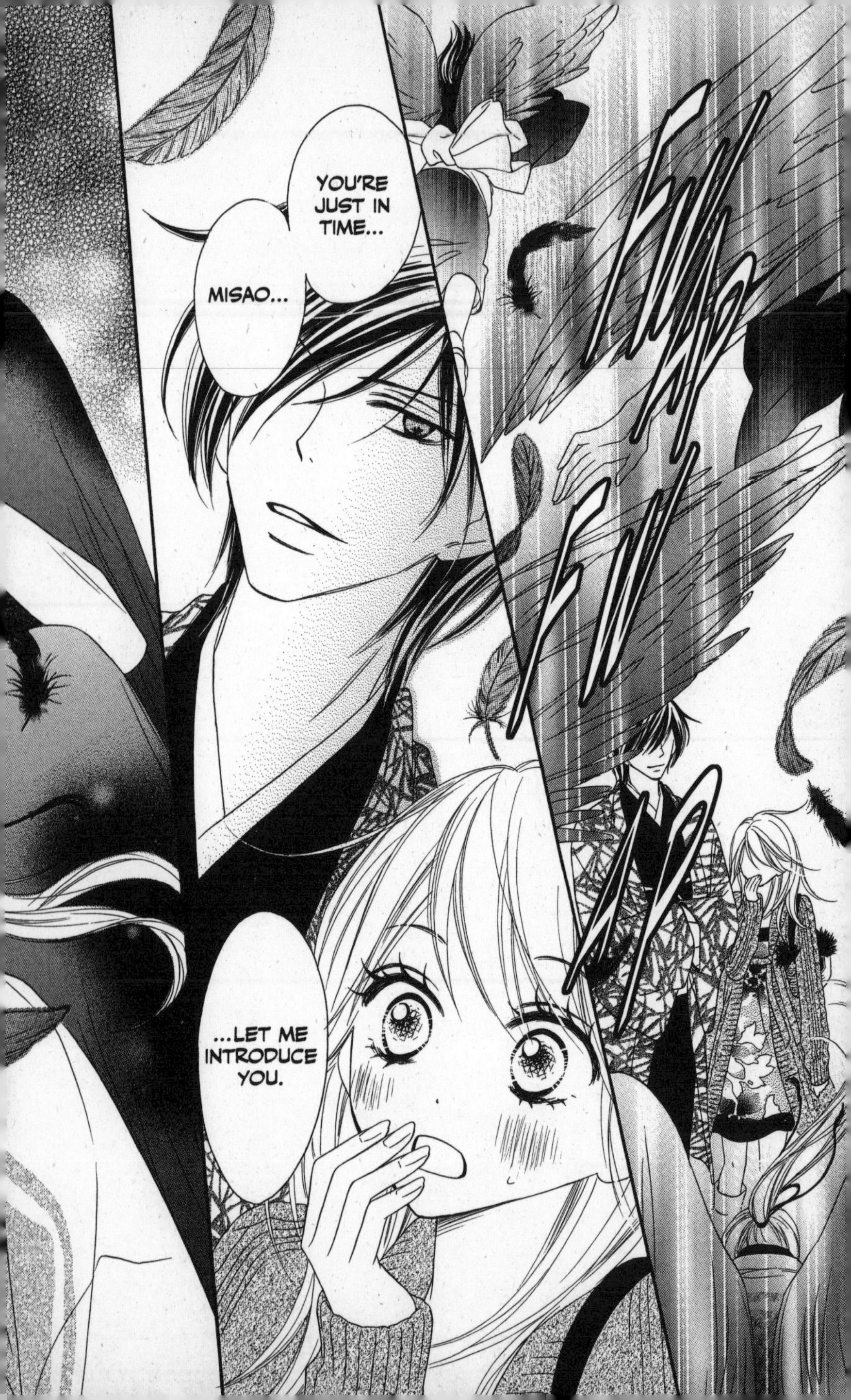
YOU'RE JUST IN TIME...
MISAO...
...LET ME INTRODUCE YOU.

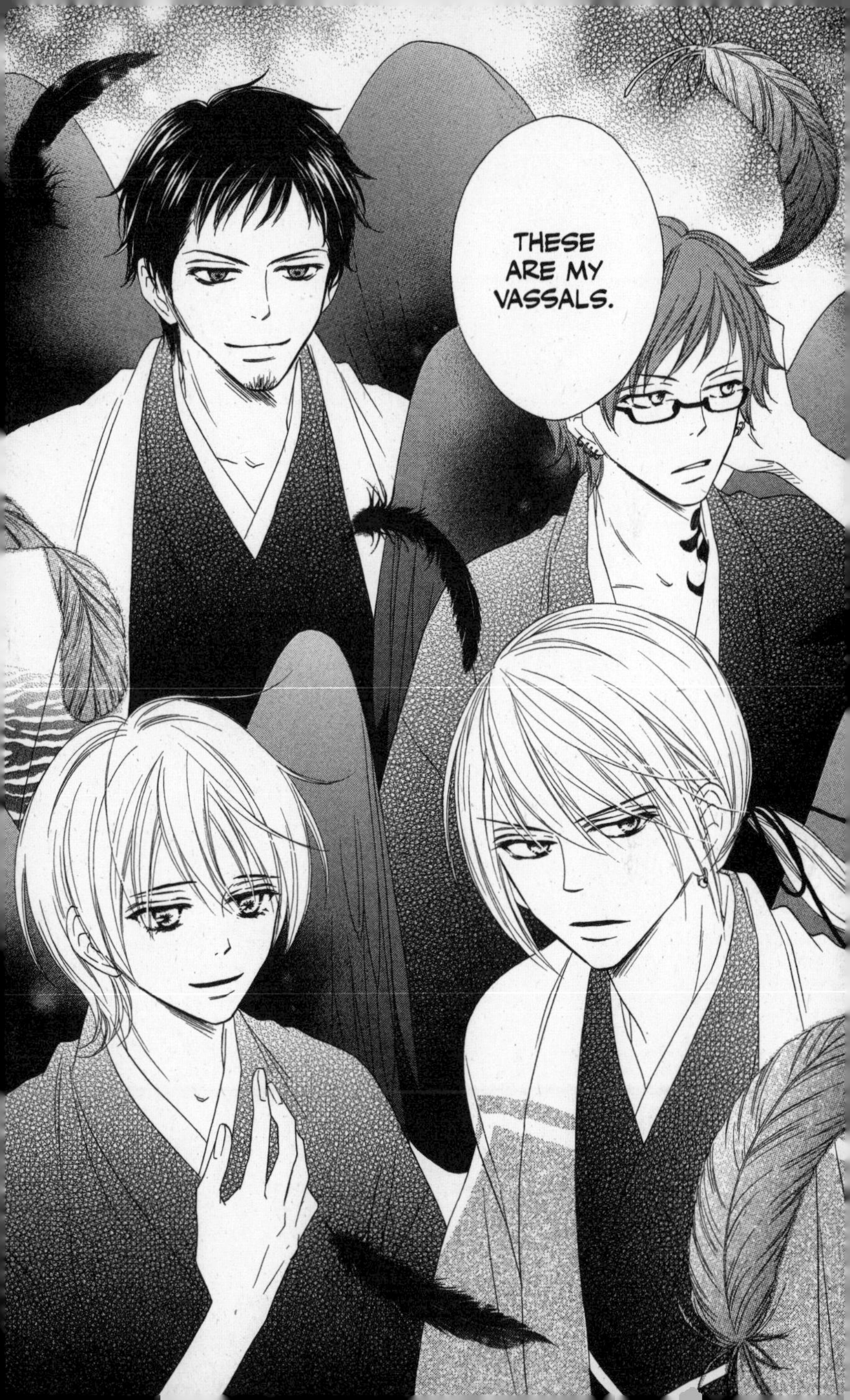
THESE ARE MY VASSALS.

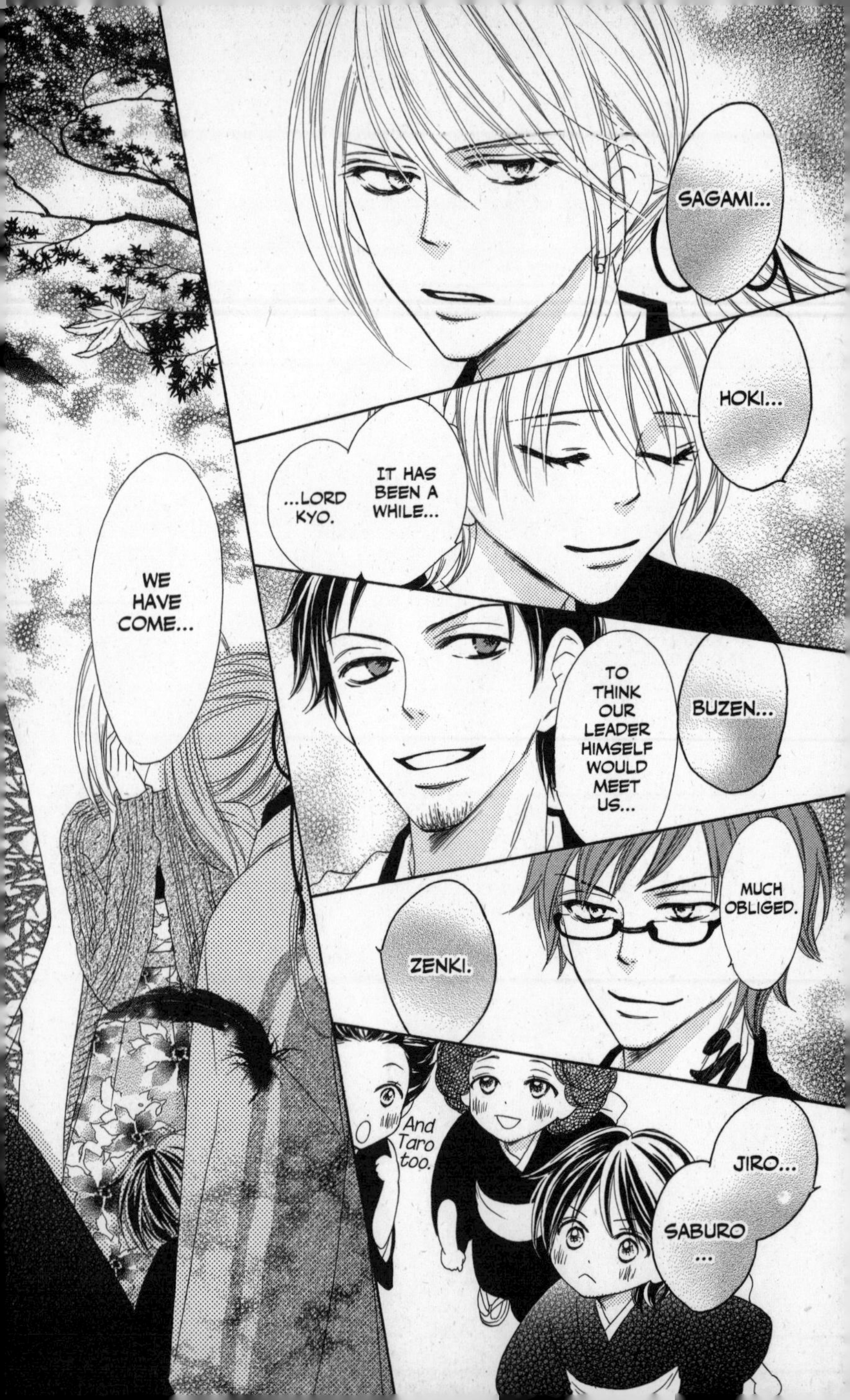
SAGAMI...
HOKI...
IT HAS BEEN A WHILE... ...LORD KYO.
BUZEN...
TO THINK OUR LEADER HIMSELF WOULD MEET US...
MUCH OBLIGED.
ZENKI.
JIRO...
SABURO ...
And Taro too.
WE HAVE COME...

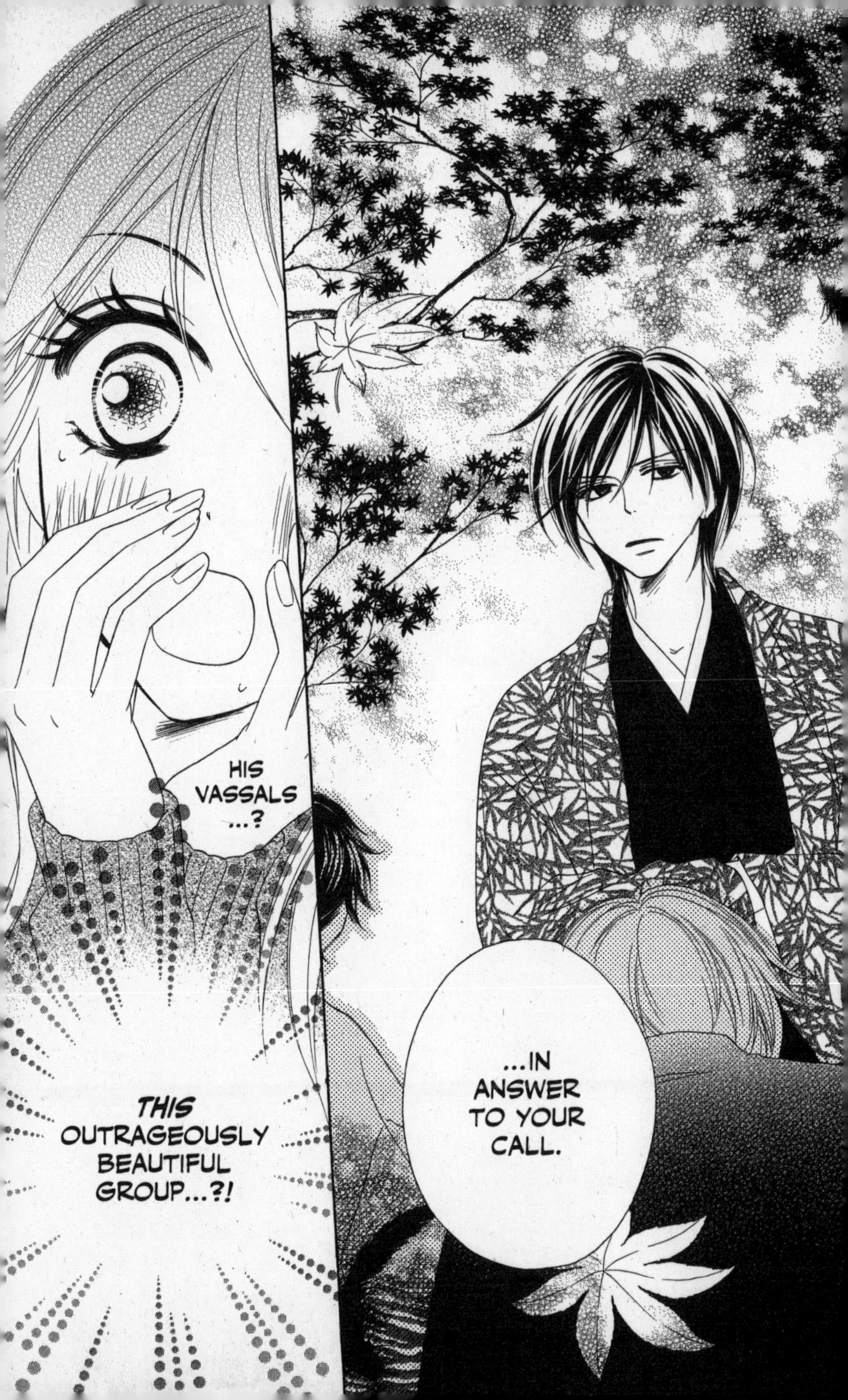
...IN ANSWER TO YOUR CALL.
HIS VASSALS ...?
THIS OUTRAGEOUSLY BEAUTIFUL GROUP...?!

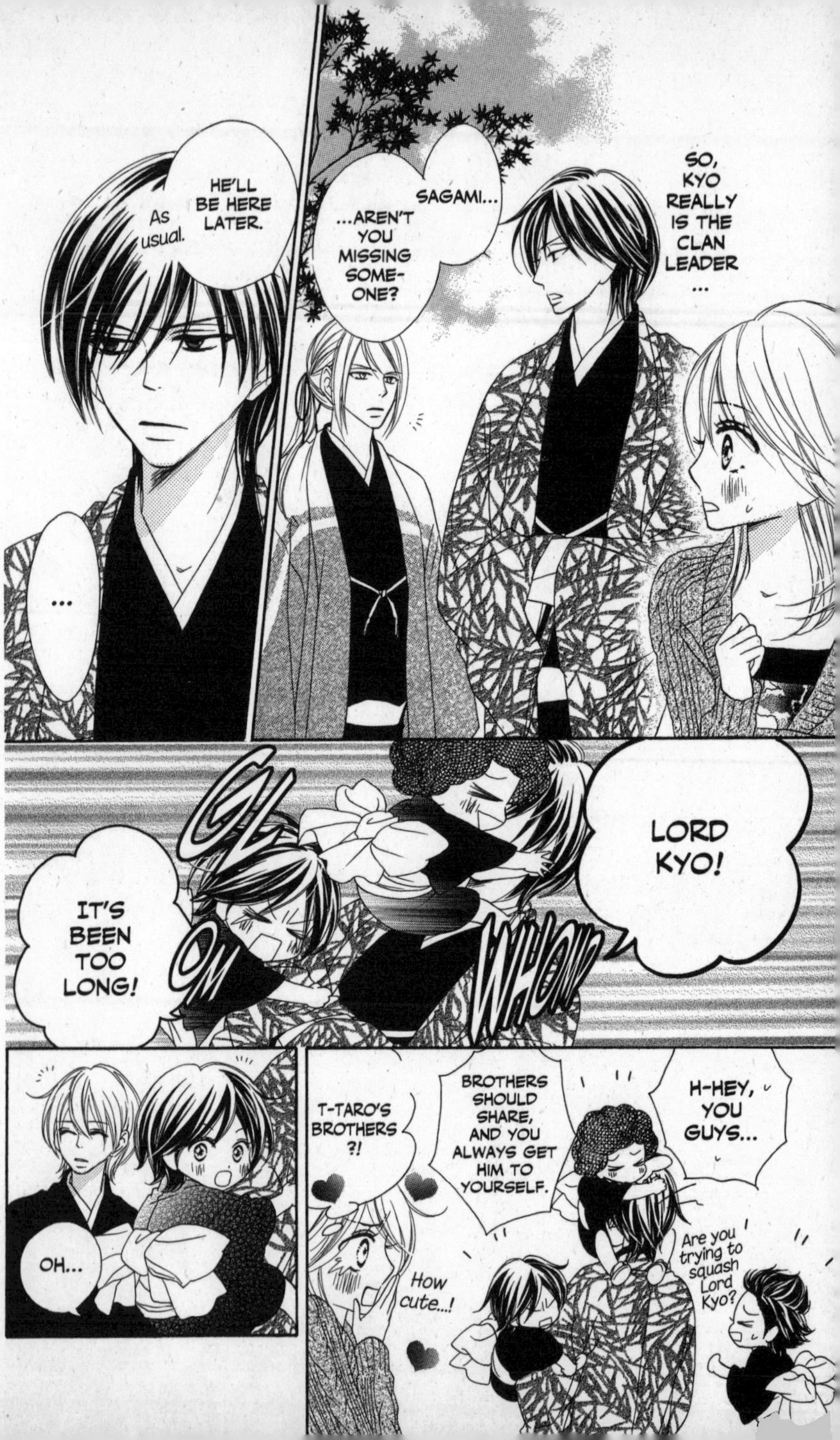
SO, KYO REALLY IS THE CLAN LEADER...
SAGAMI...
...AREN'T YOU MISSING SOME-ONE?
HE'LL BE HERE LATER.
As usual.
...
LORD KYO!
IT'S BEEN TOO LONG!
H-HEY, YOU GUYS...
BROTHERS SHOULD SHARE, AND YOU ALWAYS GET HIM TO YOURSELF.
Are you trying to squash Lord Kyo?
T-TARO'S BROTHERS?!
How cute...!
OH...

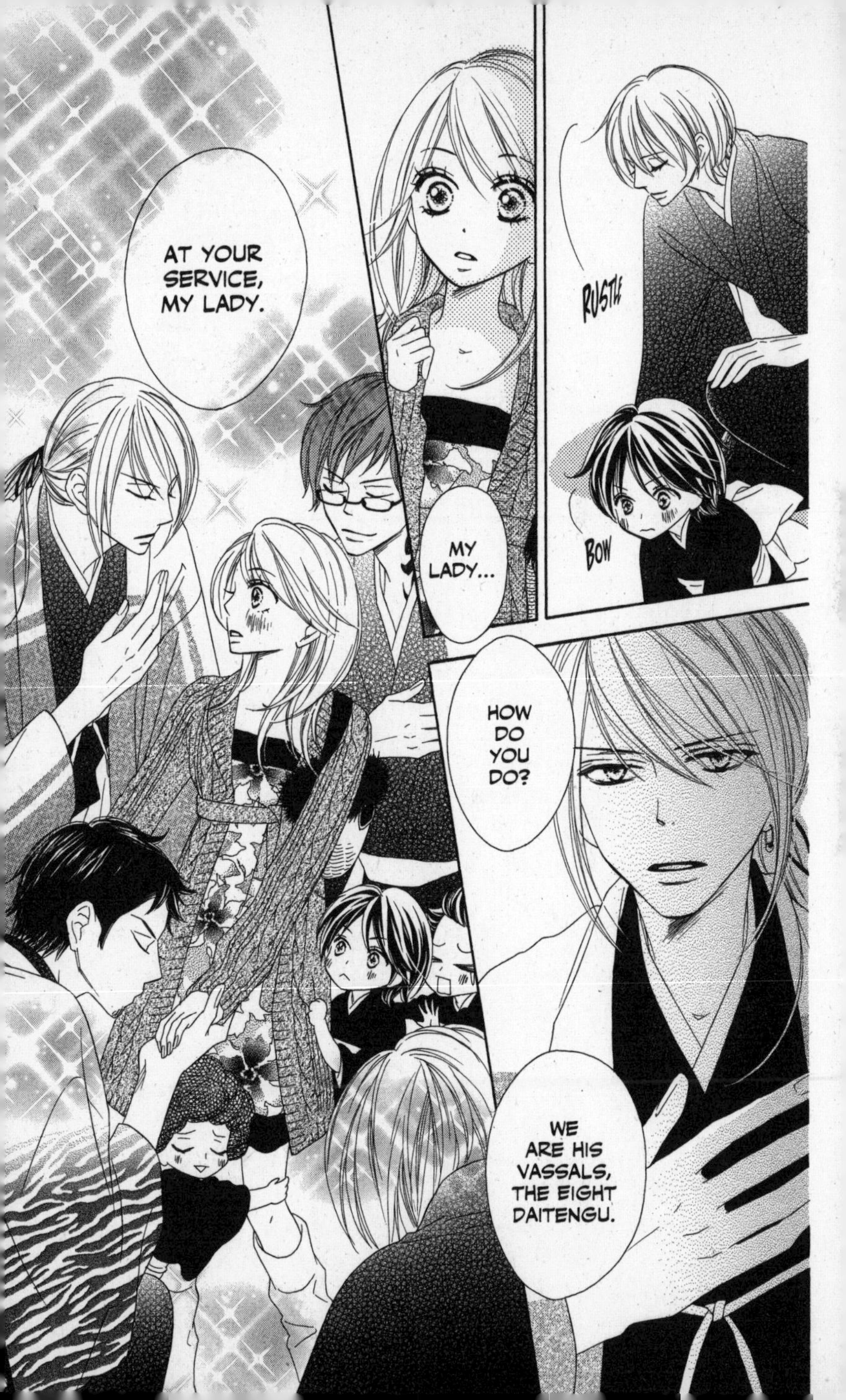
RUSTLE
BOW
MY LADY...
HOW DO YOU DO?
WE ARE HIS VASSALS, THE EIGHT DAITENGU.
AT YOUR SERVICE, MY LADY.

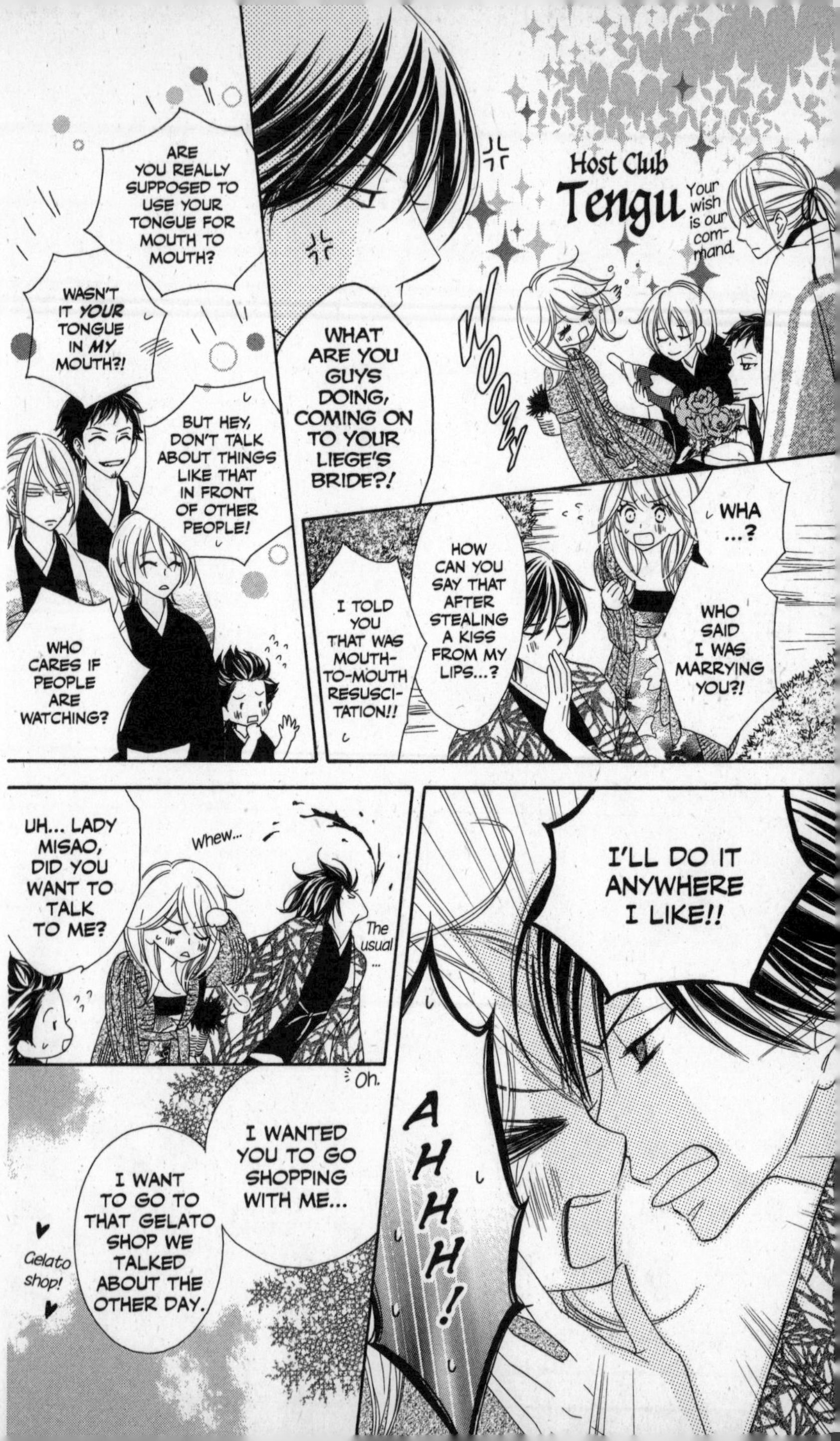

Host Club Tengu
Your wish is our command.
WOOOM
WHAT ARE YOU GUYS DOING, COMING ON TO YOUR LIEGE'S BRIDE?!
WHA ...?
WHO SAID I WAS MARRYING YOU?!
HOW CAN YOU SAY THAT AFTER STEALING A KISS FROM MY LIPS...?
I TOLD YOU THAT WAS MOUTH-TO-MOUTH RESUSCITATION!!
ARE YOU REALLY SUPPOSED TO USE YOUR TONGUE FOR MOUTH TO MOUTH?
WASN'T IT YOUR TONGUE IN MY MOUTH?!
BUT HEY, DON'T TALK ABOUT THINGS LIKE THAT IN FRONT OF OTHER PEOPLE!
WHO CARES IF PEOPLE ARE WATCHING?
I'LL DO IT ANYWHERE I LIKE!!
AHHH!
Whew...
The usual...
UH... LADY MISAO, DID YOU WANT TO TALK TO ME?
Oh.
I WANTED YOU TO GO SHOPPING WITH ME...
I WANT TO GO TO THAT GELATO SHOP WE TALKED ABOUT THE OTHER DAY.
Gelato shop!

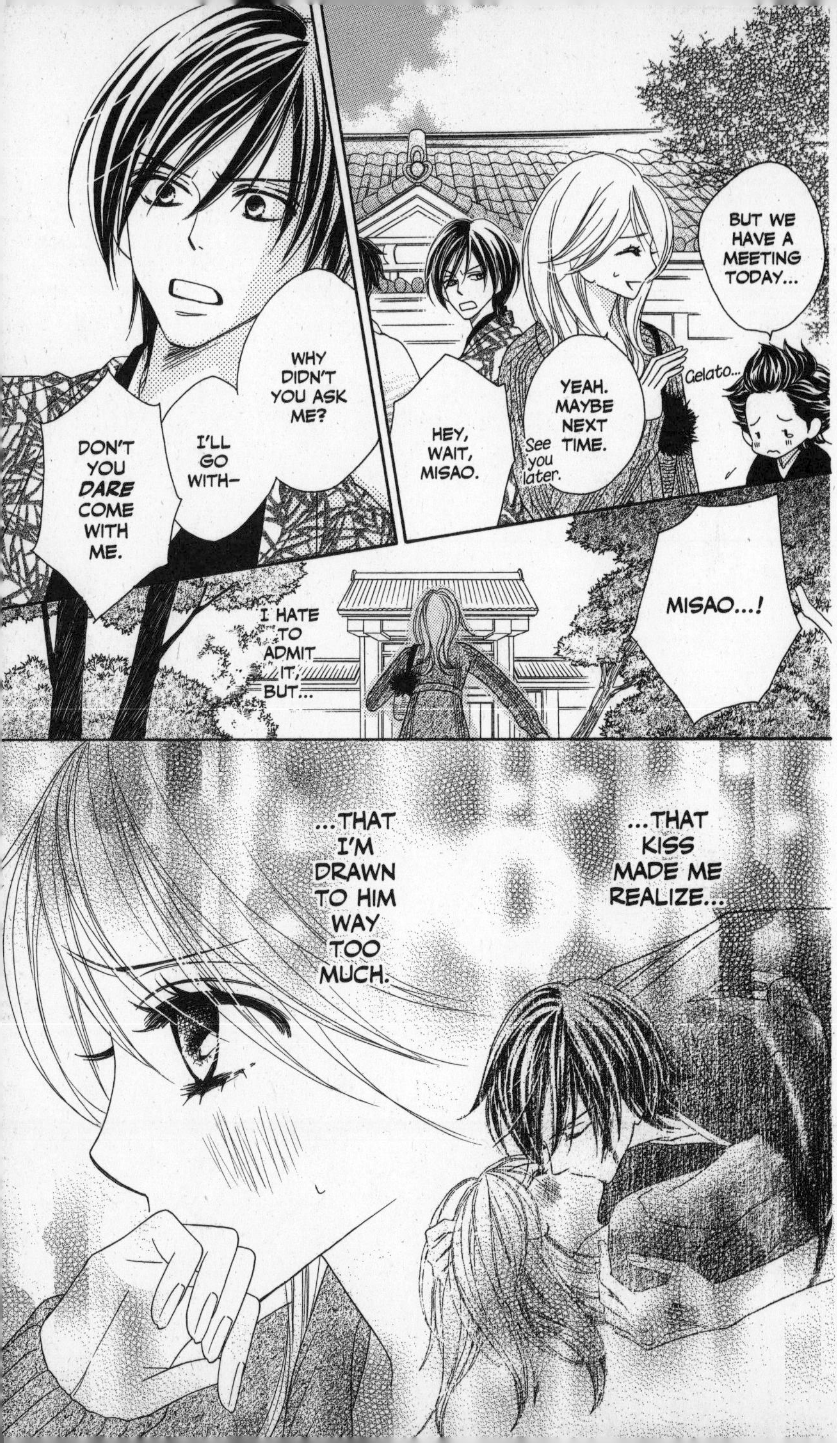
BUT WE HAVE A MEETING TODAY...
Gelato...
YEAH. MAYBE NEXT TIME.
See you later.
HEY, WAIT, MISAO.
WHY DIDN'T YOU ASK ME?
I'LL GO WITH–
DON'T YOU *DARE* COME WITH ME.
MISAO...!
I HATE TO ADMIT IT, BUT...
...THAT KISS MADE ME REALIZE...
...THAT I'M DRAWN TO HIM WAY TOO MUCH.

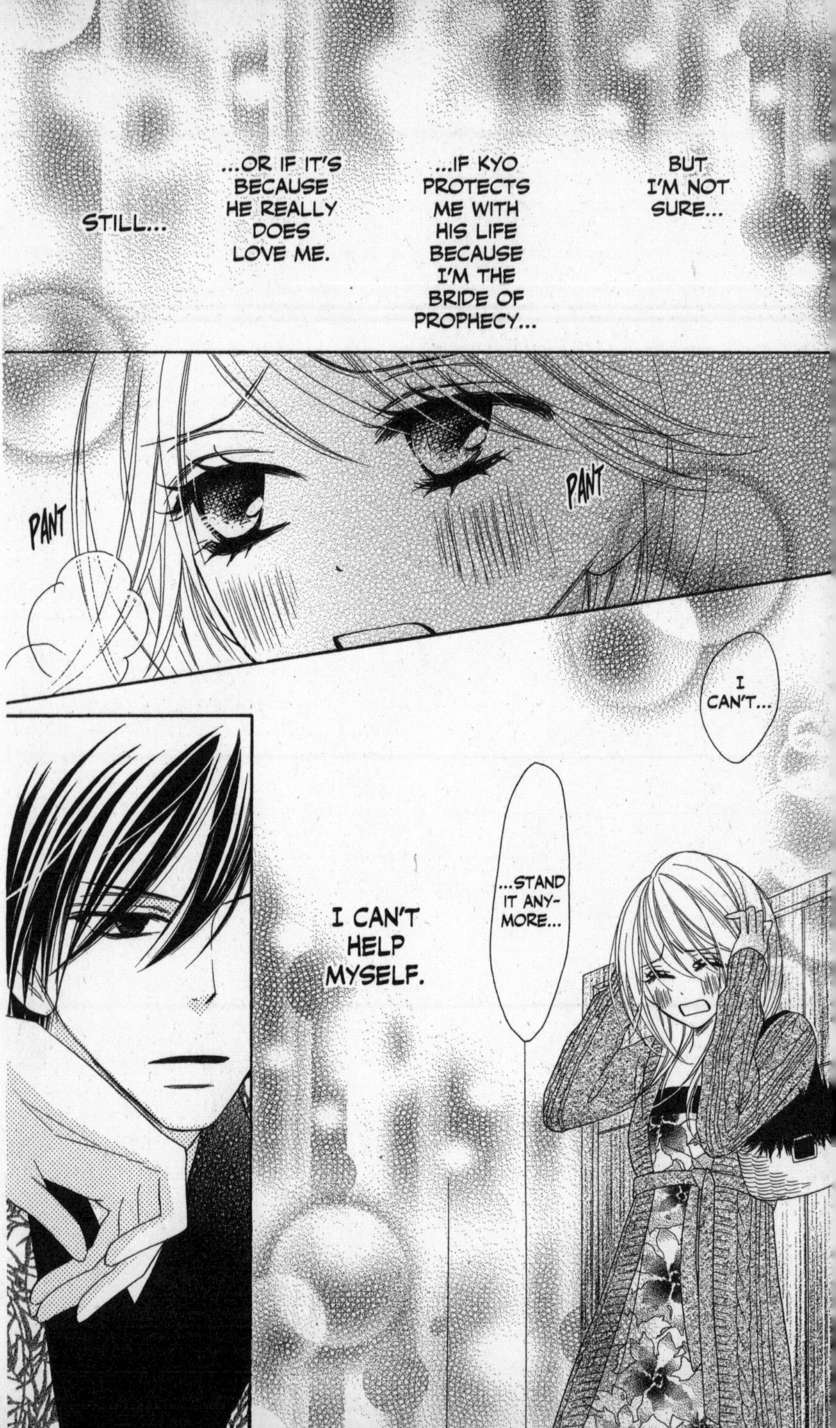
BUT I'M NOT SURE...
...IF KYO PROTECTS ME WITH HIS LIFE BECAUSE I'M THE BRIDE OF PROPHECY...
...OR IF IT'S BECAUSE HE REALLY DOES LOVE ME.
STILL...
PANT
PANT
I CAN'T...
...STAND IT ANYMORE...
I CAN'T HELP MYSELF.

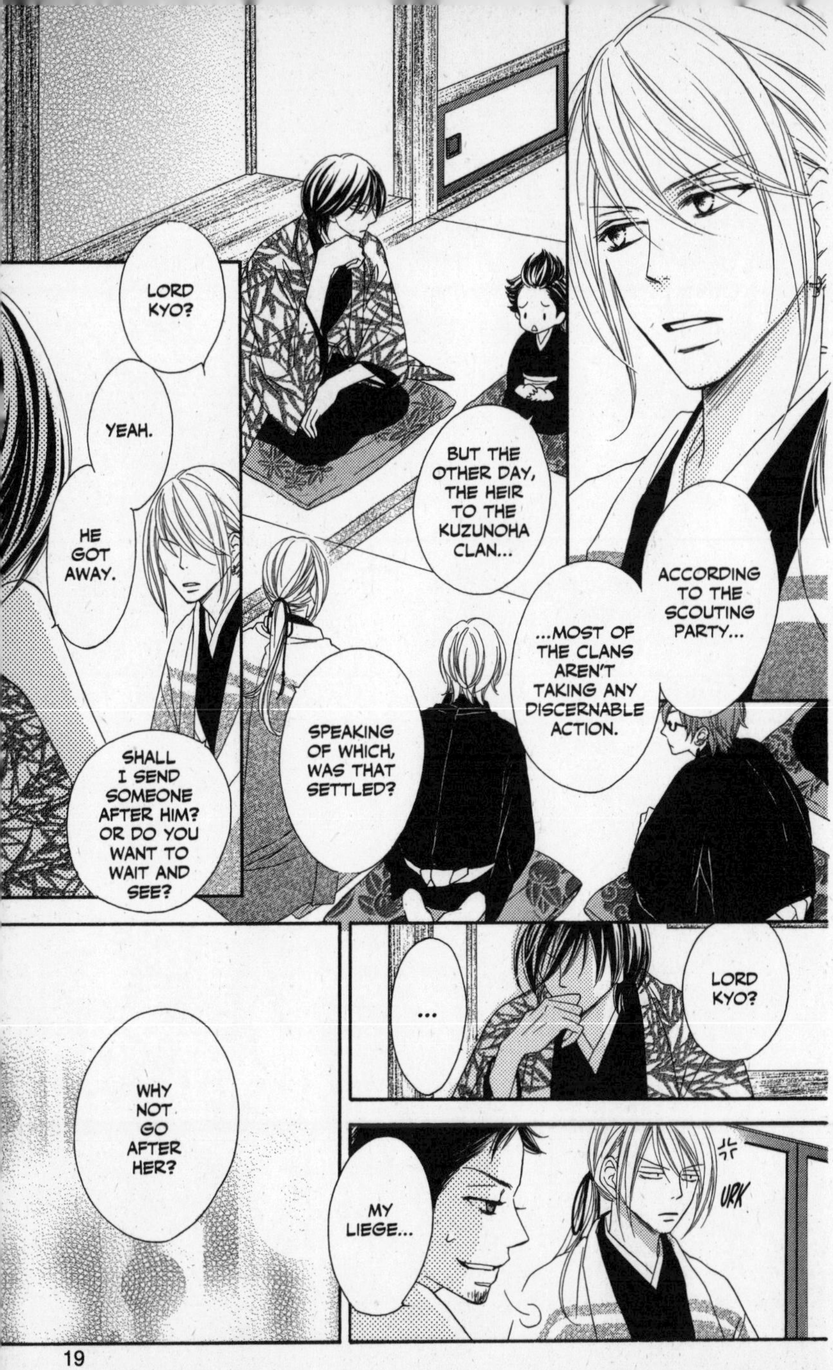
ACCORDING TO THE SCOUTING PARTY...
...MOST OF THE CLANS AREN'T TAKING ANY DISCERNABLE ACTION.
BUT THE OTHER DAY, THE HEIR TO THE KUZUNOHA CLAN...
SPEAKING OF WHICH, WAS THAT SETTLED?
LORD KYO?
YEAH.
HE GOT AWAY.
SHALL I SEND SOMEONE AFTER HIM? OR DO YOU WANT TO WAIT AND SEE?
LORD KYO?
...
URK
MY LIEGE...
WHY NOT GO AFTER HER?

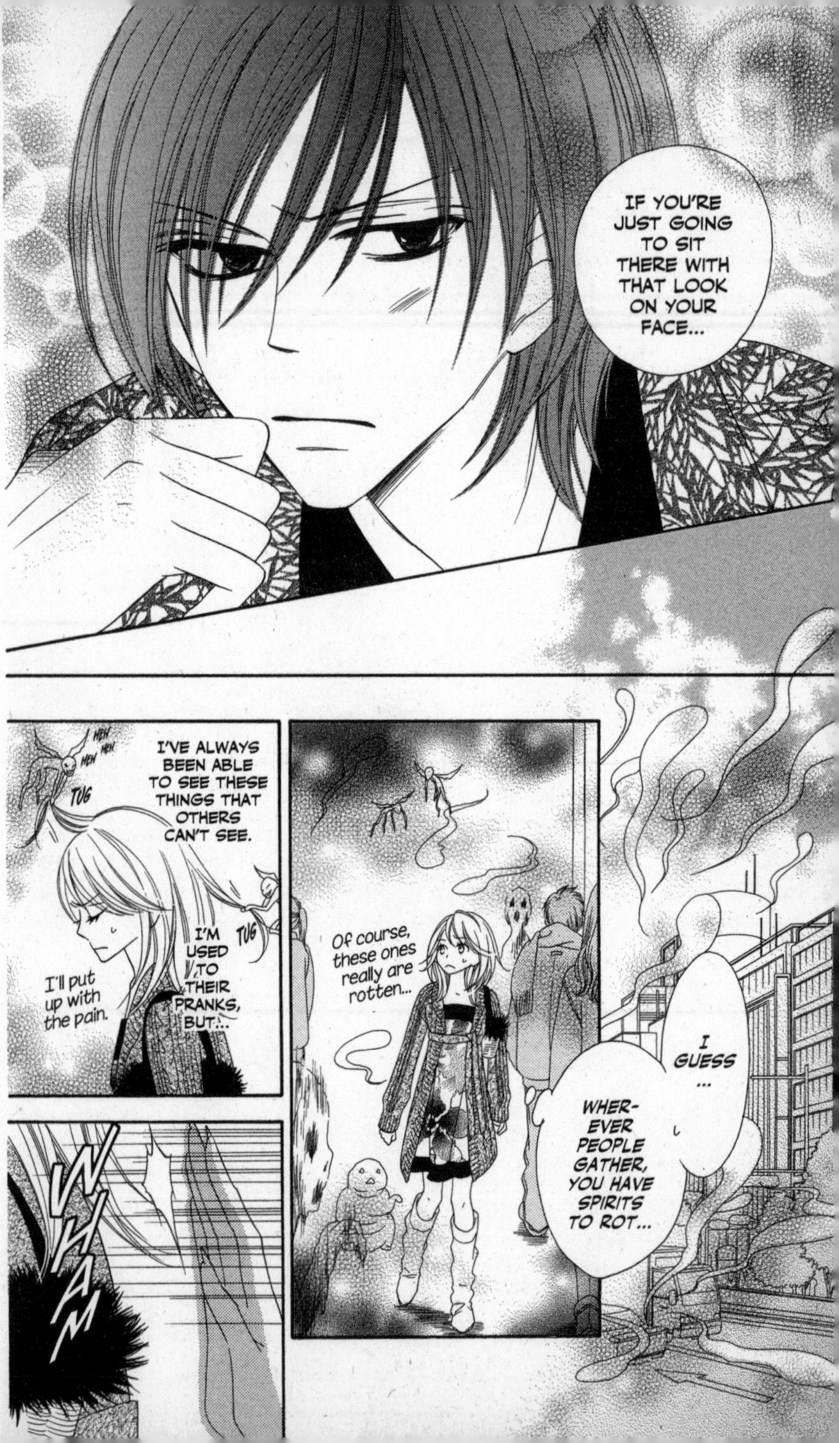
IF YOU'RE JUST GOING TO SIT THERE WITH THAT LOOK ON YOUR FACE...
I GUESS...
WHER-EVER PEOPLE GATHER, YOU HAVE SPIRITS TO ROT...
Of course, these ones really are rotten...
HEH HEH HEH
TUG
I'VE ALWAYS BEEN ABLE TO SEE THESE THINGS THAT OTHERS CAN'T SEE.
TUG
I'M USED TO THEIR PRANKS, BUT...
I'll put up with the pain.
WHAM

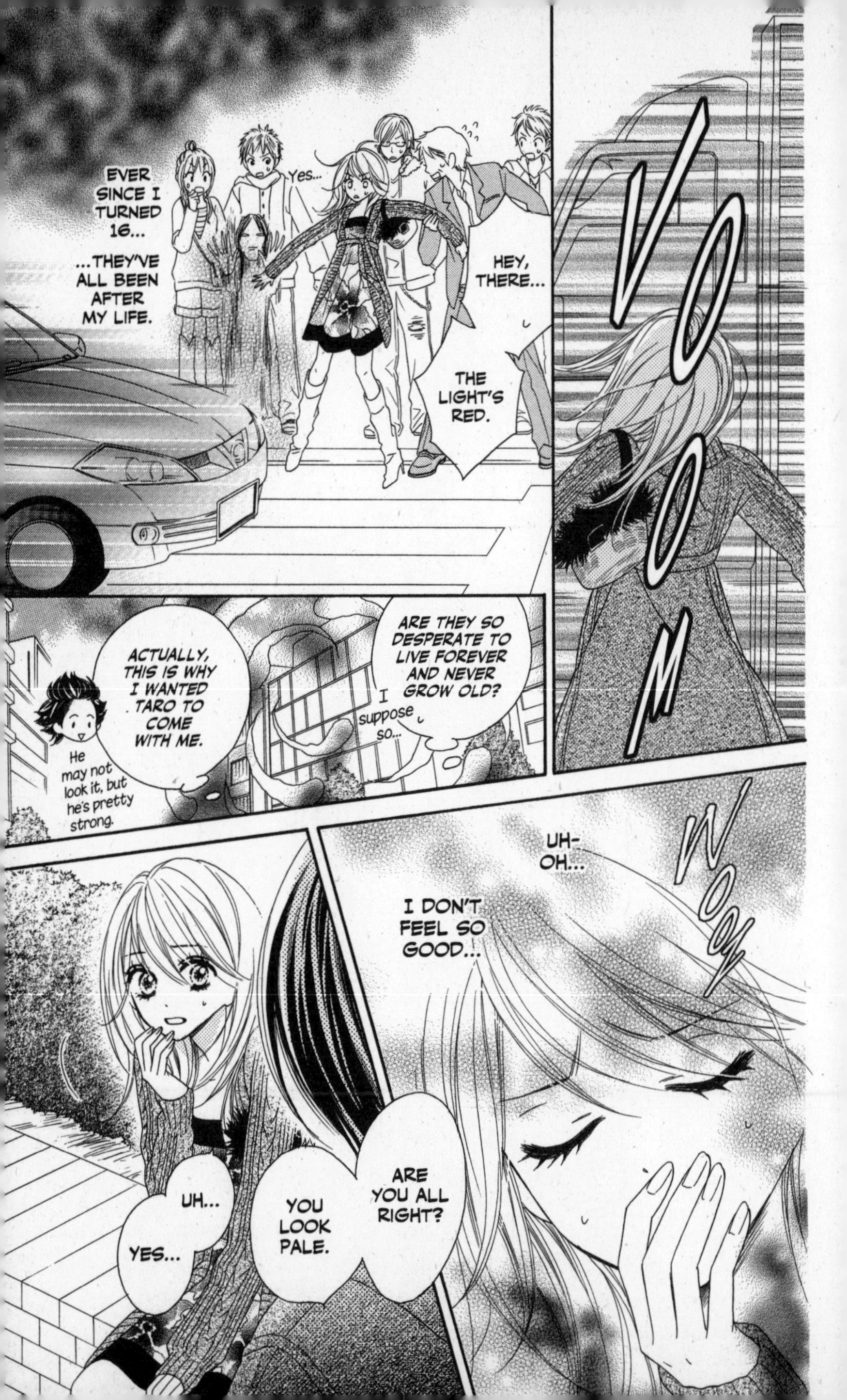
VROOM
HEY, THERE...
THE LIGHT'S RED.
Yes...
EVER SINCE I TURNED 16...
...THEY'VE ALL BEEN AFTER MY LIFE.
ARE THEY SO DESPERATE TO LIVE FOREVER AND NEVER GROW OLD?
I suppose so...
ACTUALLY, THIS IS WHY I WANTED TARO TO COME WITH ME.
He may not look it, but he's pretty strong.
UH-OH...
I DON'T FEEL SO GOOD...
ARE YOU ALL RIGHT?
YOU LOOK PALE.
UH...
YES...

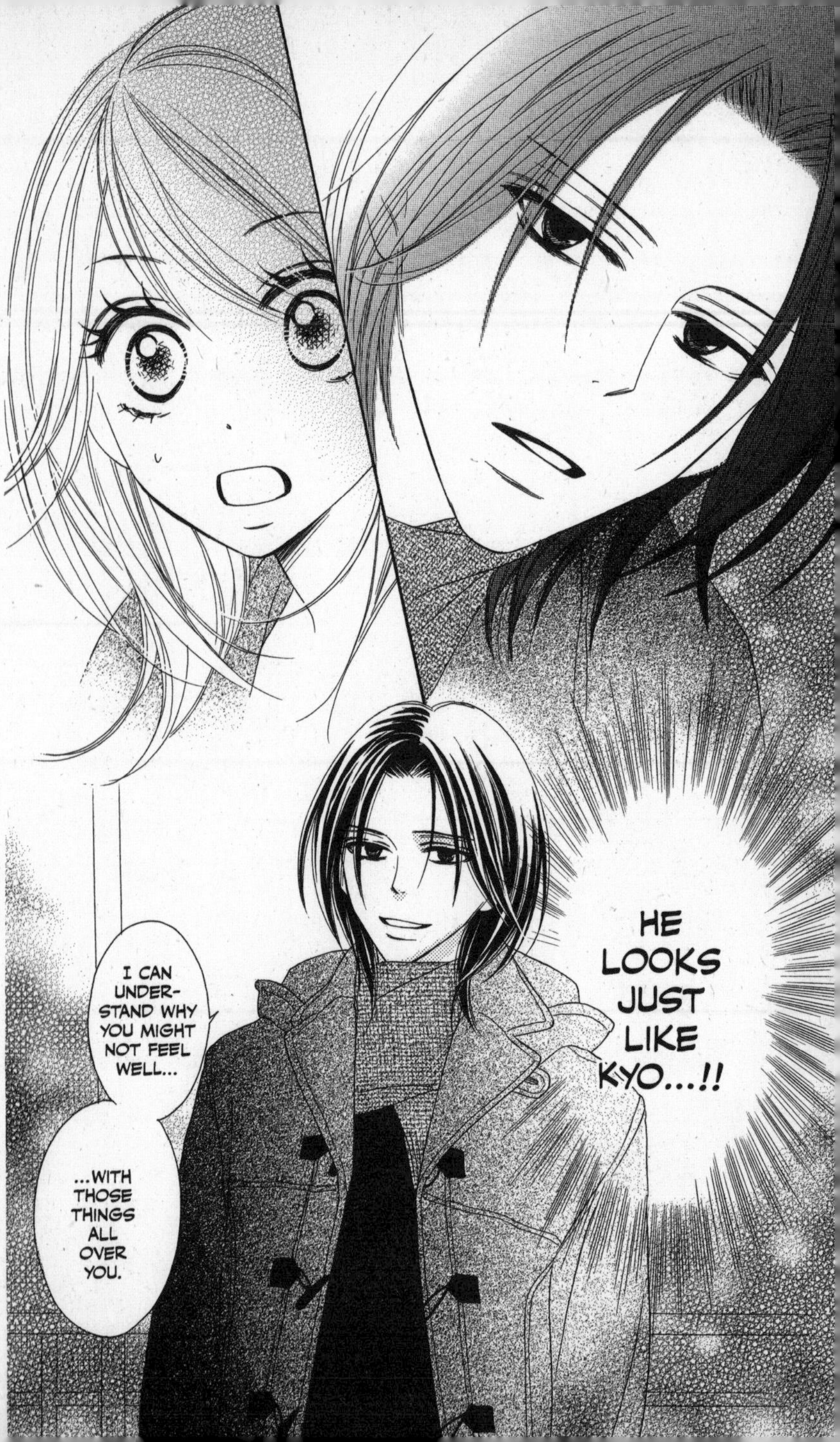
HE LOOKS JUST LIKE KYO...!!
I CAN UNDER-STAND WHY YOU MIGHT NOT FEEL WELL...
...WITH THOSE THINGS ALL OVER YOU.

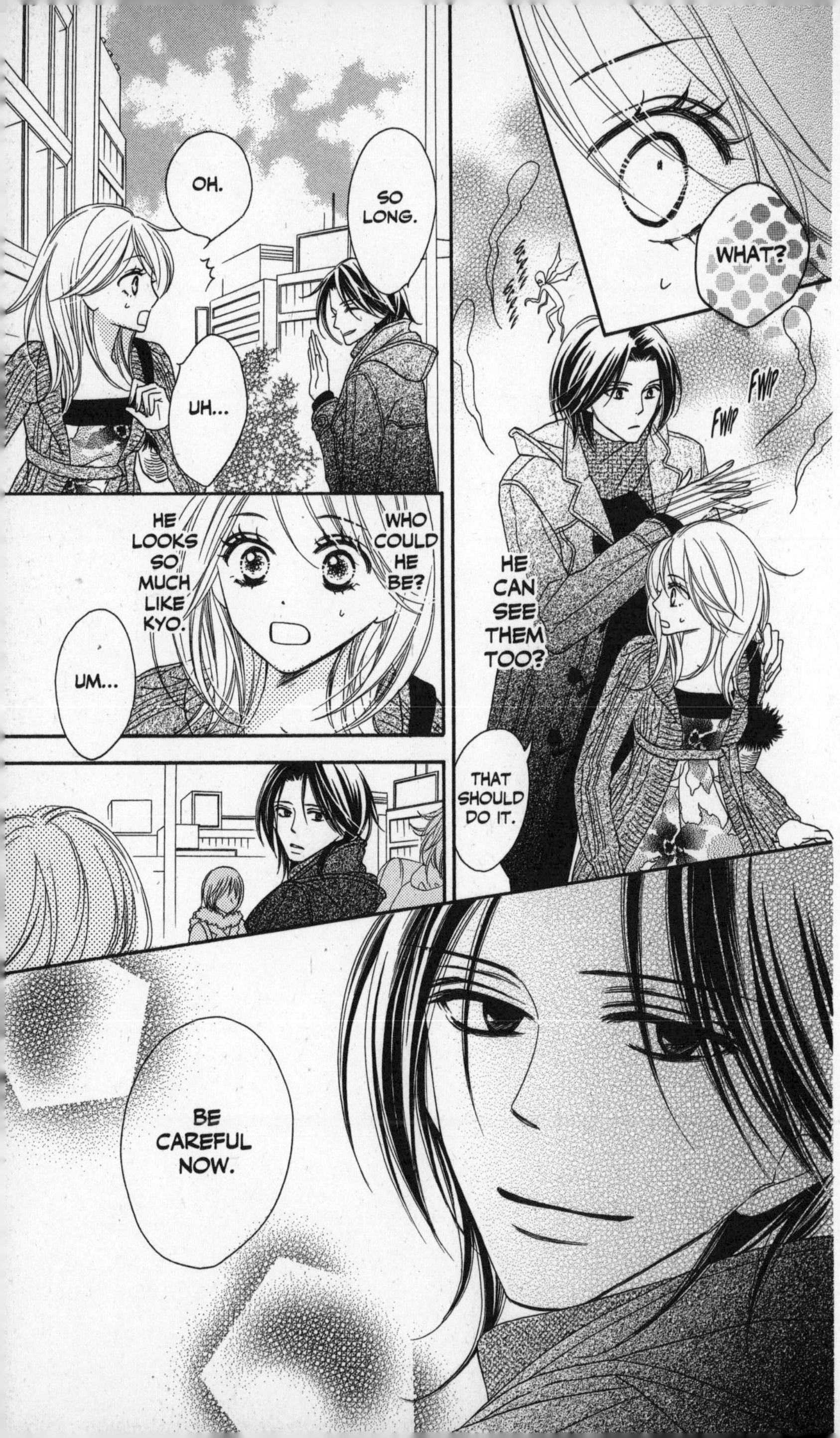
WHAT?
FWIP
FWIP
HE CAN SEE THEM TOO?
THAT SHOULD DO IT.
SO LONG.
OH.
UH...
WHO COULD HE BE?
HE LOOKS SO MUCH LIKE KYO.
UM...
BE CAREFUL NOW.

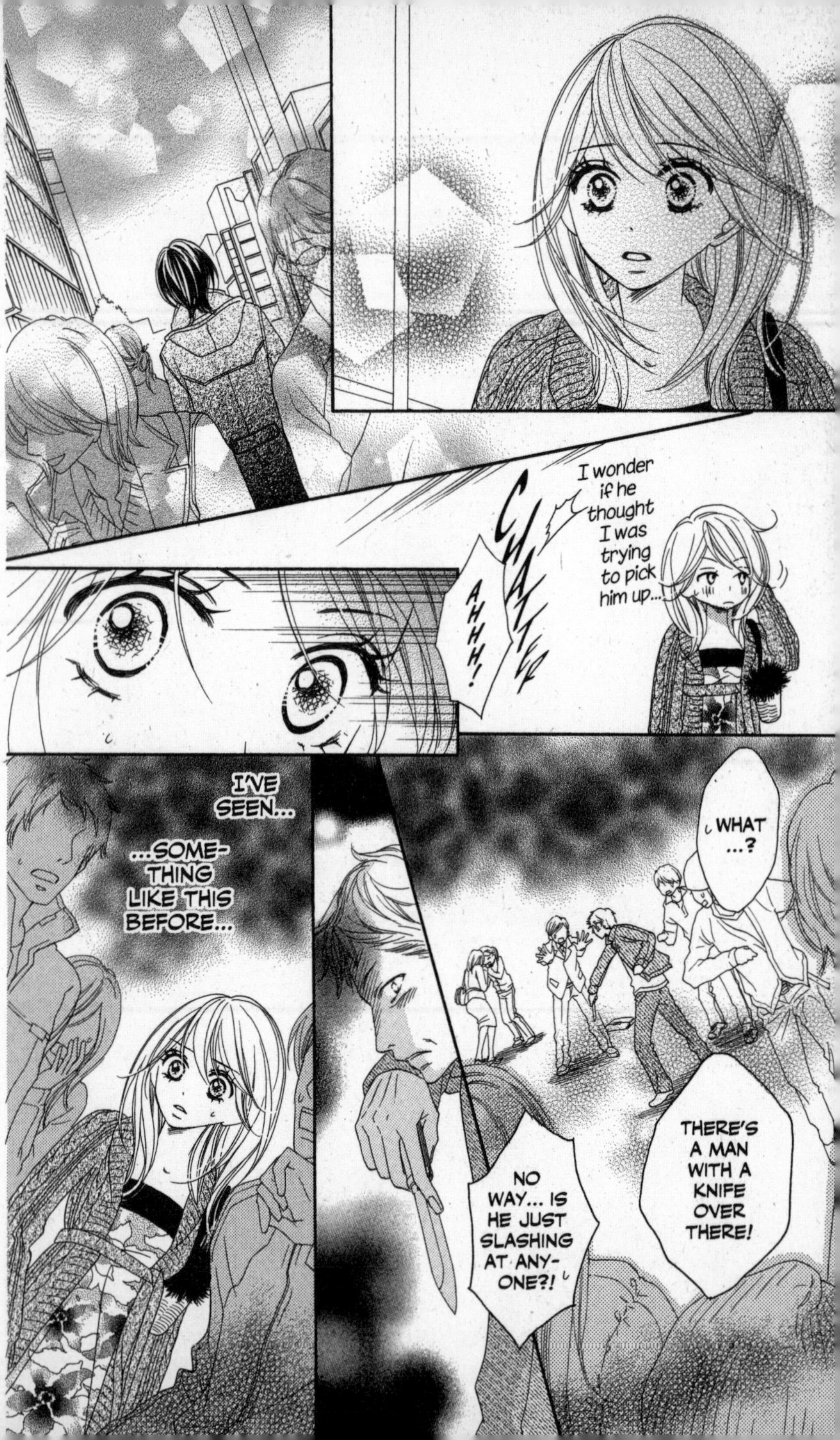
I wonder if he thought I was trying to pick him up...
AHHH!
WHAT ...?
THERE'S A MAN WITH A KNIFE OVER THERE!
NO WAY... IS HE JUST SLASHING AT ANY-ONE?!
I'VE SEEN...
...SOME-THING LIKE THIS BEFORE...

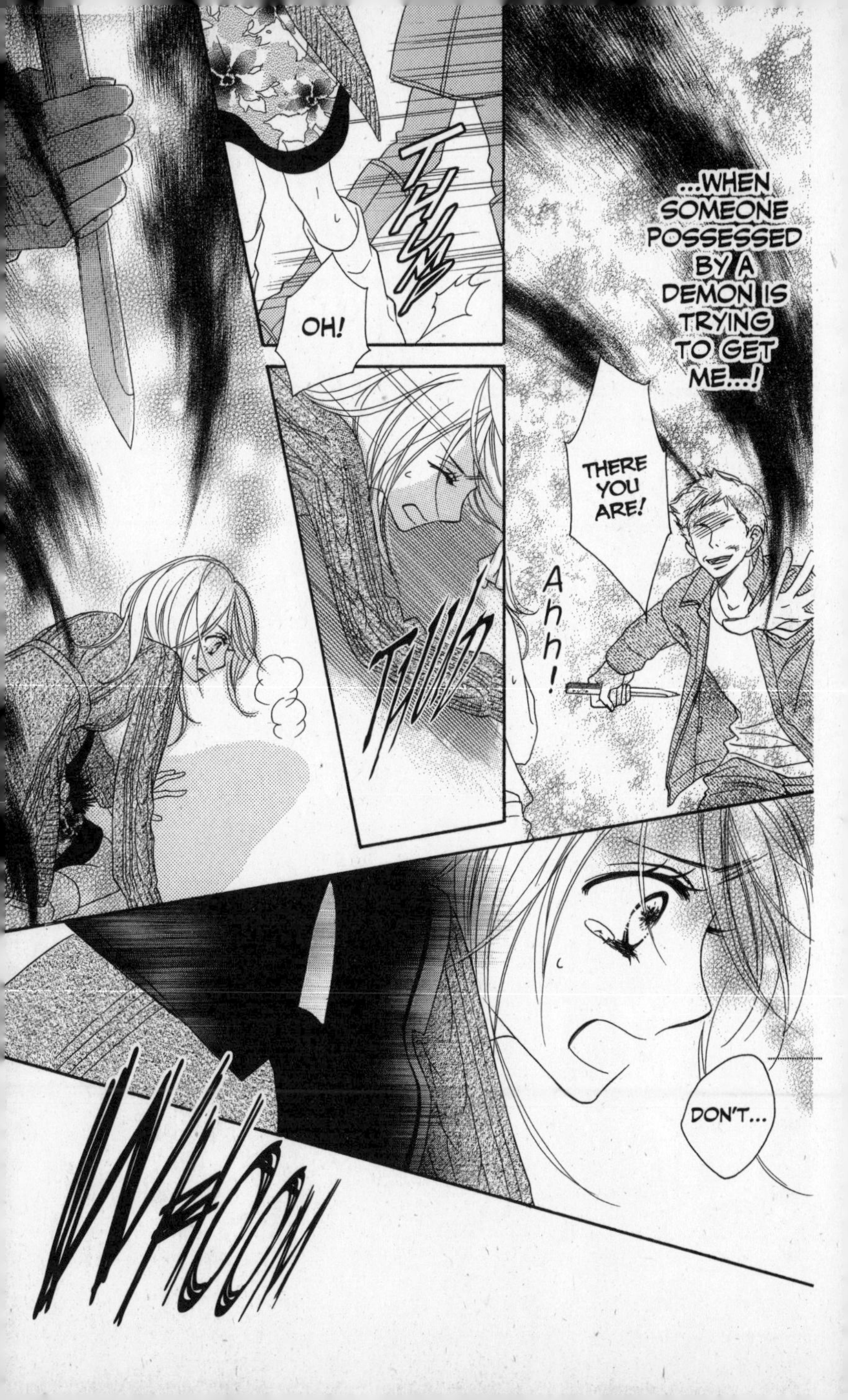
...WHEN SOMEONE POSSESSED BY A DEMON IS TRYING TO GET ME...!
THERE YOU ARE!
Anhh!
THUMP
OH!
DON'T...
WHOOM

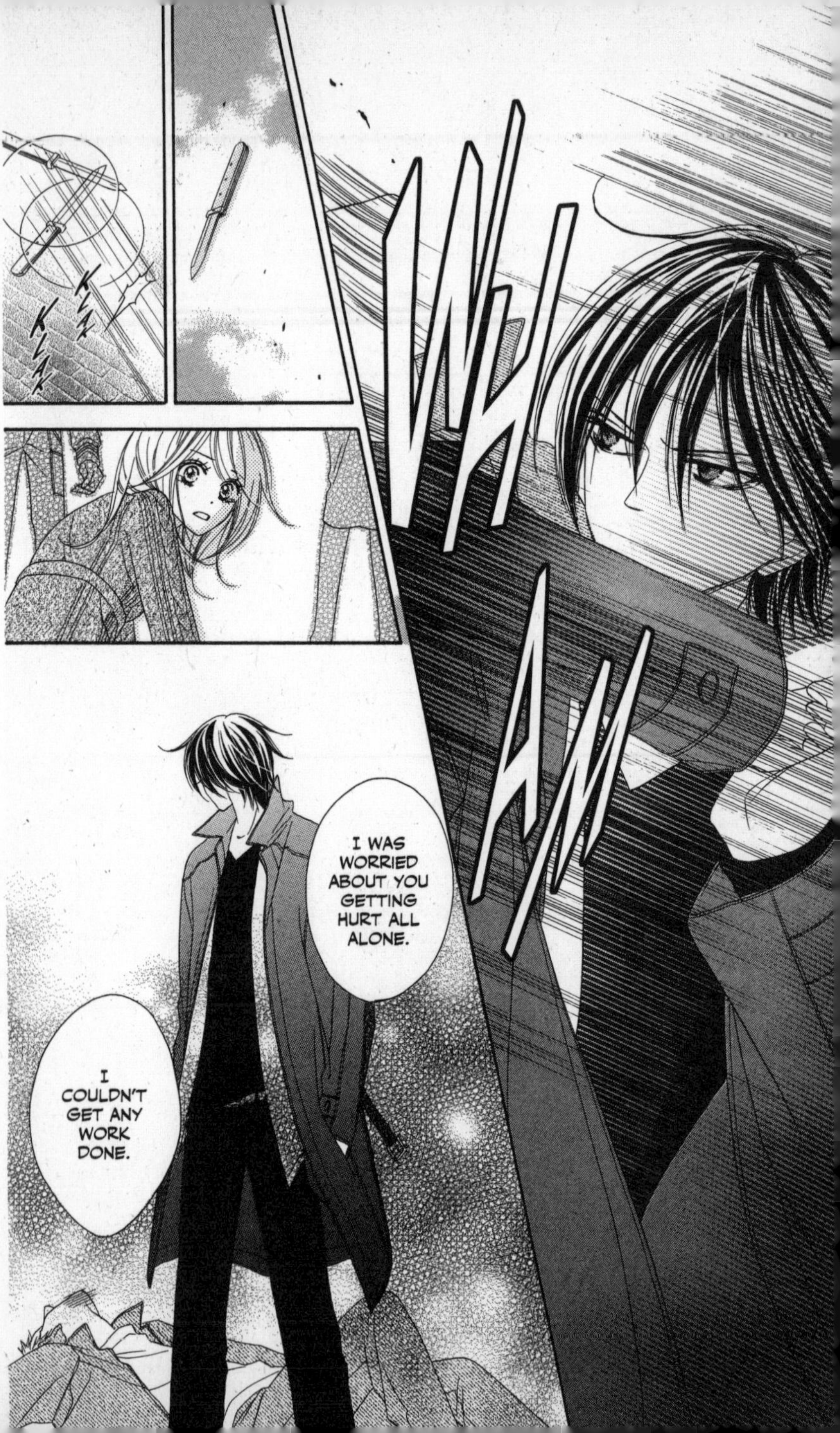
WHAM
KLAK
KLAK
I WAS WORRIED ABOUT YOU GETTING HURT ALL ALONE.
I COULDN'T GET ANY WORK DONE.

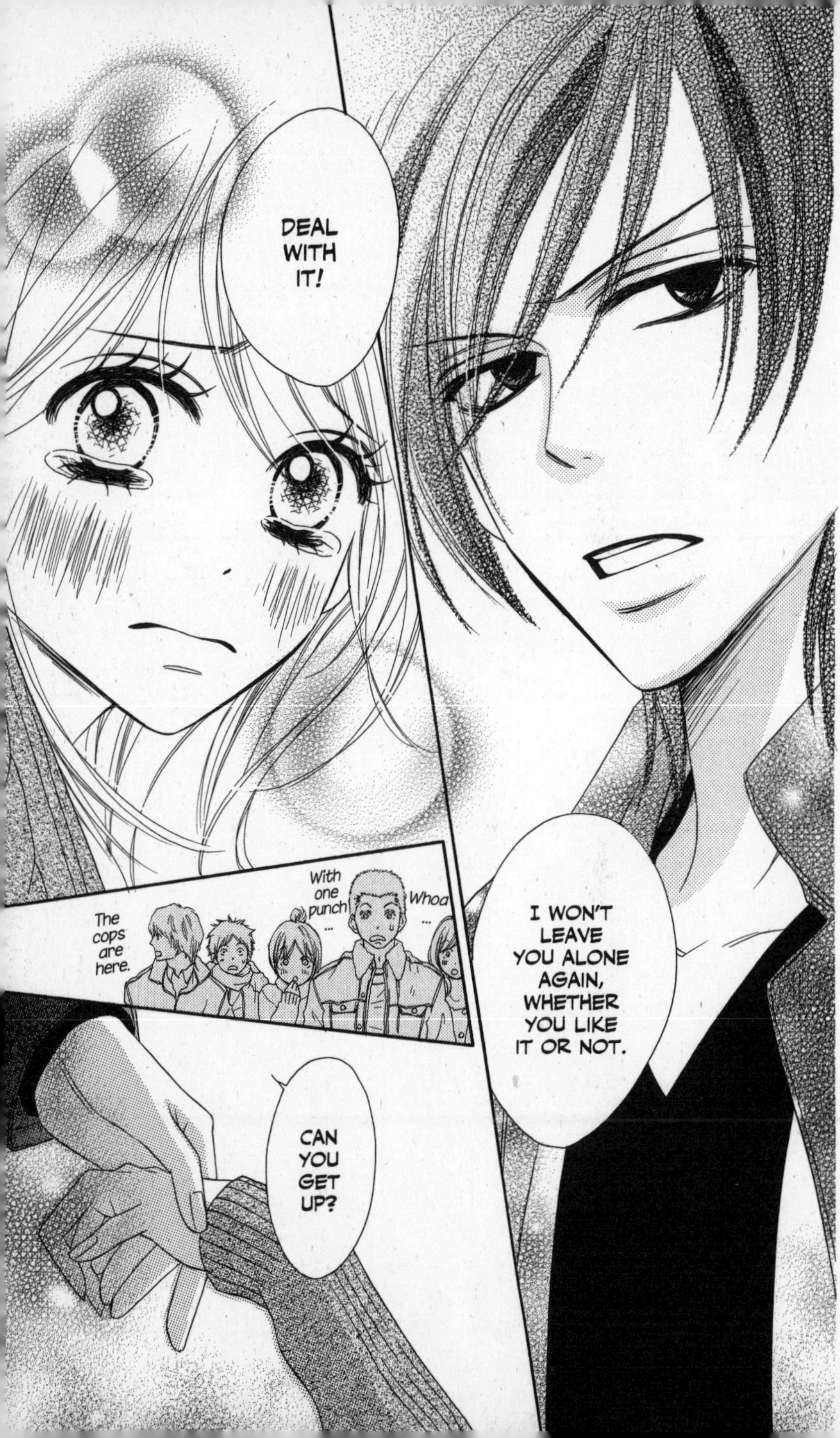
DEAL WITH IT!
I WON'T LEAVE YOU ALONE AGAIN, WHETHER YOU LIKE IT OR NOT.
Whoa ...
With one punch ...
The cops are here.
CAN YOU GET UP?

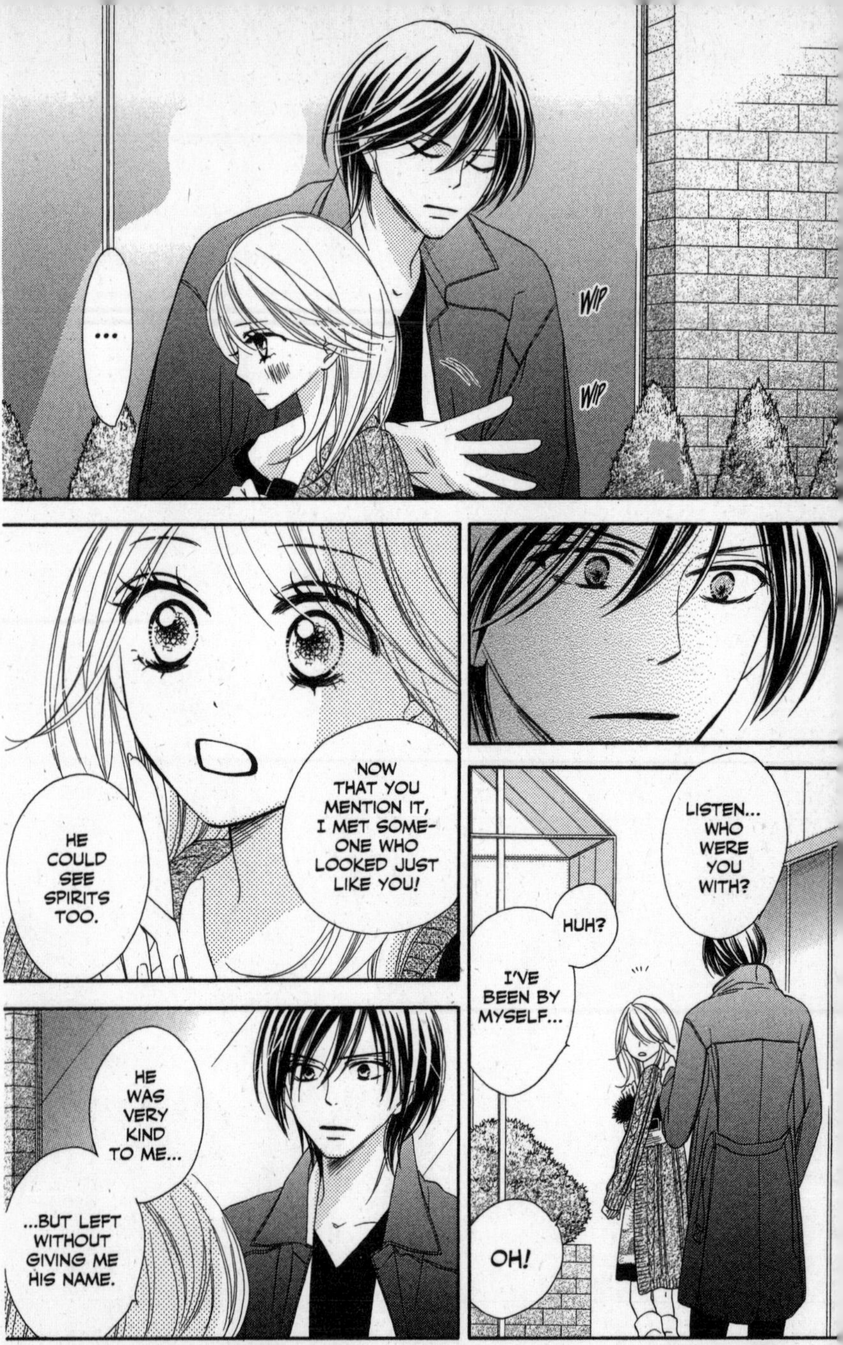
WIP
WIP
...
LISTEN... WHO WERE YOU WITH?
HUH?
I'VE BEEN BY MYSELF...
OH!
NOW THAT YOU MENTION IT, I MET SOME-ONE WHO LOOKED JUST LIKE YOU!
HE COULD SEE SPIRITS TOO.
HE WAS VERY KIND TO ME...
...BUT LEFT WITHOUT GIVING ME HIS NAME.

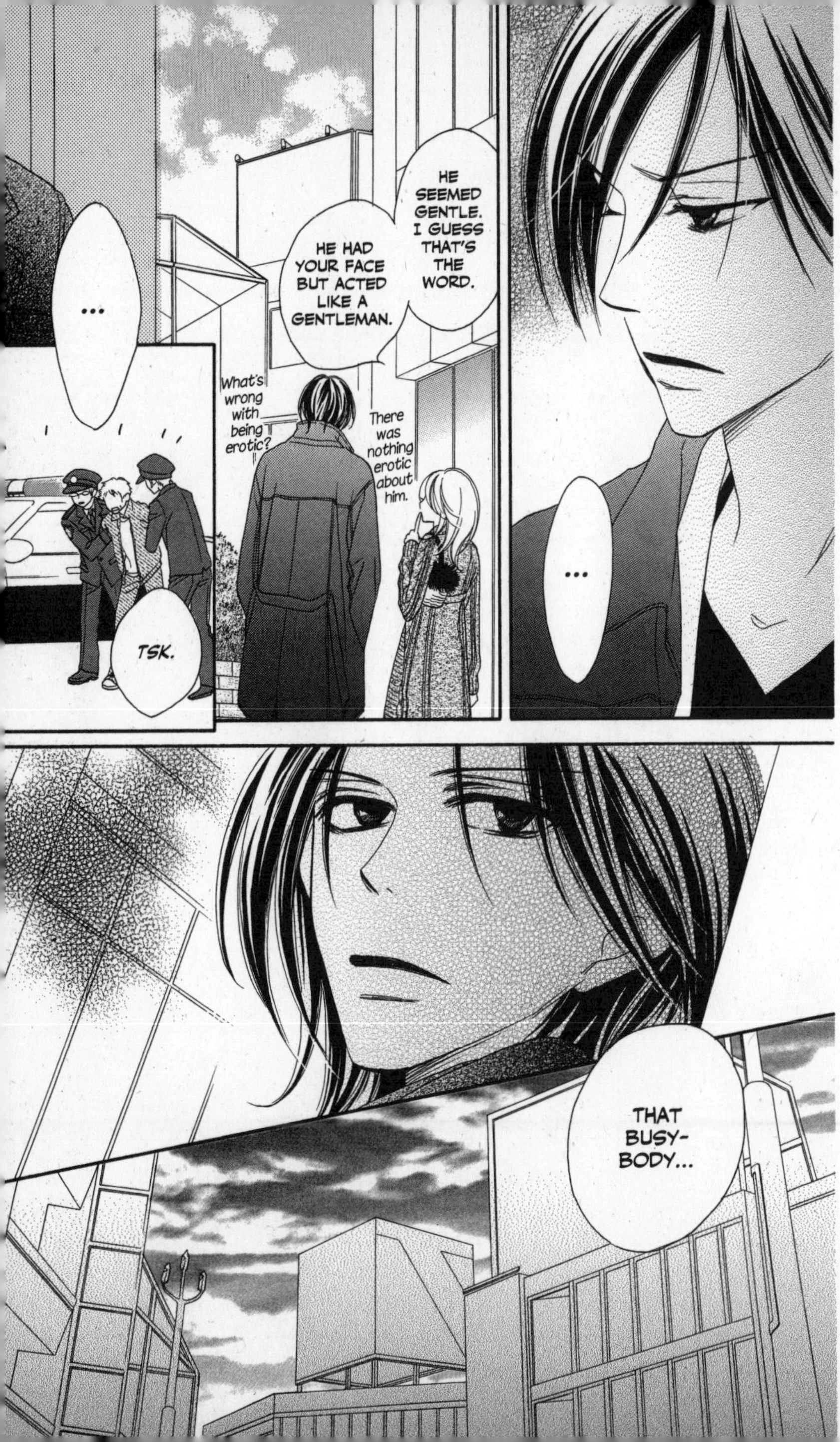
...
HE SEEMED GENTLE. I GUESS THAT'S THE WORD.
HE HAD YOUR FACE BUT ACTED LIKE A GENTLEMAN.
There was nothing erotic about him.
What's wrong with being erotic?
...
TSK.
THAT BUSY-BODY...

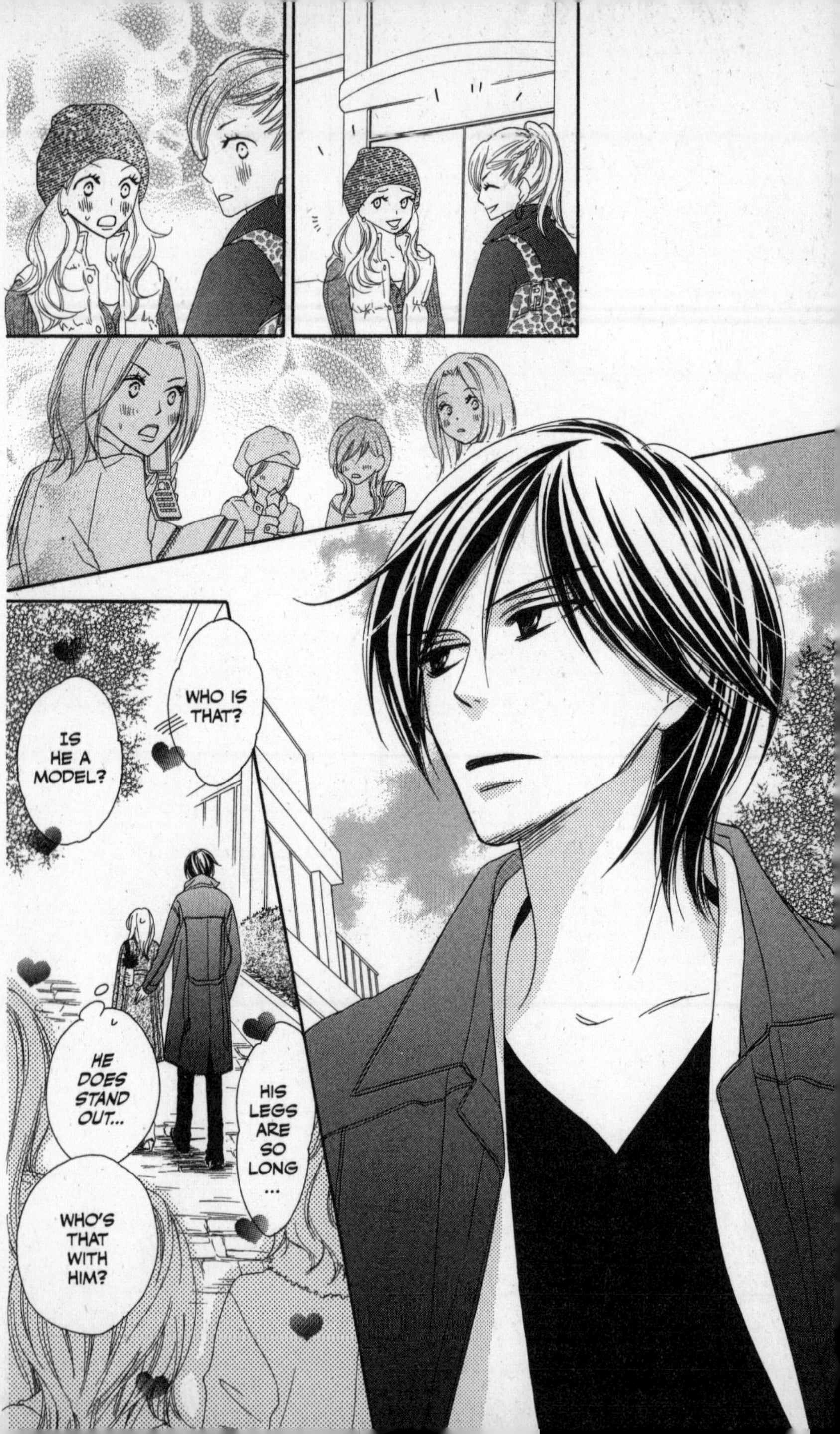
WHO IS THAT?
IS HE A MODEL?
HIS LEGS ARE SO LONG...
HE DOES STAND OUT...
WHO'S THAT WITH HIM?

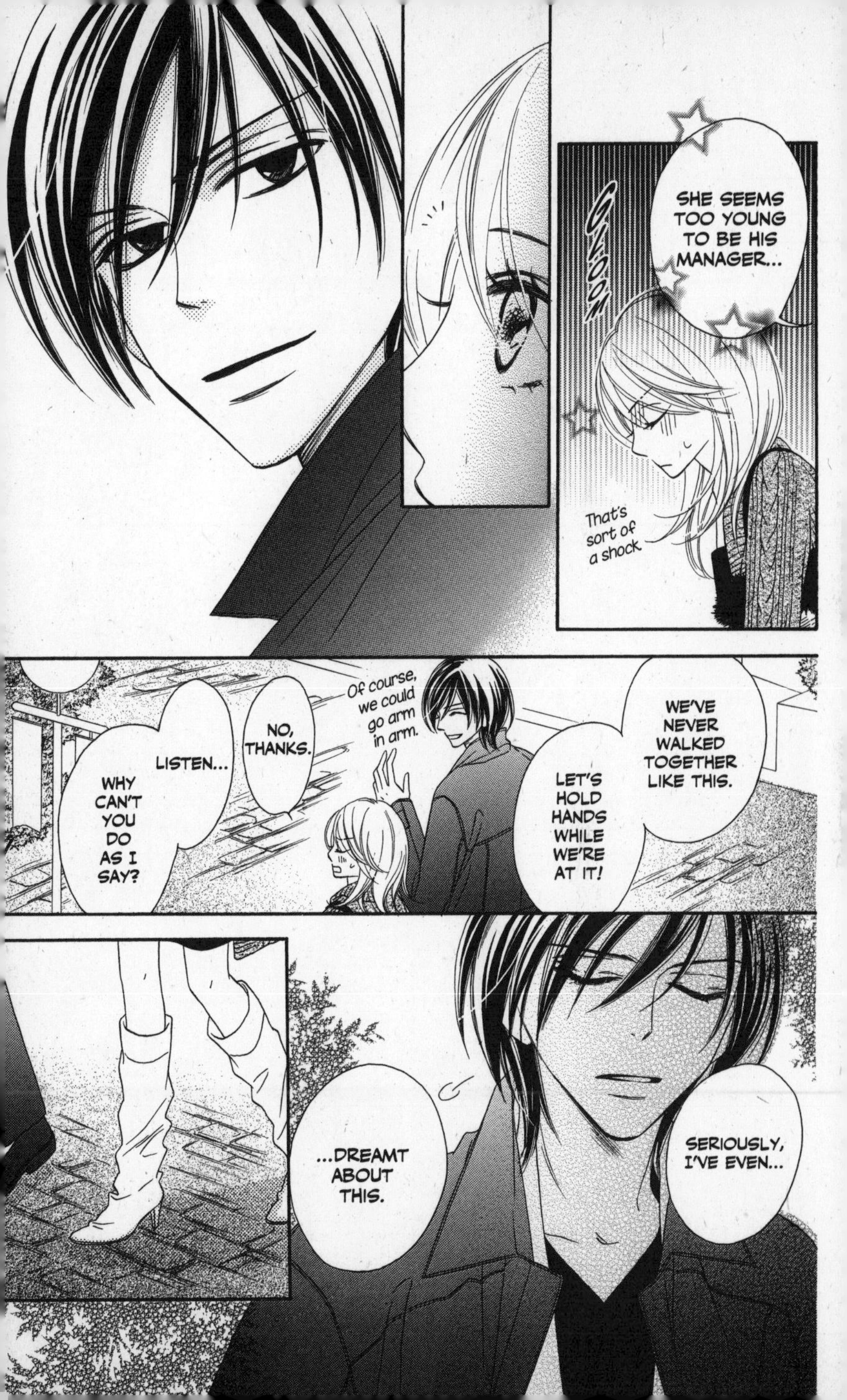
SHE SEEMS TOO YOUNG TO BE HIS MANAGER...
That's sort of a shock
WE'VE NEVER WALKED TOGETHER LIKE THIS.
LET'S HOLD HANDS WHILE WE'RE AT IT!
Of course, we could go arm in arm.
NO, THANKS.
LISTEN...
WHY CAN'T YOU DO AS I SAY?
SERIOUSLY, I'VE EVEN...
...DREAMT ABOUT THIS.

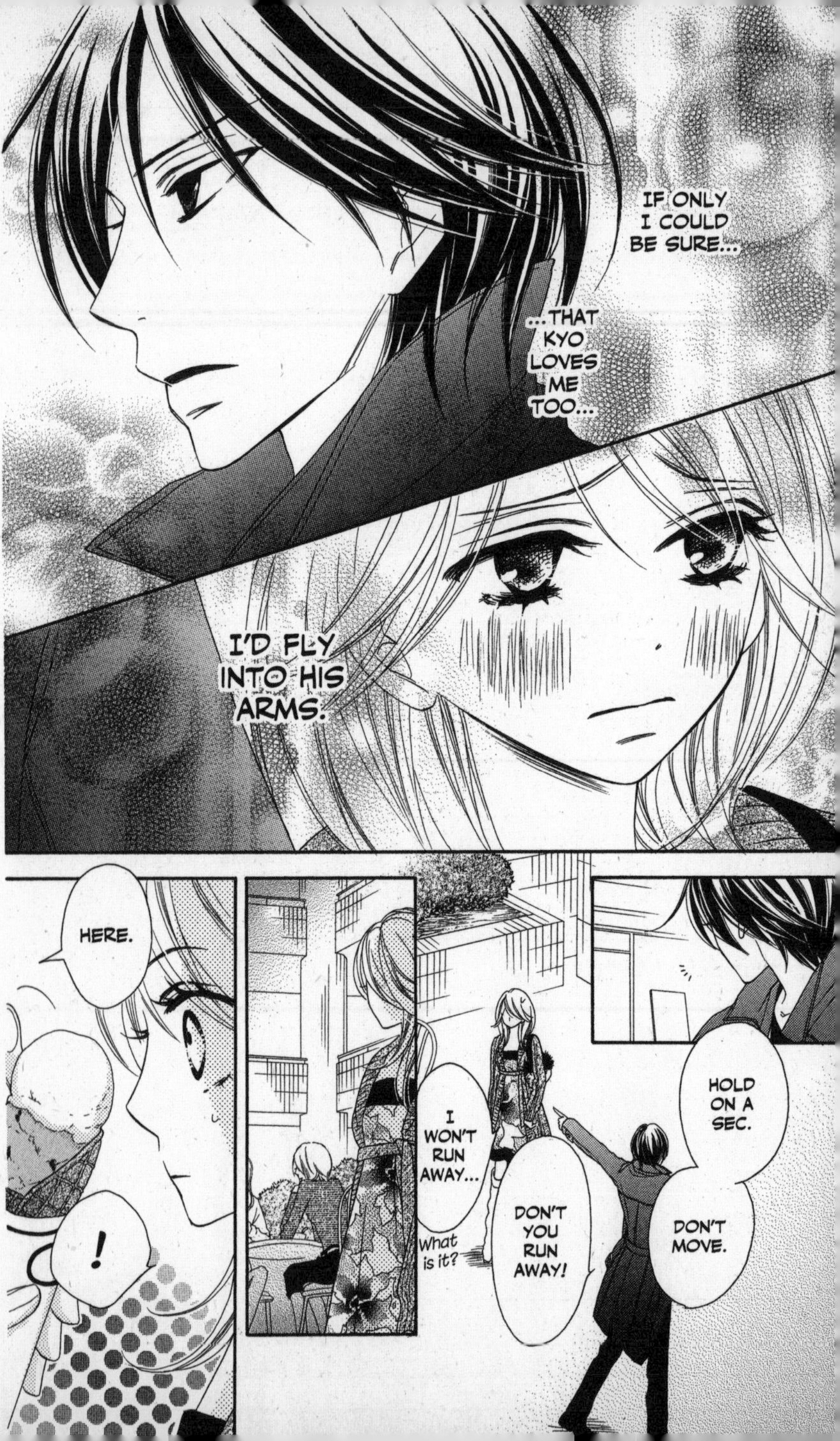
IF ONLY I COULD BE SURE...
...THAT KYO LOVES ME TOO...
I'D FLY INTO HIS ARMS.
HOLD ON A SEC.
DON'T MOVE.
DON'T YOU RUN AWAY!
I WON'T RUN AWAY...
What is it?
HERE.
!

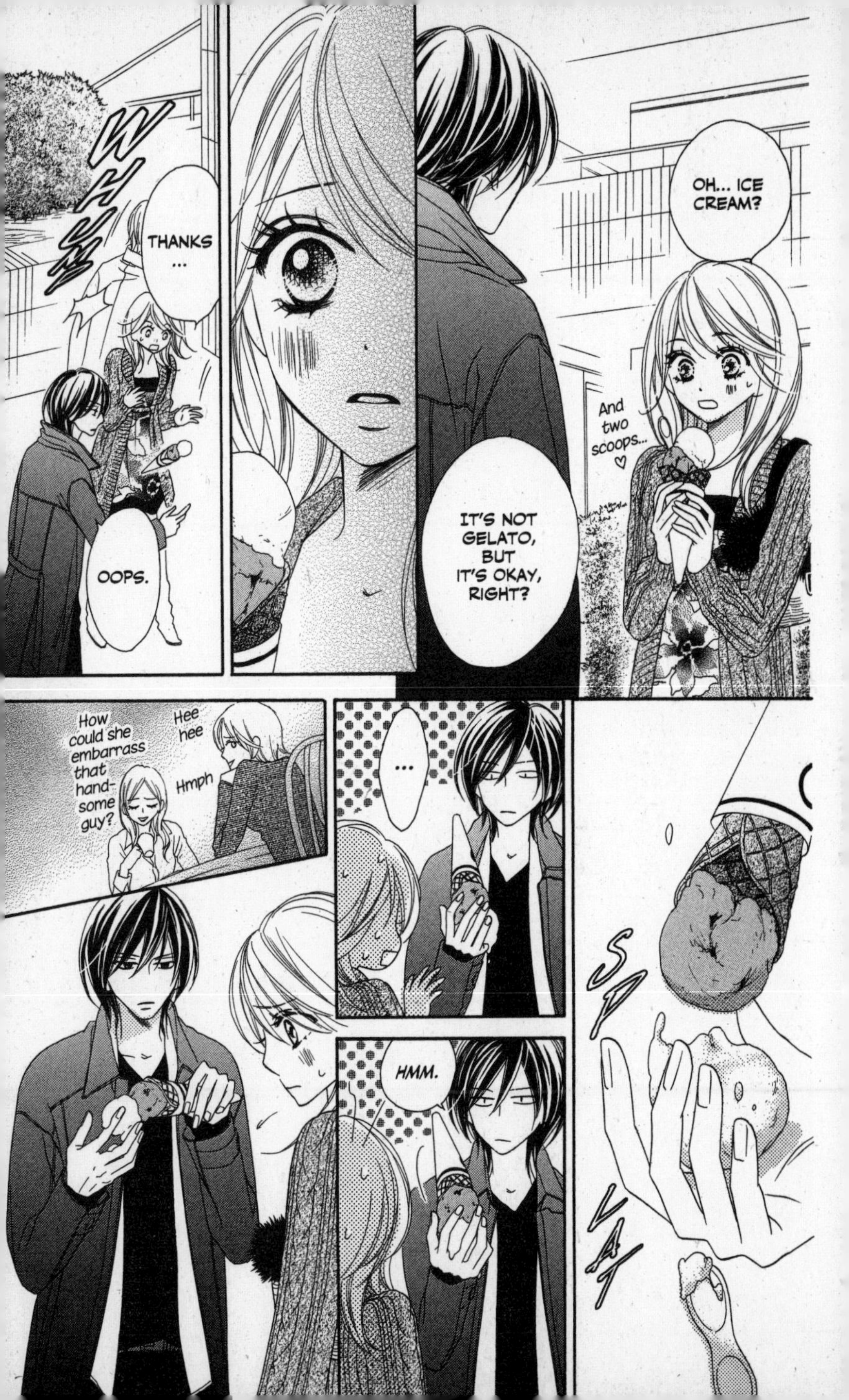
OH... ICE CREAM?
And two scoops... ♡
IT'S NOT GELATO, BUT IT'S OKAY, RIGHT?
THANKS ...
OOPS.
...
HMM.
How could she embarrass that hand-some guy?
Hee hee
Hmph

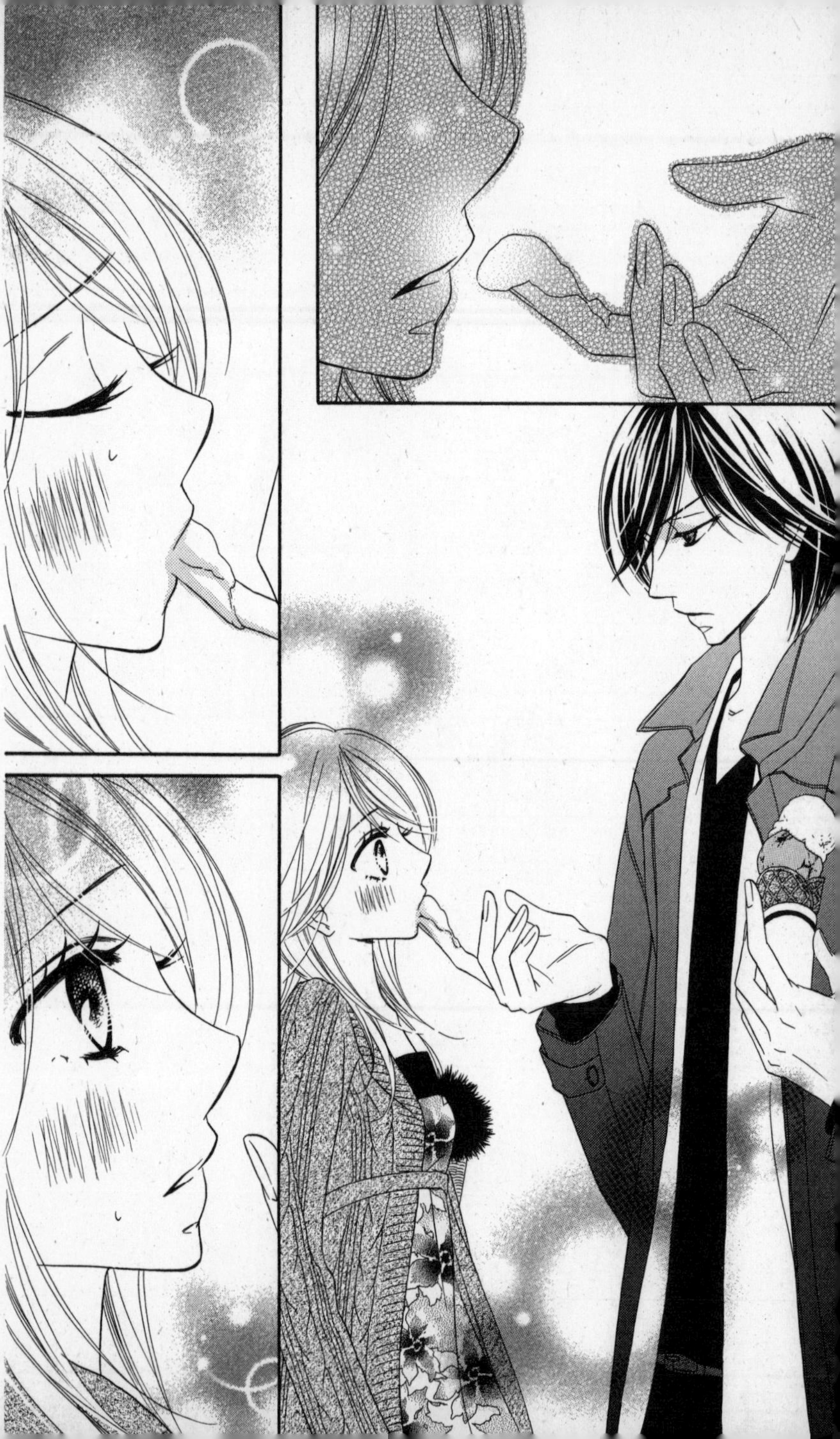

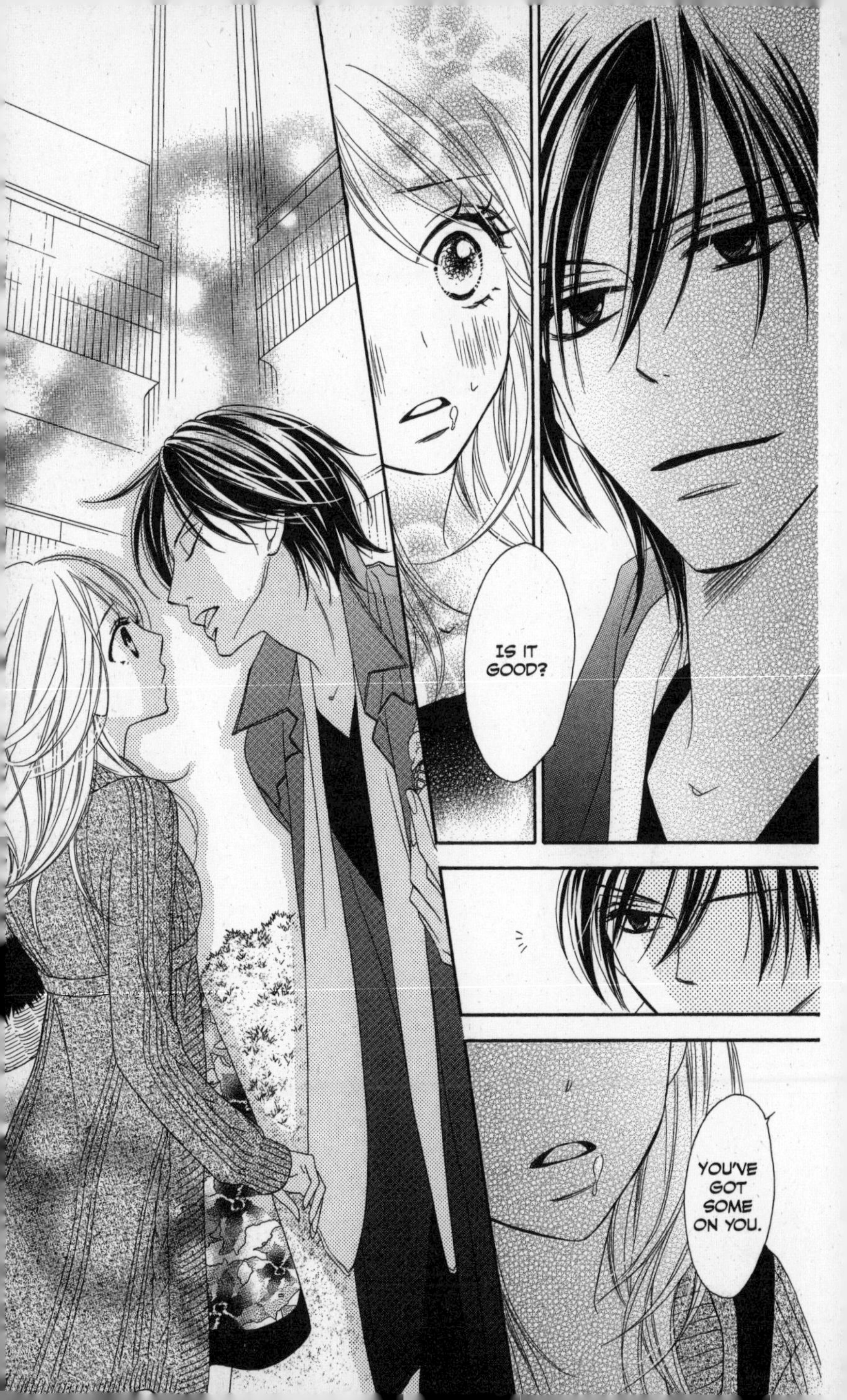
IS IT GOOD?
YOU'VE GOT SOME ON YOU.

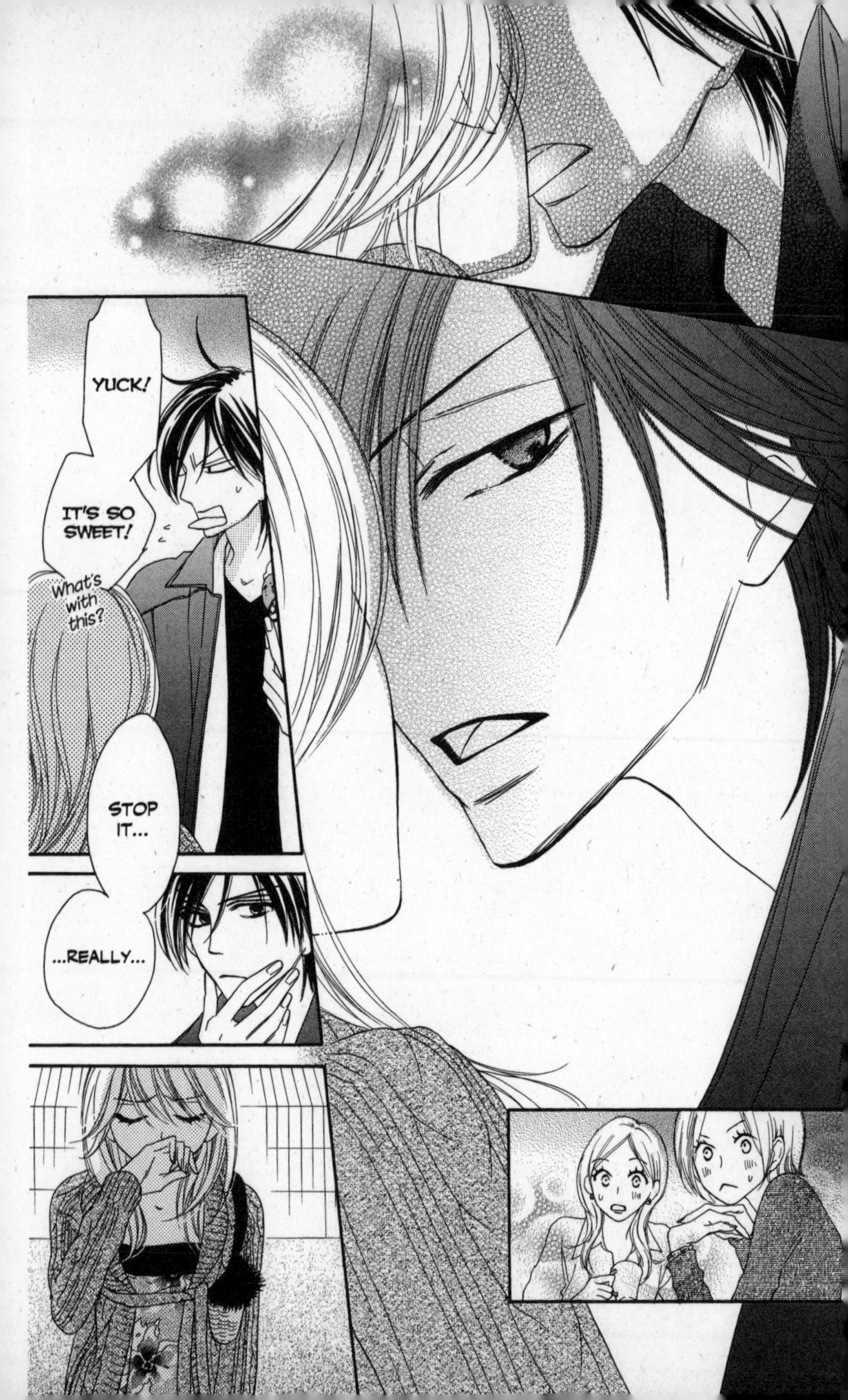
YUCK!
IT'S SO SWEET!
What's with this?
STOP IT...
...REALLY...

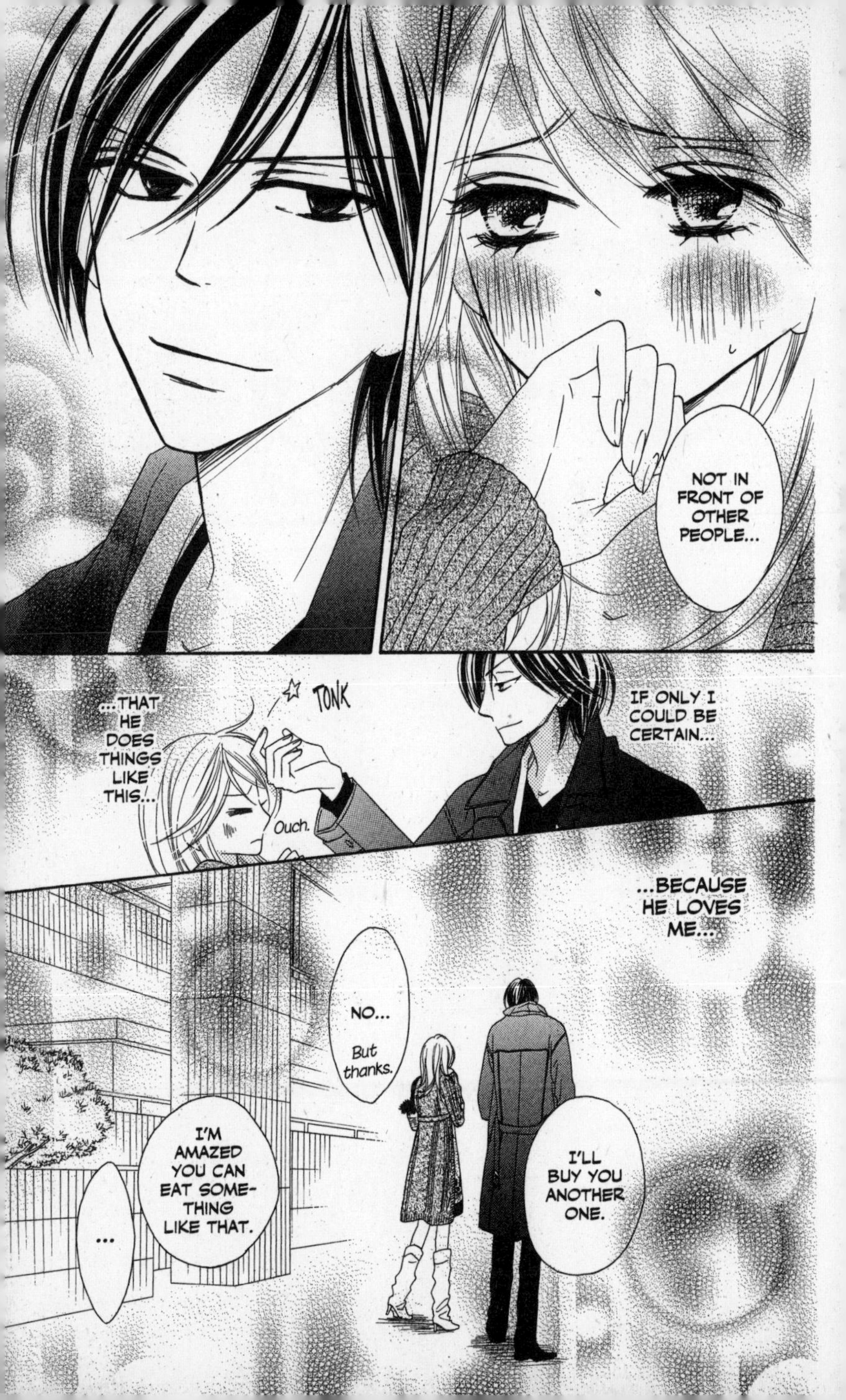
NOT IN FRONT OF OTHER PEOPLE...
IF ONLY I COULD BE CERTAIN...
TONK
Ouch.
...THAT HE DOES THINGS LIKE THIS...
...BECAUSE HE LOVES ME...
I'LL BUY YOU ANOTHER ONE.
NO...
But thanks.
I'M AMAZED YOU CAN EAT SOME-THING LIKE THAT.
...

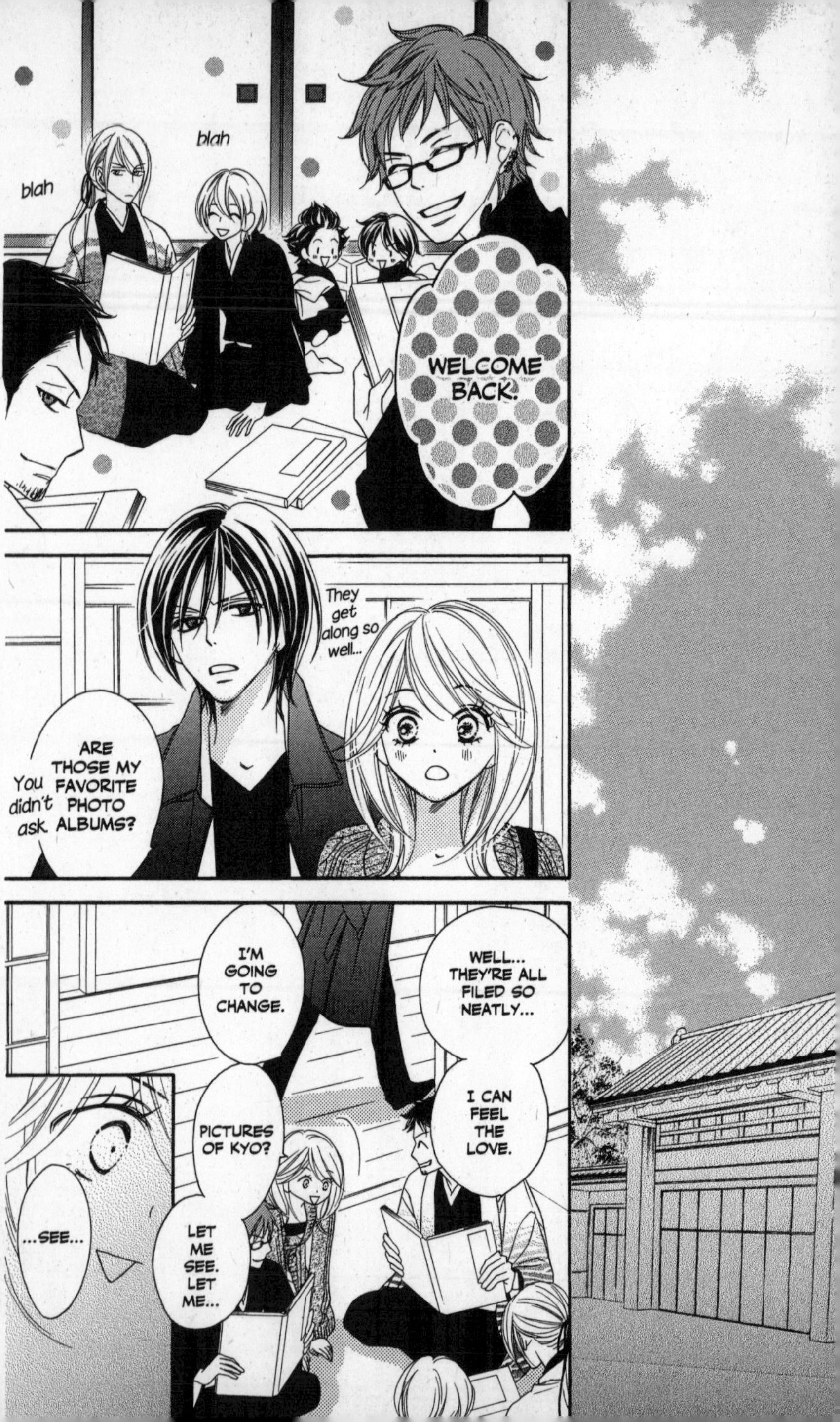
WELCOME BACK.
blah
blah
They get along so well...
ARE THOSE MY FAVORITE PHOTO ALBUMS?
You didn't ask.
WELL... THEY'RE ALL FILED SO NEATLY...
I'M GOING TO CHANGE.
I CAN FEEL THE LOVE.
PICTURES OF KYO?
LET ME SEE. LET ME...
...SEE...

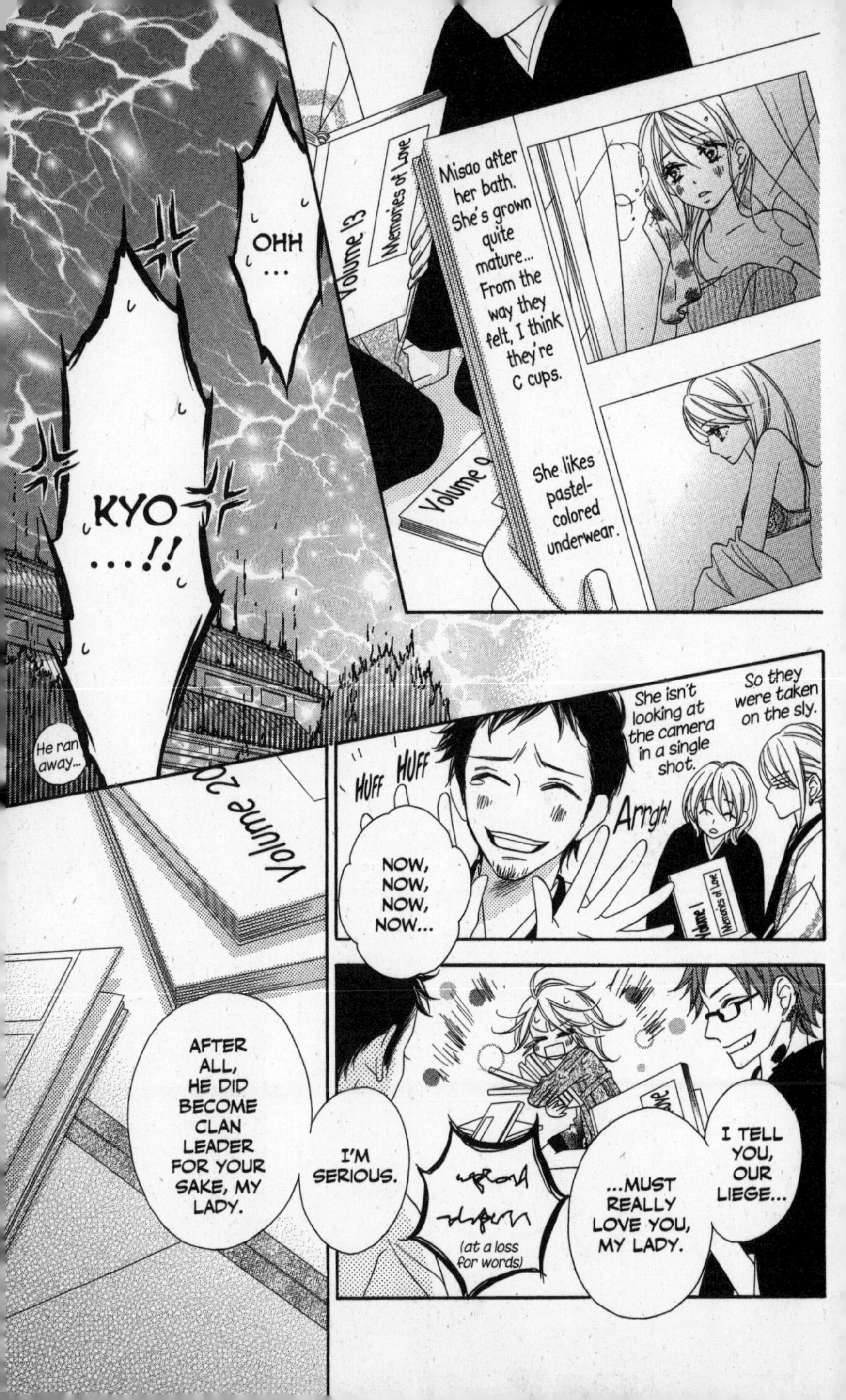
Memories of Love
Volume 13
Misao after her bath. She's grown quite mature... From the way they felt, I think they're C cups.
She likes pastel-colored underwear.
Volume 9
OHH...
KYO...!!
He ran away...
So they were taken on the sly.
She isn't looking at the camera in a single shot.
Arrgh!
Volume 1
Memories of Love
HUFF HUFF
NOW, NOW, NOW, NOW...
Volume 20
I TELL YOU, OUR LIEGE...
...MUST REALLY LOVE YOU, MY LADY.
(at a loss for words)
I'M SERIOUS.
AFTER ALL, HE DID BECOME CLAN LEADER FOR YOUR SAKE, MY LADY.

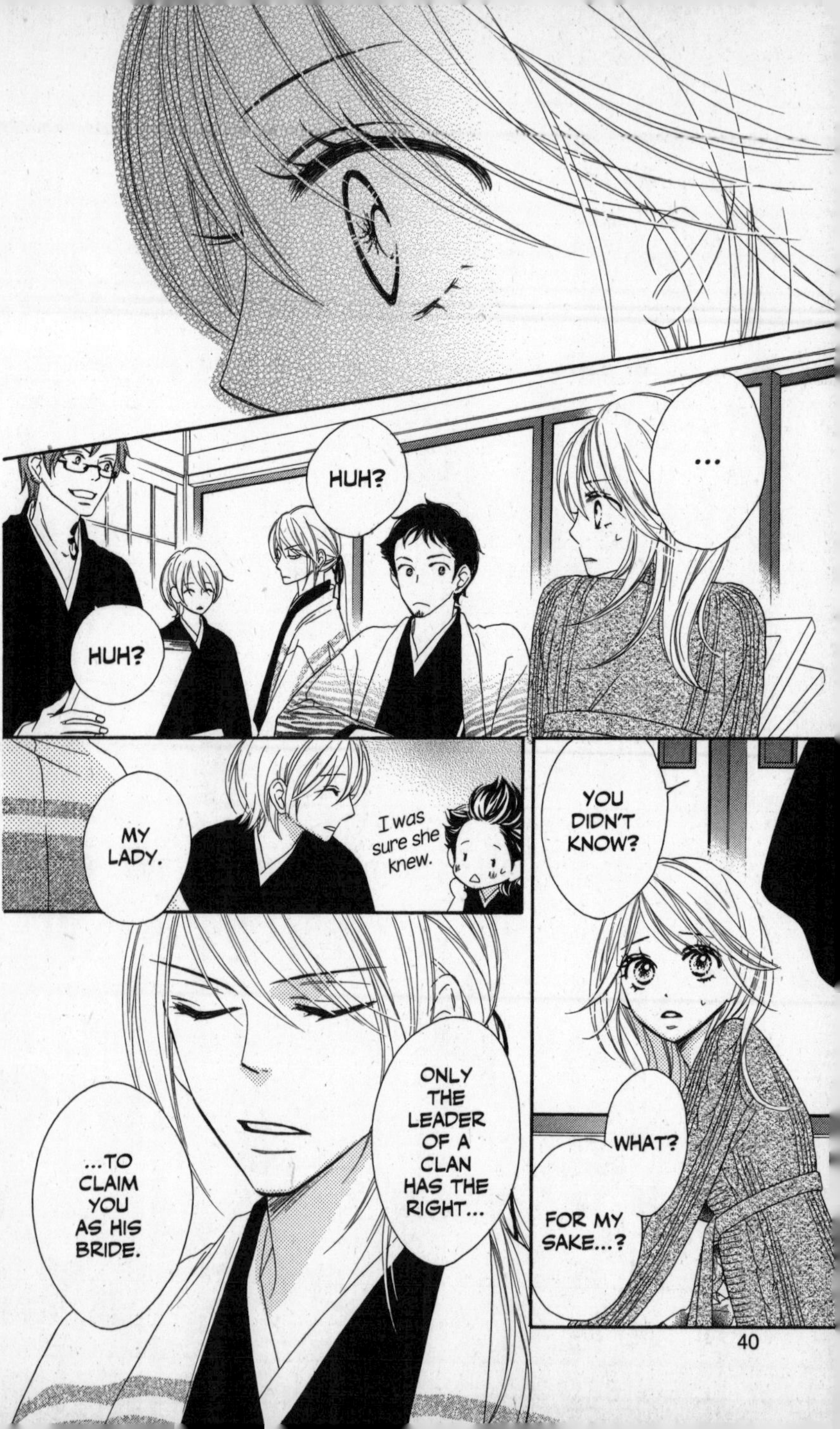
...
HUH?
HUH?
YOU DIDN'T KNOW?
WHAT?
FOR MY SAKE...?
I was sure she knew.
MY LADY.
ONLY THE LEADER OF A CLAN HAS THE RIGHT...
...TO CLAIM YOU AS HIS BRIDE.

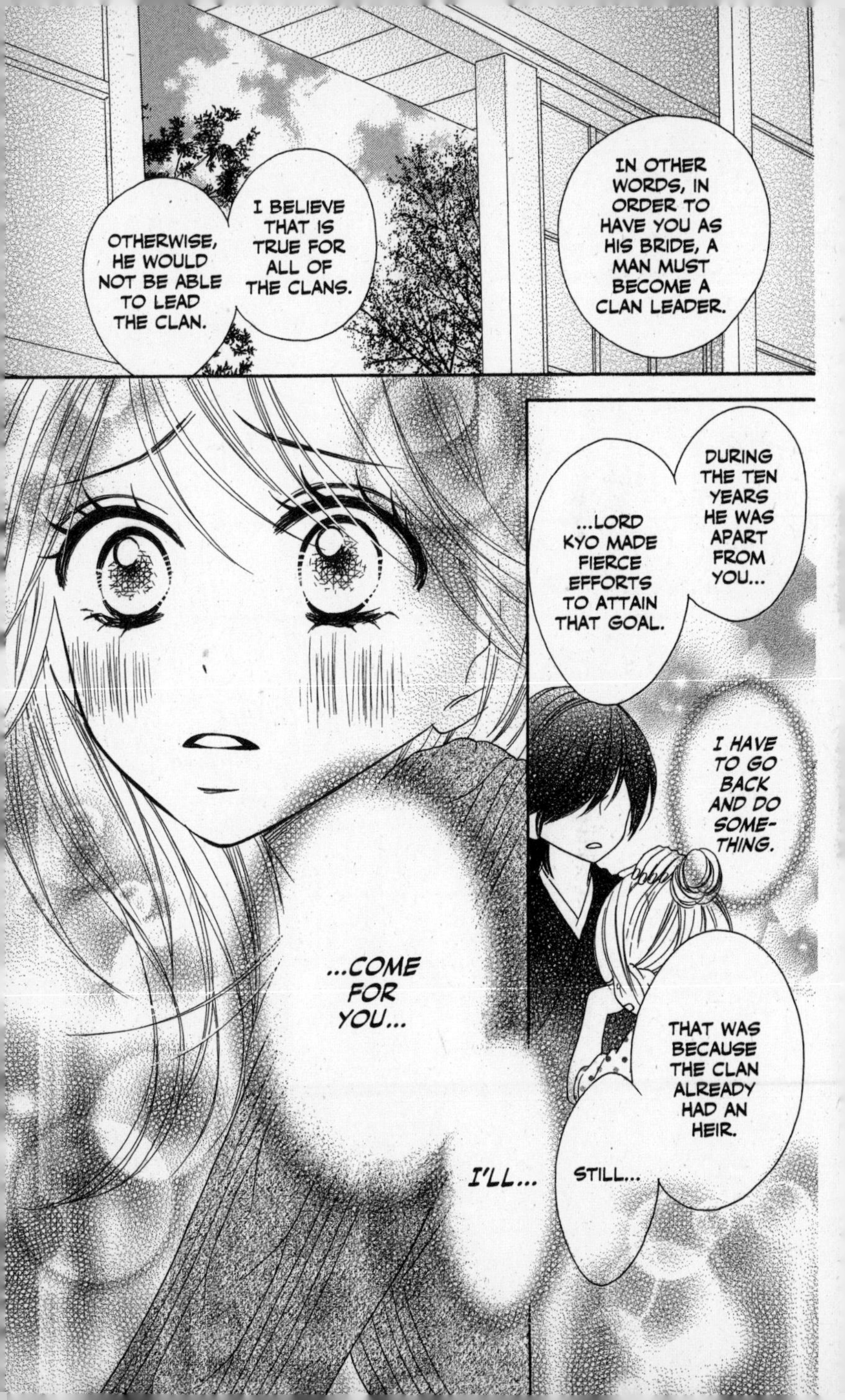
IN OTHER WORDS, IN ORDER TO HAVE YOU AS HIS BRIDE, A MAN MUST BECOME A CLAN LEADER.
I BELIEVE THAT IS TRUE FOR ALL OF THE CLANS.
OTHERWISE, HE WOULD NOT BE ABLE TO LEAD THE CLAN.
DURING THE TEN YEARS HE WAS APART FROM YOU...
...LORD KYO MADE FIERCE EFFORTS TO ATTAIN THAT GOAL.
I HAVE TO GO BACK AND DO SOME-THING.
THAT WAS BECAUSE THE CLAN ALREADY HAD AN HEIR.
STILL...
I'LL...
...COME FOR YOU...

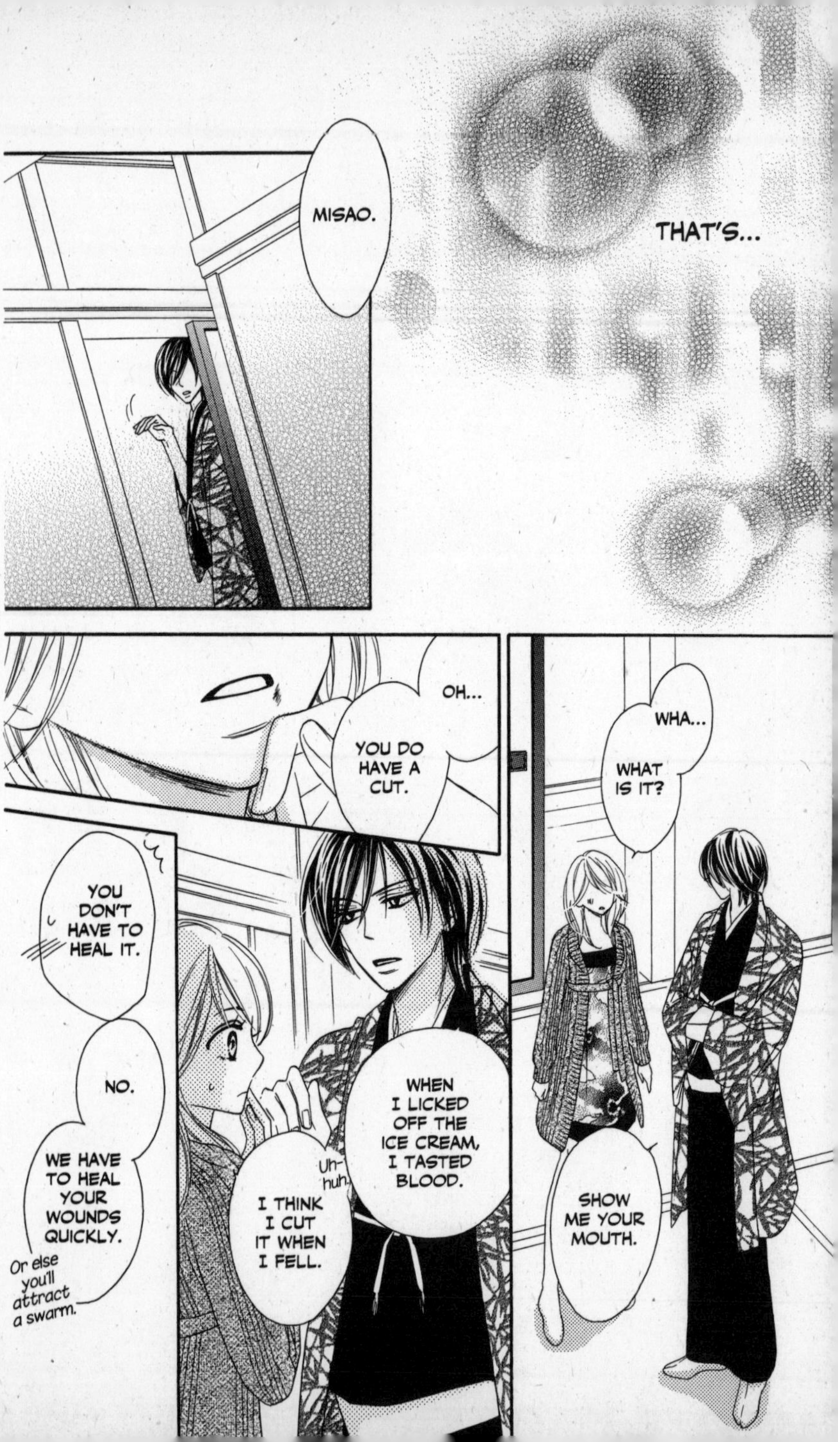
THAT'S...
MISAO.
WHA... WHAT IS IT?
SHOW ME YOUR MOUTH.
OH... YOU DO HAVE A CUT.
WHEN I LICKED OFF THE ICE CREAM, I TASTED BLOOD.
Uh-huh.
I THINK I CUT IT WHEN I FELL.
YOU DON'T HAVE TO HEAL IT.
NO.
WE HAVE TO HEAL YOUR WOUNDS QUICKLY.
Or else you'll attract a swarm.

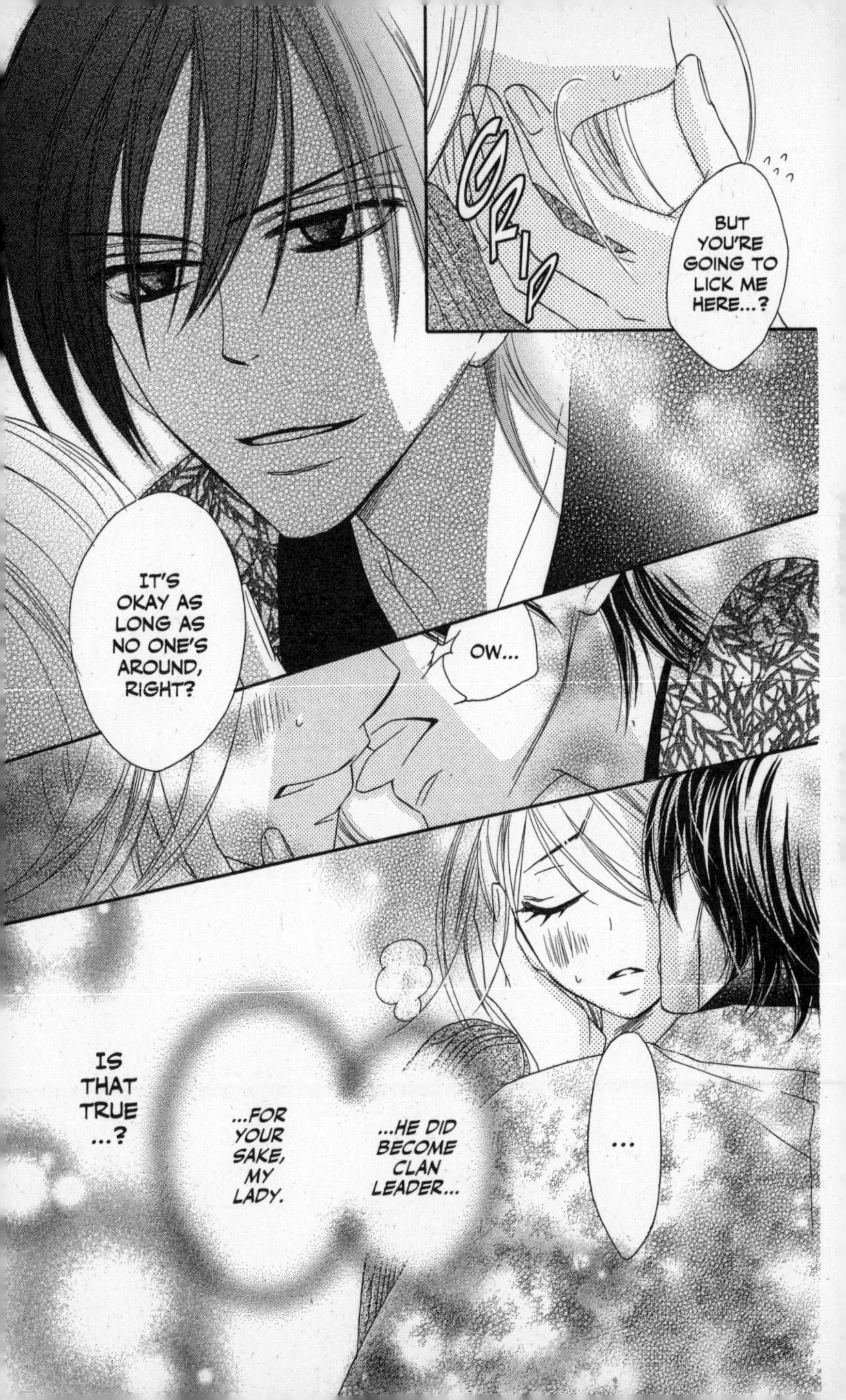
GRIP
BUT YOU'RE GOING TO LICK ME HERE...?
IT'S OKAY AS LONG AS NO ONE'S AROUND, RIGHT?
OW...
...
...HE DID BECOME CLAN LEADER...
...FOR YOUR SAKE, MY LADY.
IS THAT TRUE ...?

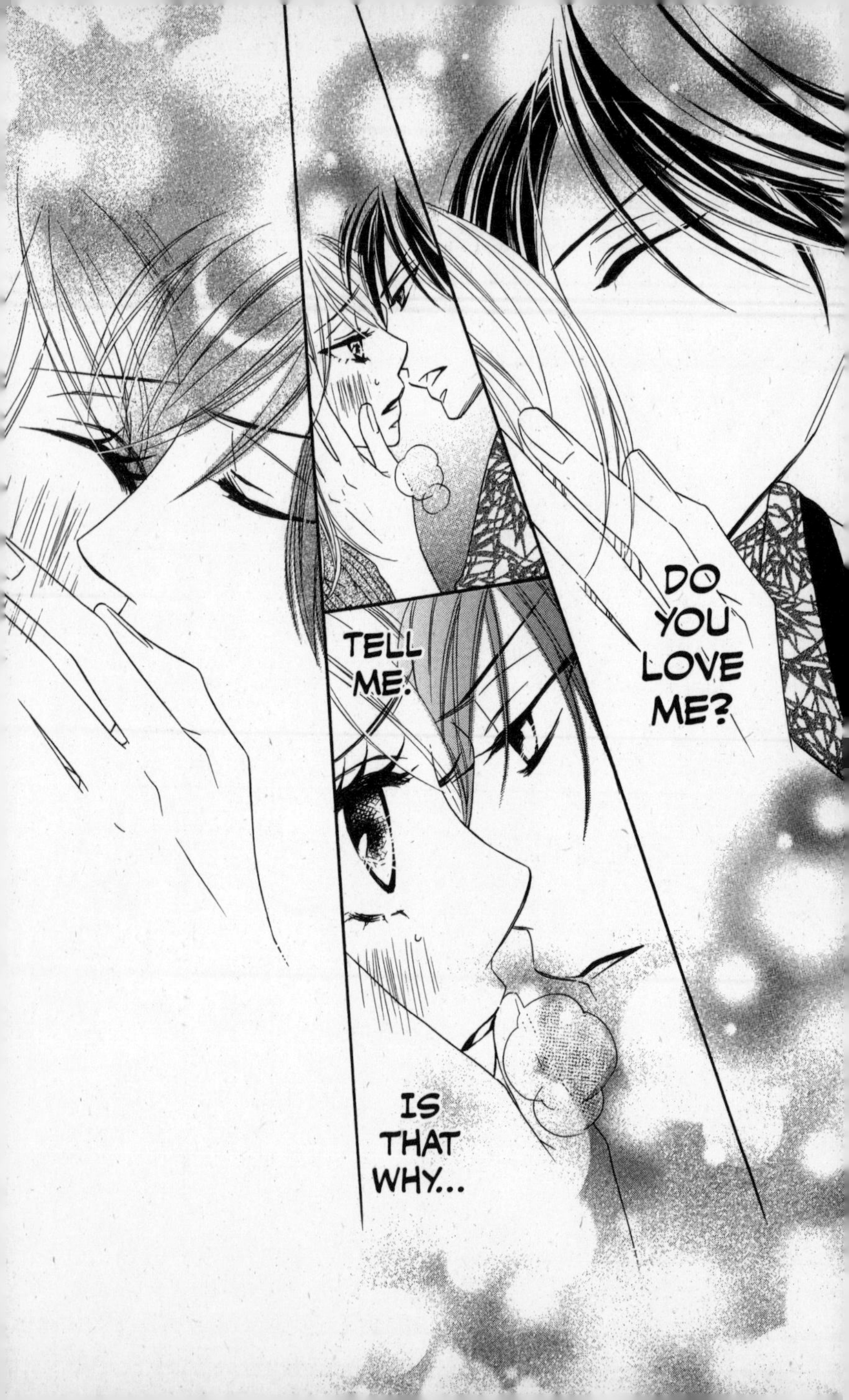
DO YOU LOVE ME?
TELL ME.
IS THAT WHY...

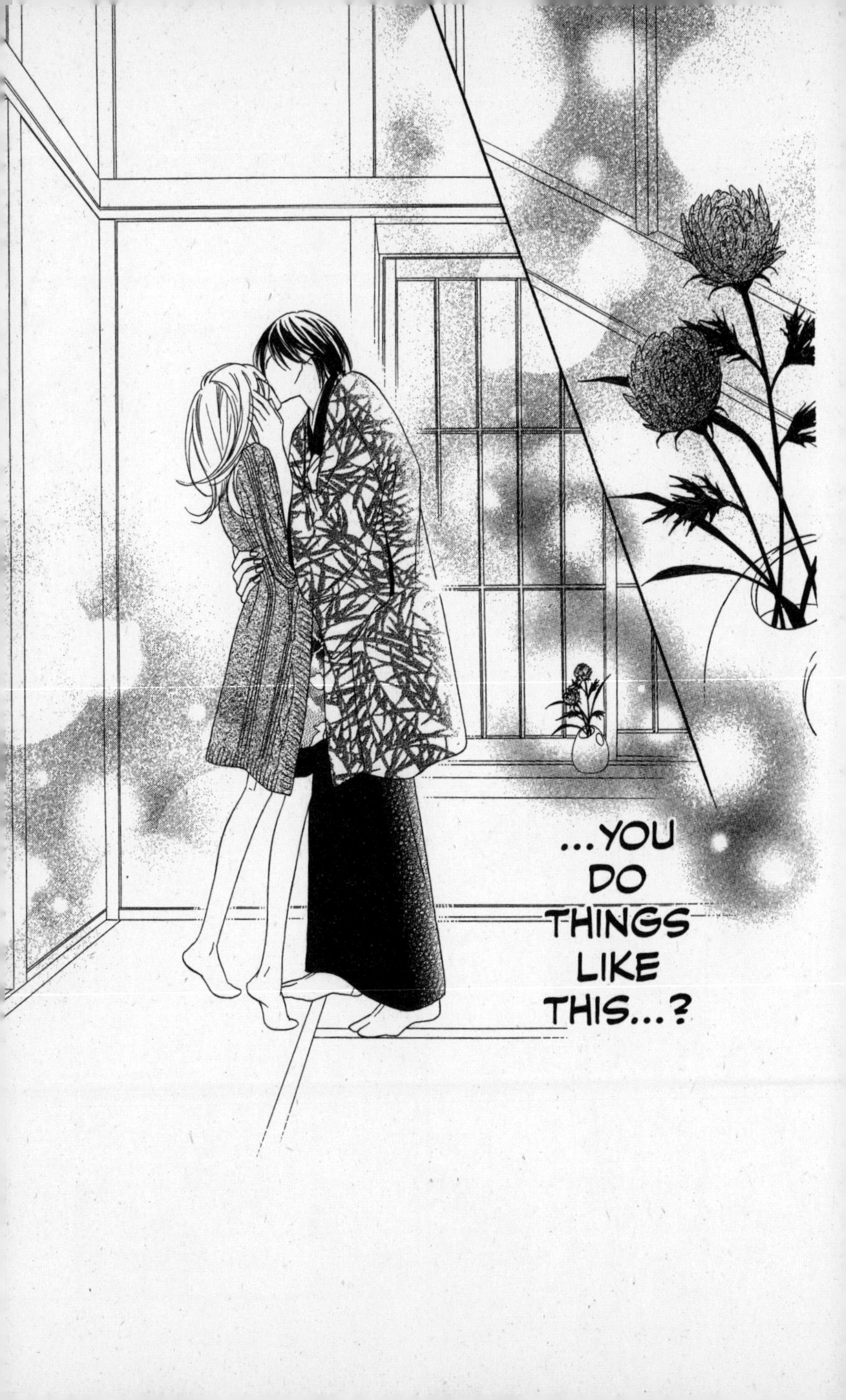
...YOU DO THINGS LIKE THIS...?

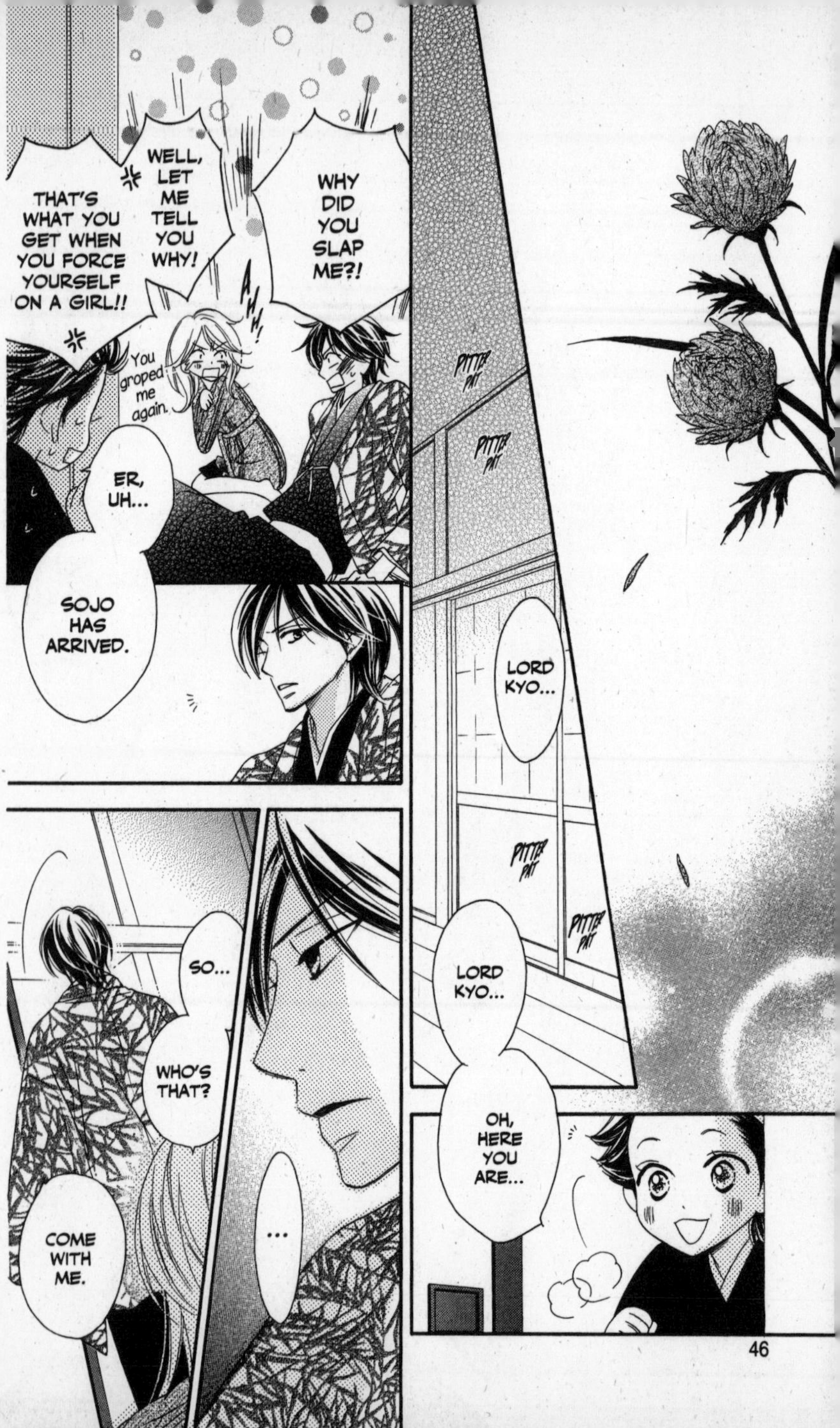
PITTER PAT
PITTER PAT
LORD KYO...
PITTER PAT
PITTER PAT
LORD KYO...
OH, HERE YOU ARE...
WHY DID YOU SLAP ME?!
AHH!
WELL, LET ME TELL YOU WHY!
THAT'S WHAT YOU GET WHEN YOU FORCE YOURSELF ON A GIRL!!
You groped me again.
ER, UH...
SOJO HAS ARRIVED.
SO...
WHO'S THAT?
...
COME WITH ME.

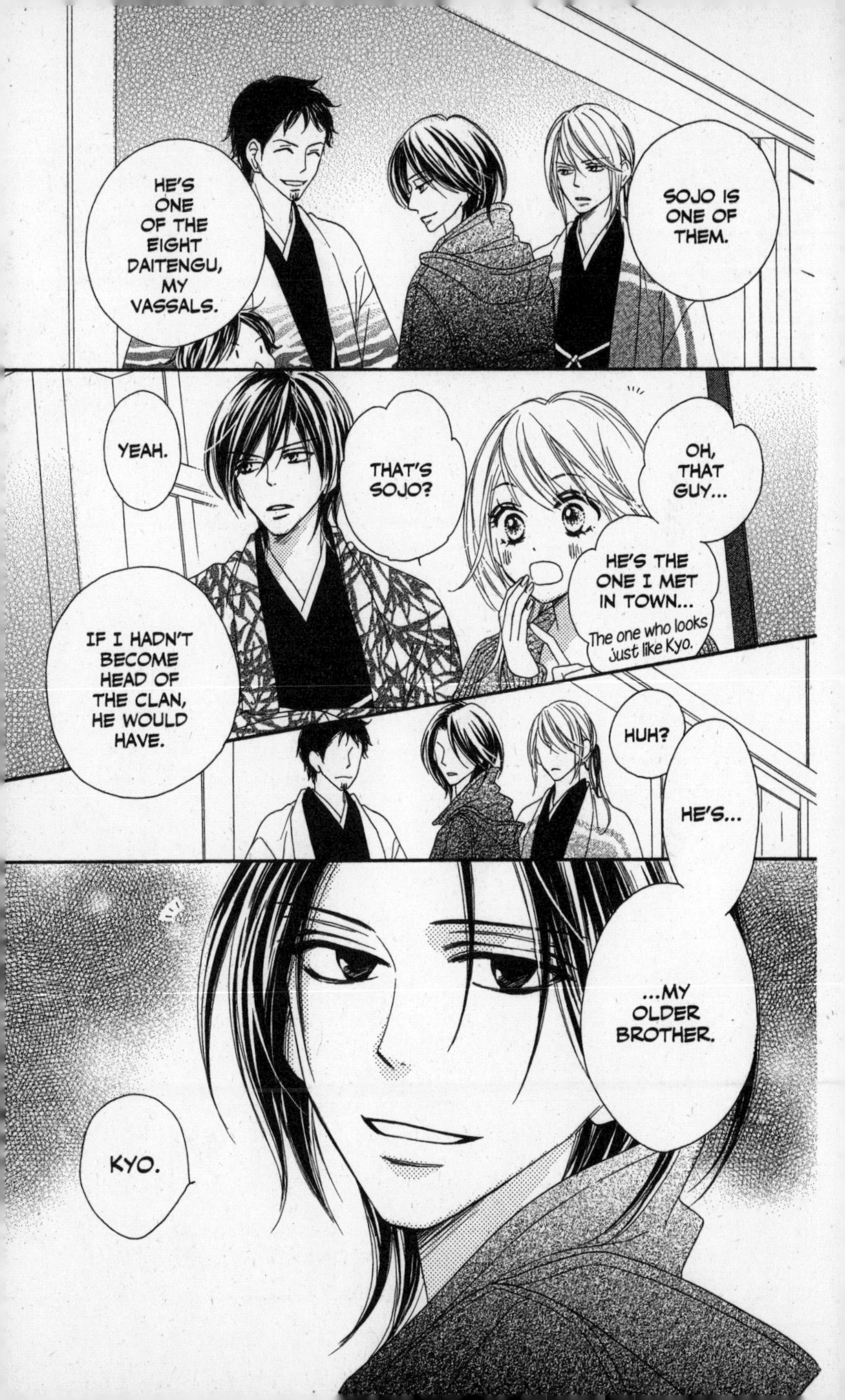
SOJO IS ONE OF THEM.
HE'S ONE OF THE EIGHT DAITENGU, MY VASSALS.
OH, THAT GUY...
HE'S THE ONE I MET IN TOWN...
The one who looks just like Kyo.
THAT'S SOJO?
YEAH.
IF I HADN'T BECOME HEAD OF THE CLAN, HE WOULD HAVE.
HUH?
HE'S...
...MY OLDER BROTHER.
KYO.

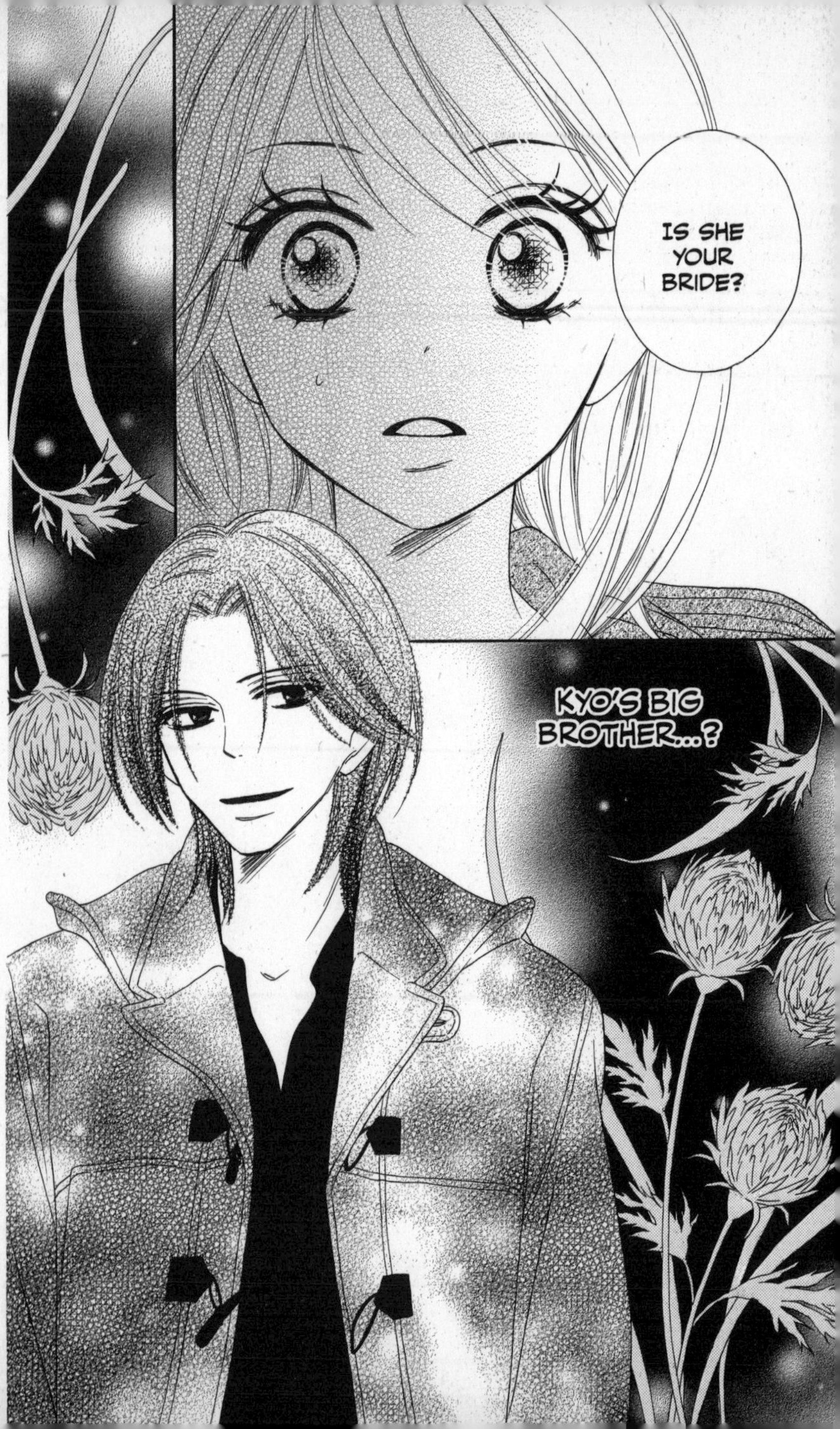
IS SHE YOUR BRIDE?
KYO'S BIG BROTHER...?

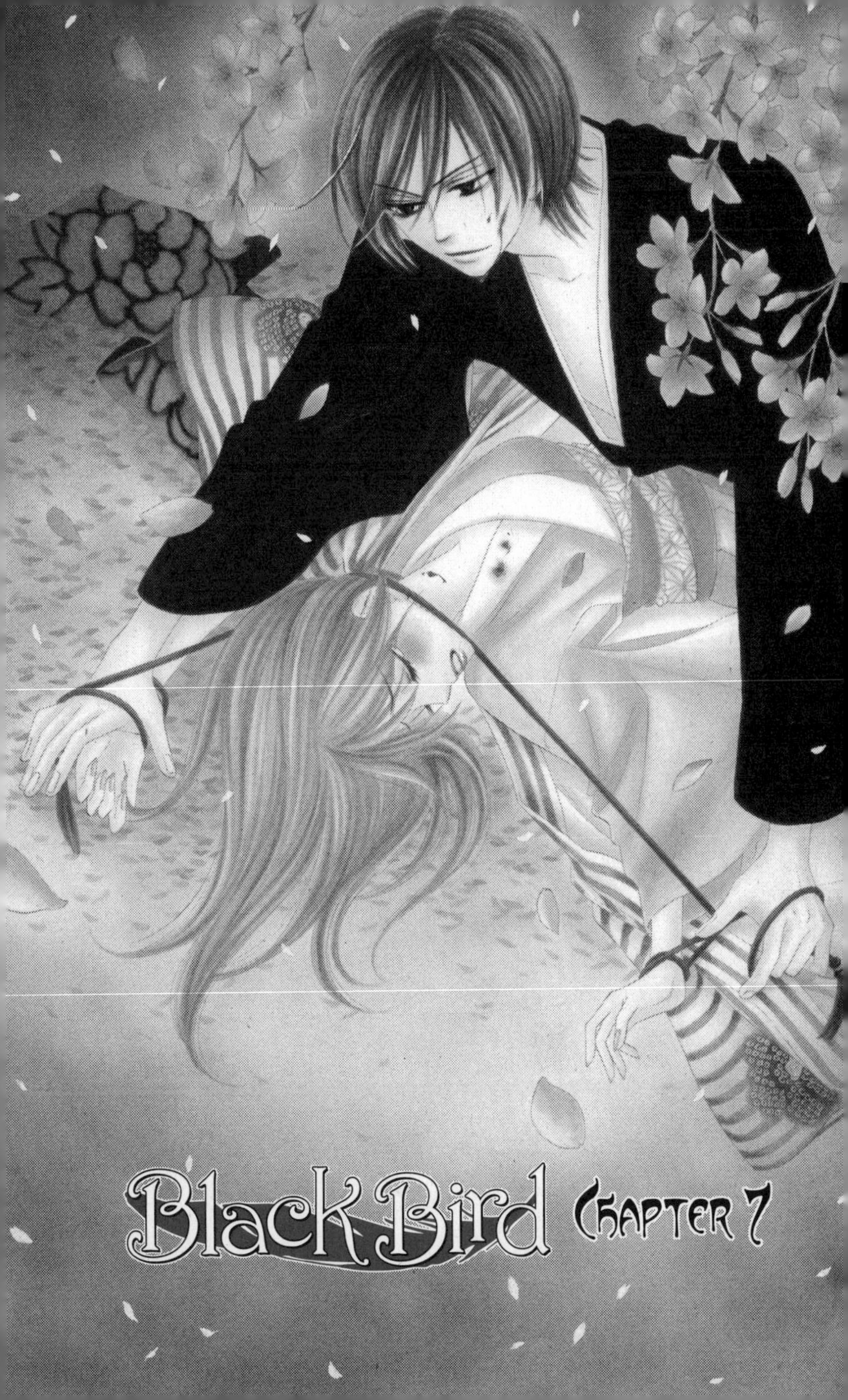
Black Bird
Chapter 7

THE EIGHT DAITENGU.

THE EIGHT VASSALS OF THE CLAN LEADER, KYO.

ONE OF THEM IS KYO'S OLDER BROTHER, WHO SHOULD HAVE BECOME LEADER.

I love to draw pictures in color. I can get so engrossed in them that I forget to eat or sleep.

And yet, for some reason, I don't get any better at it.

The cover drawing for this volume was a terrible mess that I did my best to rescue.

I'm getting better at glossing over my mistakes...

← A.M.
(This doesn't mean I got up early.)

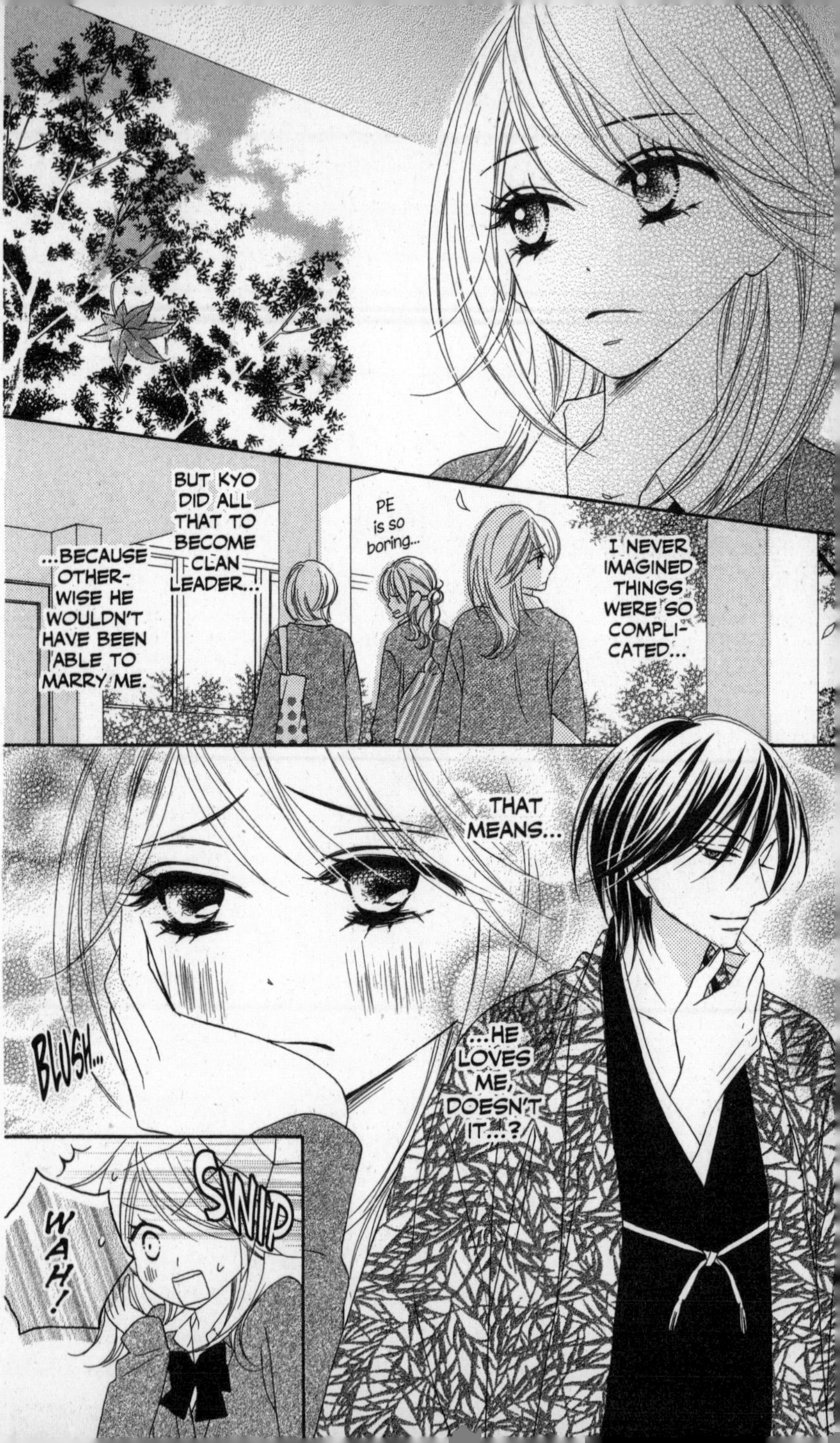
I NEVER IMAGINED THINGS WERE SO COMPLICATED...
PE is so boring...
BUT KYO DID ALL THAT TO BECOME CLAN LEADER...
...BECAUSE OTHERWISE HE WOULDN'T HAVE BEEN ABLE TO MARRY ME.
THAT MEANS...
...HE LOVES ME, DOESN'T IT...?
BLUSH...
SNIP
WAH!

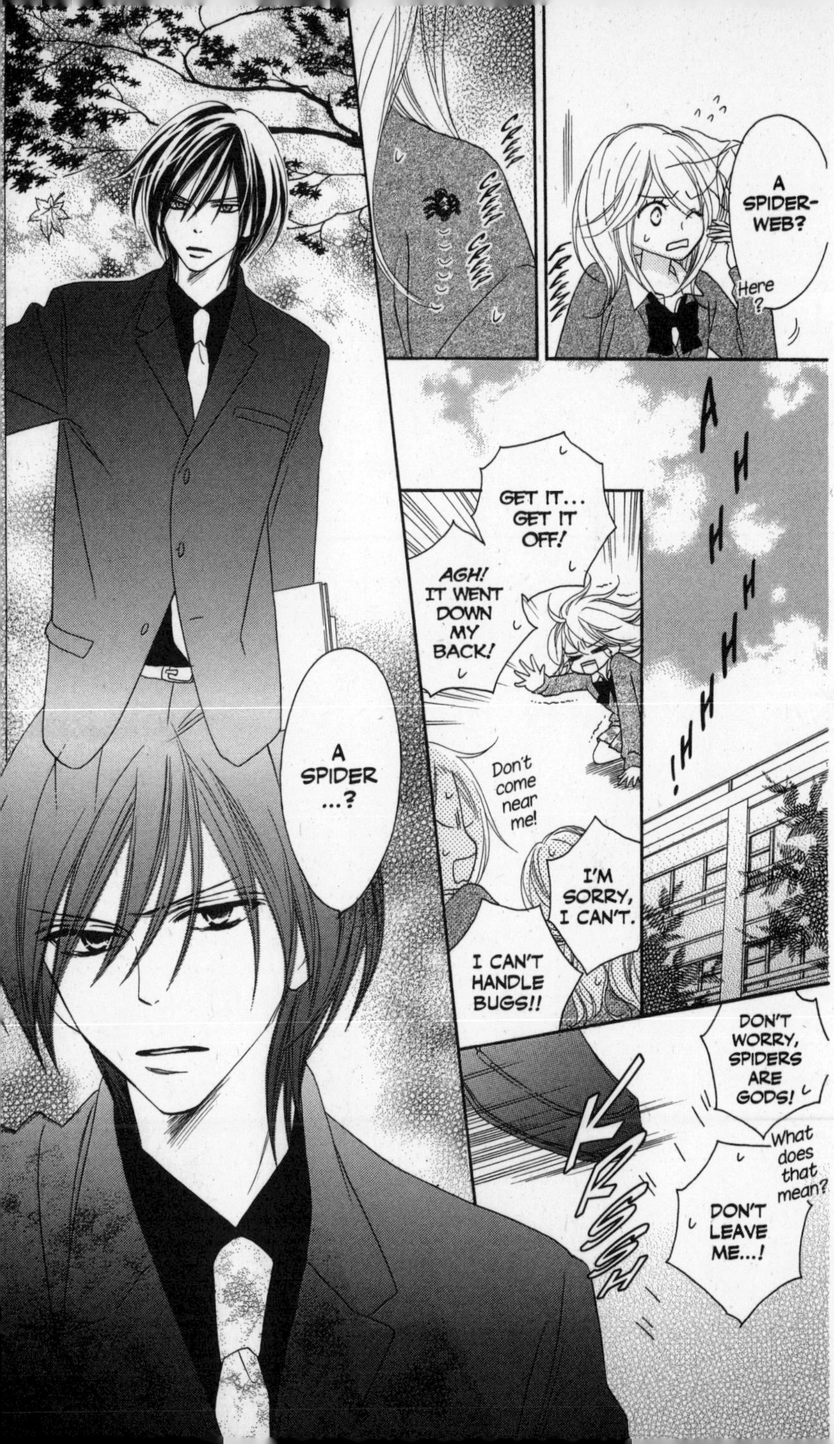
A SPIDER-WEB?
Here?
AHHHHHHHH!!
GET IT... GET IT OFF!
AGH! IT WENT DOWN MY BACK!
Don't come near me!
I'M SORRY, I CAN'T.
I CAN'T HANDLE BUGS!!
DON'T WORRY, SPIDERS ARE GODS!
What does that mean?
DON'T LEAVE ME...!
A SPIDER ...?

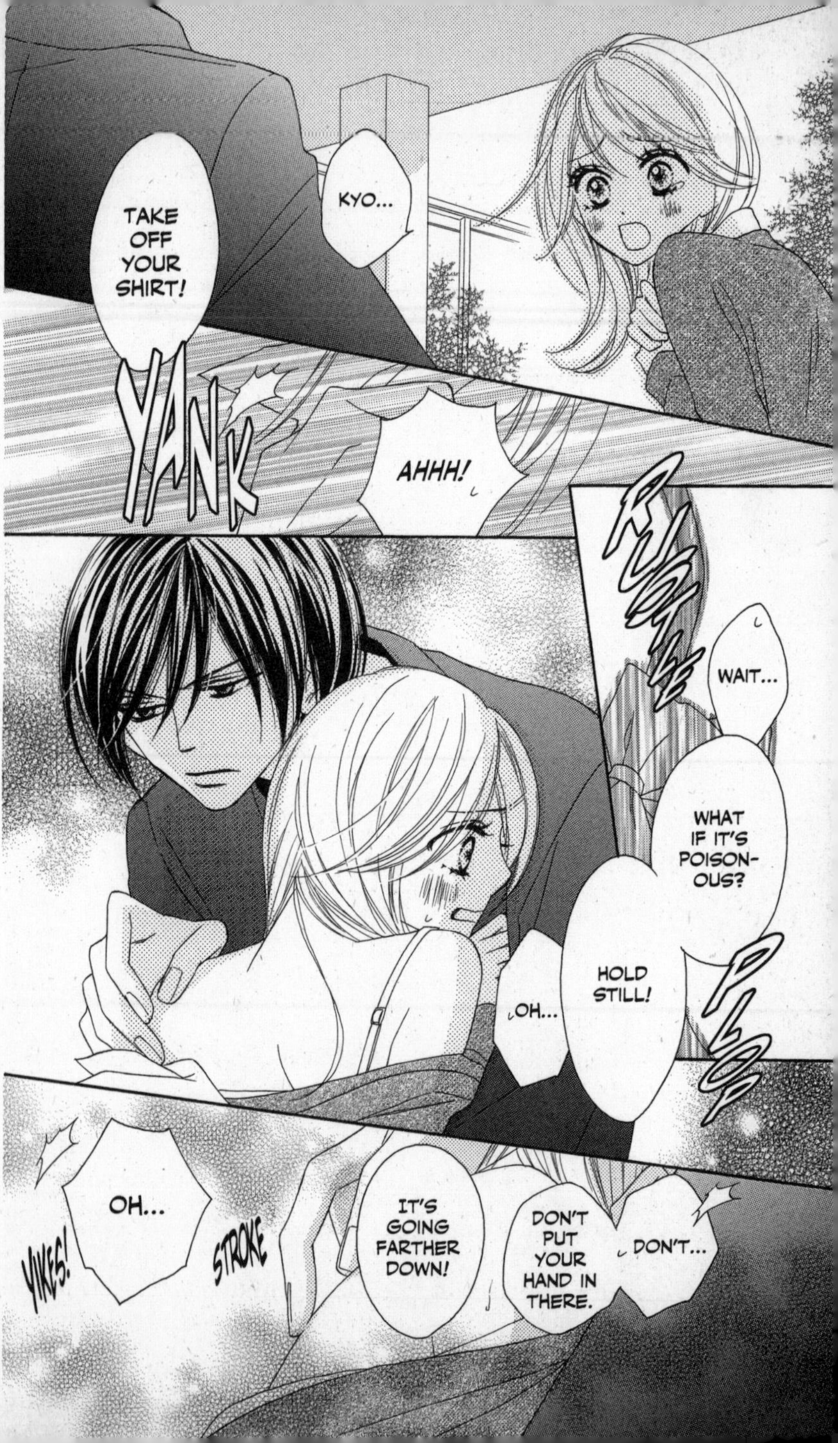
KYO...
TAKE OFF YOUR SHIRT!
YANK
AHHH!
WAIT...
WHAT IF IT'S POISON-OUS?
HOLD STILL!
OH...
DON'T...
DON'T PUT YOUR HAND IN THERE.
IT'S GOING FARTHER DOWN!
STROKE
OH...
YIKES!

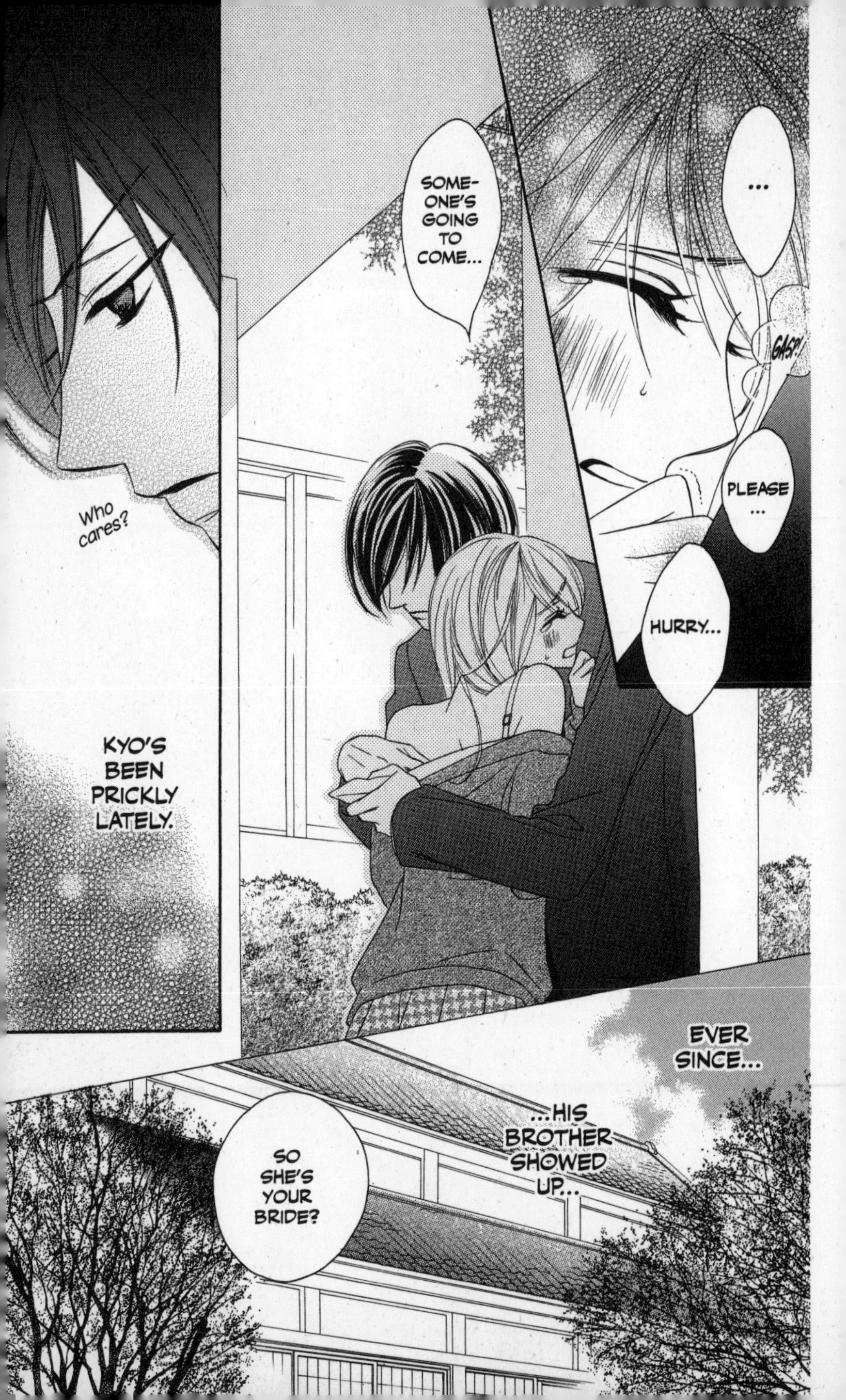
...
GASP!
PLEASE...
HURRY...
SOME-ONE'S GOING TO COME...
Who cares?
KYO'S BEEN PRICKLY LATELY.
EVER SINCE...
...HIS BROTHER SHOWED UP...
SO SHE'S YOUR BRIDE?

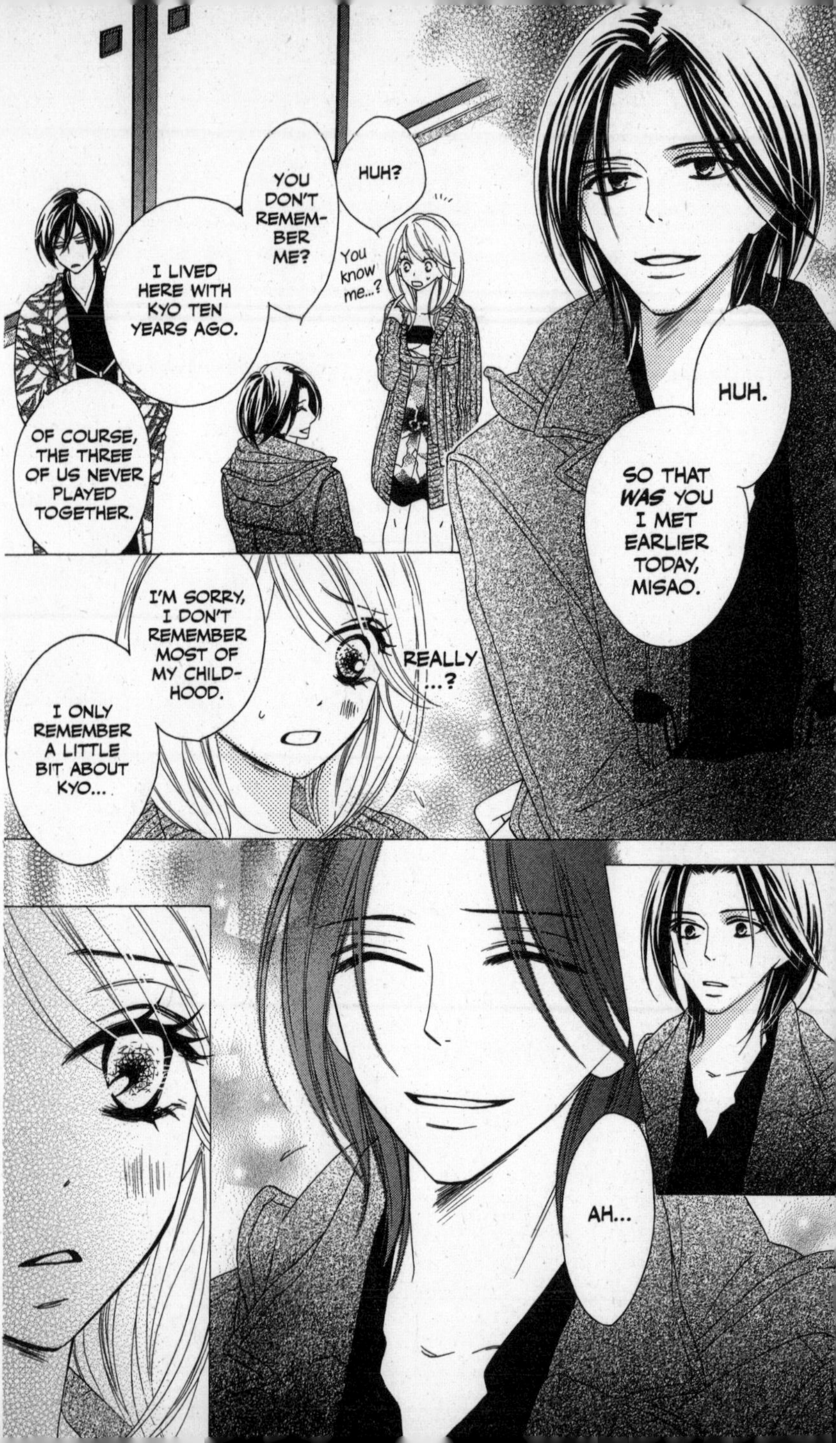
HUH.
SO THAT *WAS* YOU I MET EARLIER TODAY, MISAO.
HUH?
You know me...?
YOU DON'T REMEMBER ME?
I LIVED HERE WITH KYO TEN YEARS AGO.
OF COURSE, THE THREE OF US NEVER PLAYED TOGETHER.
REALLY ...?
I'M SORRY, I DON'T REMEMBER MOST OF MY CHILDHOOD.
I ONLY REMEMBER A LITTLE BIT ABOUT KYO...
AH...

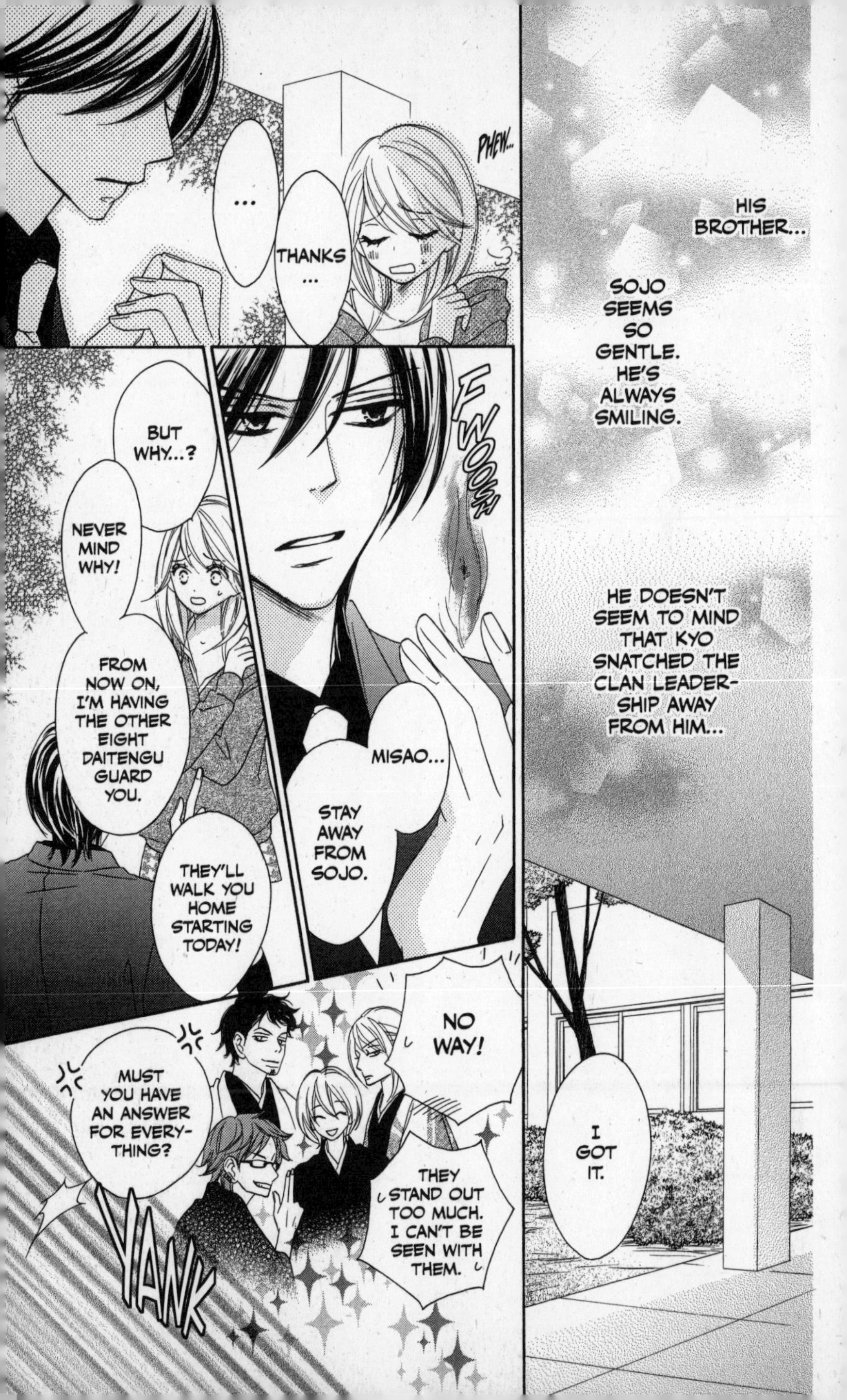
HIS BROTHER...
SOJO SEEMS SO GENTLE. HE'S ALWAYS SMILING.
HE DOESN'T SEEM TO MIND THAT KYO SNATCHED THE CLAN LEADER-SHIP AWAY FROM HIM...
I GOT IT.
PHEW...
...
THANKS ...
FWOOOH
MISAO...
STAY AWAY FROM SOJO.
BUT WHY...?
NEVER MIND WHY!
FROM NOW ON, I'M HAVING THE OTHER EIGHT DAITENGU GUARD YOU.
THEY'LL WALK YOU HOME STARTING TODAY!
NO WAY!
THEY STAND OUT TOO MUCH. I CAN'T BE SEEN WITH THEM.
MUST YOU HAVE AN ANSWER FOR EVERY-THING?
YANK

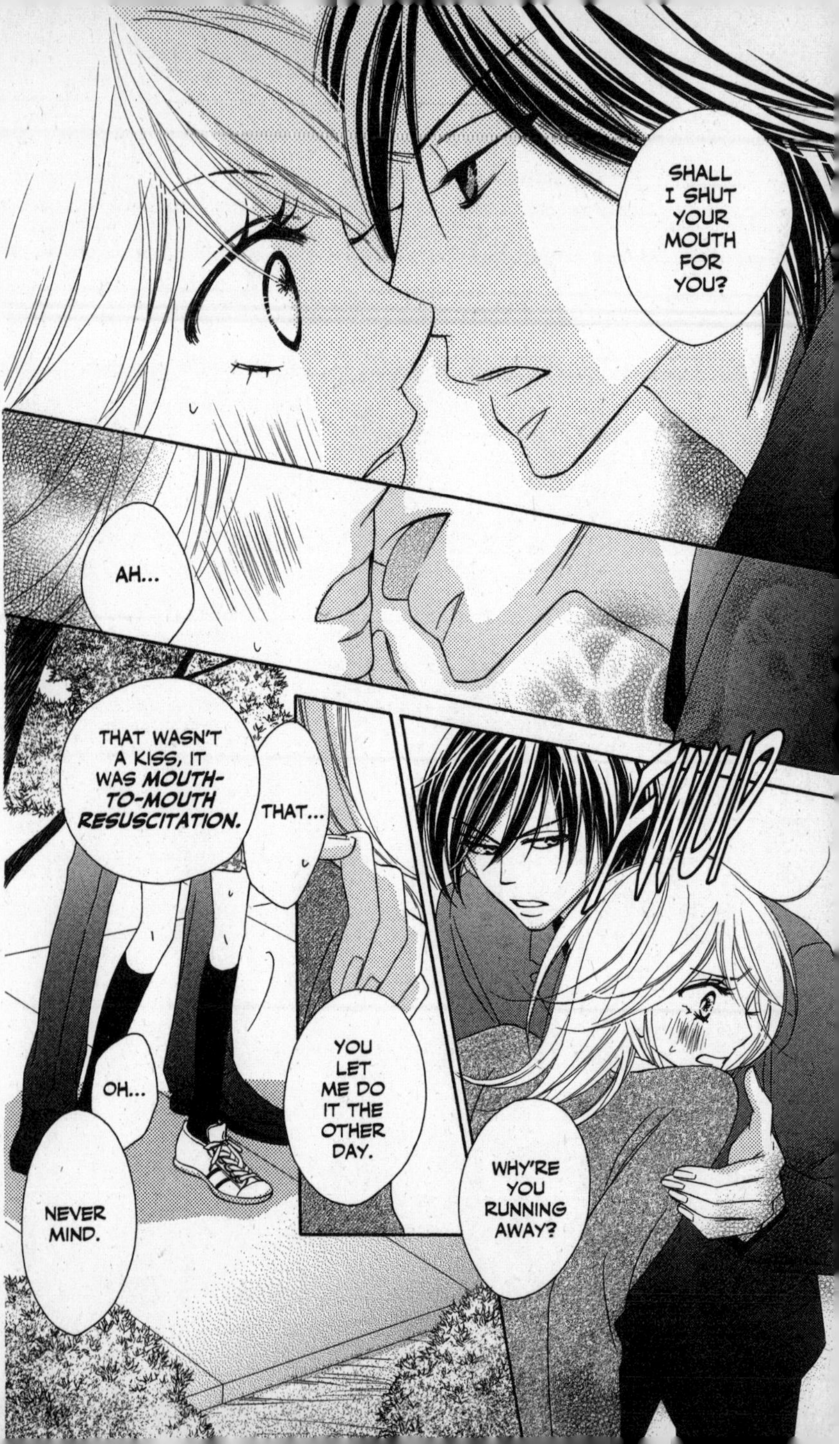
SHALL I SHUT YOUR MOUTH FOR YOU?
AH...
WHY'RE YOU RUNNING AWAY?
YOU LET ME DO IT THE OTHER DAY.
THAT...
THAT WASN'T A KISS, IT WAS *MOUTH-TO-MOUTH RESUSCITATION.*
OH...
NEVER MIND.

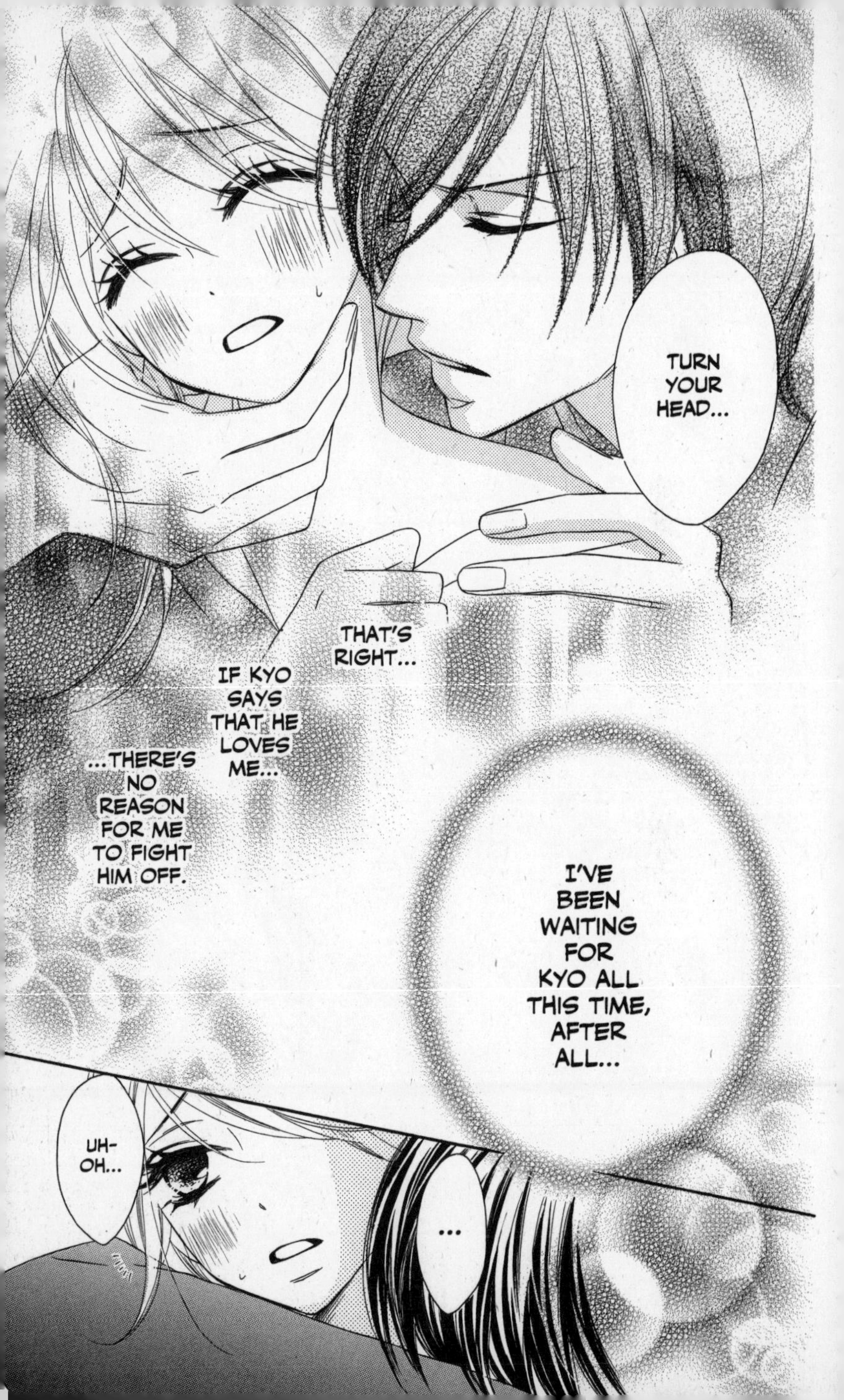
TURN YOUR HEAD...
THAT'S RIGHT...
IF KYO SAYS THAT HE LOVES ME...
...THERE'S NO REASON FOR ME TO FIGHT HIM OFF.
I'VE BEEN WAITING FOR KYO ALL THIS TIME, AFTER ALL...
...
UH-OH...

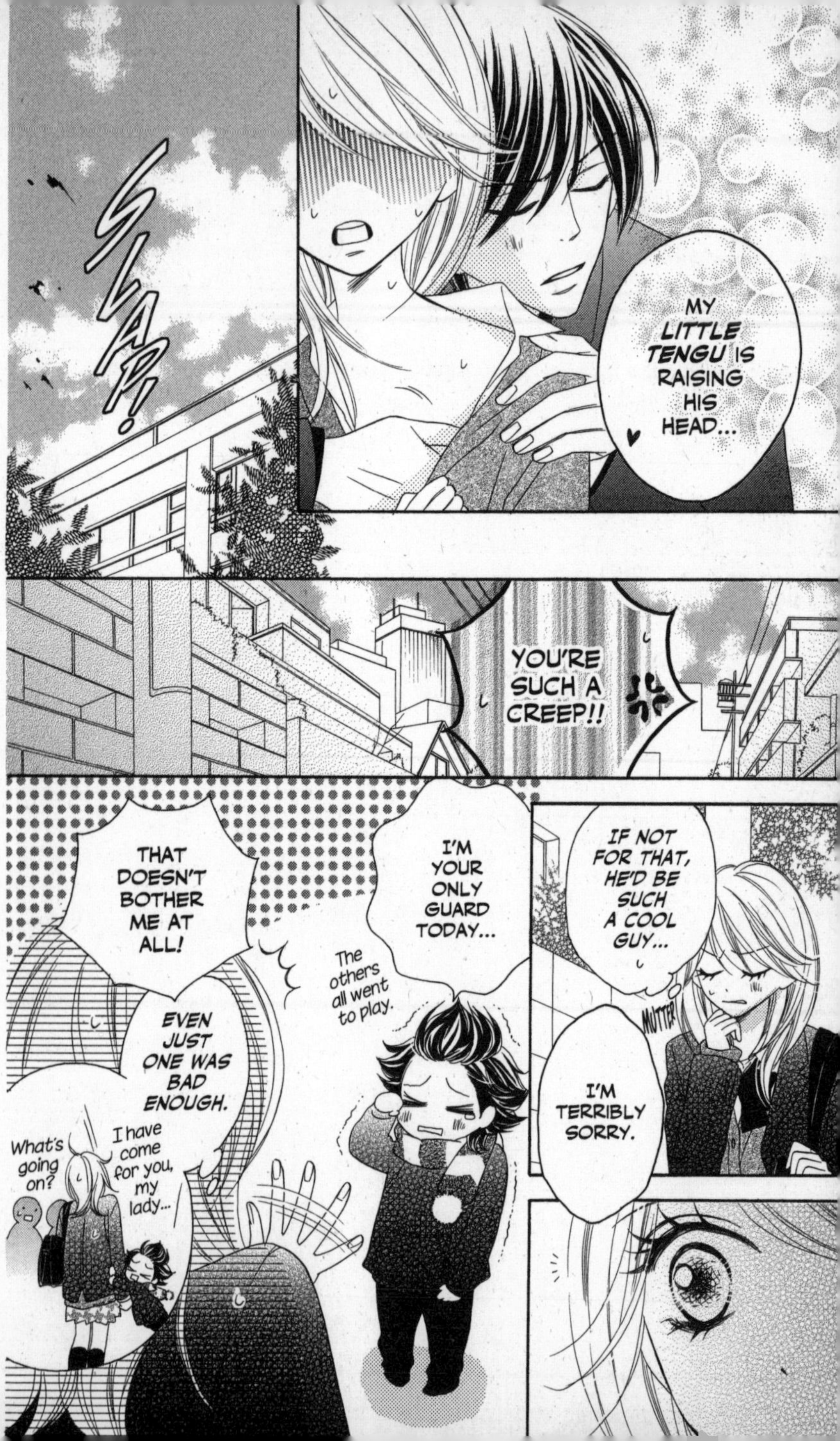
MY LITTLE TENGU IS RAISING HIS HEAD...
SLAP!
YOU'RE SUCH A CREEP!!
IF NOT FOR THAT, HE'D BE SUCH A COOL GUY...
MUTTER
I'M TERRIBLY SORRY.
I'M YOUR ONLY GUARD TODAY...
The others all went to play.
THAT DOESN'T BOTHER ME AT ALL!
EVEN JUST ONE WAS BAD ENOUGH.
I have come for you, my lady...
What's going on?

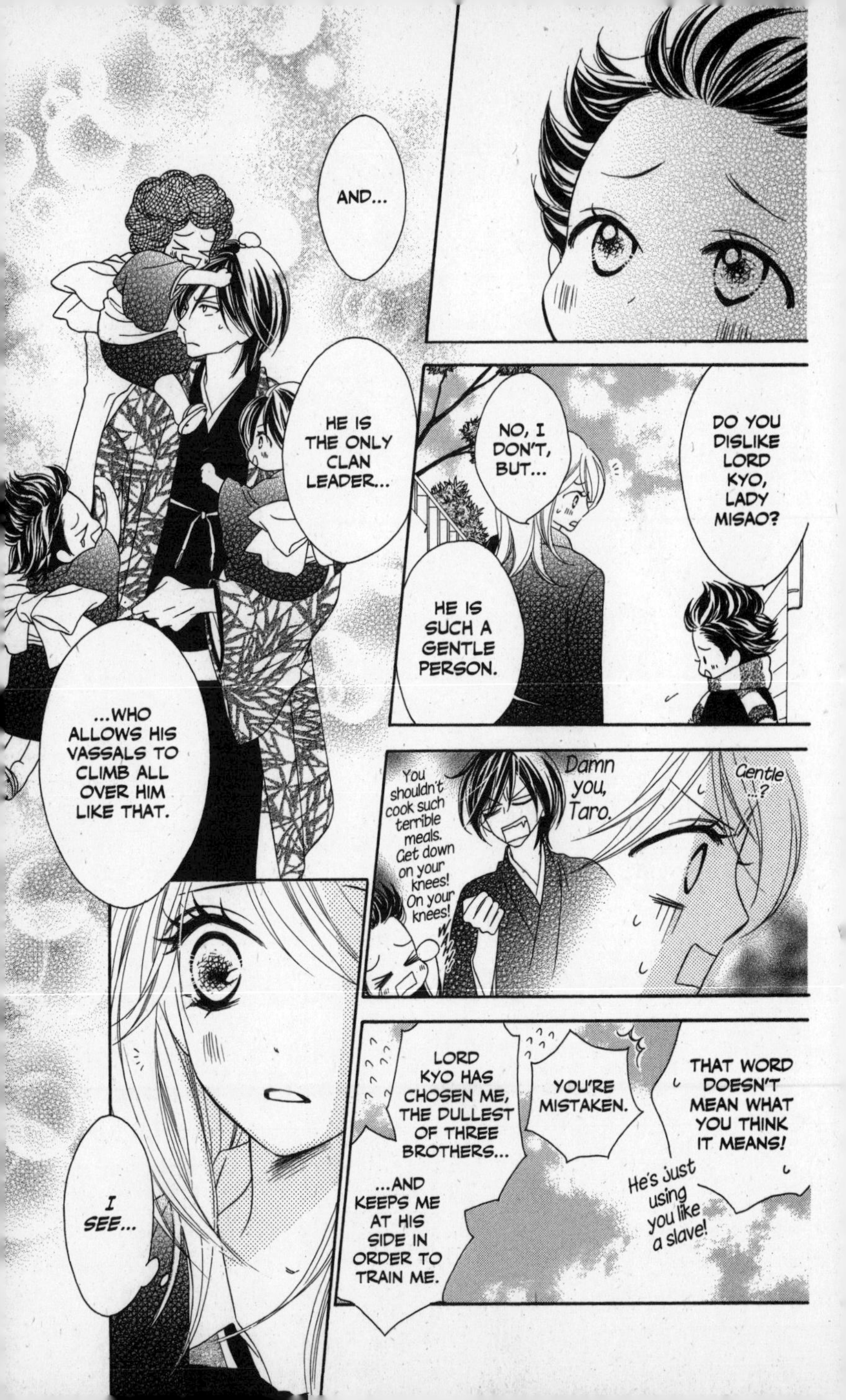
DO YOU DISLIKE LORD KYO, LADY MISAO?
NO, I DON'T, BUT...
HE IS SUCH A GENTLE PERSON.
Gentle ...?
Damn you, Taro.
You shouldn't cook such terrible meals. Get down on your knees! On your knees!
THAT WORD DOESN'T MEAN WHAT YOU THINK IT MEANS!
He's just using you like a slave!
YOU'RE MISTAKEN.
LORD KYO HAS CHOSEN ME, THE DULLEST OF THREE BROTHERS...
...AND KEEPS ME AT HIS SIDE IN ORDER TO TRAIN ME.
AND...
HE IS THE ONLY CLAN LEADER...
...WHO ALLOWS HIS VASSALS TO CLIMB ALL OVER HIM LIKE THAT.
I SEE...

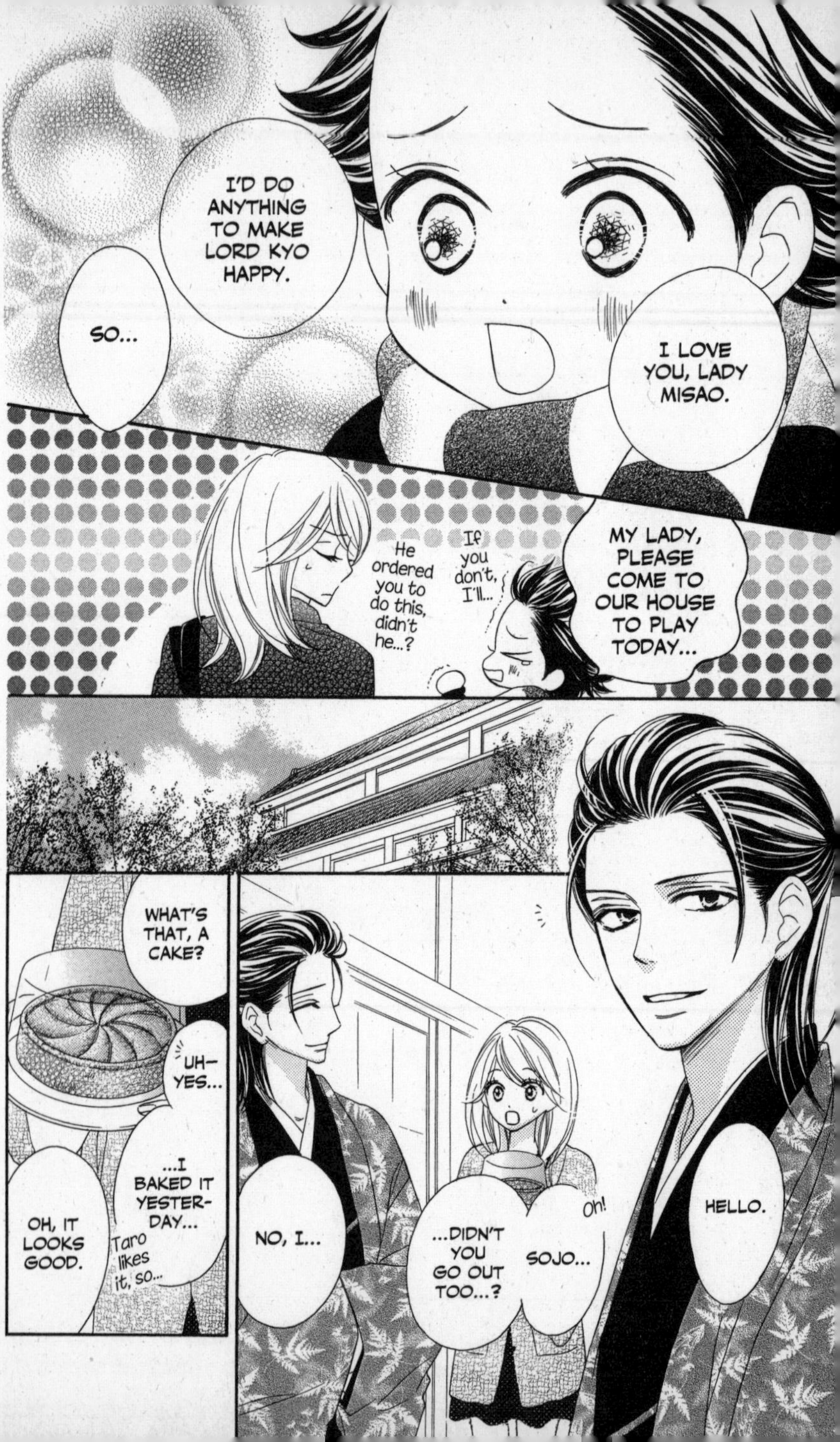
I LOVE YOU, LADY MISAO.
I'D DO ANYTHING TO MAKE LORD KYO HAPPY.
SO...
MY LADY, PLEASE COME TO OUR HOUSE TO PLAY TODAY...
If you don't, I'll...
He ordered you to do this, didn't he...?
HELLO.
Oh!
SOJO...
...DIDN'T YOU GO OUT TOO...?
NO, I...
WHAT'S THAT, A CAKE?
UH- YES...
...I BAKED IT YESTER-DAY...
Taro likes it, so...
OH, IT LOOKS GOOD.

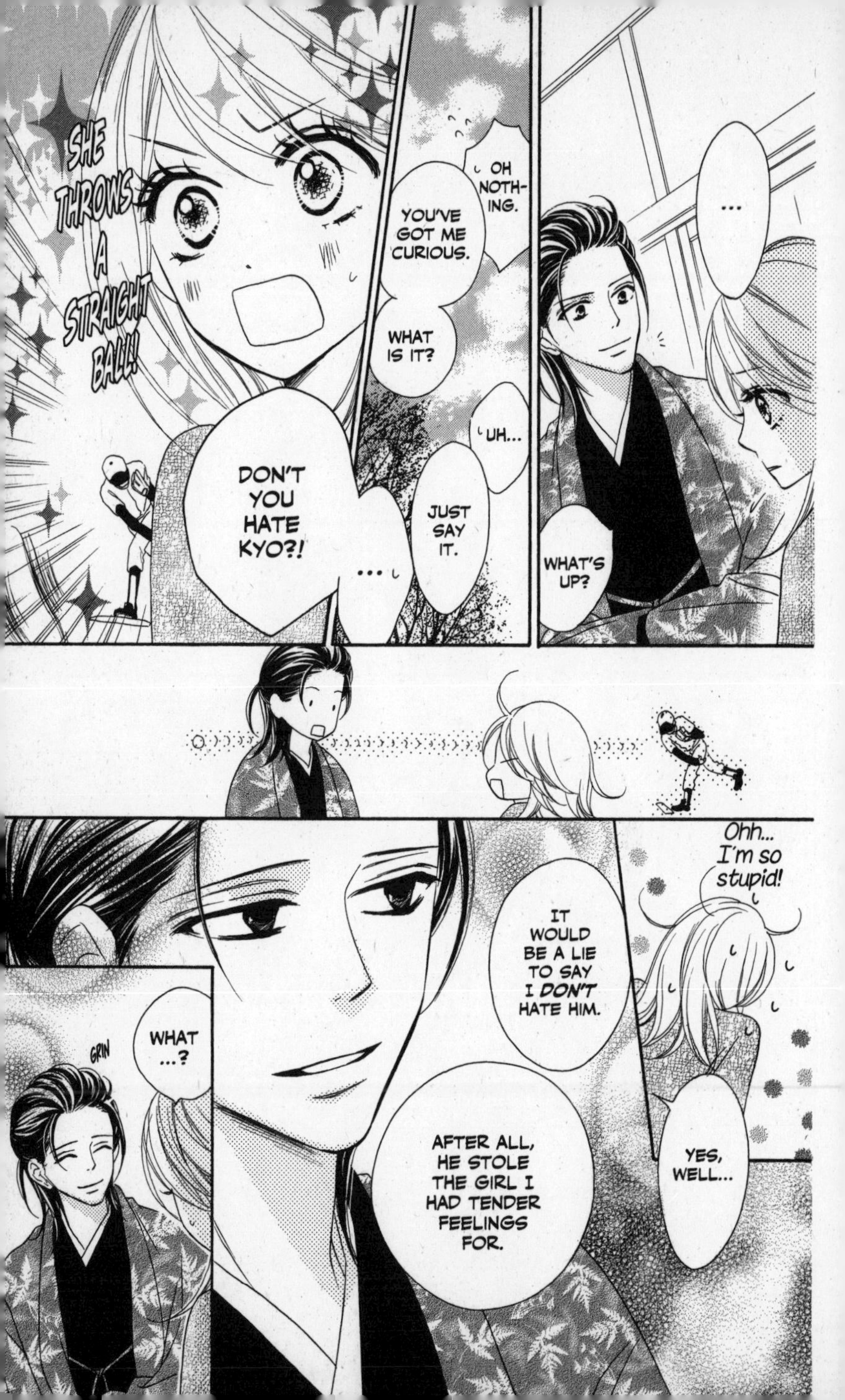
...
WHAT'S UP?
OH NOTHING.
YOU'VE GOT ME CURIOUS.
WHAT IS IT?
UH...
JUST SAY IT.
...
DON'T YOU HATE KYO?!
SHE THROWS A STRAIGHT BALL!!
Ohh... I'm so stupid!
YES, WELL...
IT WOULD BE A LIE TO SAY I *DON'T* HATE HIM.
AFTER ALL, HE STOLE THE GIRL I HAD TENDER FEELINGS FOR.
WHAT ...?
GRIN

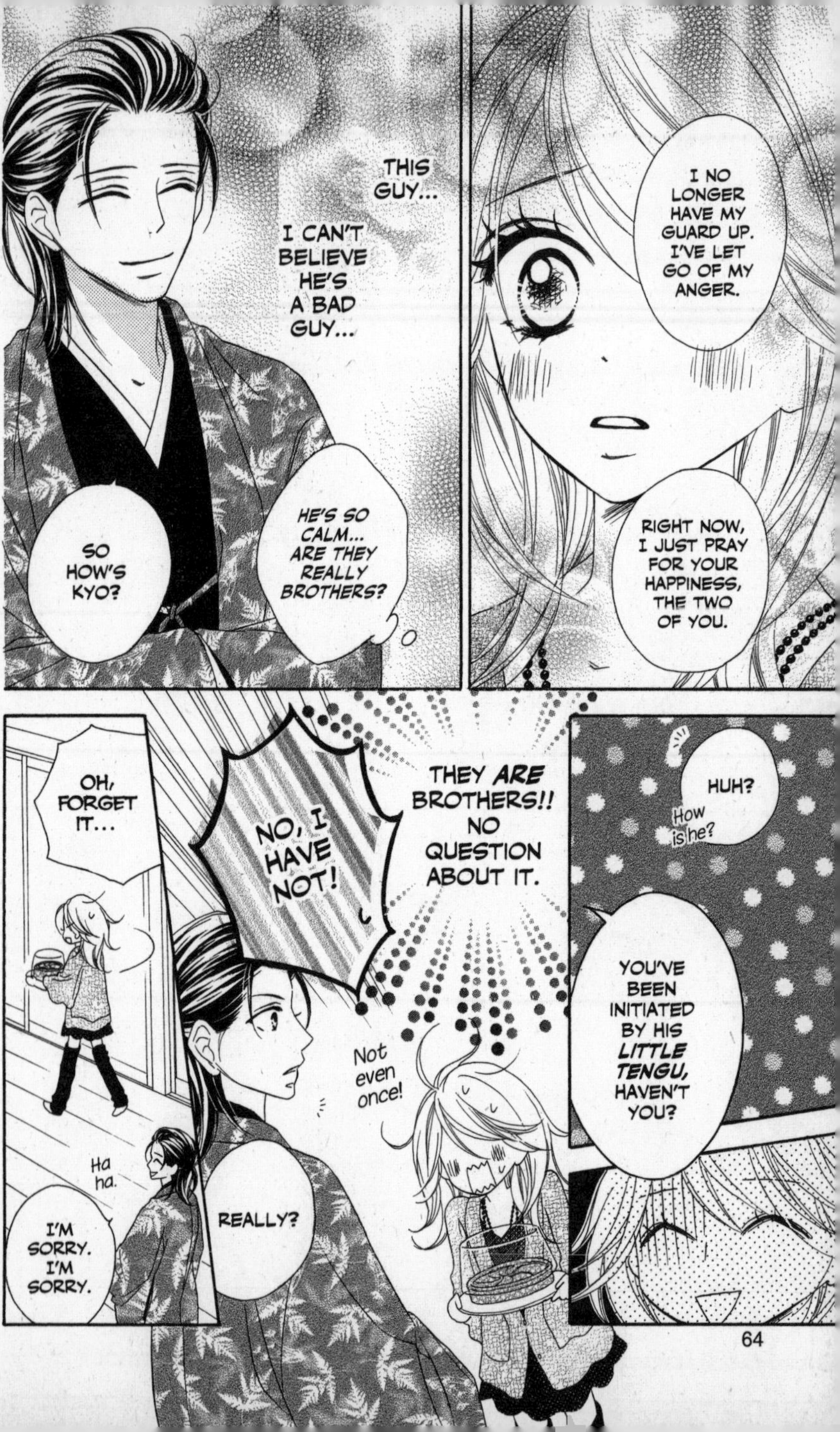

I NO LONGER HAVE MY GUARD UP. I'VE LET GO OF MY ANGER.
RIGHT NOW, I JUST PRAY FOR YOUR HAPPINESS, THE TWO OF YOU.
THIS GUY...
I CAN'T BELIEVE HE'S A BAD GUY...
HE'S SO CALM... ARE THEY REALLY BROTHERS?
SO HOW'S KYO?
HUH?
How is he?
YOU'VE BEEN INITIATED BY HIS *LITTLE TENGU,* HAVEN'T YOU?
NO, I HAVE NOT!
THEY *ARE* BROTHERS!! NO QUESTION ABOUT IT.
Not even once!
REALLY?
OH, FORGET IT...
Ha ha.
I'M SORRY. I'M SORRY.

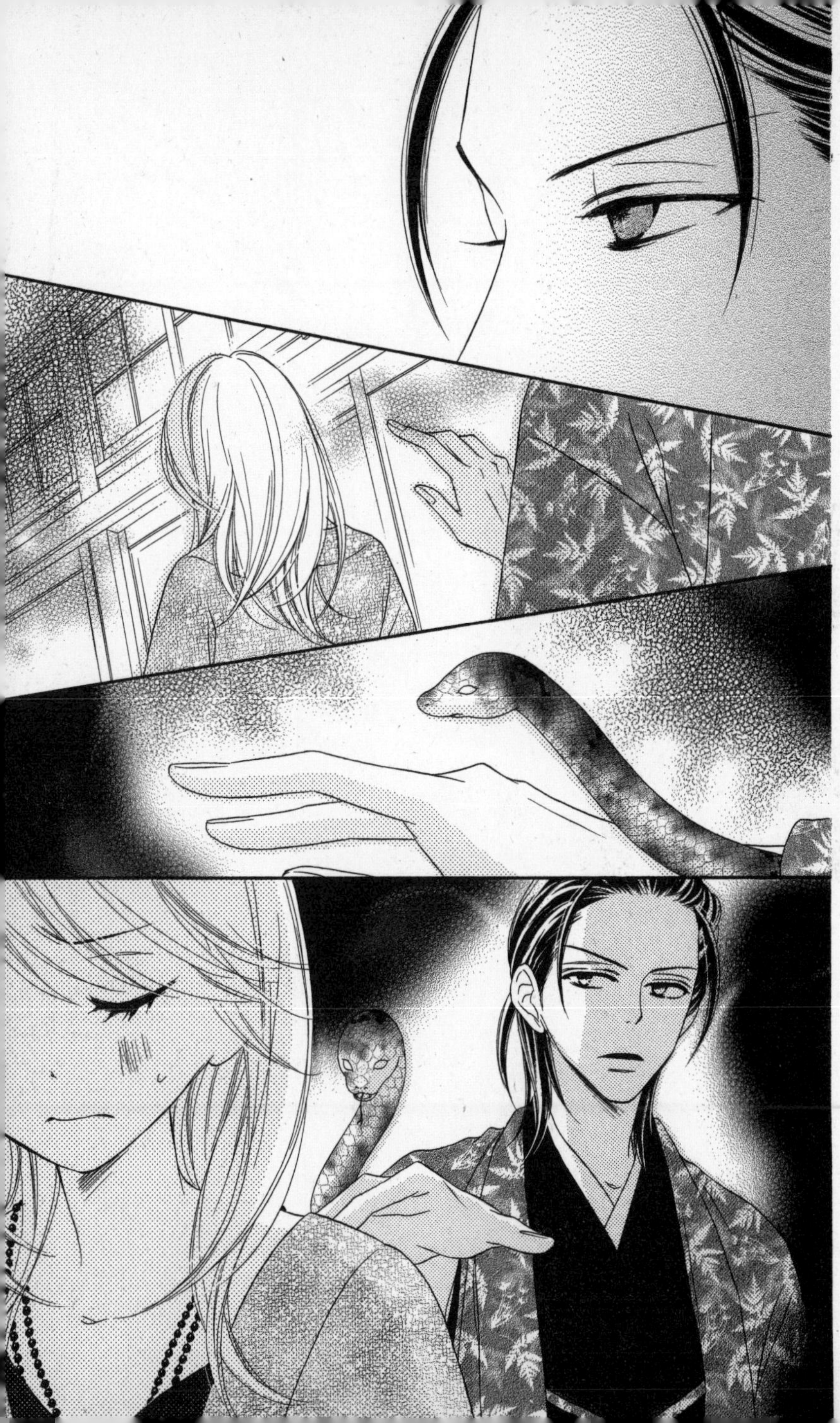

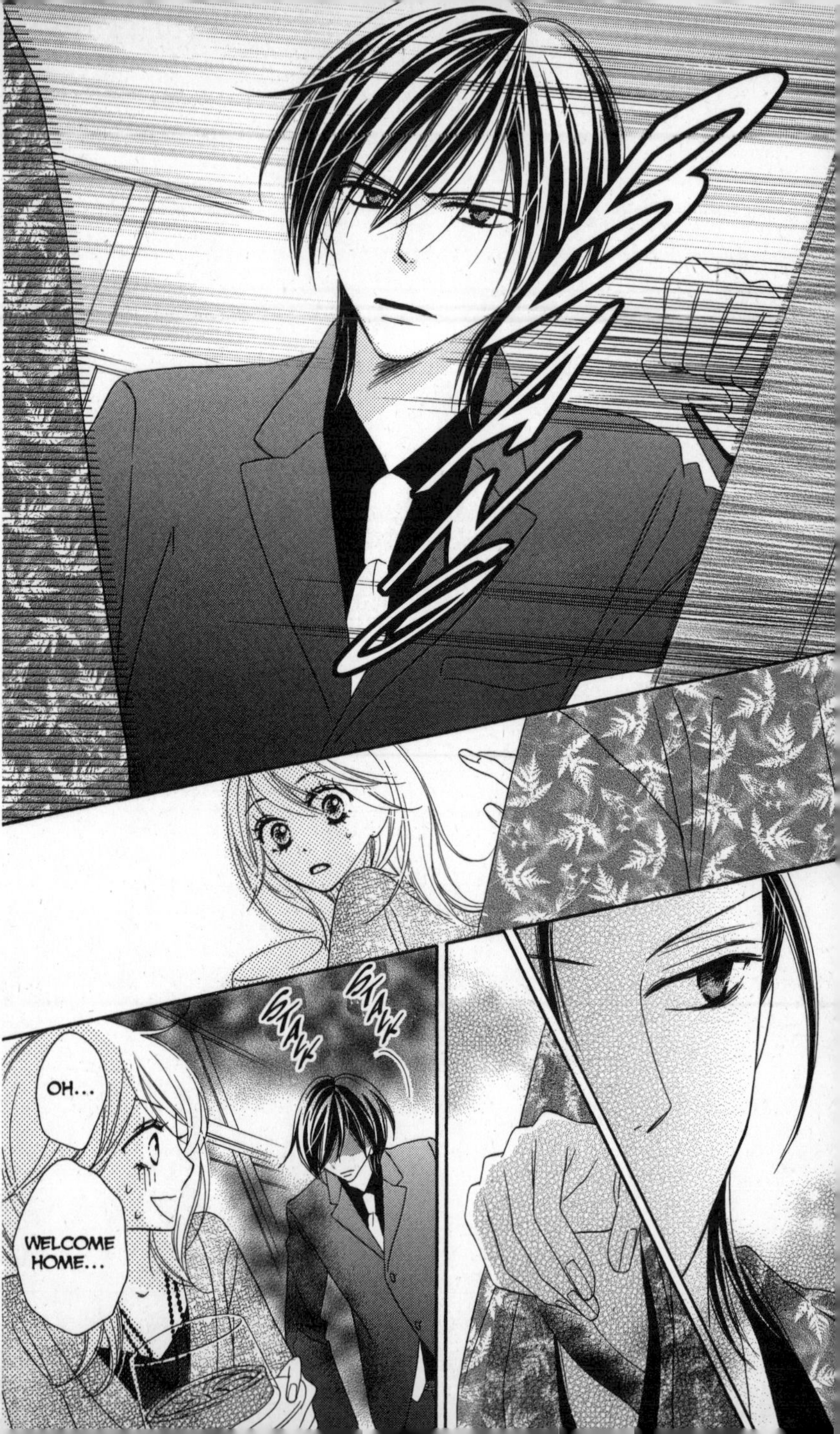
OH...
WELCOME HOME...

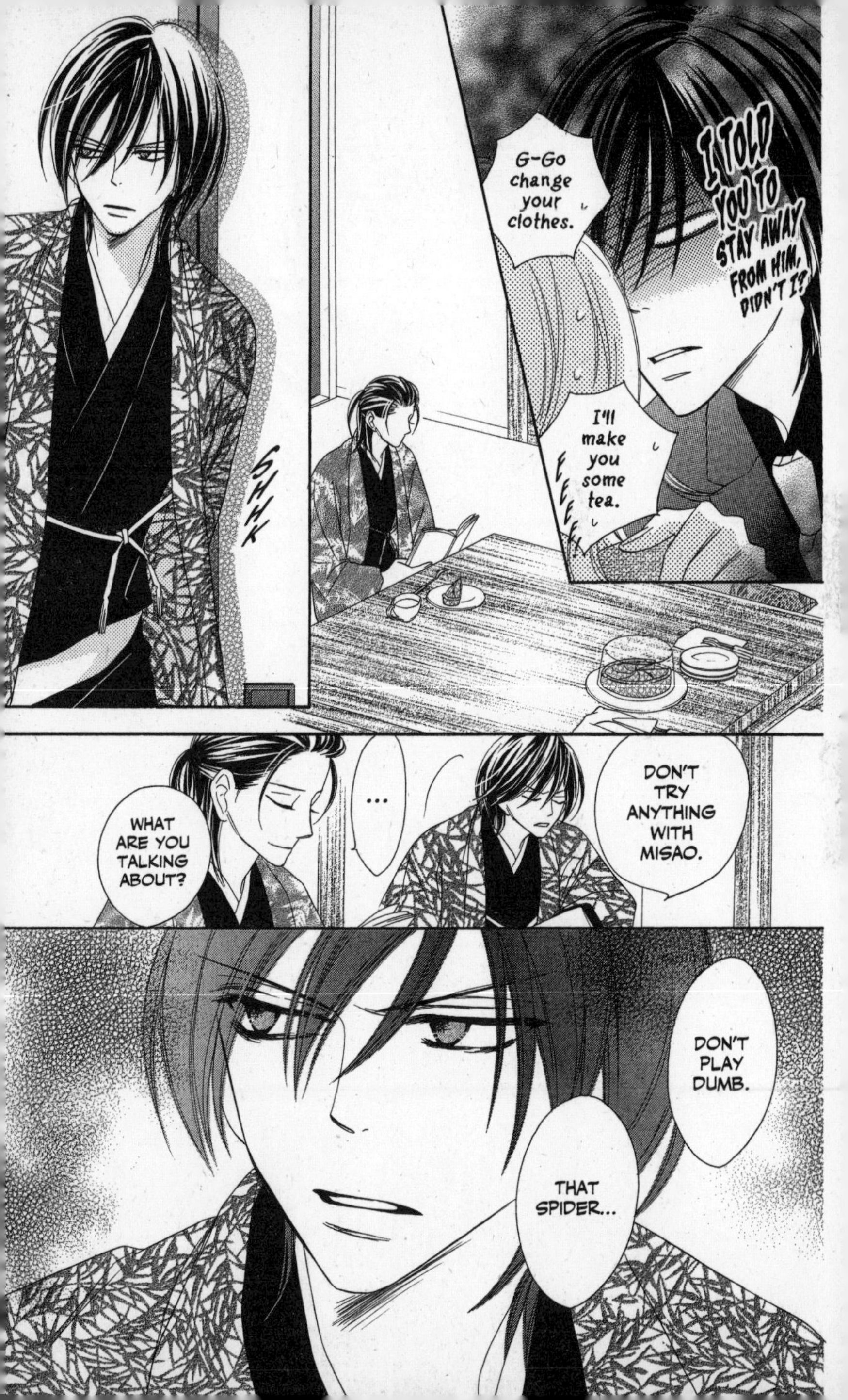
I TOLD YOU TO STAY AWAY FROM HIM, DIDN'T I?
G-Go change your clothes.
I'll make you some tea.
SHHK
DON'T TRY ANYTHING WITH MISAO.
...
WHAT ARE YOU TALKING ABOUT?
DON'T PLAY DUMB.
THAT SPIDER...

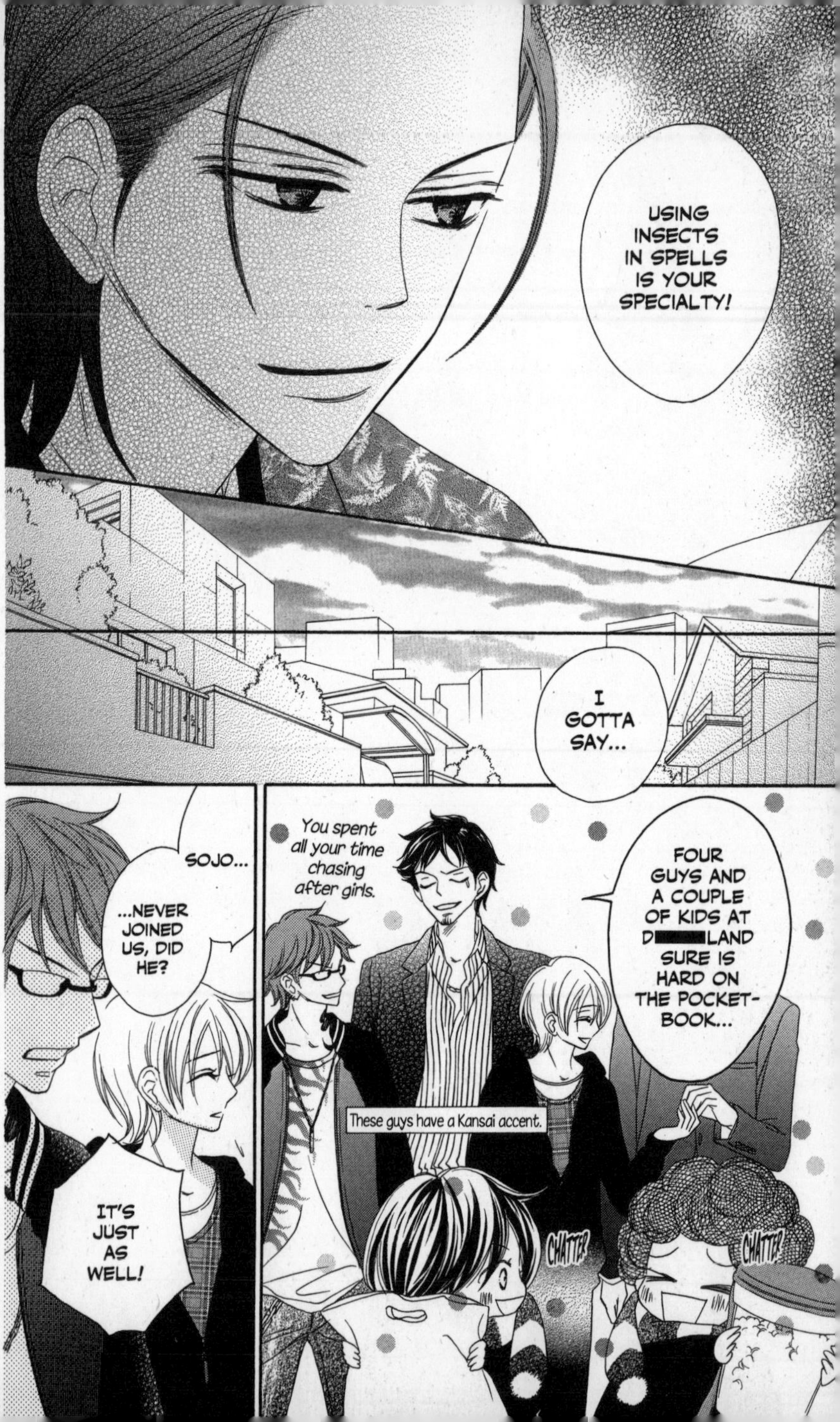
USING INSECTS IN SPELLS IS YOUR SPECIALTY!
I GOTTA SAY...
FOUR GUYS AND A COUPLE OF KIDS AT D[redacted]LAND SURE IS HARD ON THE POCKET-BOOK...
You spent all your time chasing after girls.
These guys have a Kansai accent.
CHATTER
CHATTER
SOJO...
...NEVER JOINED US, DID HE?
IT'S JUST AS WELL!

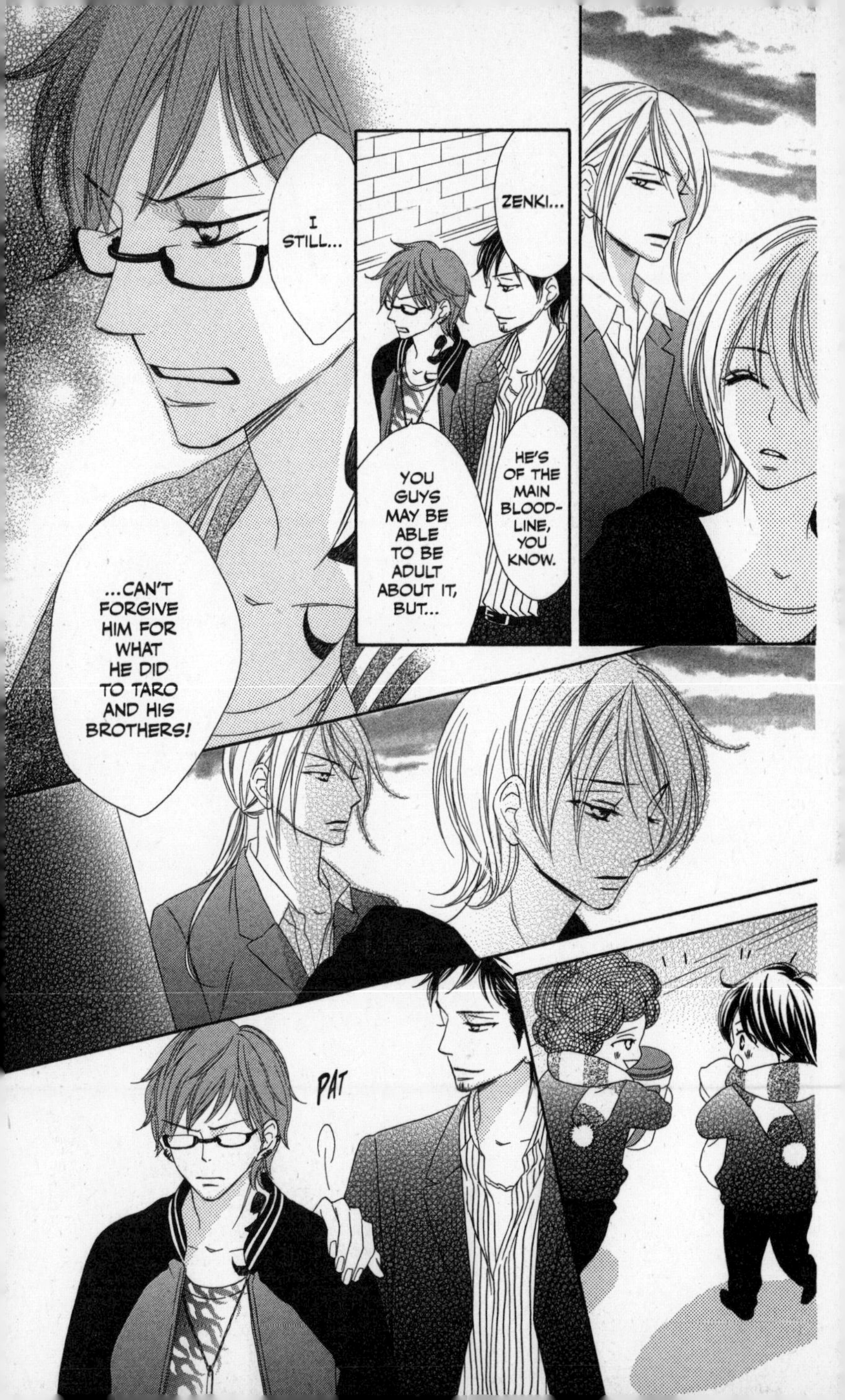
ZENKI...
HE'S OF THE MAIN BLOOD-LINE, YOU KNOW.
YOU GUYS MAY BE ABLE TO BE ADULT ABOUT IT, BUT...
I STILL...
...CAN'T FORGIVE HIM FOR WHAT HE DID TO TARO AND HIS BROTHERS!
PAT

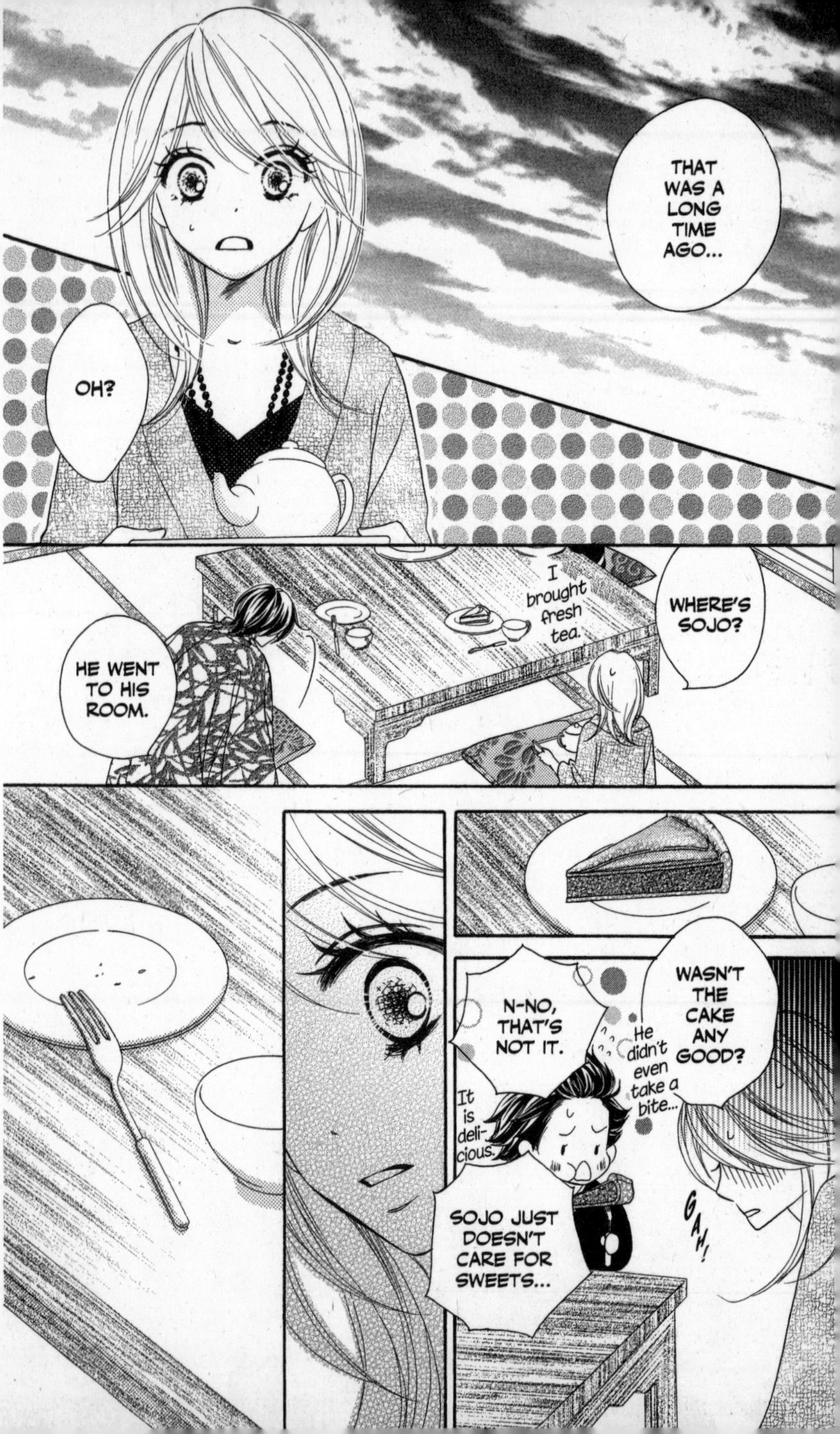
THAT WAS A LONG TIME AGO...
OH?
WHERE'S SOJO?
I brought fresh tea.
HE WENT TO HIS ROOM.
WASN'T THE CAKE ANY GOOD?
He didn't even take a bite...
N-NO, THAT'S NOT IT.
It is delicious.
SOJO JUST DOESN'T CARE FOR SWEETS...
GAH!

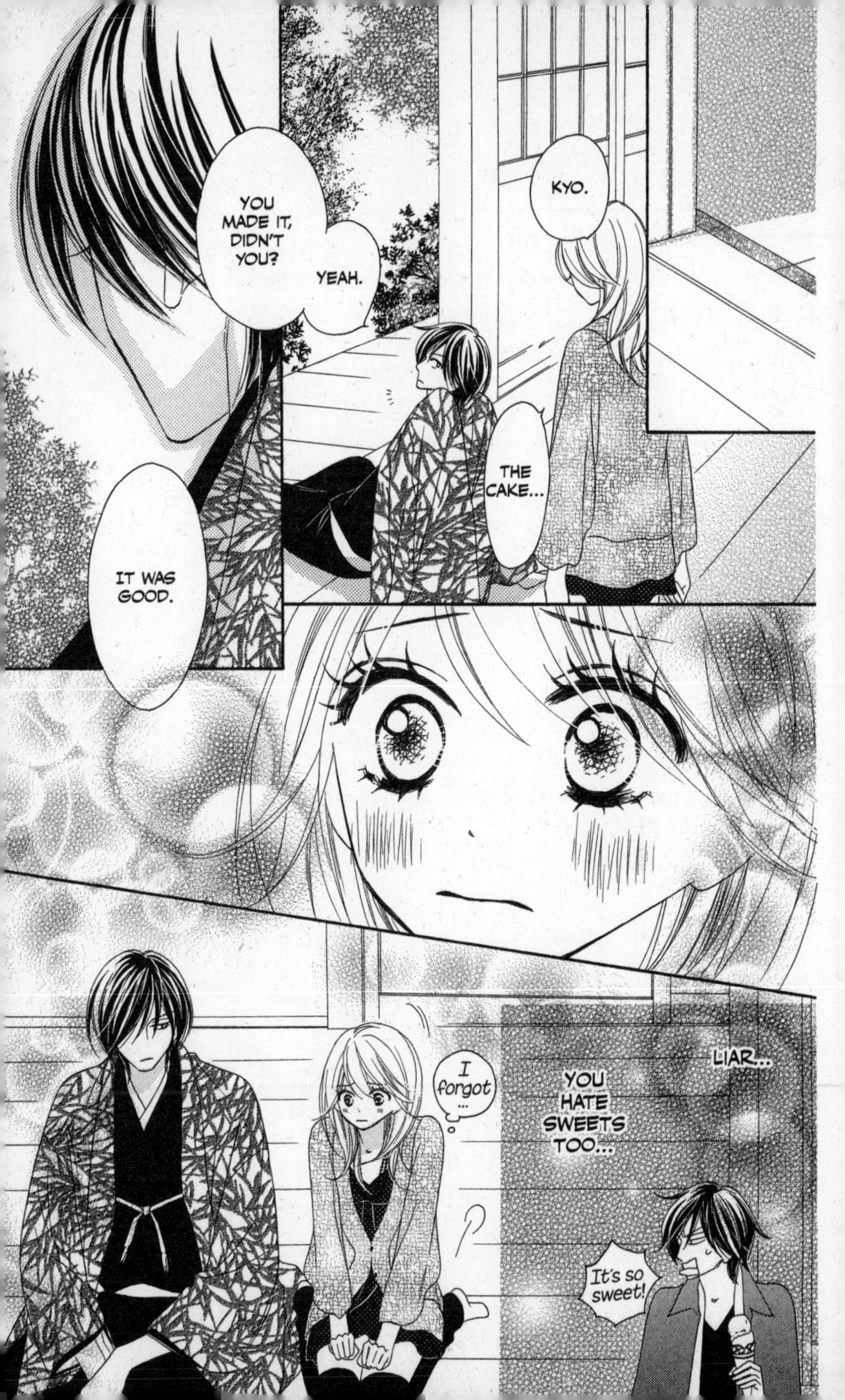
KYO.
THE CAKE...
YOU MADE IT, DIDN'T YOU?
YEAH.
IT WAS GOOD.
LIAR...
YOU HATE SWEETS TOO...
It's so sweet!
I forgot...

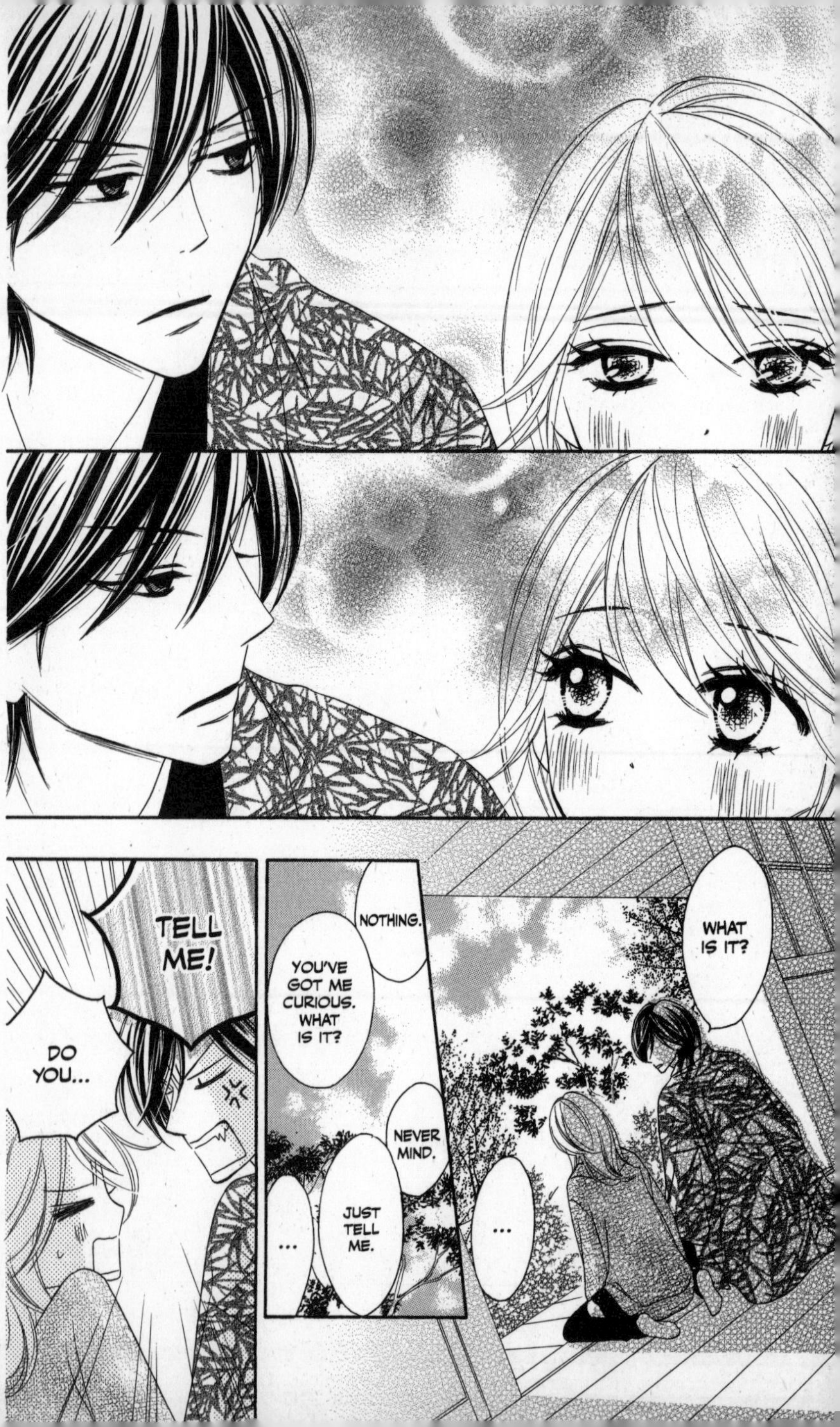
WHAT IS IT?
...
NOTHING.
YOU'VE GOT ME CURIOUS. WHAT IS IT?
NEVER MIND.
JUST TELL ME.
...
TELL ME!
DO YOU...

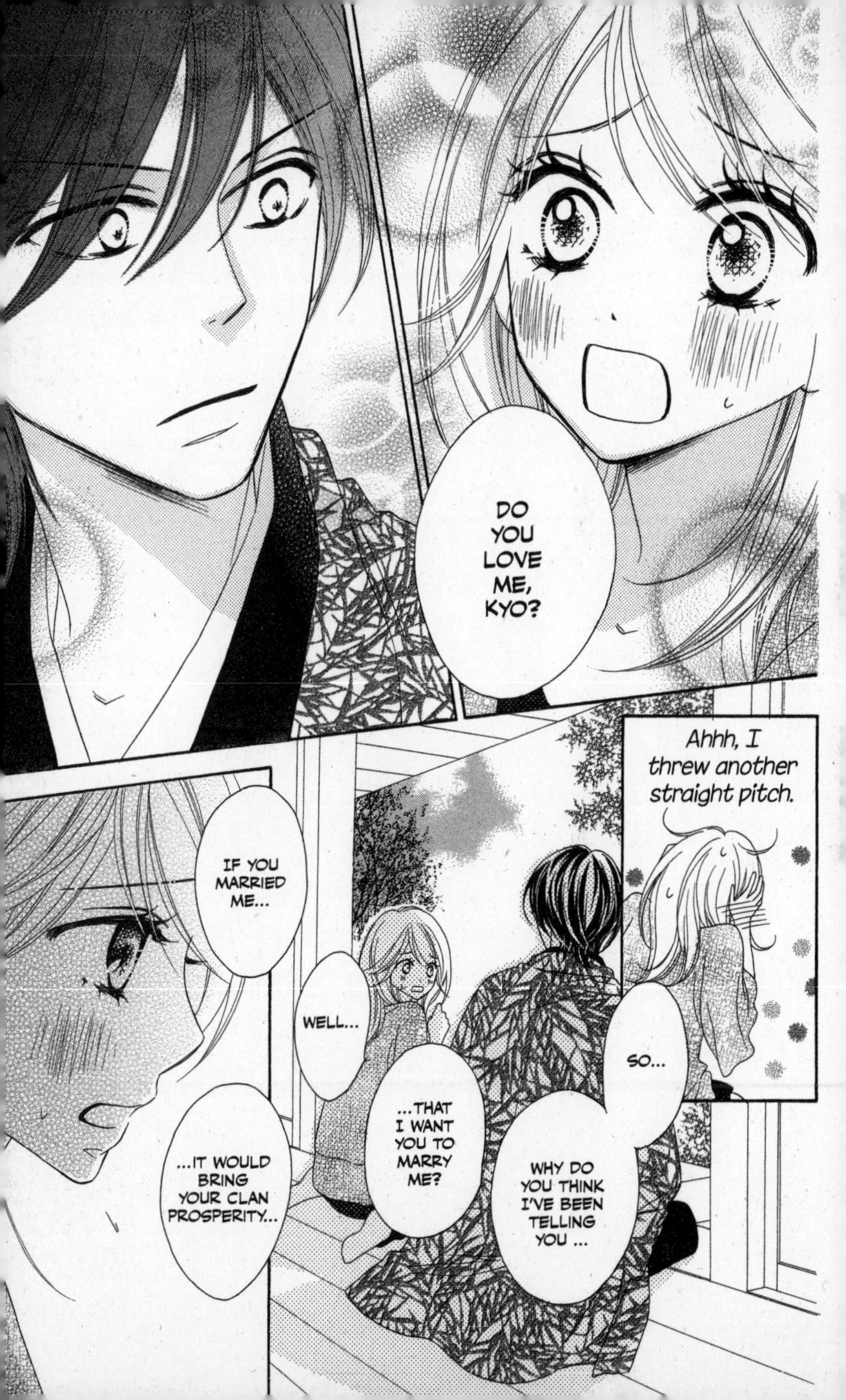
DO YOU LOVE ME, KYO?
Ahhh, I threw another straight pitch.
SO...
WHY DO YOU THINK I'VE BEEN TELLING YOU ...
...THAT I WANT YOU TO MARRY ME?
WELL...
IF YOU MARRIED ME...
...IT WOULD BRING YOUR CLAN PROSPERITY...

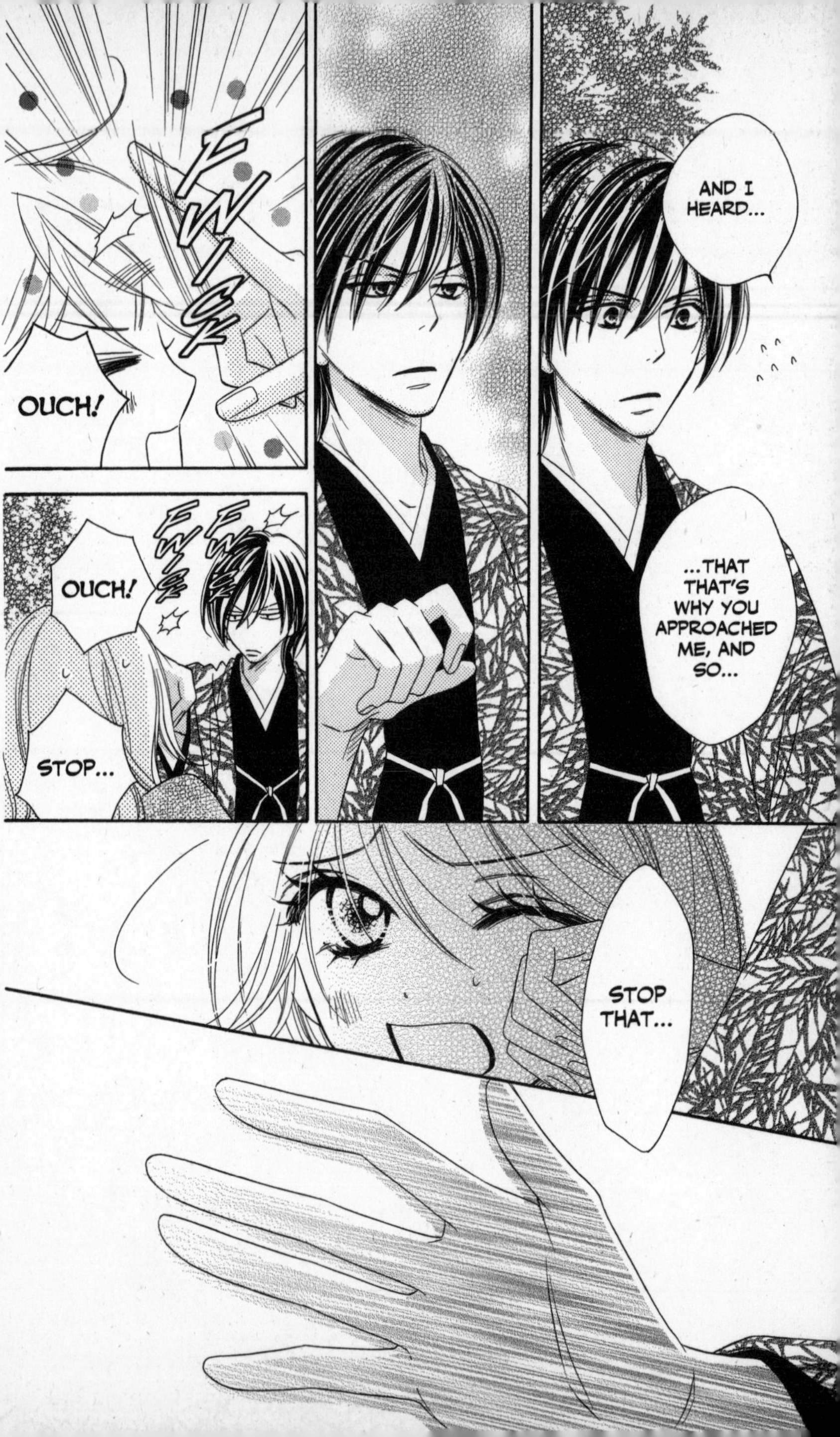
AND I HEARD...
...THAT THAT'S WHY YOU APPROACHED ME, AND SO...
FWICK
OUCH!
FWICK FWICK
OUCH!
STOP...
STOP THAT...

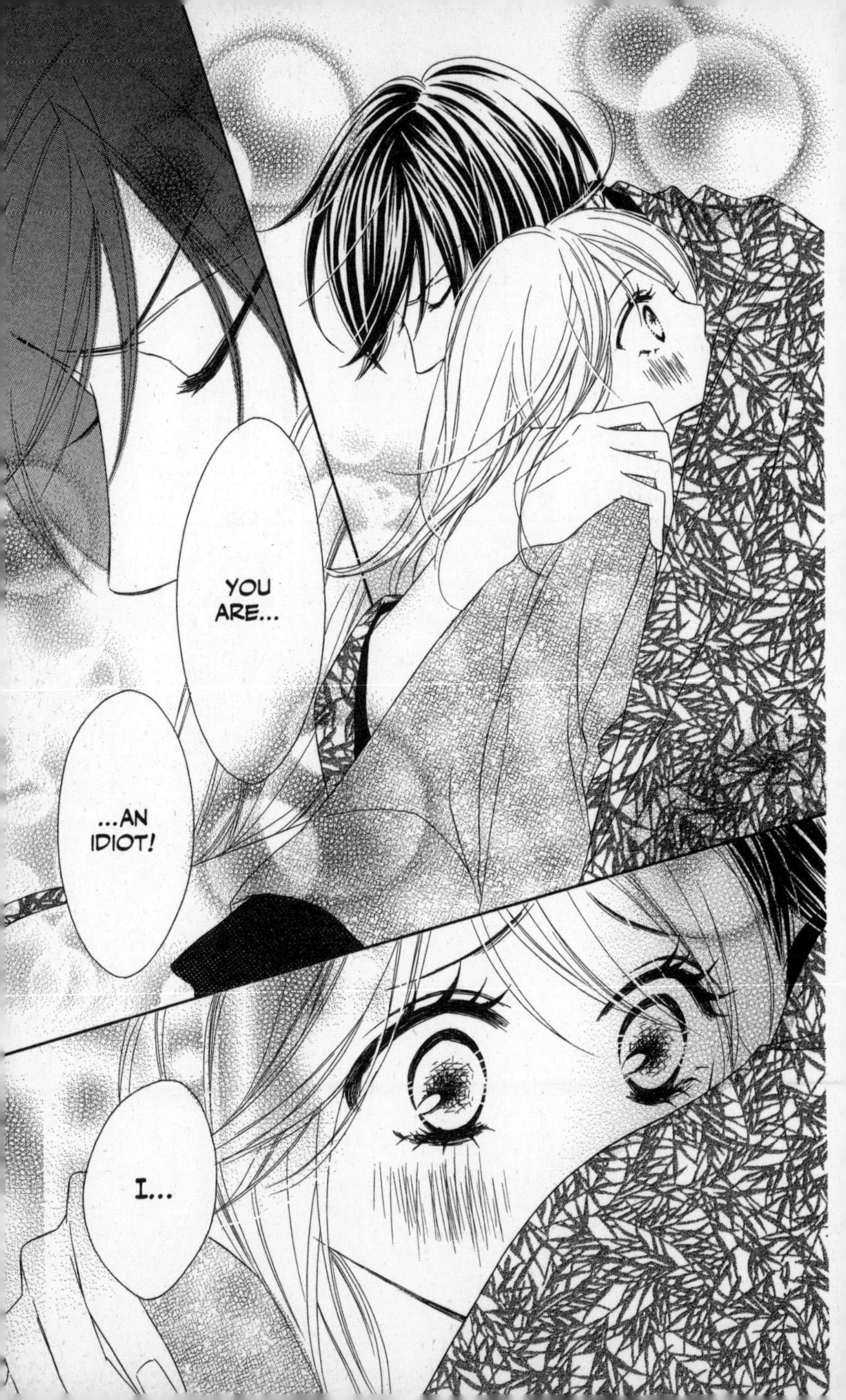
YOU ARE...
...AN IDIOT!
I...

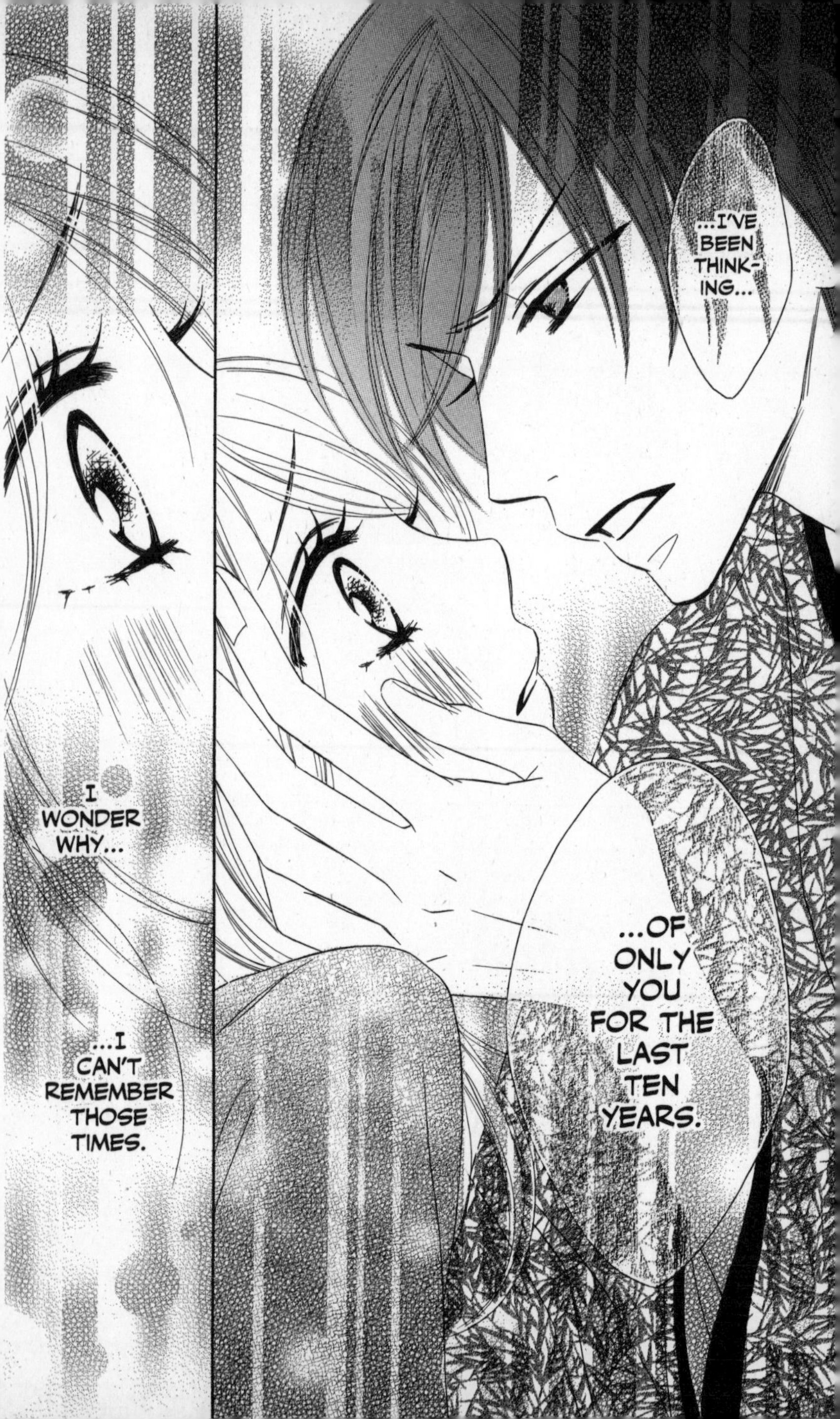
...I'VE BEEN THINKING...
...OF ONLY YOU FOR THE LAST TEN YEARS.
I WONDER WHY...
...I CAN'T REMEMBER THOSE TIMES.

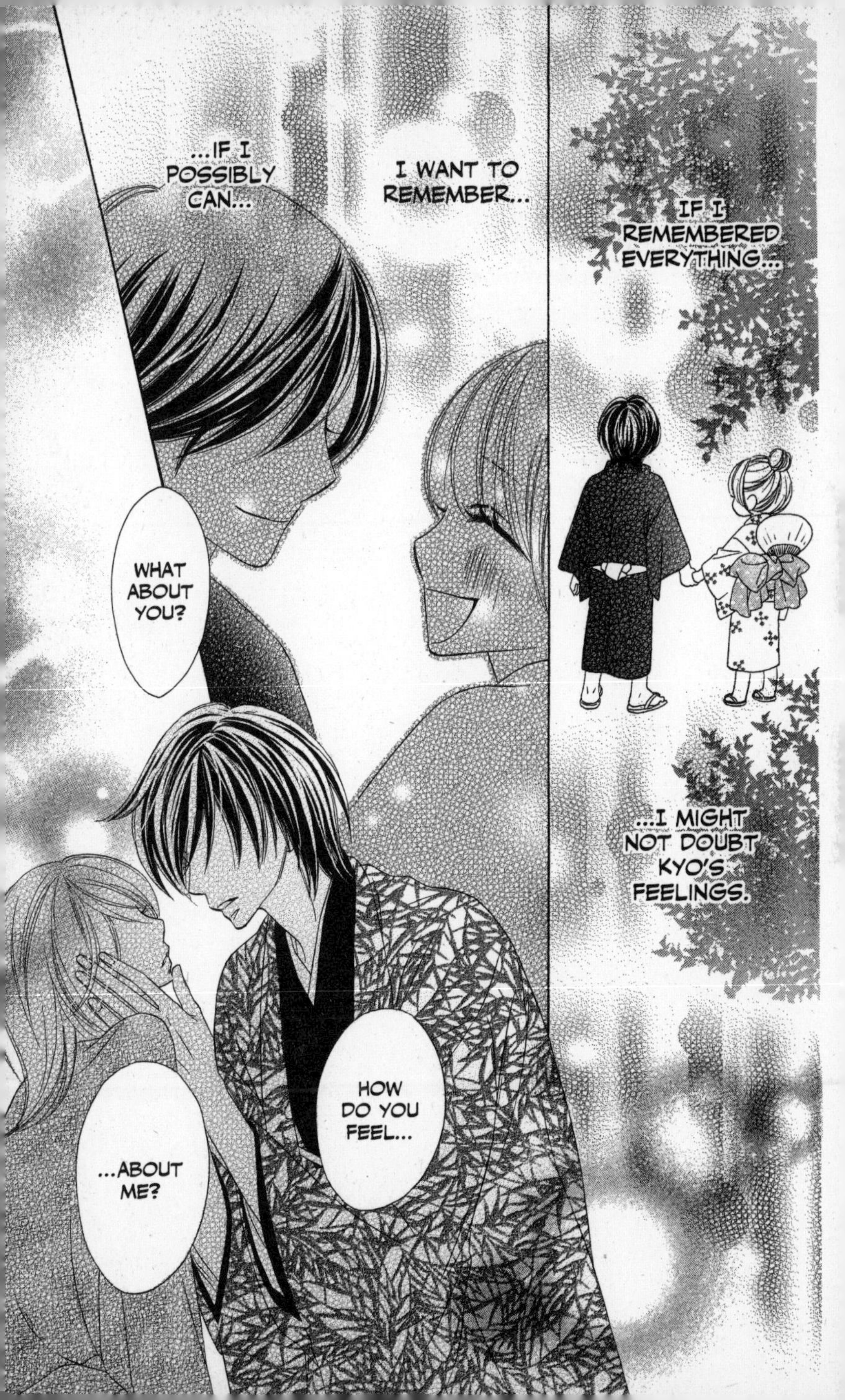
IF I REMEMBERED EVERYTHING...
...I MIGHT NOT DOUBT KYO'S FEELINGS.
I WANT TO REMEMBER...
...IF I POSSIBLY CAN...
WHAT ABOUT YOU?
HOW DO YOU FEEL...
...ABOUT ME?

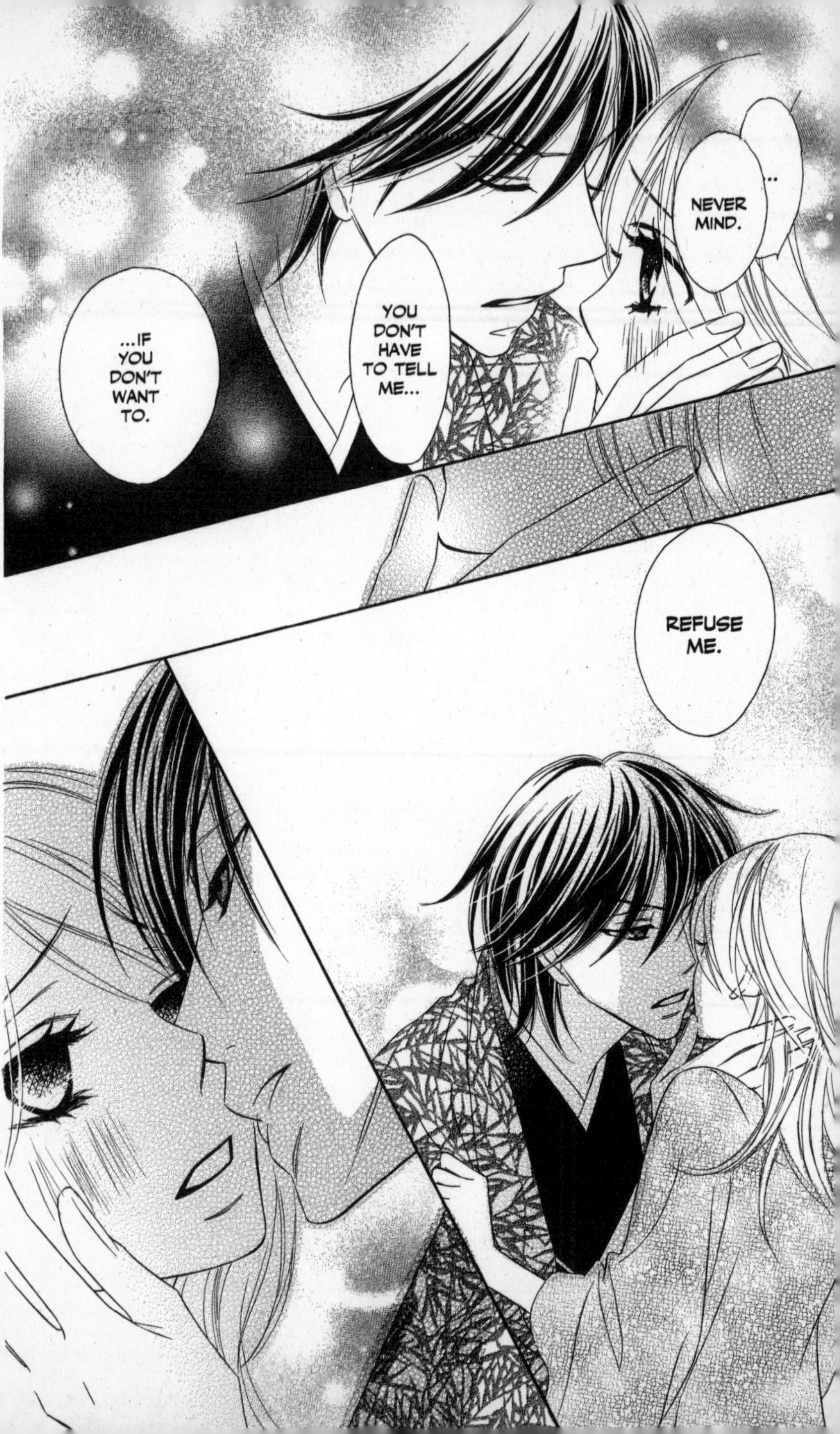
..
NEVER MIND.
YOU DON'T HAVE TO TELL ME...
...IF YOU DON'T WANT TO.
REFUSE ME.

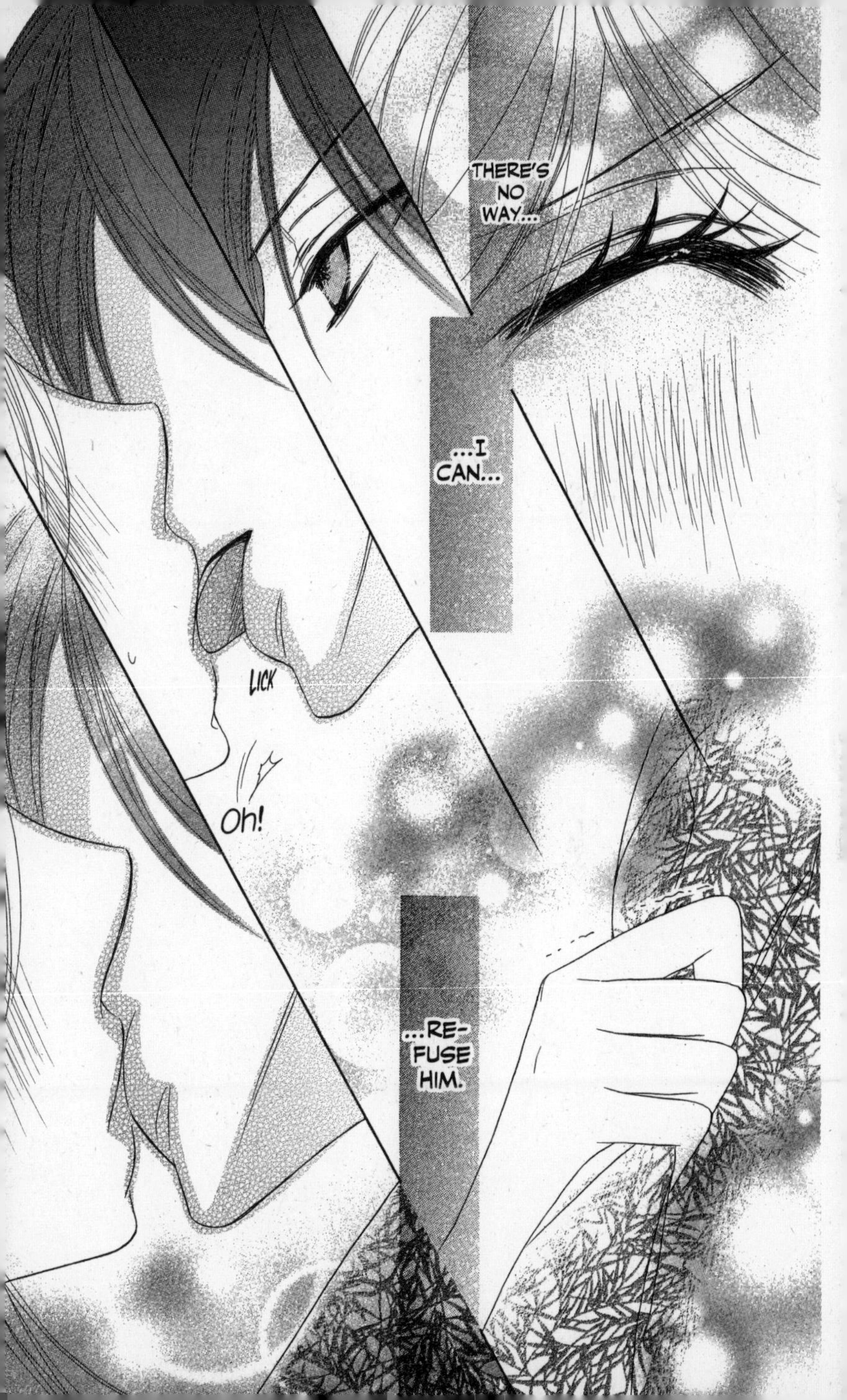
THERE'S NO WAY...
...I CAN...
LICK
Oh!
...RE-FUSE HIM.

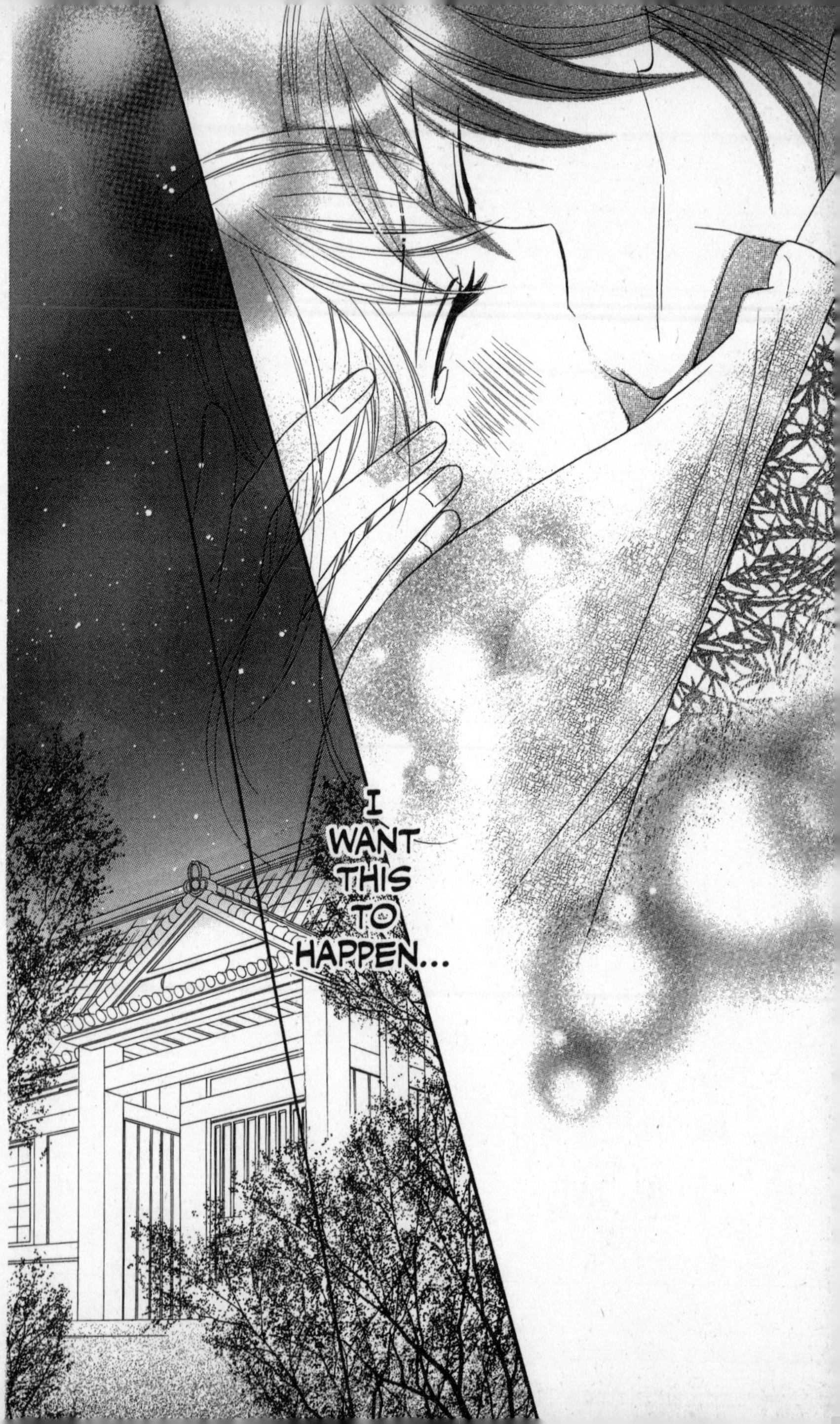
I WANT THIS TO HAPPEN...

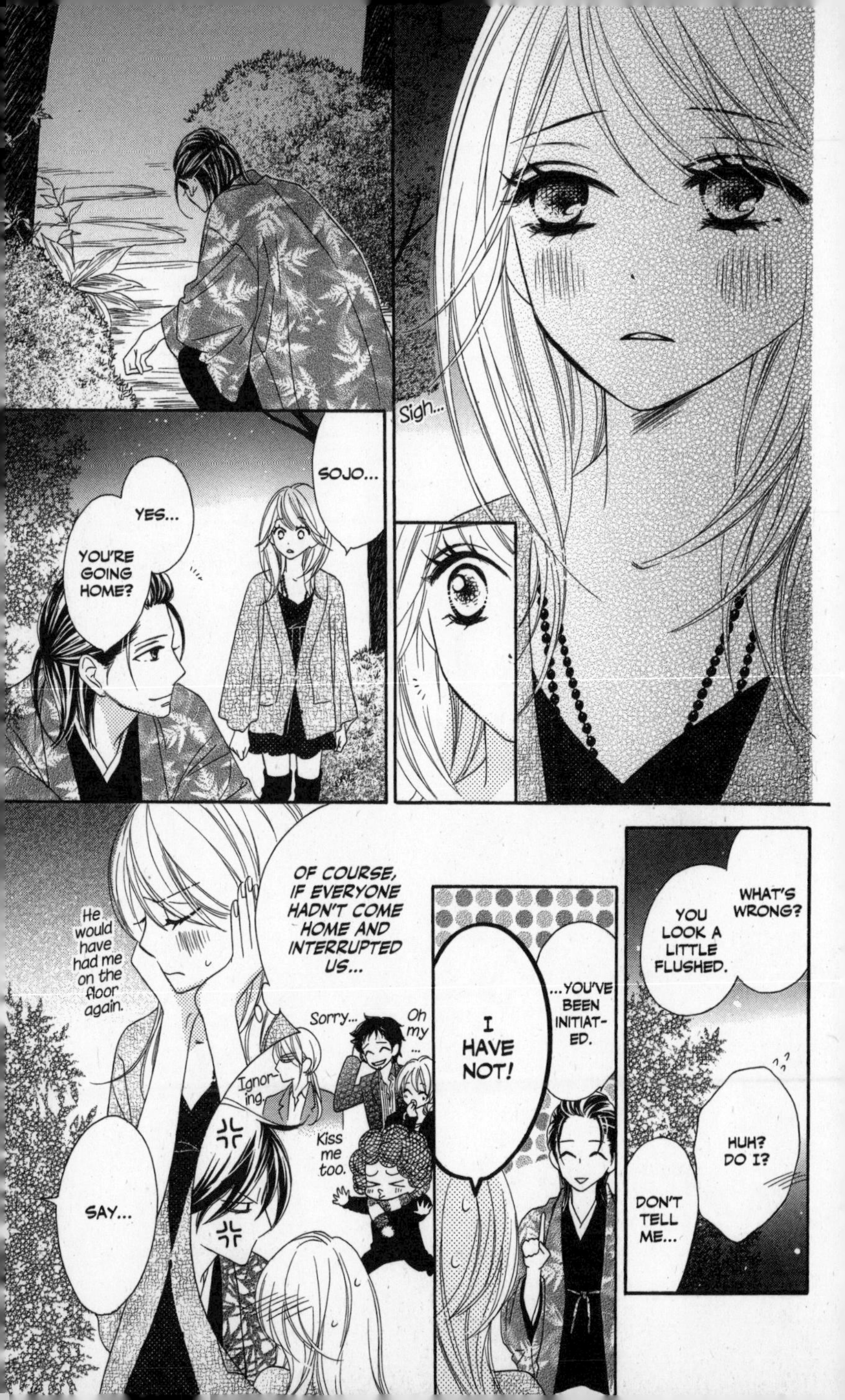
Sigh...
SOJO...
YES...
YOU'RE GOING HOME?
WHAT'S WRONG?
YOU LOOK A LITTLE FLUSHED.
HUH? DO I?
DON'T TELL ME...
...YOU'VE BEEN INITIAT-ED.
I HAVE NOT!
OF COURSE, IF EVERYONE HADN'T COME HOME AND INTERRUPTED US...
He would have had me on the floor again.
Oh my...
Sorry...
Ignor-ing.
Kiss me too.
SAY...

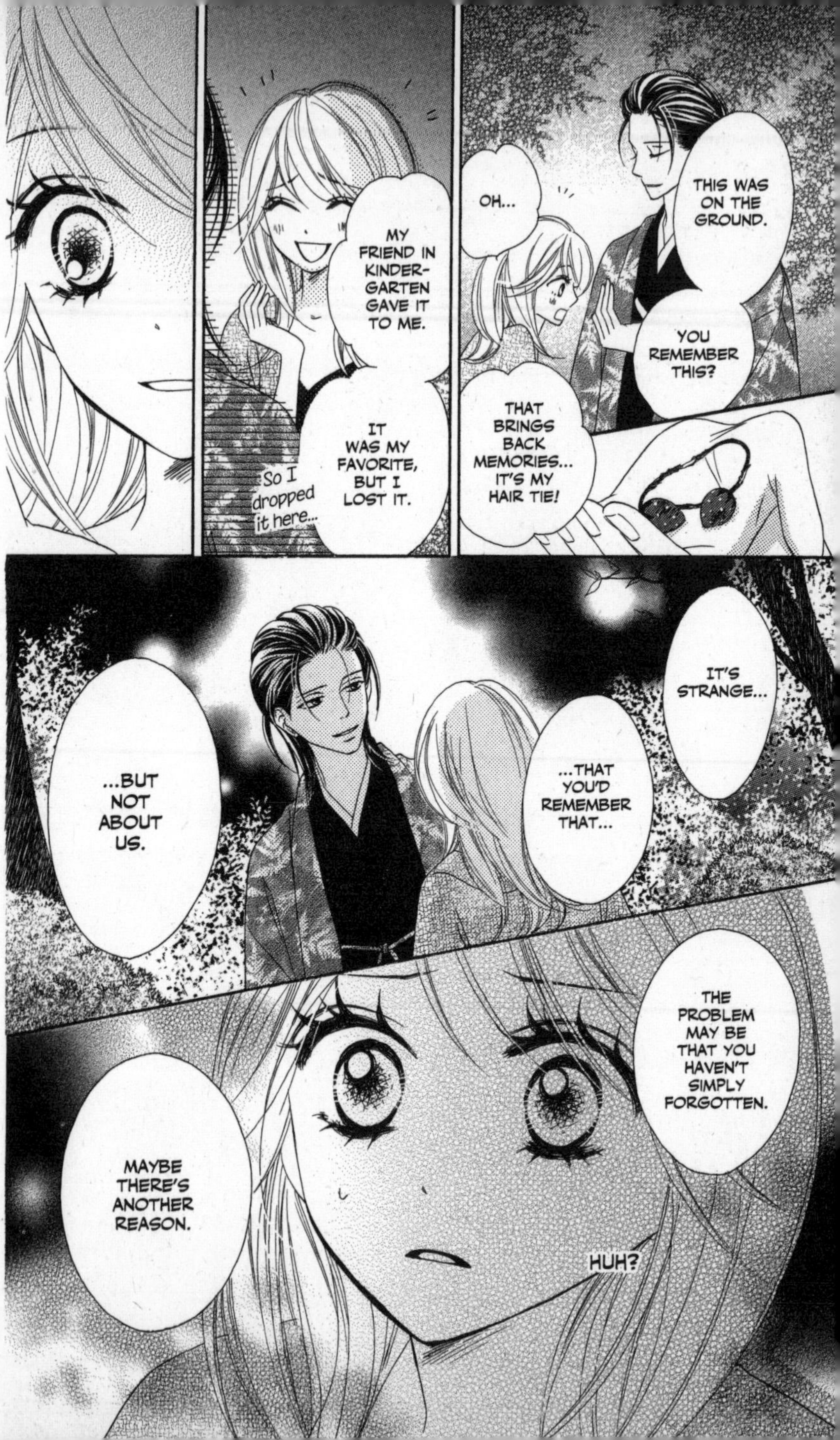
THIS WAS ON THE GROUND.
YOU REMEMBER THIS?
OH...
THAT BRINGS BACK MEMORIES... IT'S MY HAIR TIE!
MY FRIEND IN KINDER-GARTEN GAVE IT TO ME.
IT WAS MY FAVORITE, BUT I LOST IT.
So I dropped it here...
IT'S STRANGE...
...THAT YOU'D REMEMBER THAT...
...BUT NOT ABOUT US.
THE PROBLEM MAY BE THAT YOU HAVEN'T SIMPLY FORGOTTEN.
HUH?
MAYBE THERE'S ANOTHER REASON.

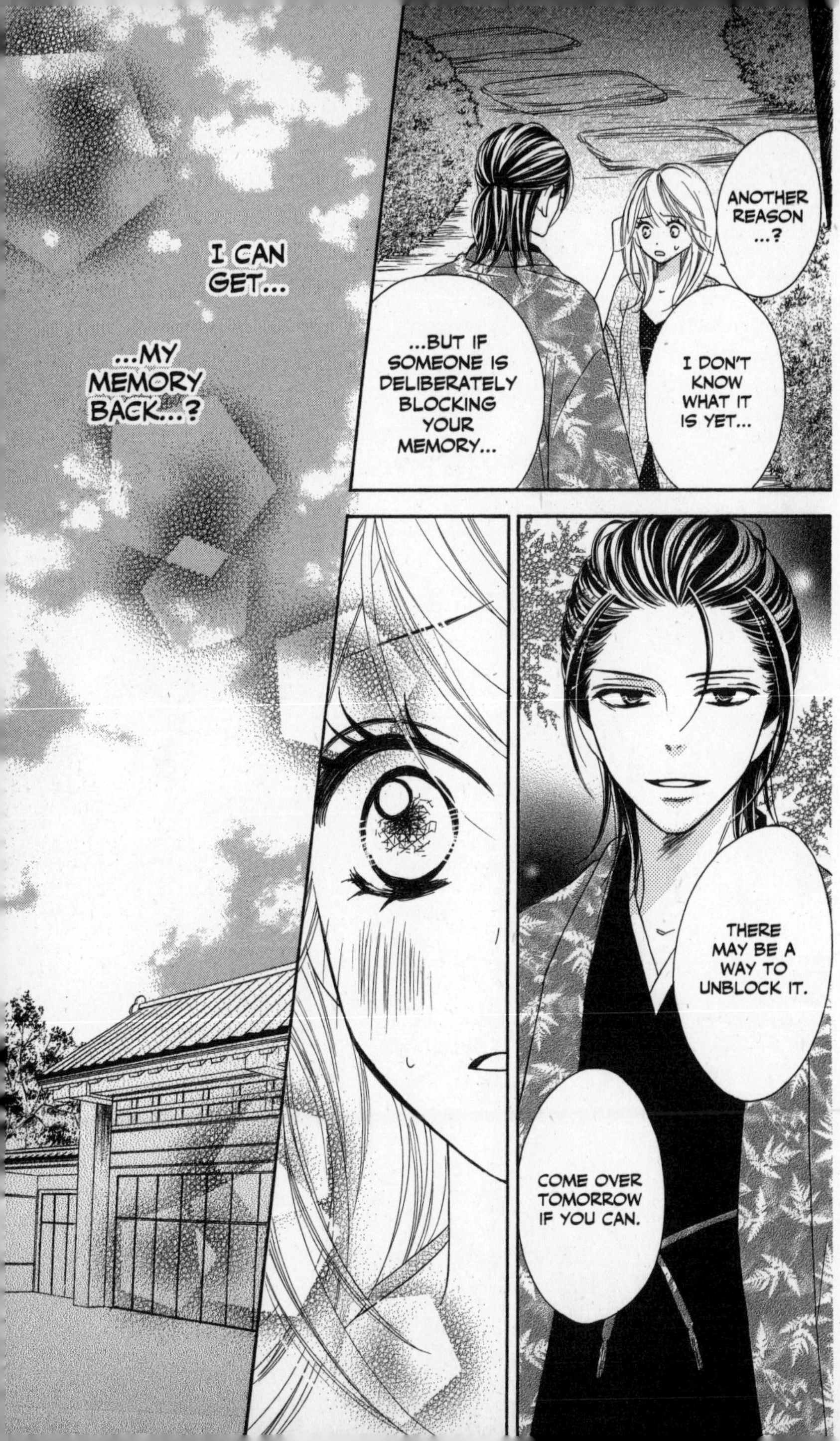
ANOTHER REASON ...?
I DON'T KNOW WHAT IT IS YET...
...BUT IF SOMEONE IS DELIBERATELY BLOCKING YOUR MEMORY...
THERE MAY BE A WAY TO UNBLOCK IT.
COME OVER TOMORROW IF YOU CAN.
I CAN GET...
...MY MEMORY BACK...?

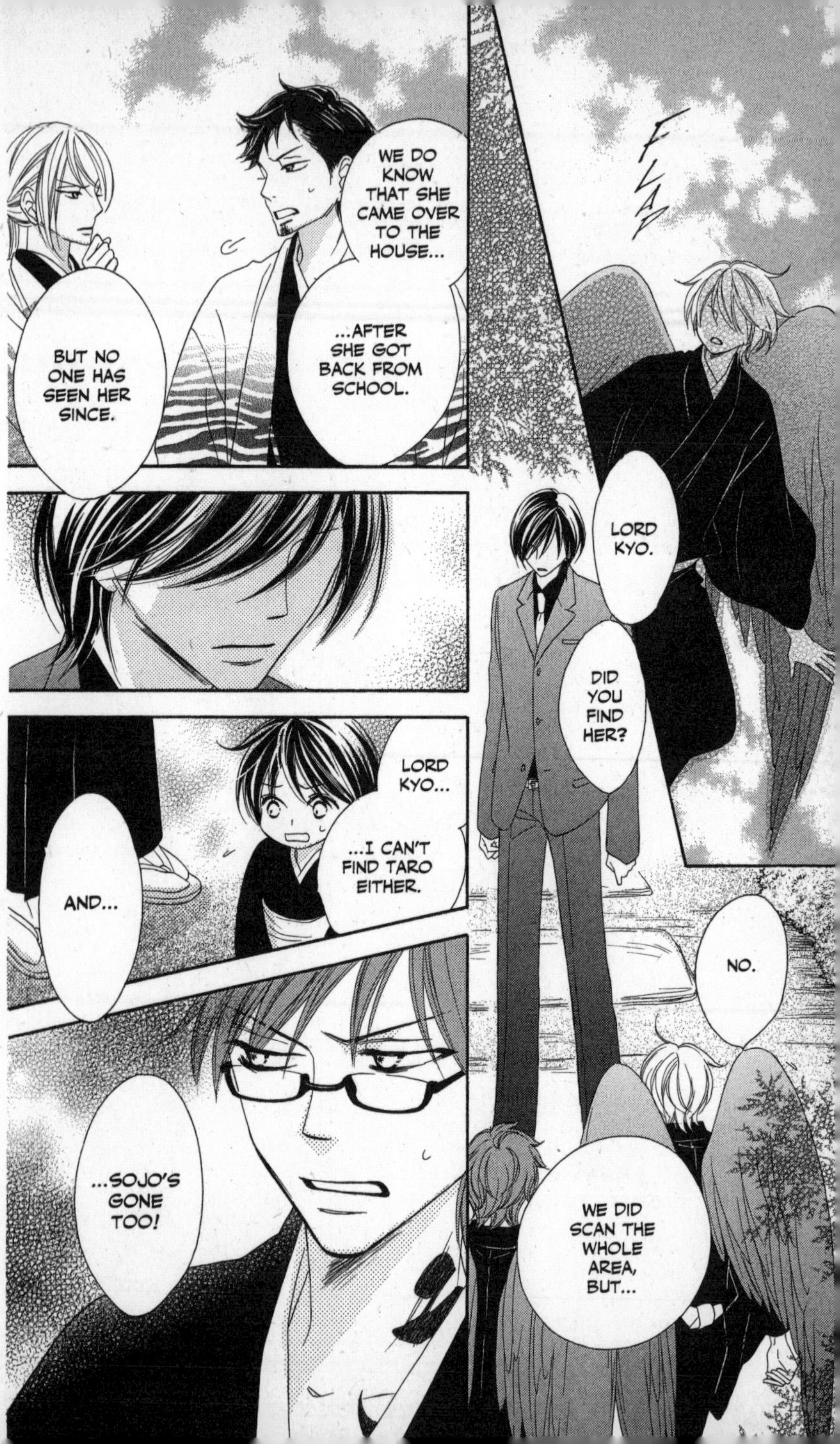
FLAP
LORD KYO.
DID YOU FIND HER?
NO.
WE DID SCAN THE WHOLE AREA, BUT...
WE DO KNOW THAT SHE CAME OVER TO THE HOUSE...
...AFTER SHE GOT BACK FROM SCHOOL.
BUT NO ONE HAS SEEN HER SINCE.
LORD KYO...
...I CAN'T FIND TARO EITHER.
AND...
...SOJO'S GONE TOO!

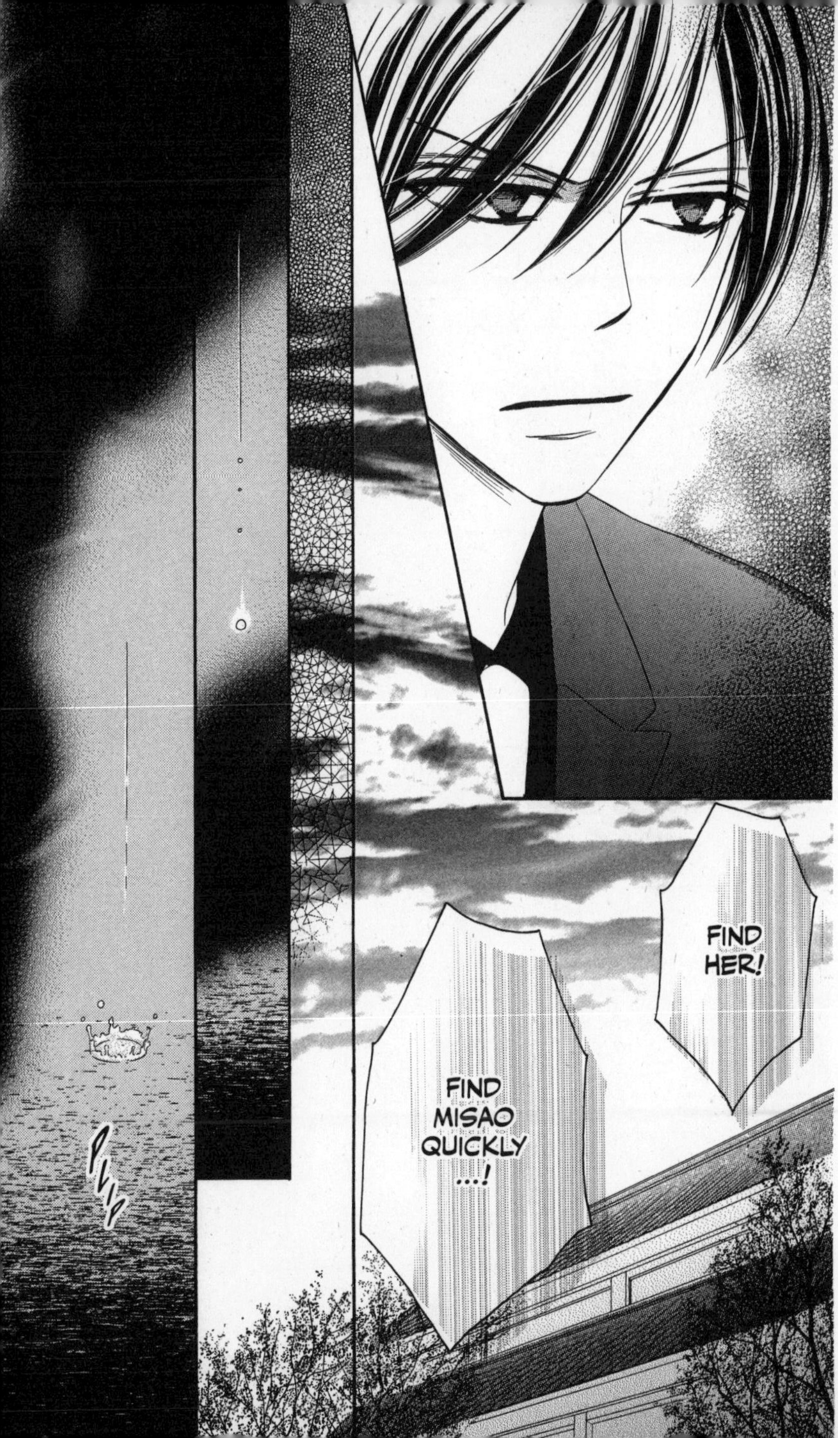
FIND HER!
FIND MISAO QUICKLY ...!
PLIP

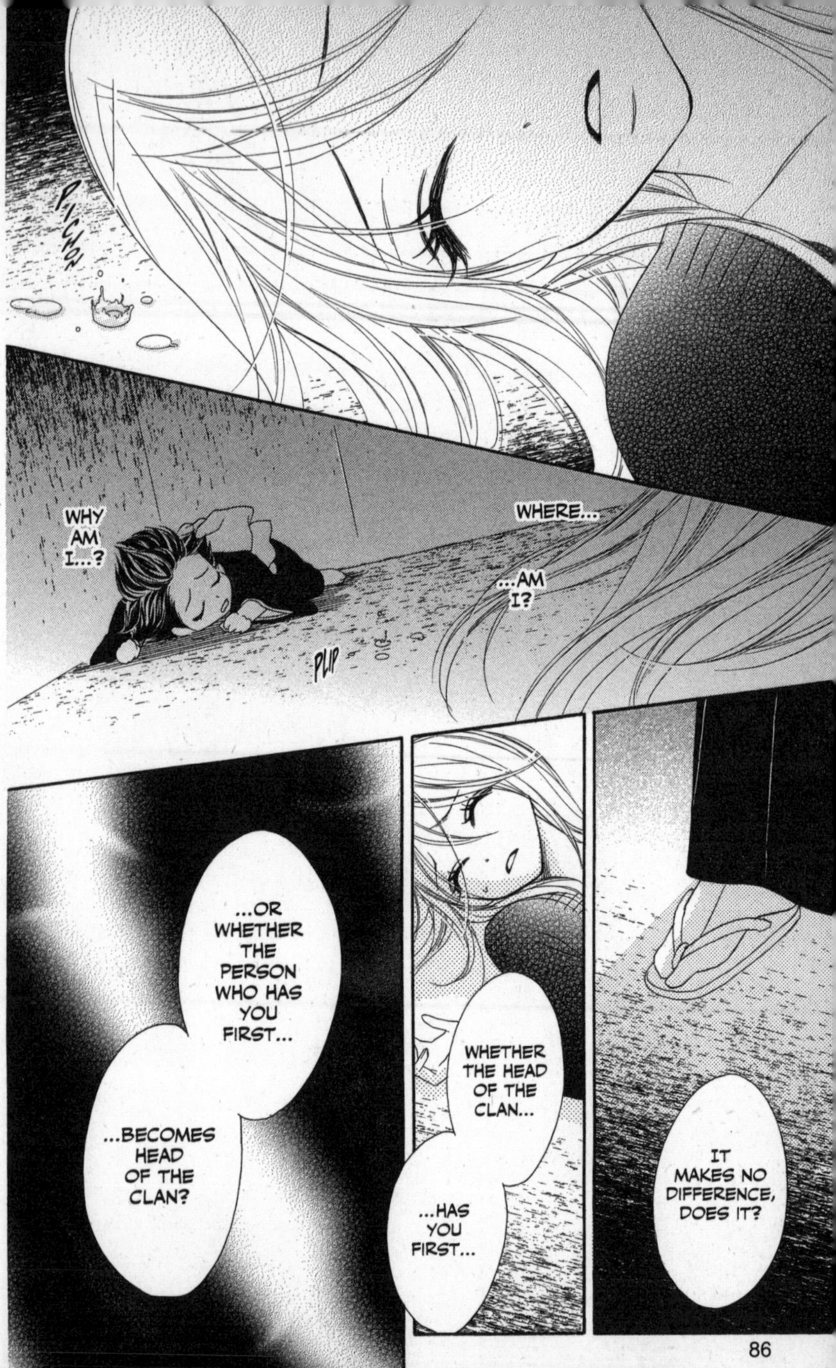
PICHON
WHERE...
...AM I?
PLIP
WHY AM I...?
IT MAKES NO DIFFERENCE, DOES IT?
WHETHER THE HEAD OF THE CLAN...
...HAS YOU FIRST...
...OR WHETHER THE PERSON WHO HAS YOU FIRST...
...BECOMES HEAD OF THE CLAN?

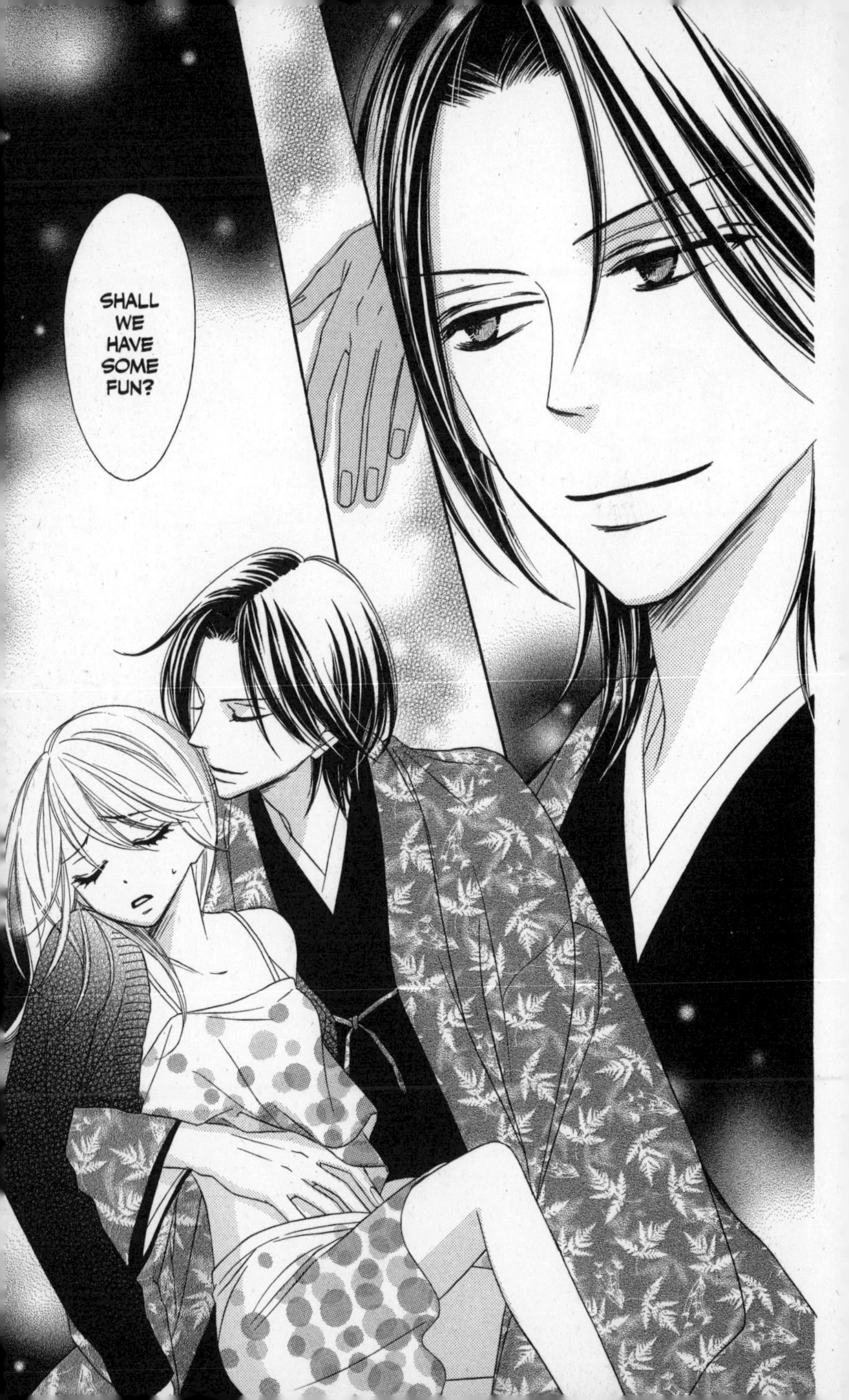
SHALL WE HAVE SOME FUN?

On the Eight Daitengu

• One •

Since ancient times, legends of tengu have abounded in Japan. The names of many tengu that lived in the mountains are still remembered today.

Among them are eight powerful tengu called the Eight Daitengu of Japan.

So I did not make up the names Sagami or Buzen. Not even Taro...

There are various versions of the list of the Eight Daitengu, and actually Darani of Mt. Fuji is more appropriate, but ~~his name is too complicated to write.~~ I thought Zenki would fit the character better.

Hello, my name is Darani!
...It just doesn't fit.

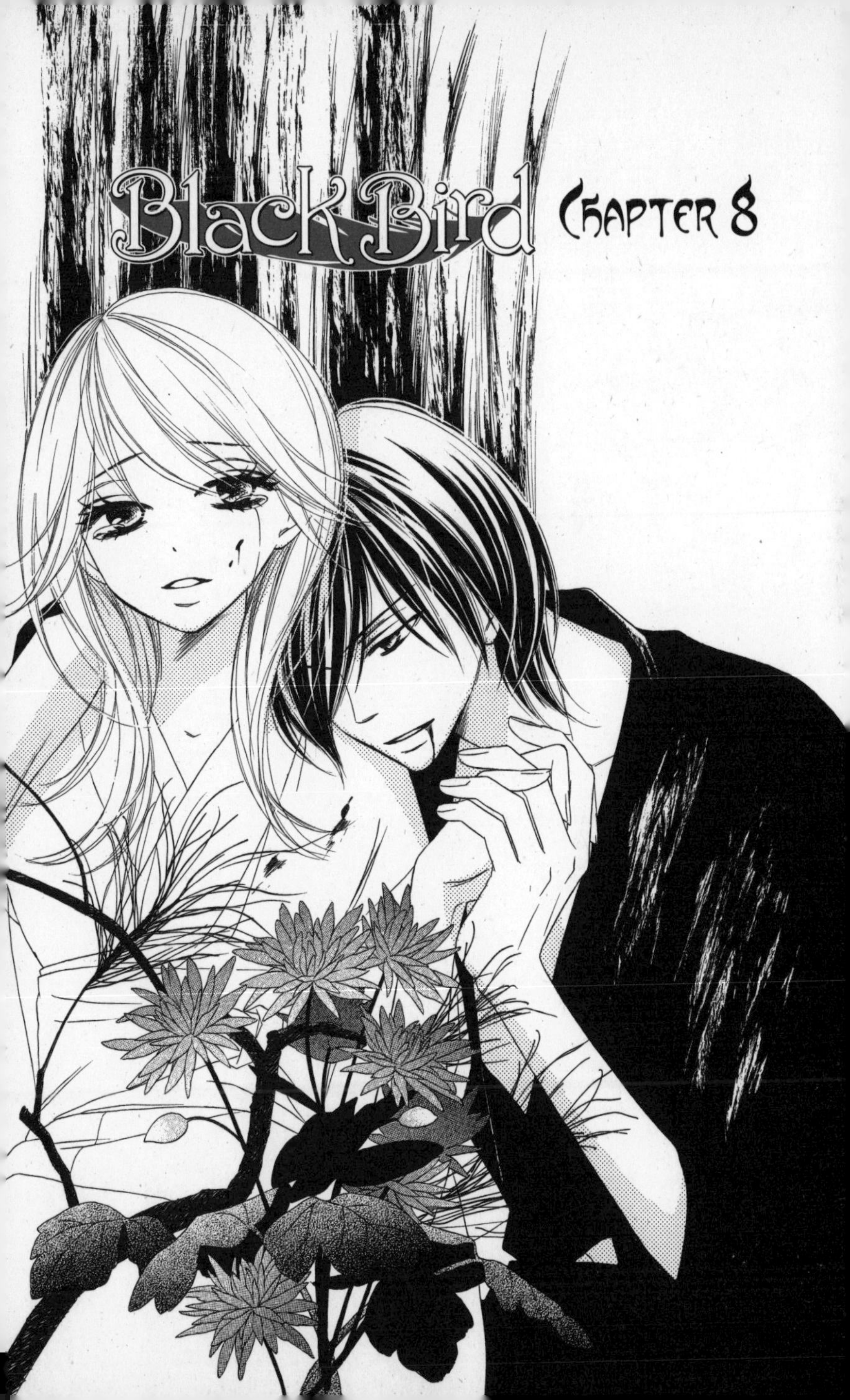
Black Bird
Chapter 8

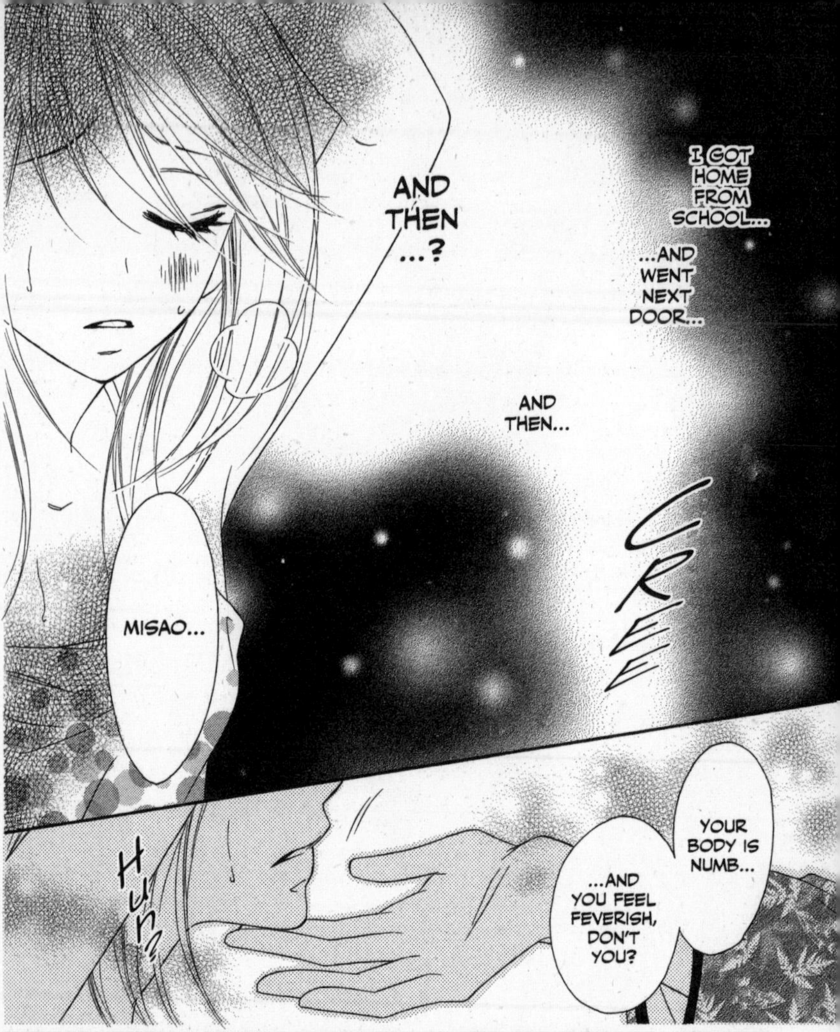
I GOT HOME FROM SCHOOL...
...AND WENT NEXT DOOR...
AND THEN...
CREEE
AND THEN ...?
MISAO...
YOUR BODY IS NUMB...
...AND YOU FEEL FEVERISH, DON'T YOU?
HUN?

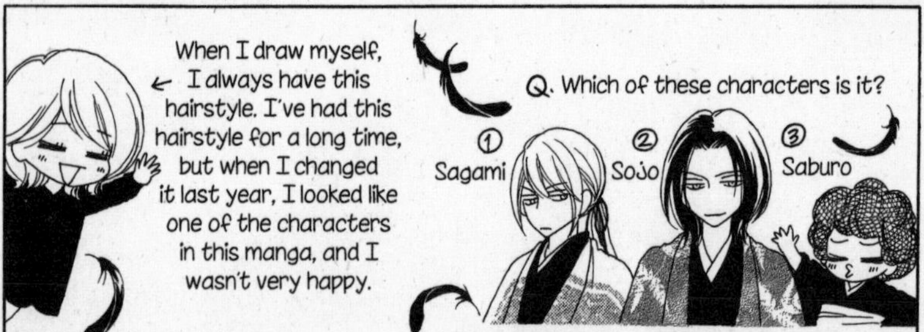
When I draw myself, ← I always have this hairstyle. I've had this hairstyle for a long time, but when I changed it last year, I looked like one of the characters in this manga, and I wasn't very happy.
Q. Which of these characters is it?
① Sagami
② Sojo
③ Saburo
The answer is in the next character introduction box.

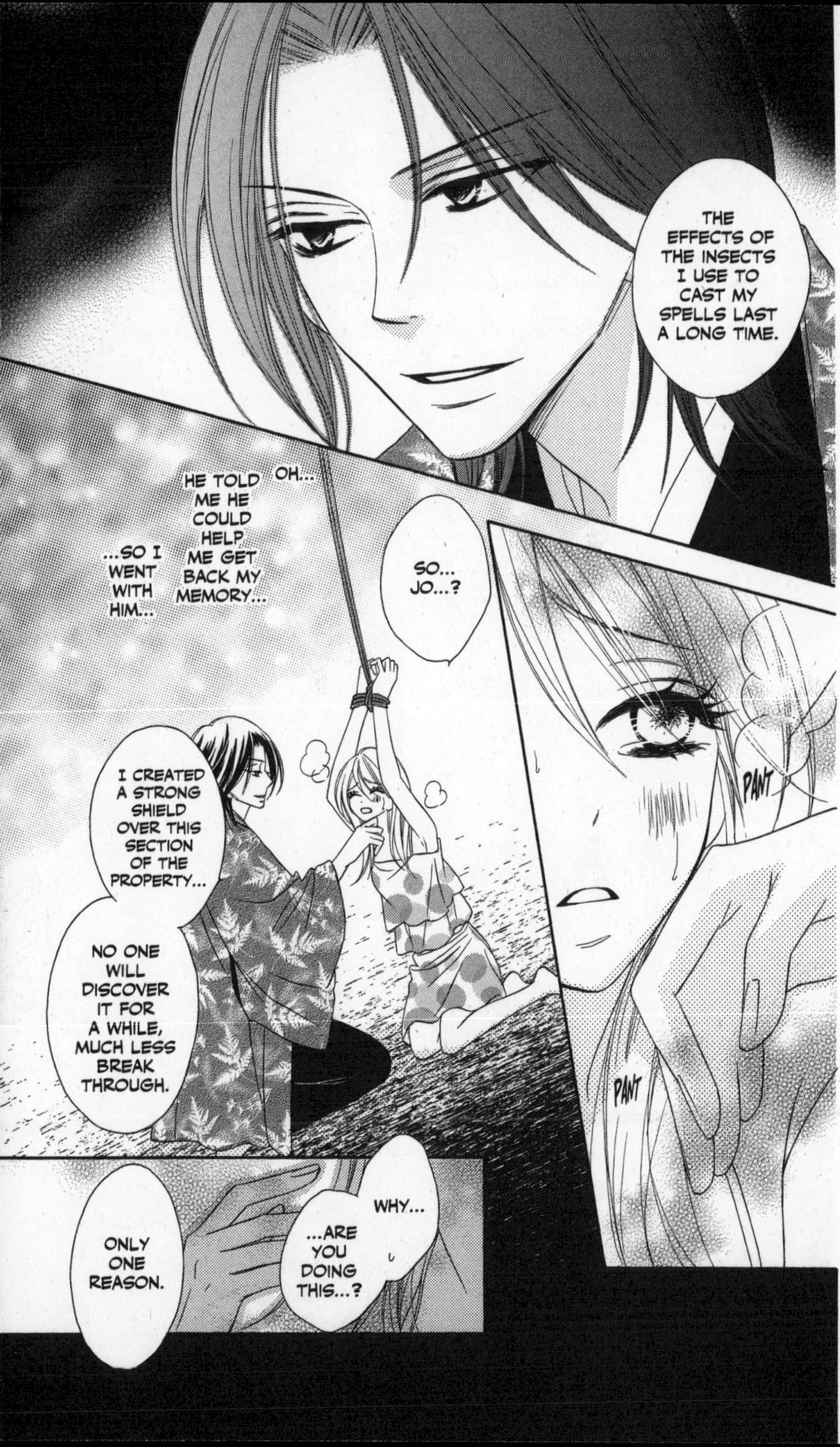
THE EFFECTS OF THE INSECTS I USE TO CAST MY SPELLS LAST A LONG TIME.
PANT
PANT
SO... JO...?
OH...
HE TOLD ME HE COULD HELP ME GET BACK MY MEMORY...
...SO I WENT WITH HIM...
I CREATED A STRONG SHIELD OVER THIS SECTION OF THE PROPERTY...
NO ONE WILL DISCOVER IT FOR A WHILE, MUCH LESS BREAK THROUGH.
WHY...
...ARE YOU DOING THIS...?
ONLY ONE REASON.

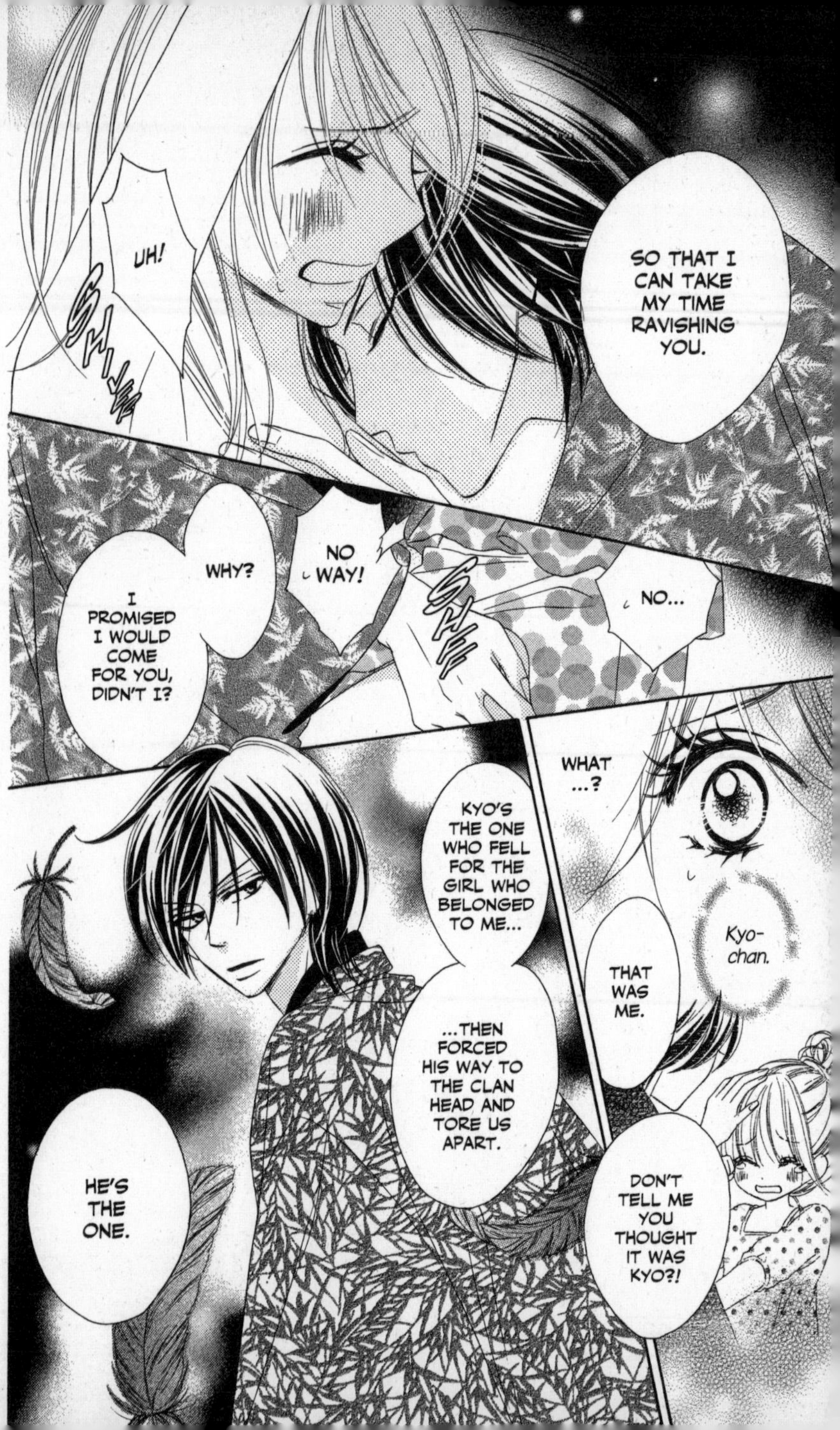
SO THAT I CAN TAKE MY TIME RAVISHING YOU.
UH!
NO...
NO WAY!
WHY?
I PROMISED I WOULD COME FOR YOU, DIDN'T I?
WHAT ...?
Kyo-chan.
THAT WAS ME.
DON'T TELL ME YOU THOUGHT IT WAS KYO?!
KYO'S THE ONE WHO FELL FOR THE GIRL WHO BELONGED TO ME...
...THEN FORCED HIS WAY TO THE CLAN HEAD AND TORE US APART.
HE'S THE ONE.

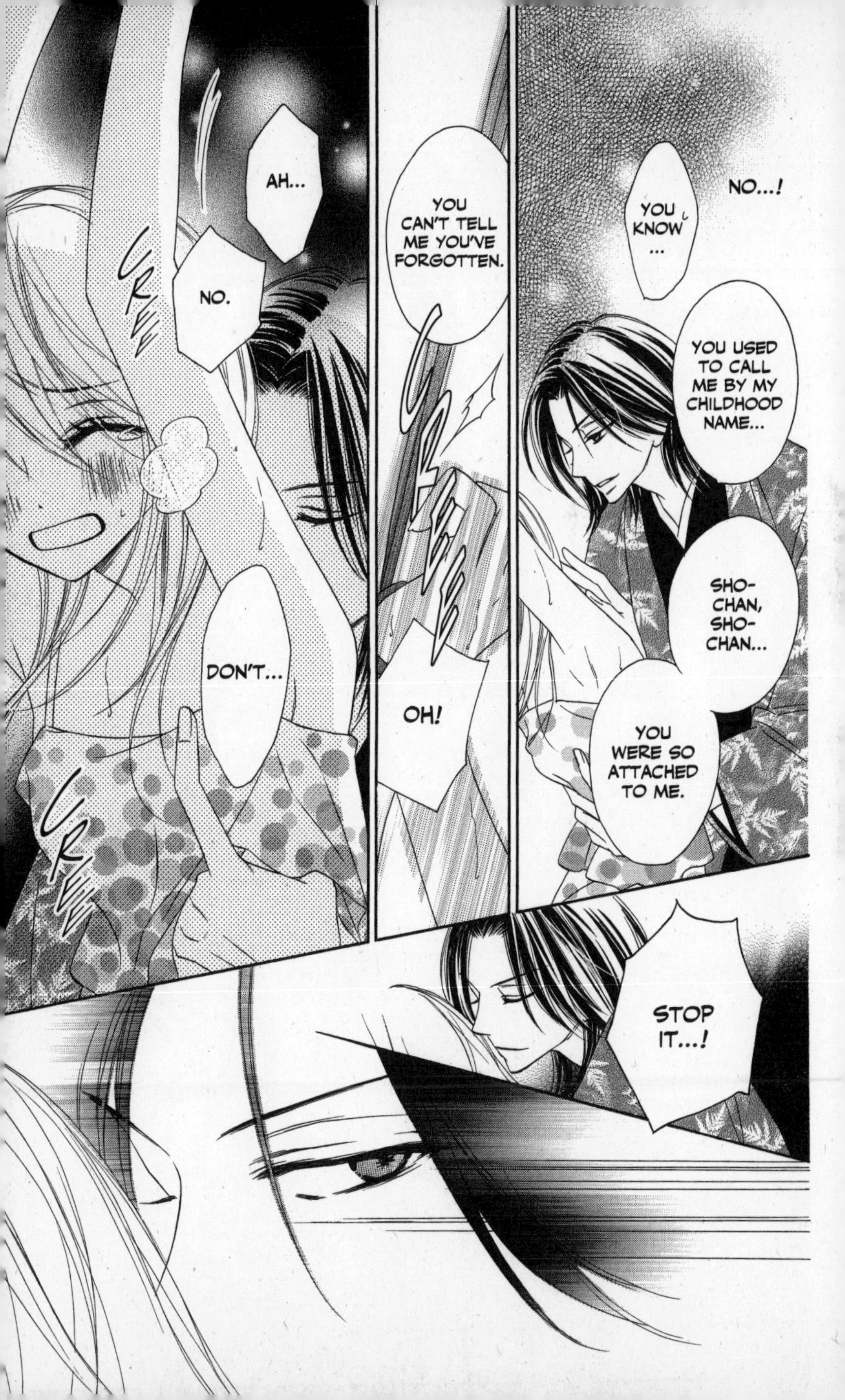
NO...!
YOU KNOW ...
YOU USED TO CALL ME BY MY CHILDHOOD NAME...
SHO-CHAN, SHO-CHAN...
YOU WERE SO ATTACHED TO ME.
YOU CAN'T TELL ME YOU'VE FORGOTTEN.
OH!
AH...
NO.
DON'T...
STOP IT...!

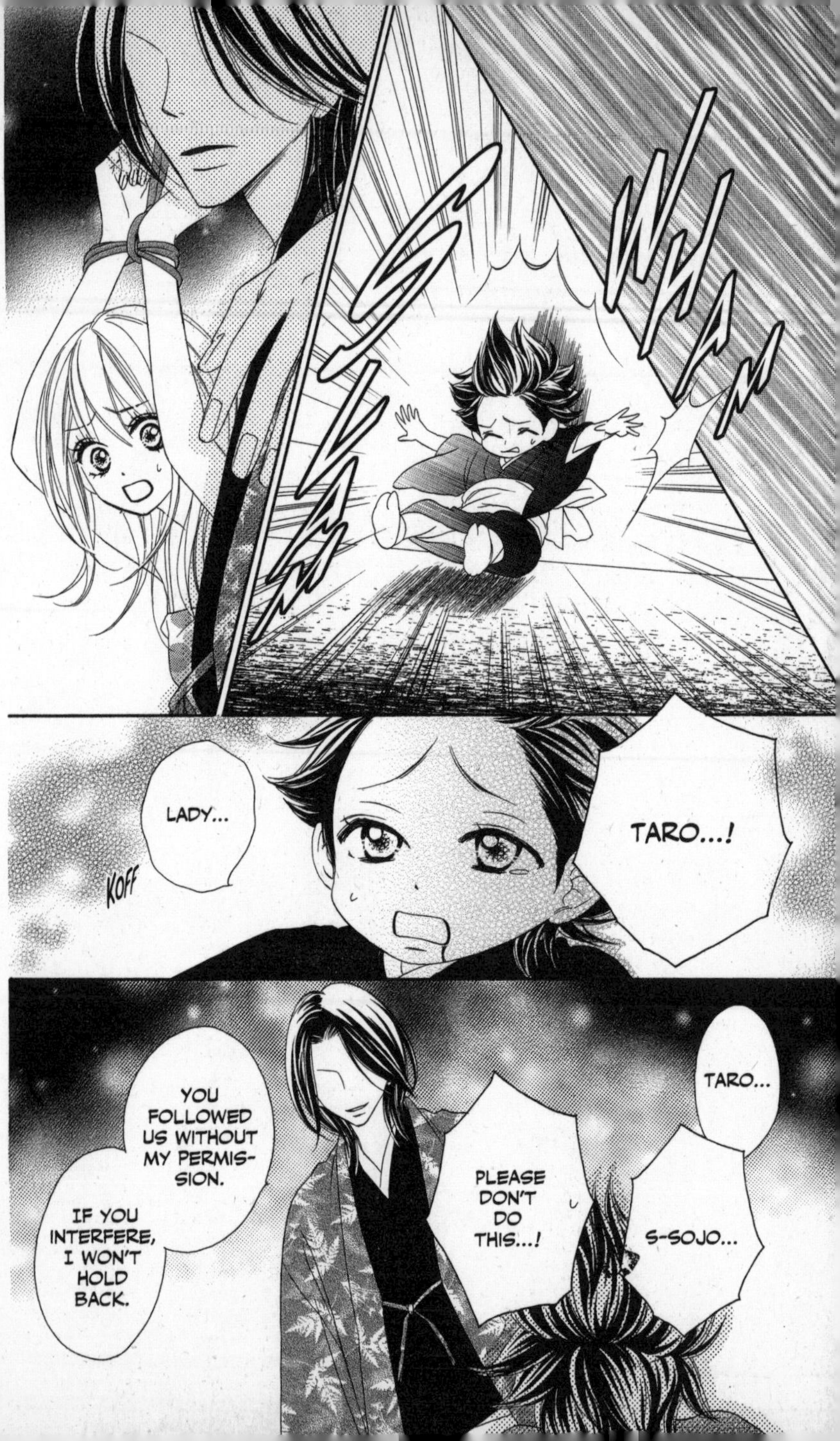
WHAM
TARO...!
LADY...
KOFF
TARO...
S-SOJO...
PLEASE DON'T DO THIS...!
YOU FOLLOWED US WITHOUT MY PERMISSION.
IF YOU INTERFERE, I WON'T HOLD BACK.

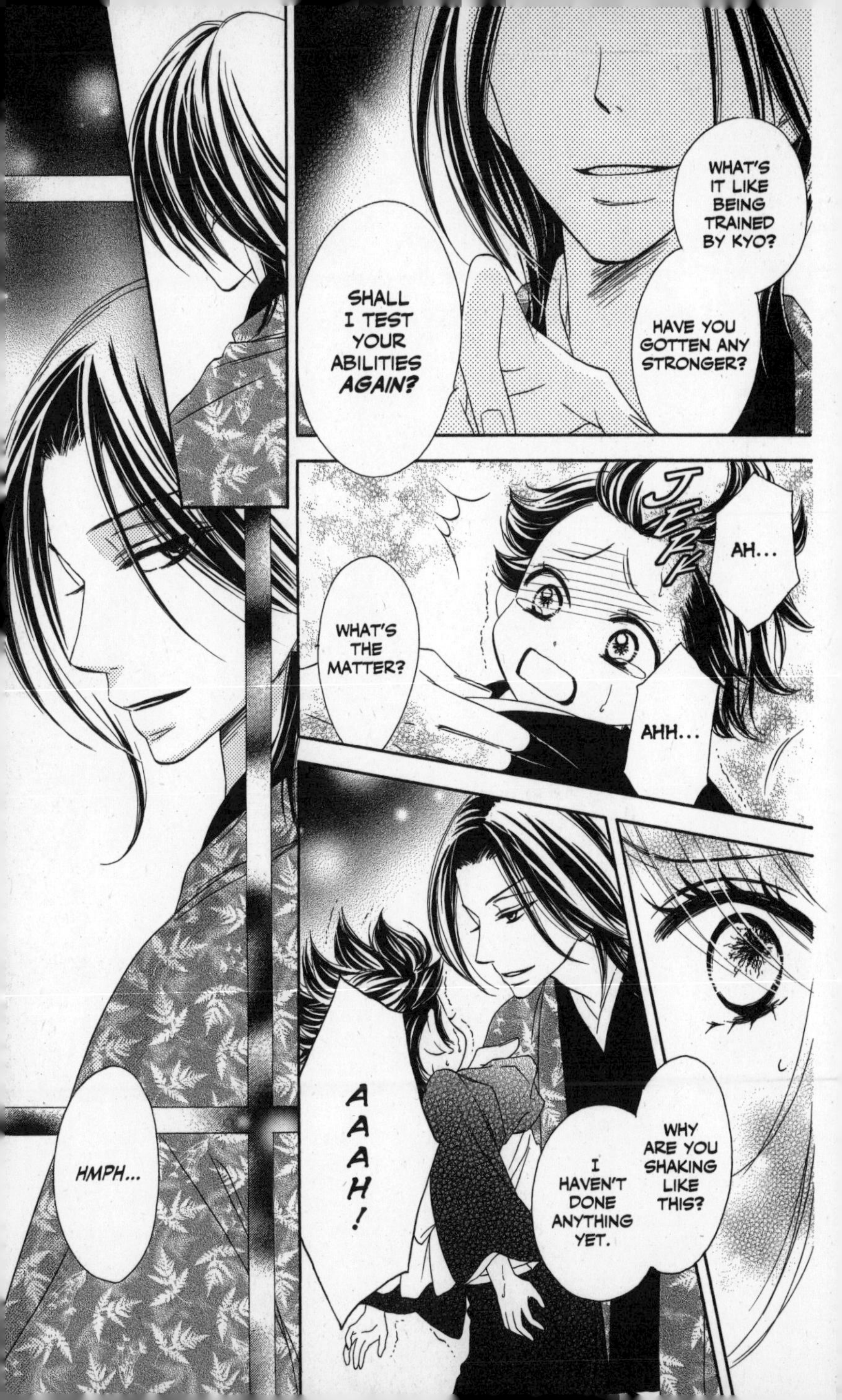
WHAT'S IT LIKE BEING TRAINED BY KYO?
HAVE YOU GOTTEN ANY STRONGER?
SHALL I TEST YOUR ABILITIES *AGAIN?*
JERK
AH...
AHH...
WHAT'S THE MATTER?
WHY ARE YOU SHAKING LIKE THIS?
I HAVEN'T DONE ANYTHING YET.
AAAAH!
HMPH...

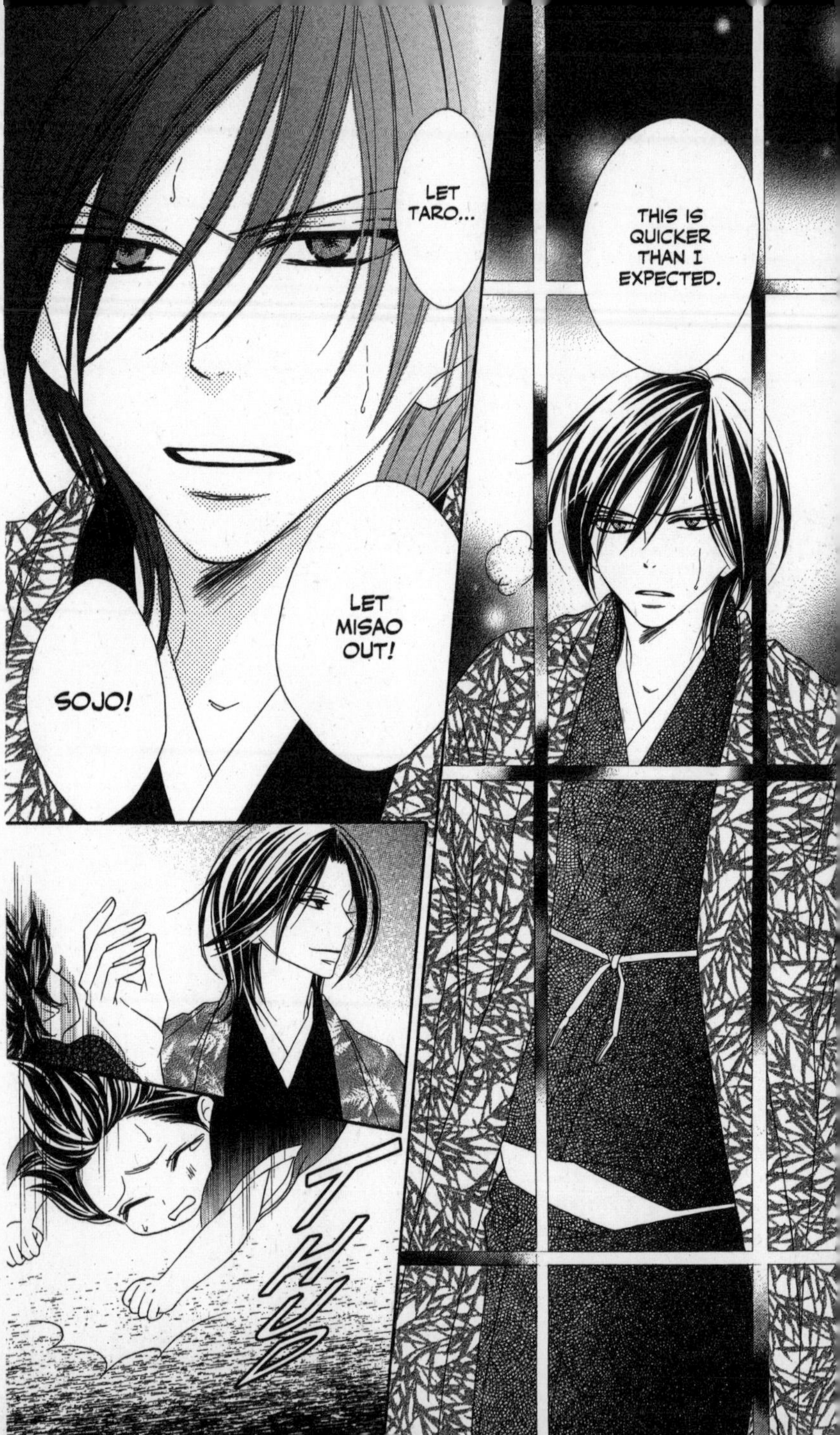
THIS IS QUICKER THAN I EXPECTED.
LET TARO...
LET MISAO OUT!
SOJO!

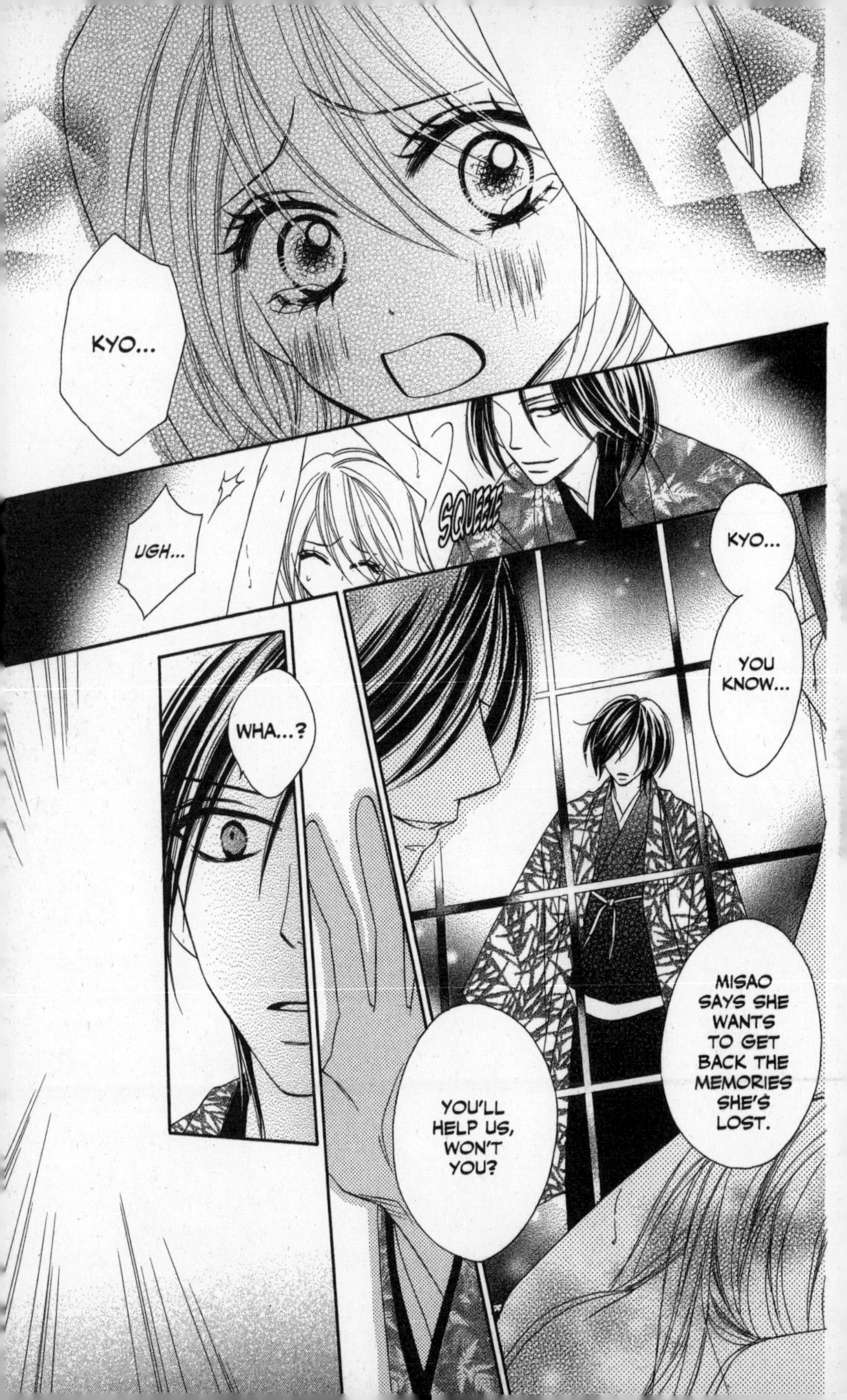
KYO...
SQUEEEE
UGH...
KYO...
YOU KNOW...
MISAO SAYS SHE WANTS TO GET BACK THE MEMORIES SHE'S LOST.
YOU'LL HELP US, WON'T YOU?
WHA...?

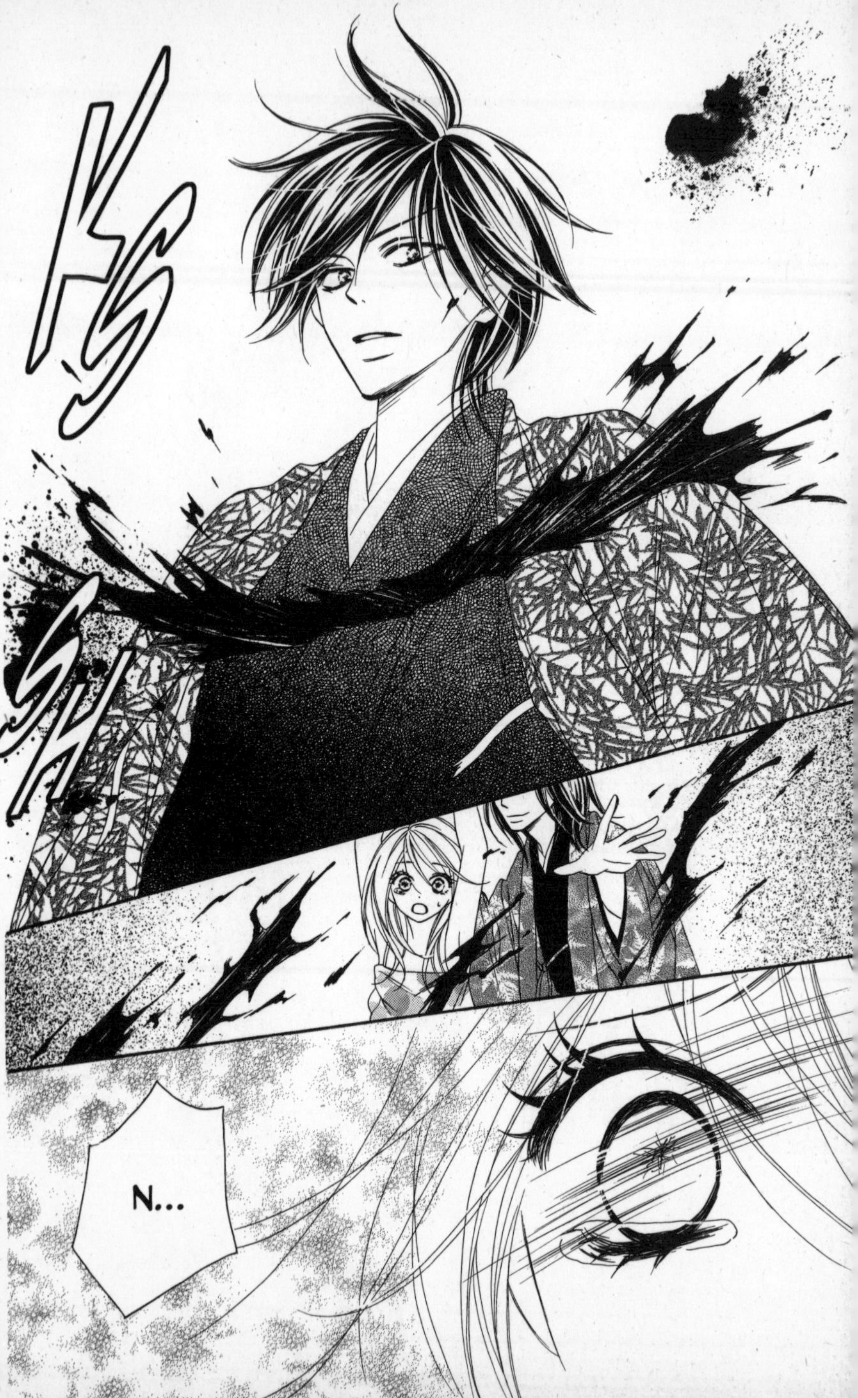
KSSSH
N...

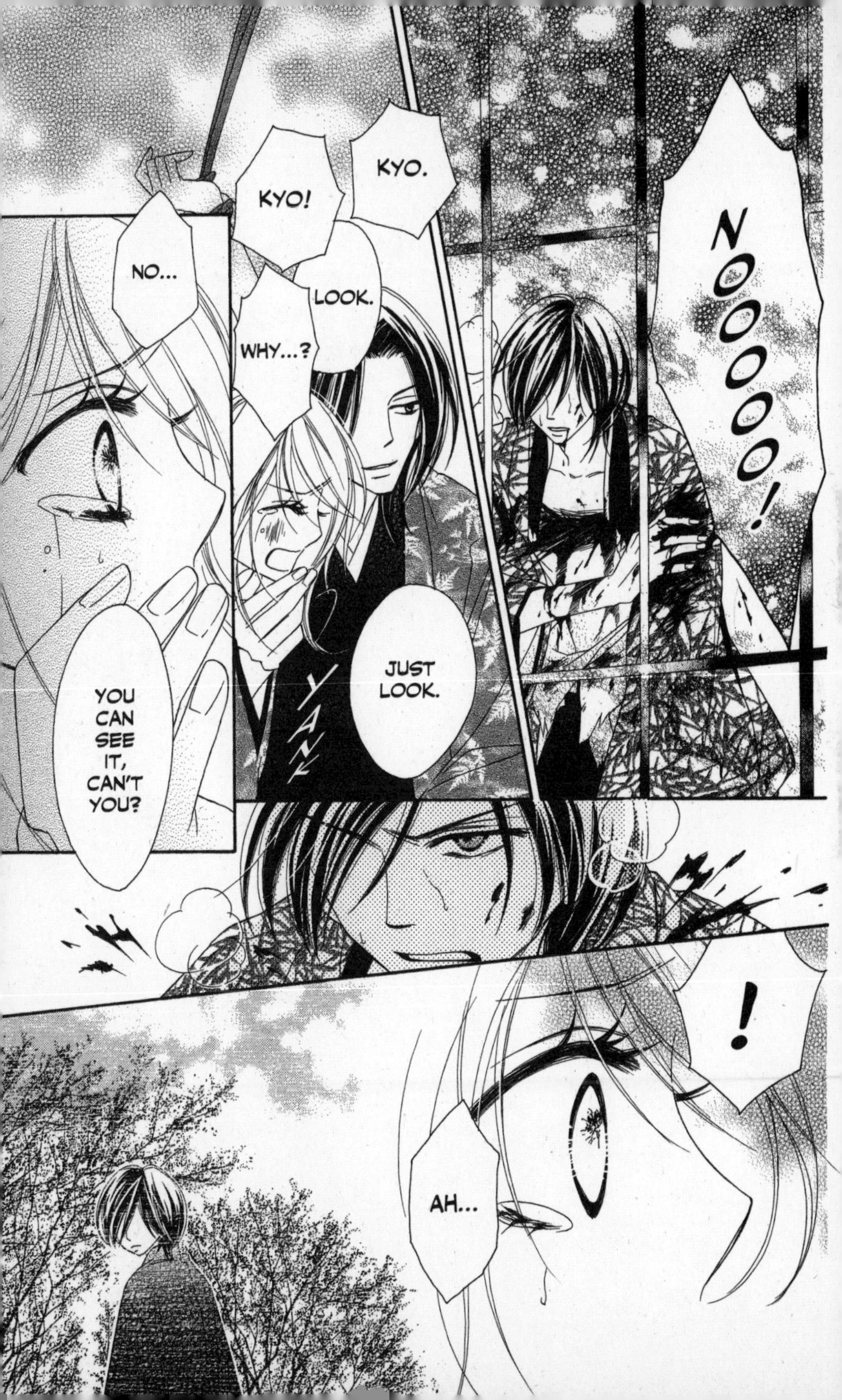
NOOOOOO!
KYO.
KYO!
LOOK.
WHY...?
YANK
JUST LOOK.
NO...
YOU CAN SEE IT, CAN'T YOU?
!
AH...

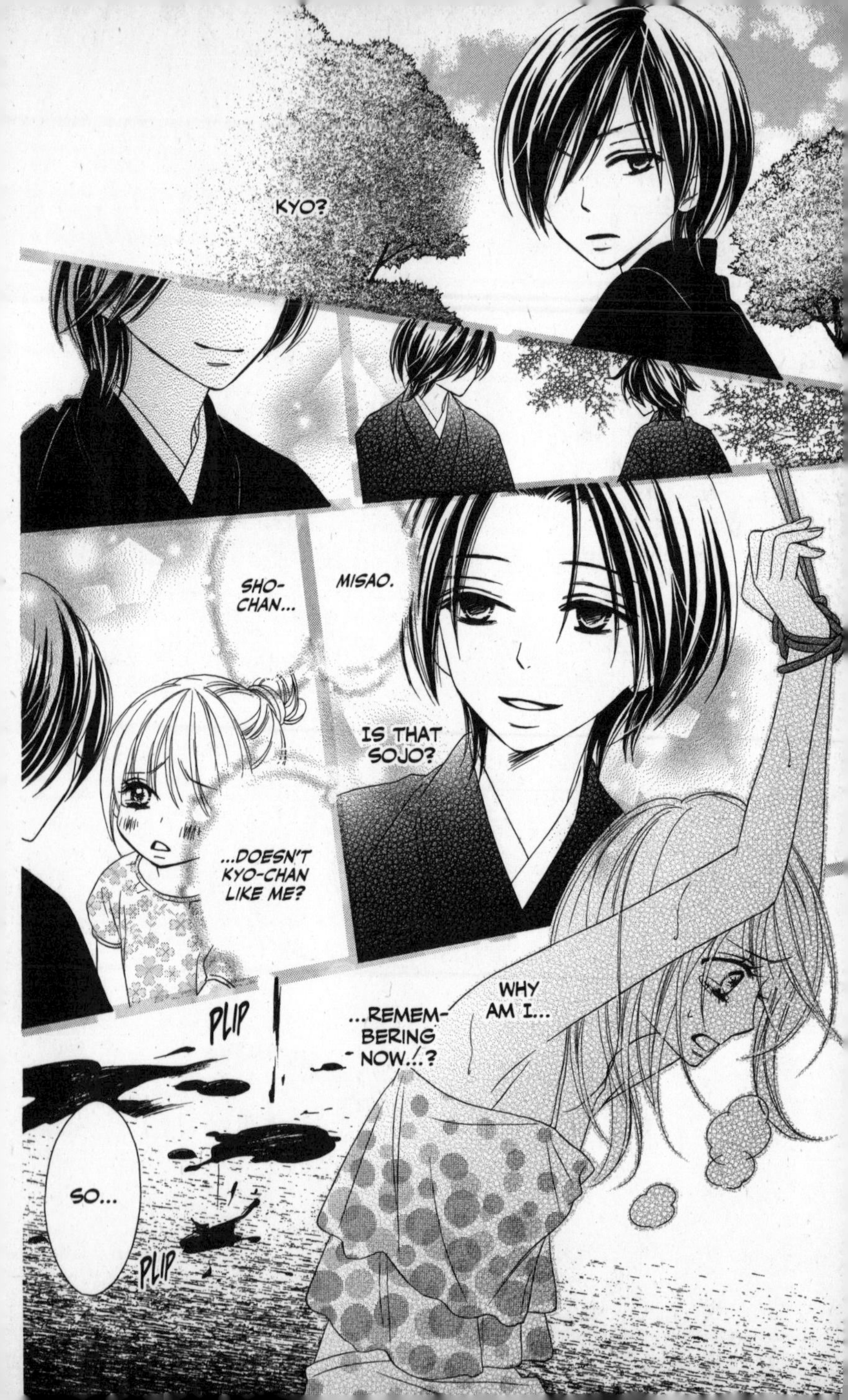
KYO?
MISAO.
IS THAT SOJO?
SHO-CHAN...
...DOESN'T KYO-CHAN LIKE ME?
WHY AM I...
...REMEMBERING NOW!?
PLIP
SO...
PLIP

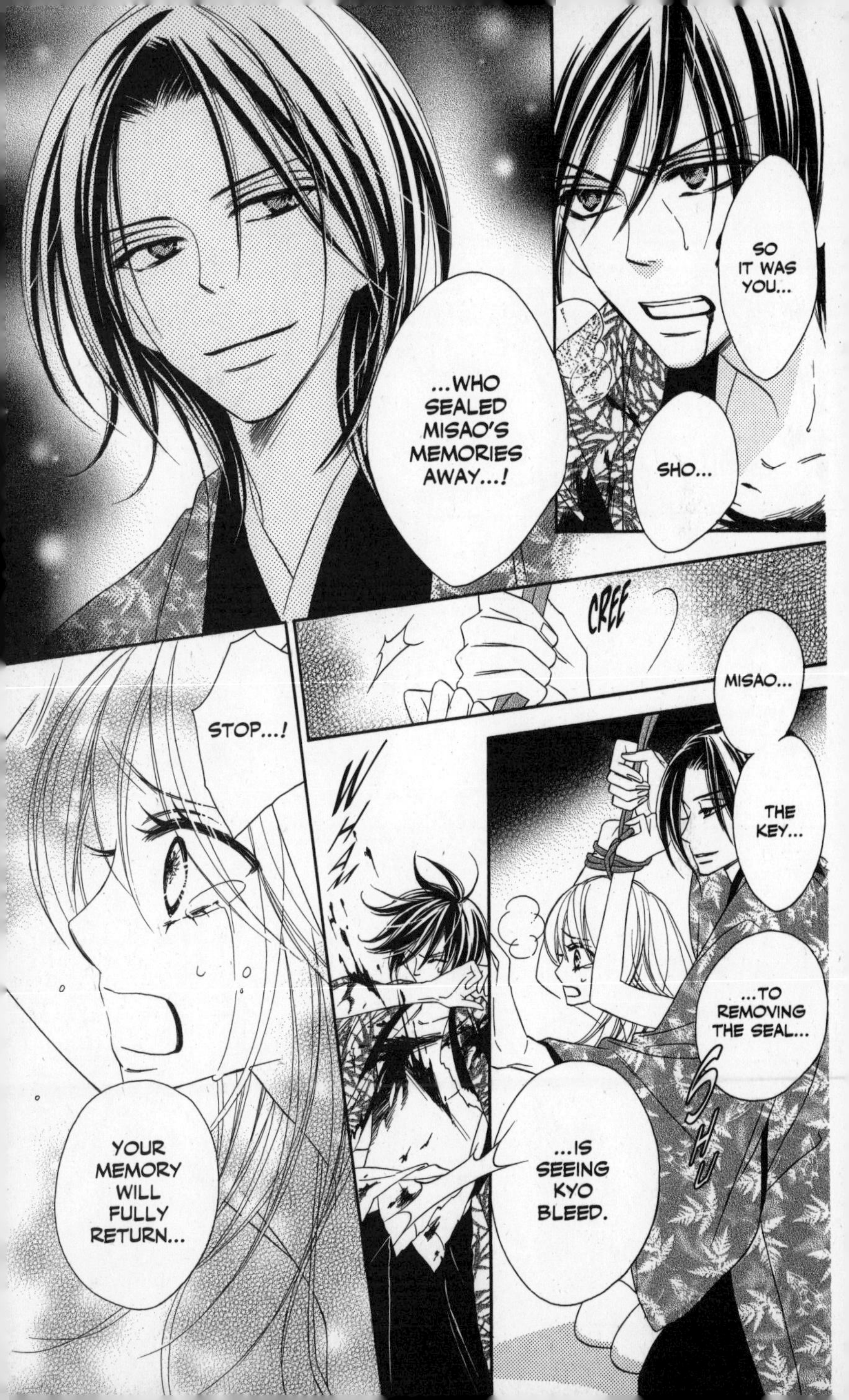
SO IT WAS YOU...
SHO...
...WHO SEALED MISAO'S MEMORIES AWAY...!
CREE
MISAO...
THE KEY...
...TO REMOVING THE SEAL...
...IS SEEING KYO BLEED.
STOP...!
YOUR MEMORY WILL FULLY RETURN...

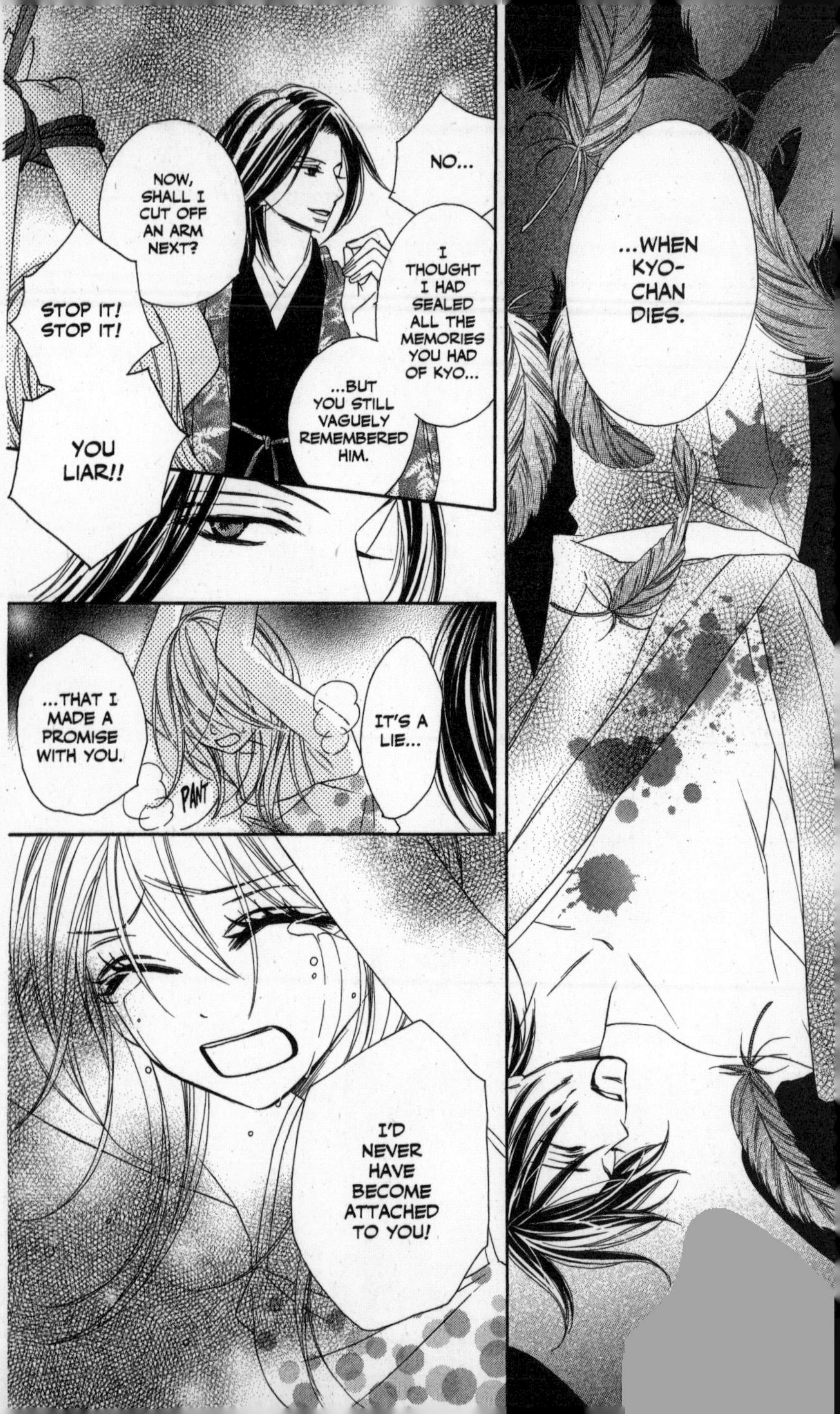
...WHEN KYO-CHAN DIES.
NO...
I THOUGHT I HAD SEALED ALL THE MEMORIES YOU HAD OF KYO...
...BUT YOU STILL VAGUELY REMEMBERED HIM.
NOW, SHALL I CUT OFF AN ARM NEXT?
STOP IT! STOP IT!
YOU LIAR!!
IT'S A LIE...
...THAT I MADE A PROMISE WITH YOU.
PANT
I'D NEVER HAVE BECOME ATTACHED TO YOU!

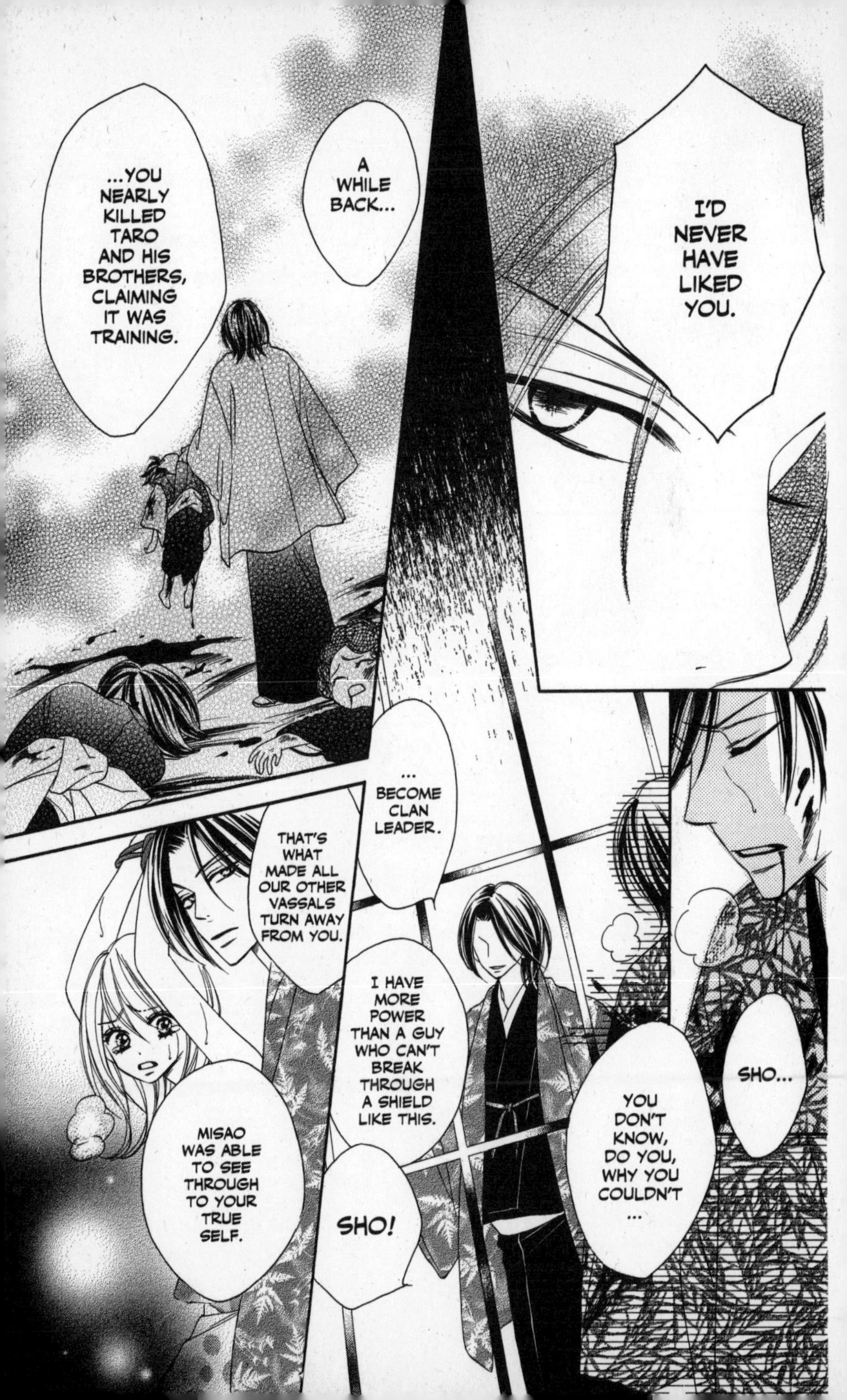
I'D NEVER HAVE LIKED YOU.
A WHILE BACK...
...YOU NEARLY KILLED TARO AND HIS BROTHERS, CLAIMING IT WAS TRAINING.
SHO...
YOU DON'T KNOW, DO YOU, WHY YOU COULDN'T ...
... BECOME CLAN LEADER.
THAT'S WHAT MADE ALL OUR OTHER VASSALS TURN AWAY FROM YOU.
I HAVE MORE POWER THAN A GUY WHO CAN'T BREAK THROUGH A SHIELD LIKE THIS.
SHO!
MISAO WAS ABLE TO SEE THROUGH TO YOUR TRUE SELF.

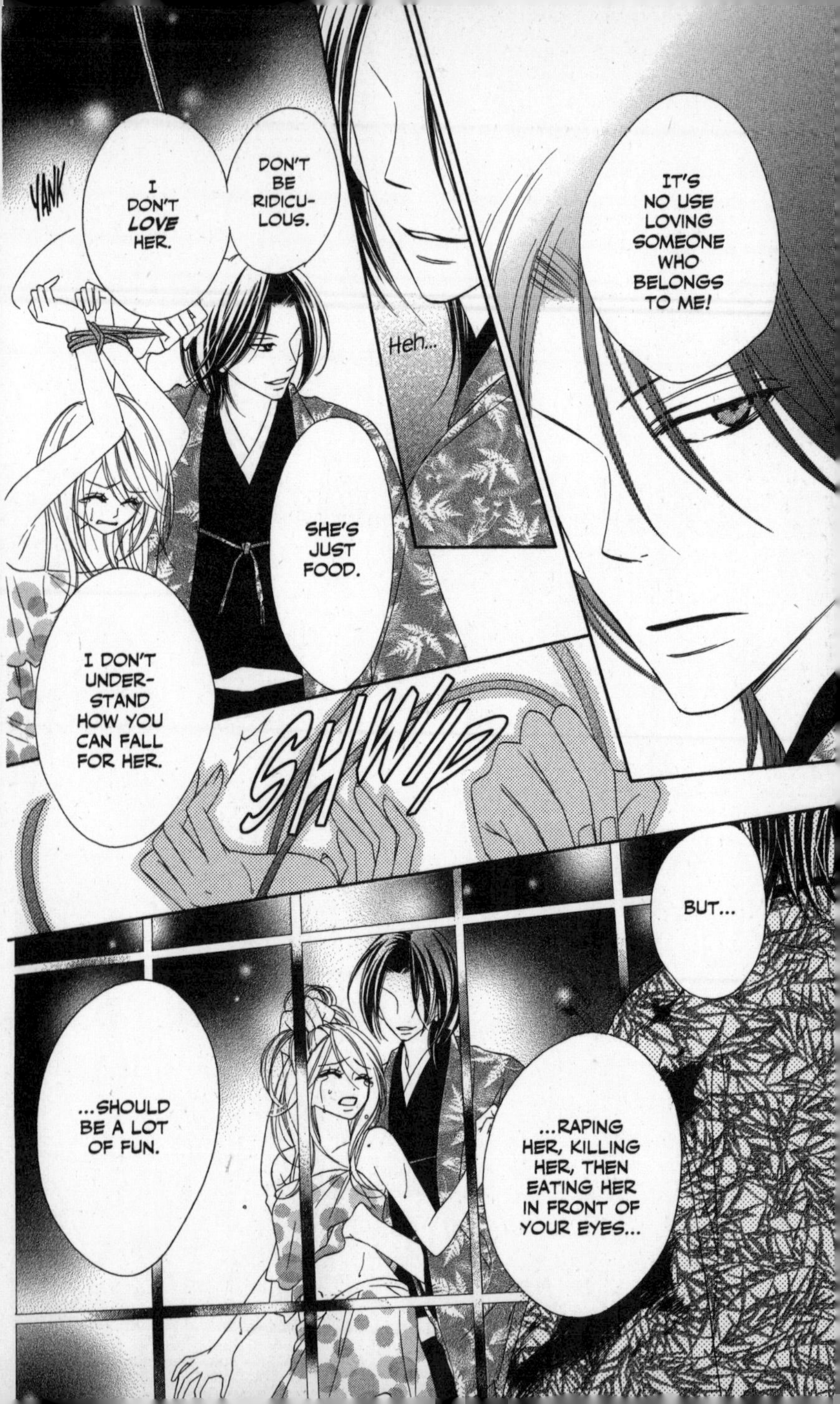
IT'S NO USE LOVING SOMEONE WHO BELONGS TO ME!
Heh...
DON'T BE RIDICULOUS.
I DON'T LOVE HER.
YANK
SHE'S JUST FOOD.
I DON'T UNDER-STAND HOW YOU CAN FALL FOR HER.
SHWIP
BUT...
...RAPING HER, KILLING HER, THEN EATING HER IN FRONT OF YOUR EYES...
...SHOULD BE A LOT OF FUN.

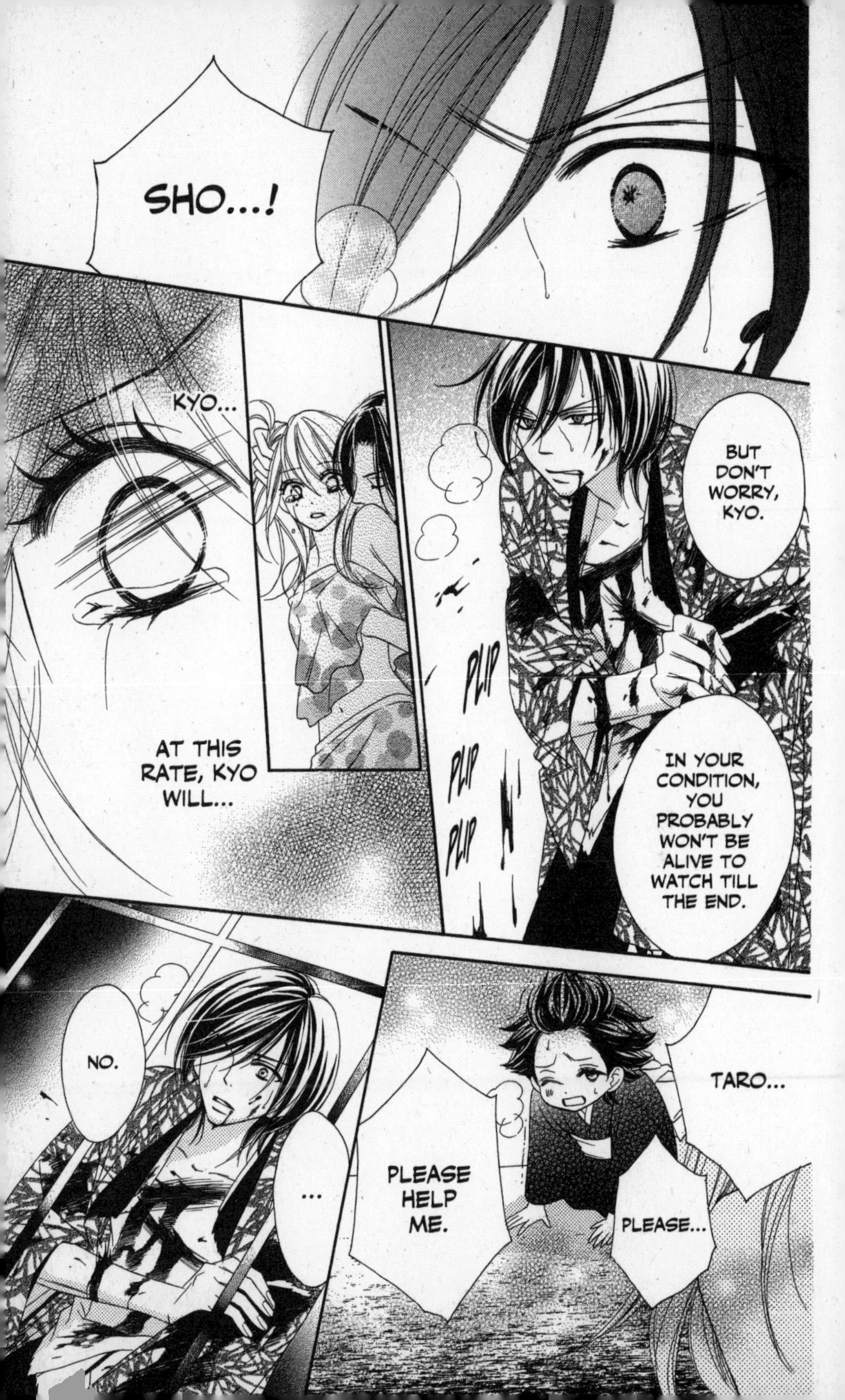
SHO...!
BUT DON'T WORRY, KYO.
PLIP
PLIP
PLIP
IN YOUR CONDITION, YOU PROBABLY WON'T BE ALIVE TO WATCH TILL THE END.
KYO...
AT THIS RATE, KYO WILL...
TARO...
PLEASE...
PLEASE HELP ME.
...
NO.

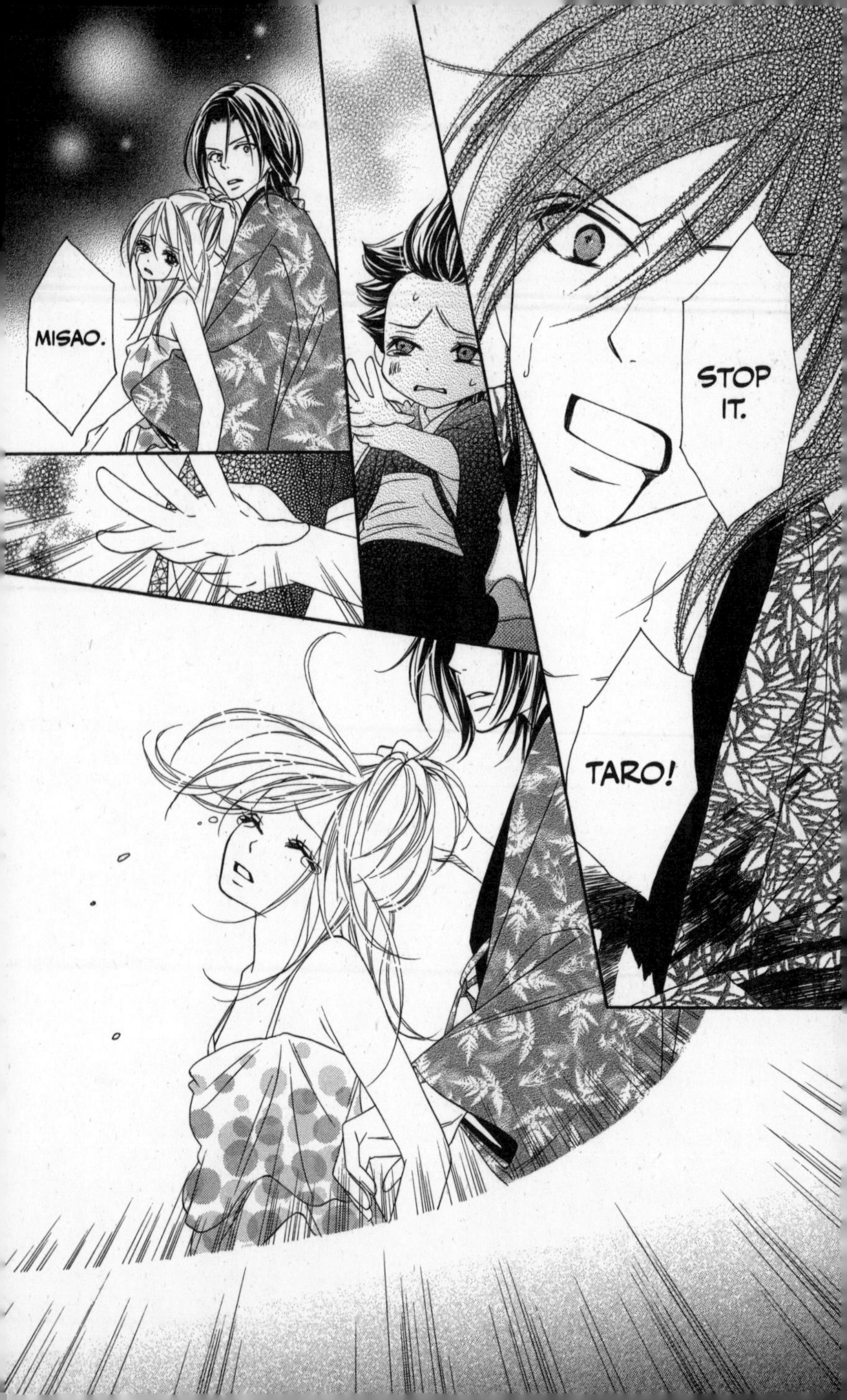
STOP IT.
TARO!
MISAO.

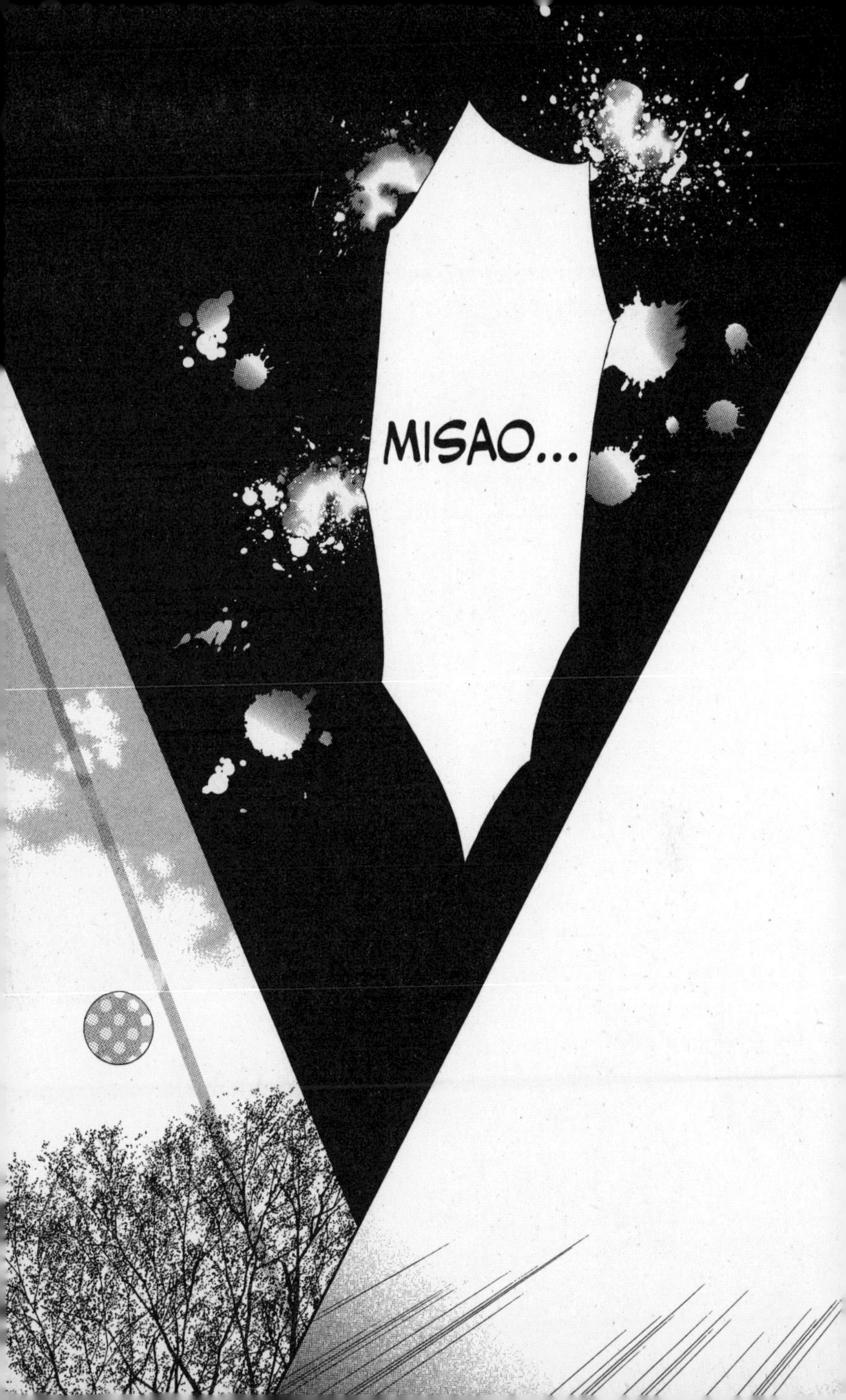
MISAO...

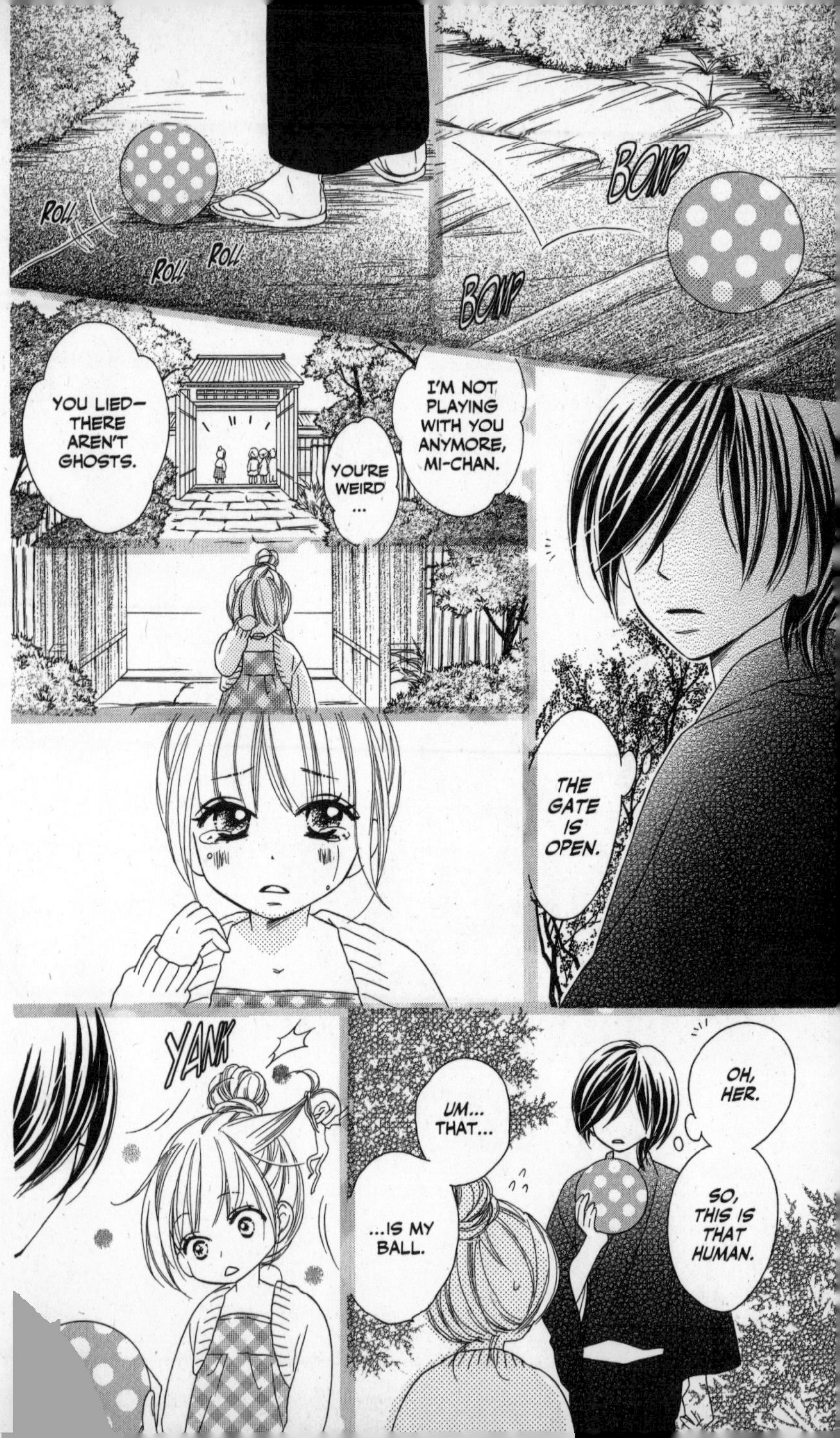
BOMP
BOMP
ROLL
ROLL
ROLL
THE GATE IS OPEN.
I'M NOT PLAYING WITH YOU ANYMORE, MI-CHAN.
YOU'RE WEIRD...
YOU LIED—THERE AREN'T GHOSTS.
OH, HER.
SO, THIS IS THAT HUMAN.
UM... THAT...
...IS MY BALL.
YANK

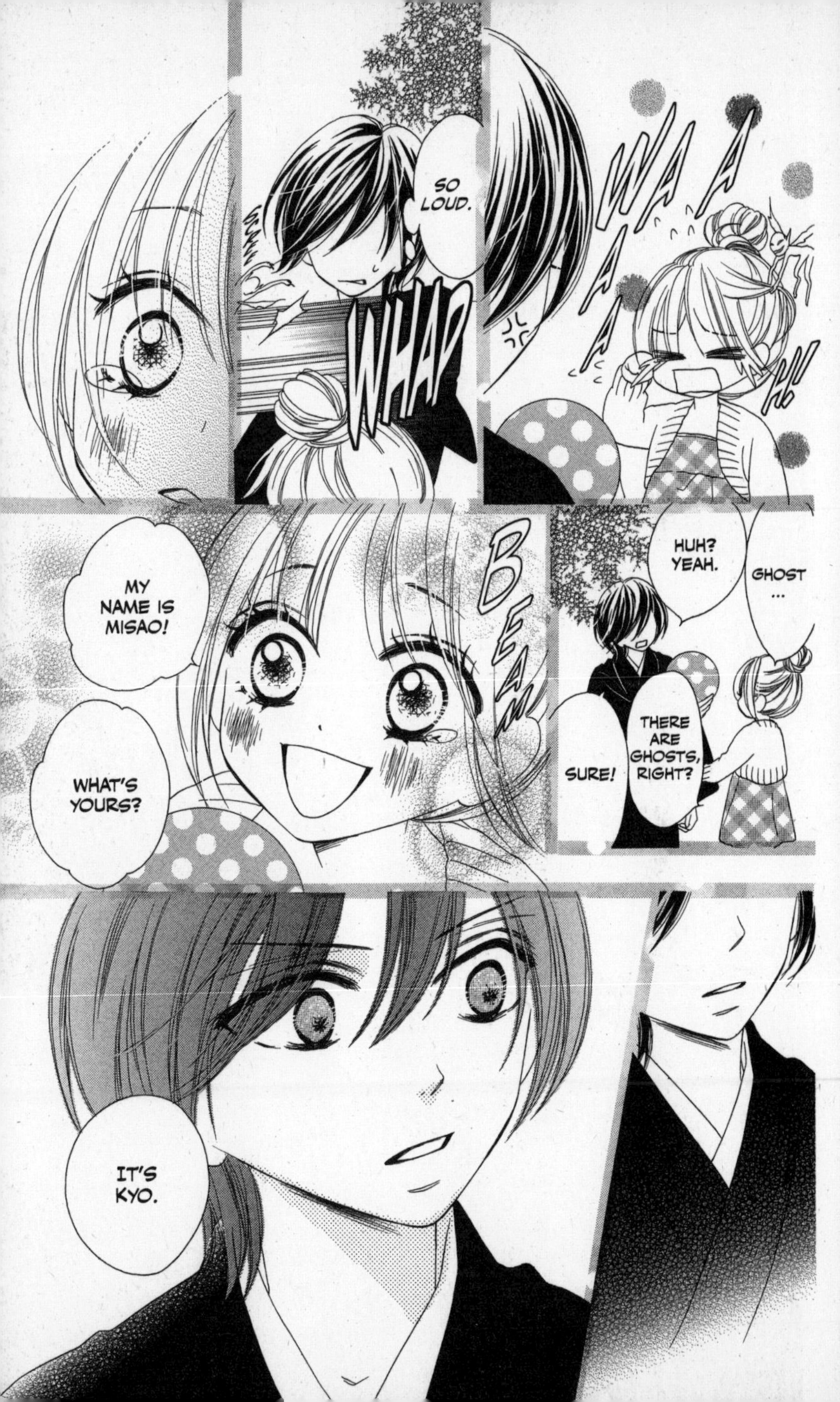
WAAAAAH!
SO LOUD.
WHAP
GHOST...
HUH? YEAH.
THERE ARE GHOSTS, RIGHT?
SURE!
BEAM
MY NAME IS MISAO!
WHAT'S YOURS?
IT'S KYO.

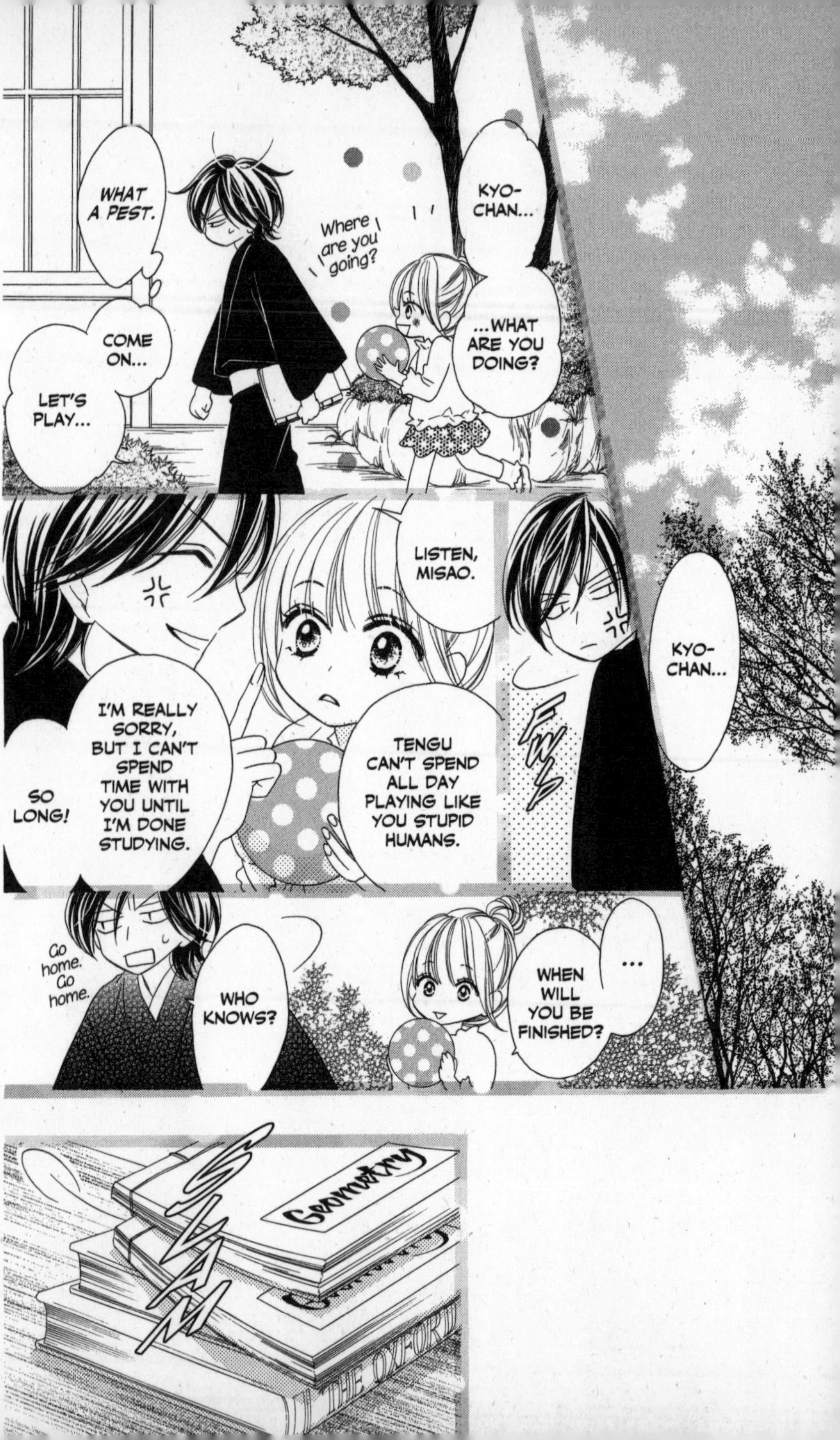
KYO-CHAN...
...WHAT ARE YOU DOING?
Where are you going?
WHAT A PEST.
COME ON...
LET'S PLAY...
KYO-CHAN...
FWIP
LISTEN, MISAO.
TENGU CAN'T SPEND ALL DAY PLAYING LIKE YOU STUPID HUMANS.
I'M REALLY SORRY, BUT I CAN'T SPEND TIME WITH YOU UNTIL I'M DONE STUDYING.
SO LONG!
...
WHEN WILL YOU BE FINISHED?
WHO KNOWS?
Go home. Go home.
SLAM
Geometry
THE OXFORD

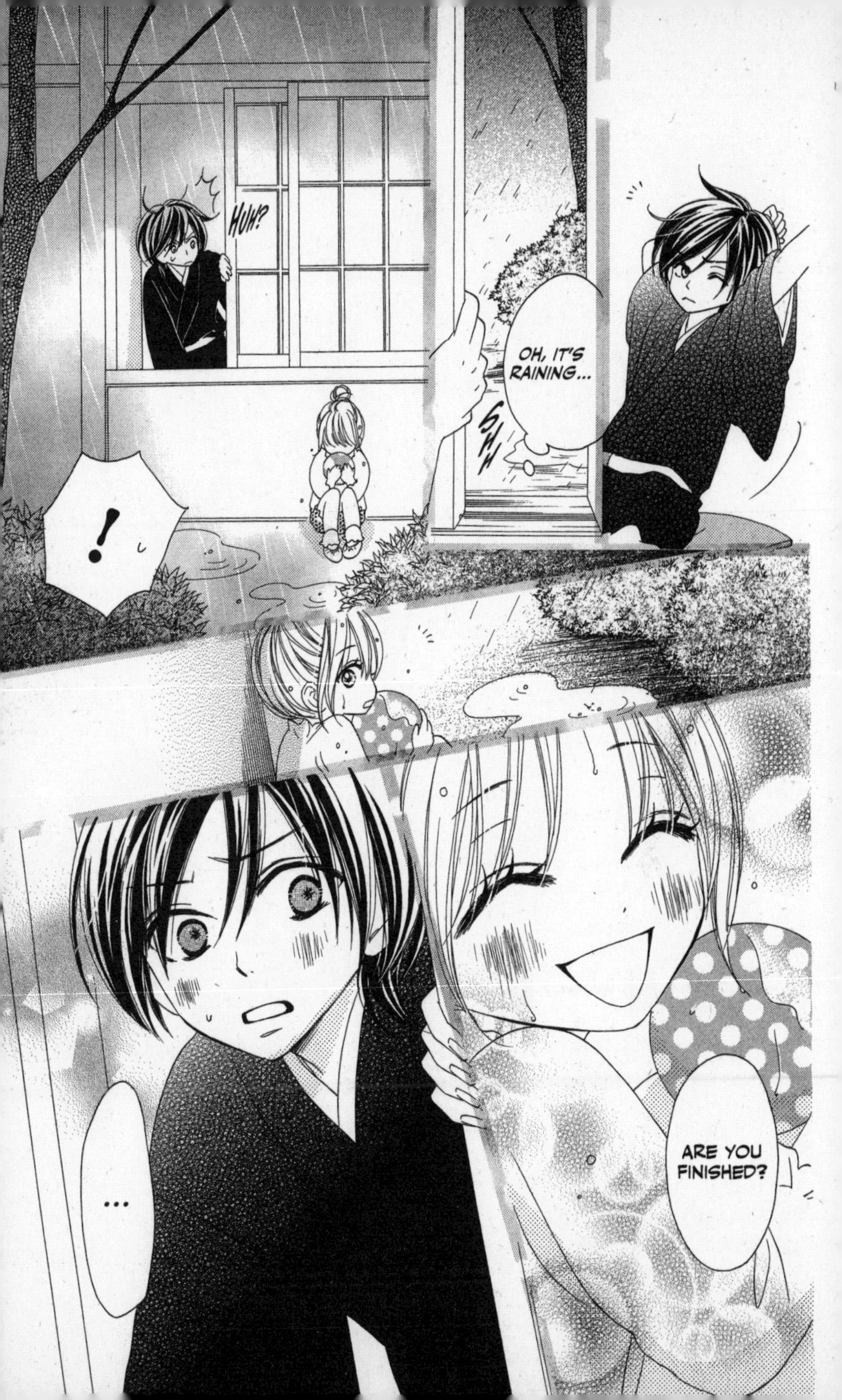
OH, IT'S RAINING...
SHH
HUH?
!
ARE YOU FINISHED?
...

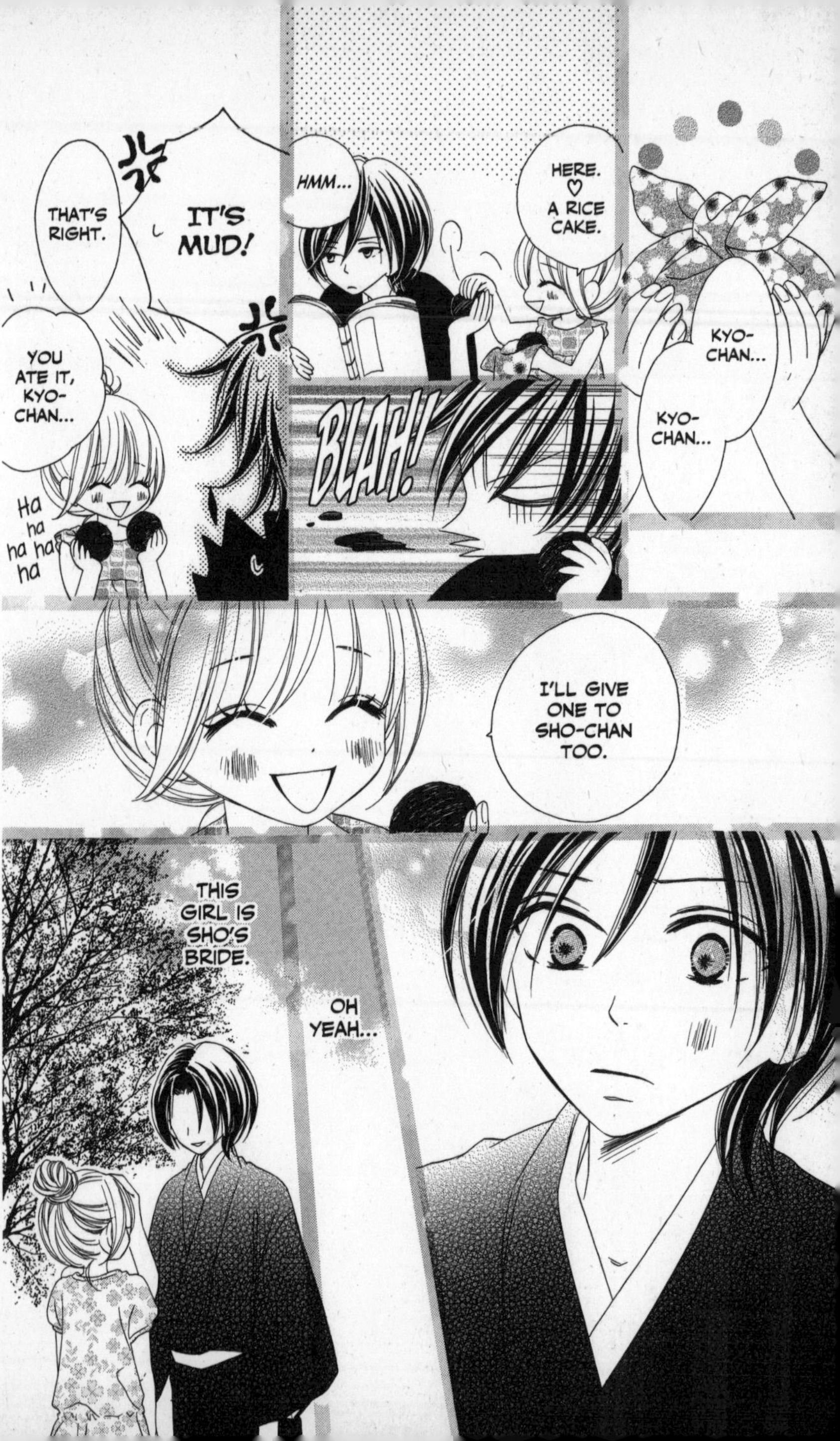
KYO-CHAN...
KYO-CHAN...
HERE. ♡ A RICE CAKE.
HMM...
BLAH!
IT'S MUD!
THAT'S RIGHT.
YOU ATE IT, KYO-CHAN...
Ha ha ha ha ha
I'LL GIVE ONE TO SHO-CHAN TOO.
OH YEAH...
THIS GIRL IS SHO'S BRIDE.

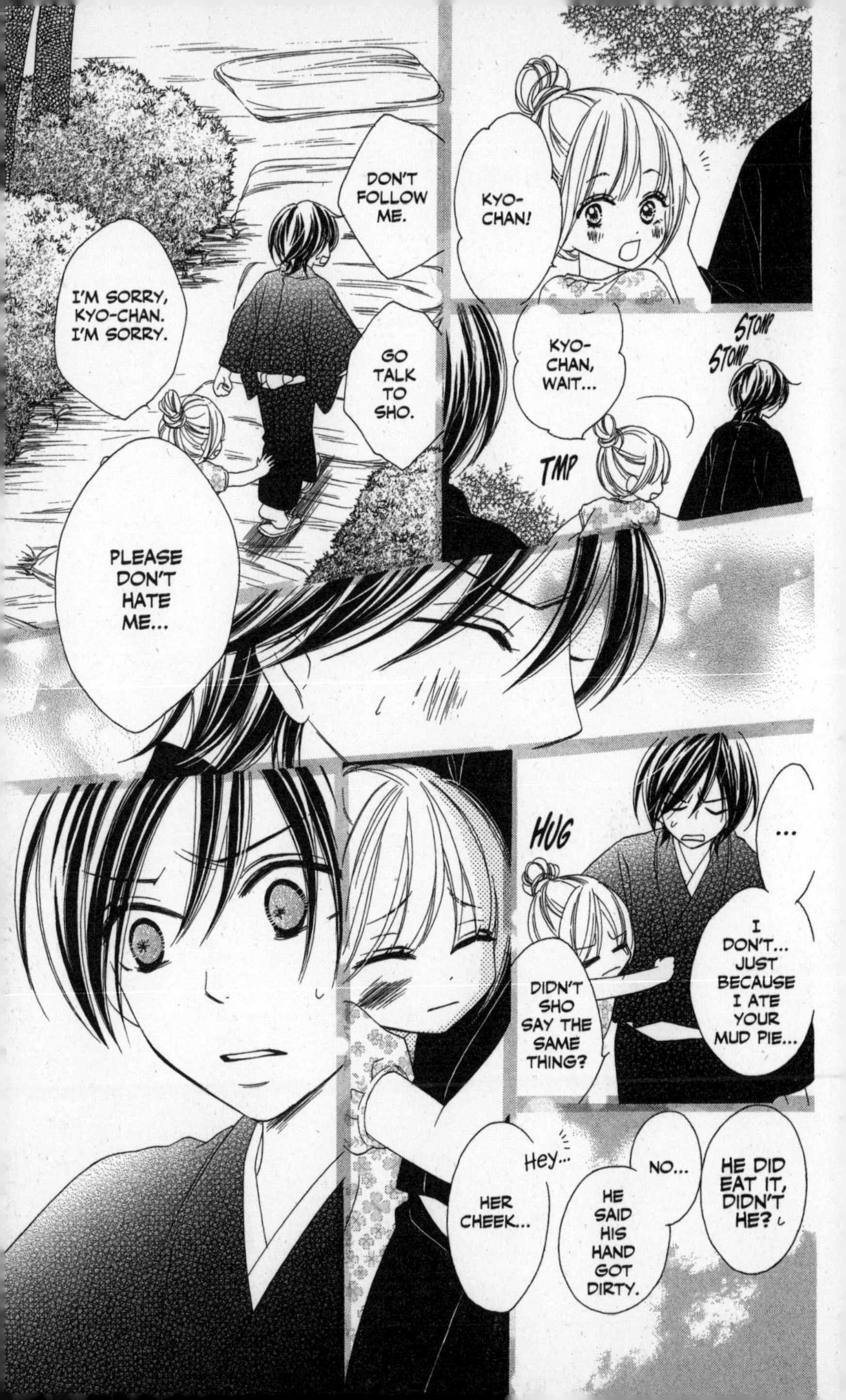
KYO-CHAN!
KYO-CHAN, WAIT...
STOMP
STOMP
TMP
DON'T FOLLOW ME.
GO TALK TO SHO.
I'M SORRY, KYO-CHAN. I'M SORRY.
PLEASE DON'T HATE ME...
HUG
...
I DON'T... JUST BECAUSE I ATE YOUR MUD PIE...
DIDN'T SHO SAY THE SAME THING?
HE DID EAT IT, DIDN'T HE?
NO...
HE SAID HIS HAND GOT DIRTY.
Hey...
HER CHEEK...

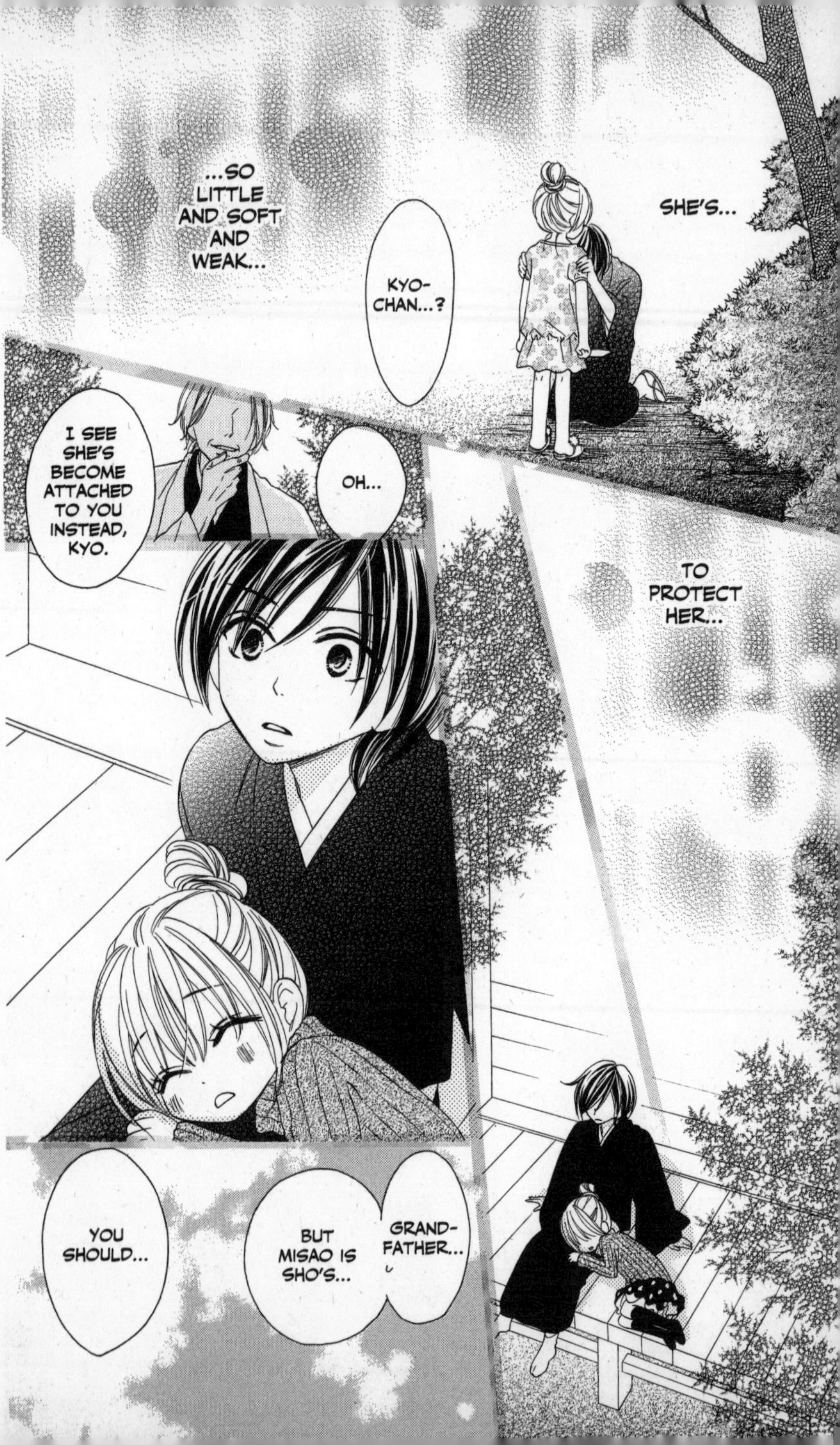
SHE'S...
KYO-CHAN...?
...SO LITTLE AND SOFT AND WEAK...
TO PROTECT HER...
OH...
I SEE SHE'S BECOME ATTACHED TO YOU INSTEAD, KYO.
GRAND-FATHER...
BUT MISAO IS SHO'S...
YOU SHOULD...

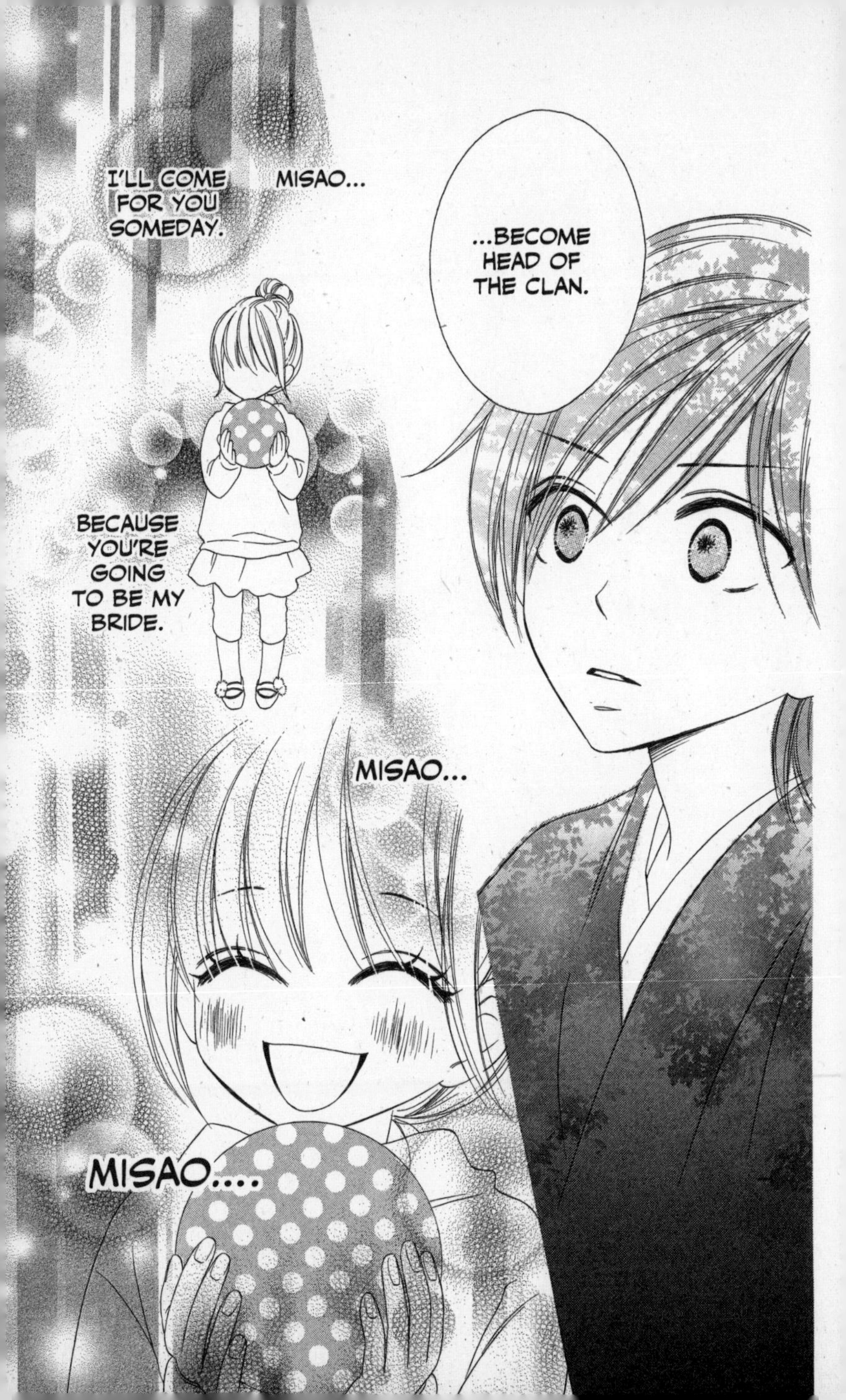
...BECOME HEAD OF THE CLAN.
MISAO...
I'LL COME FOR YOU SOMEDAY.
BECAUSE YOU'RE GOING TO BE MY BRIDE.
MISAO...
MISAO....

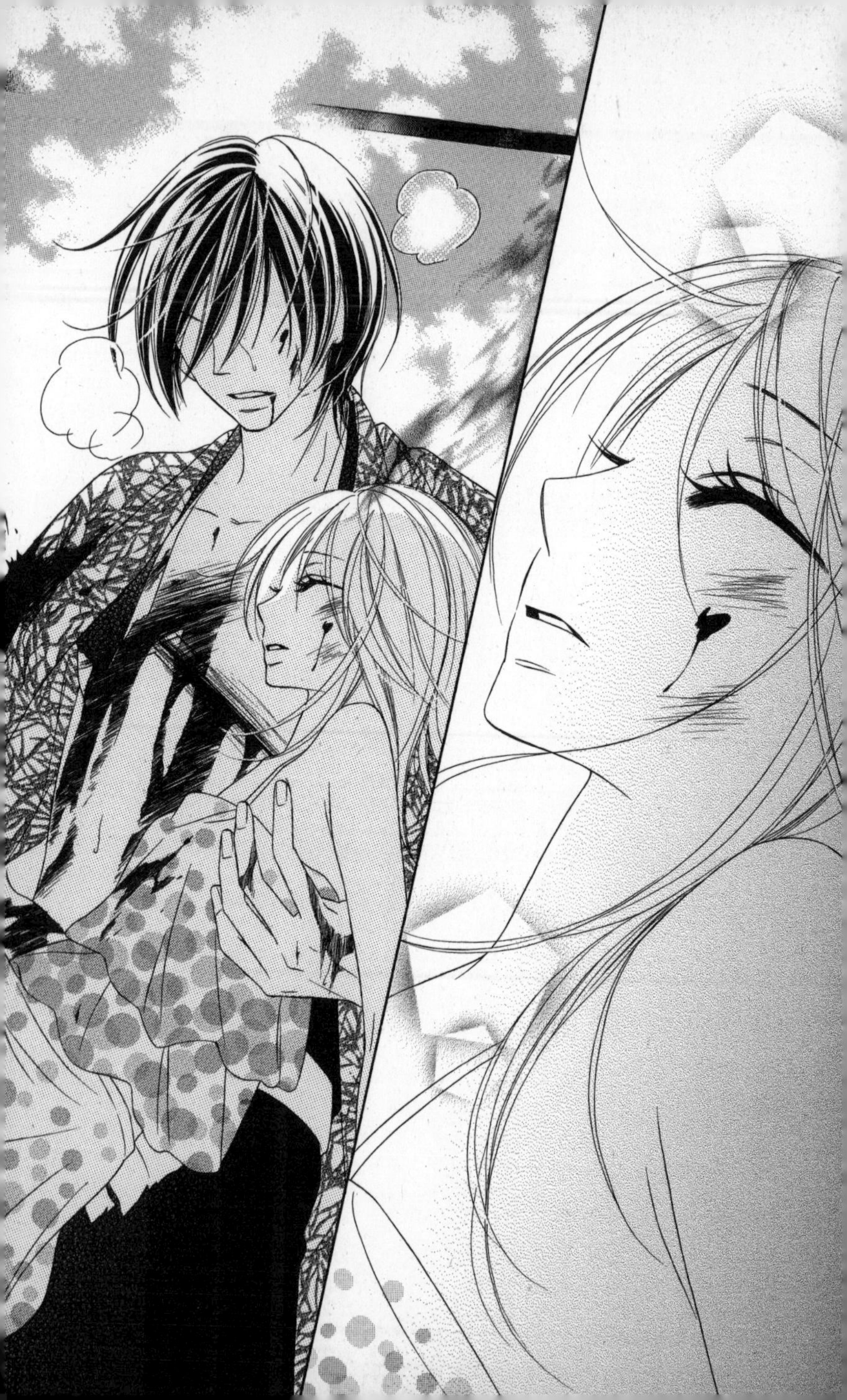

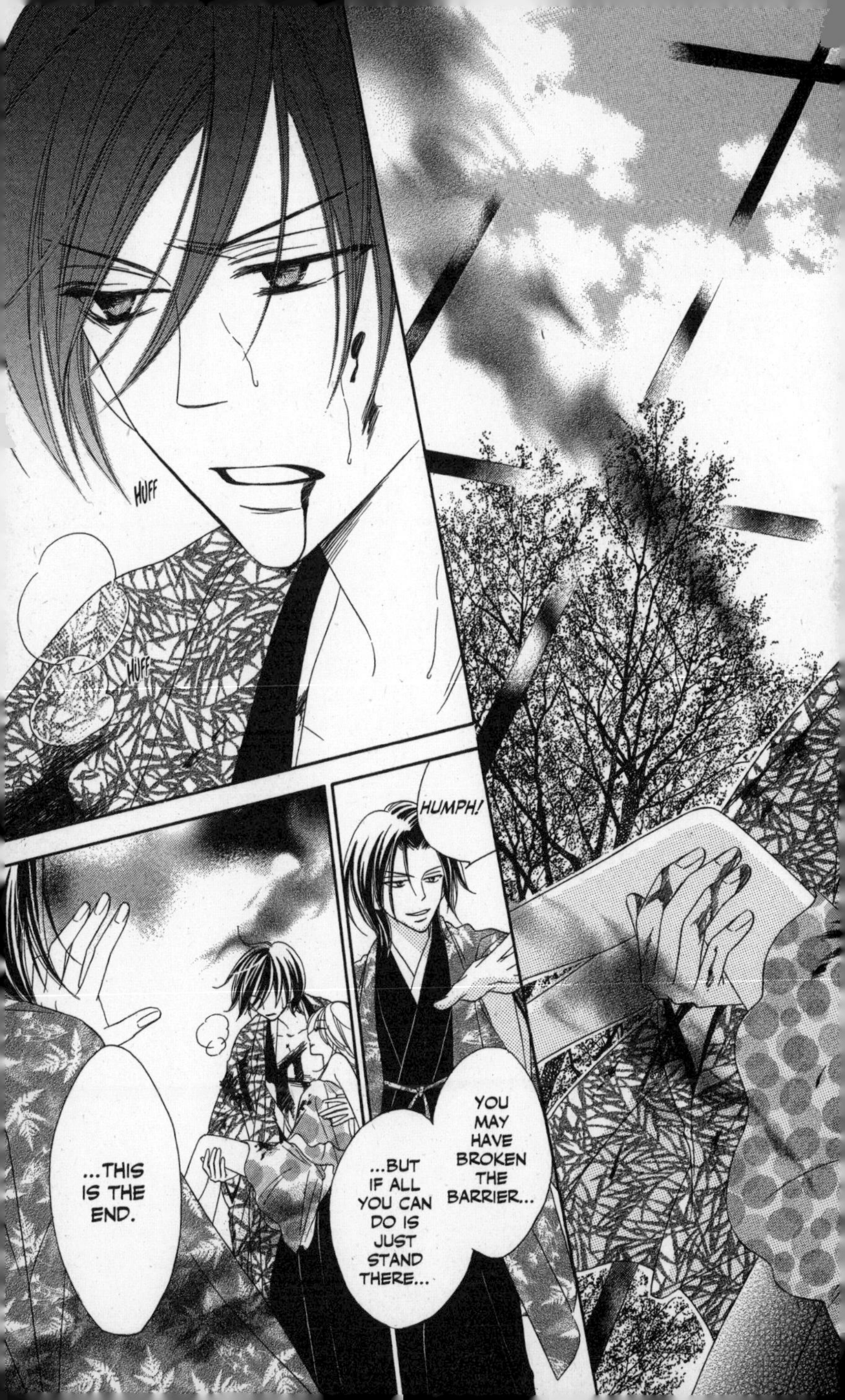
HUFF
HUFF
HUMPH!
YOU MAY HAVE BROKEN THE BARRIER...
...BUT IF ALL YOU CAN DO IS JUST STAND THERE...
...THIS IS THE END.

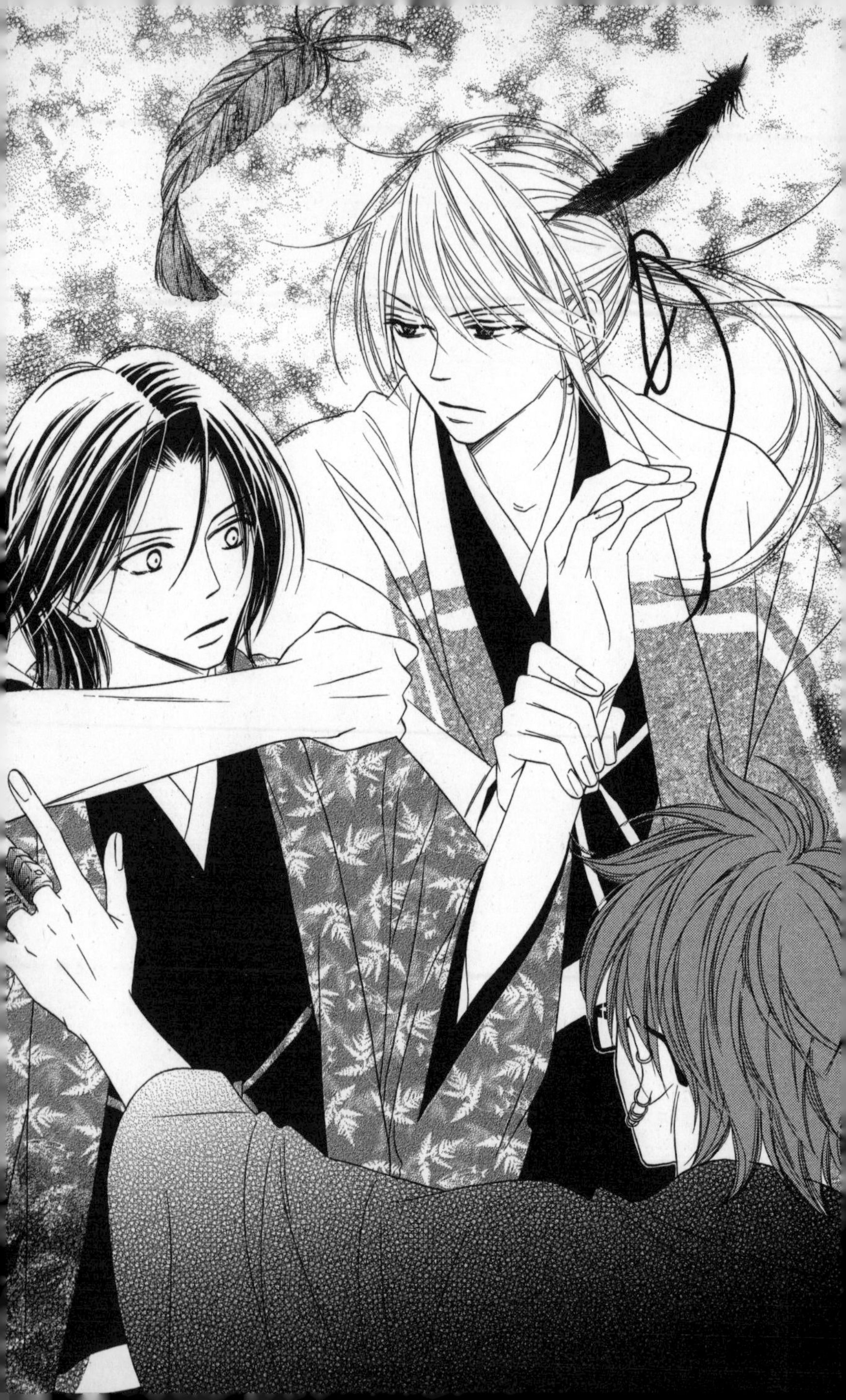

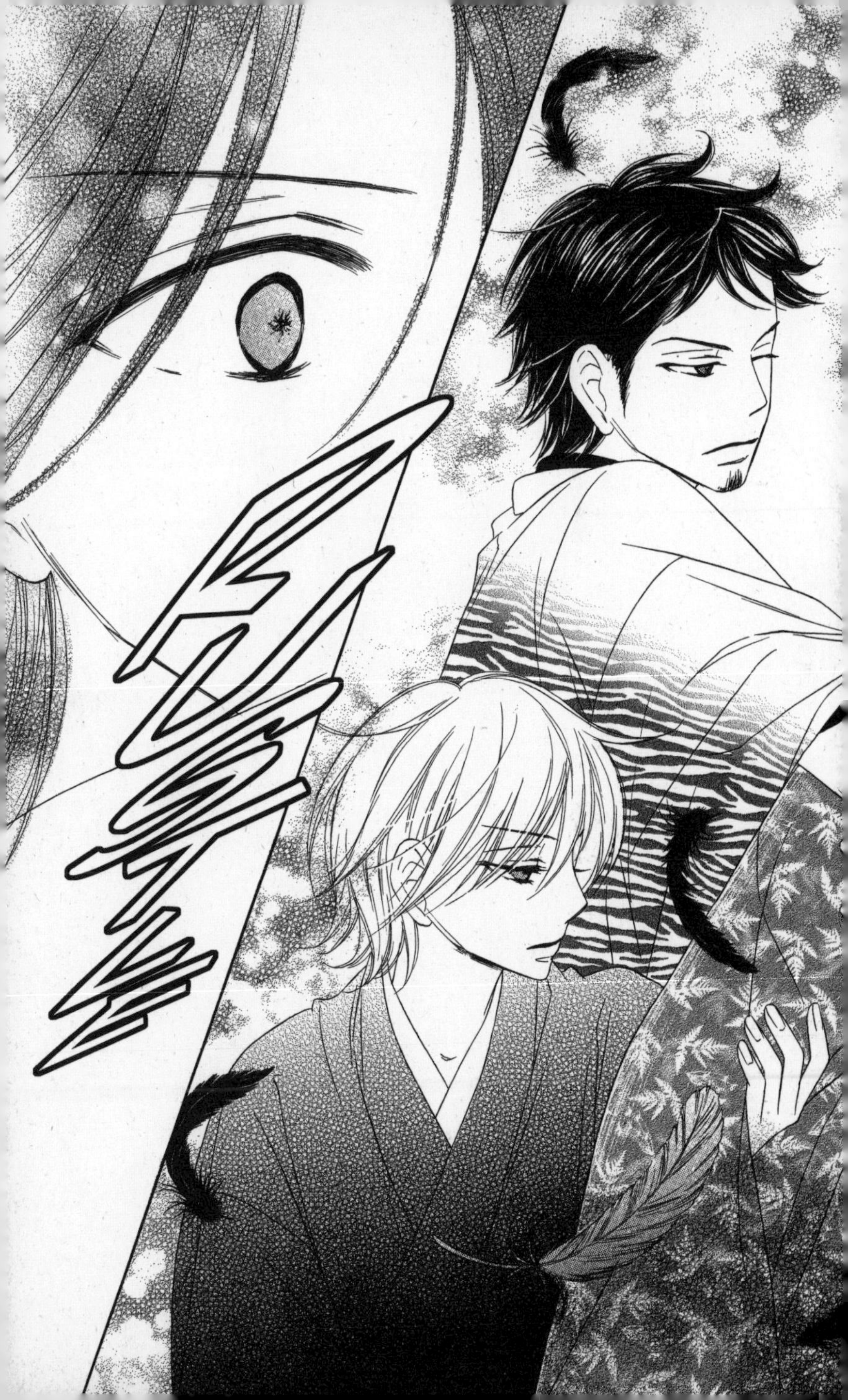

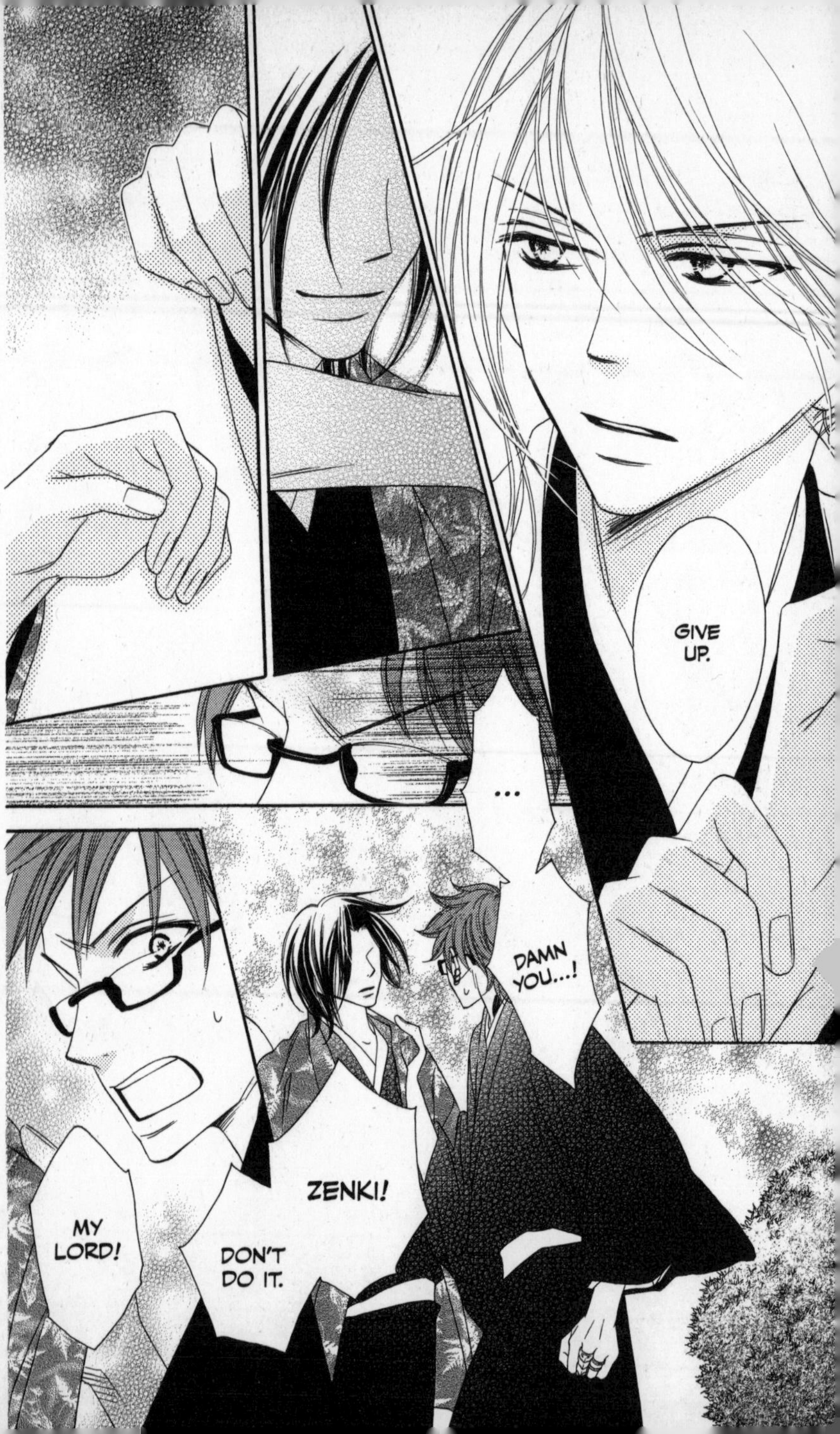
GIVE UP.
...
DAMN YOU...!
ZENKI!
DON'T DO IT.
MY LORD!

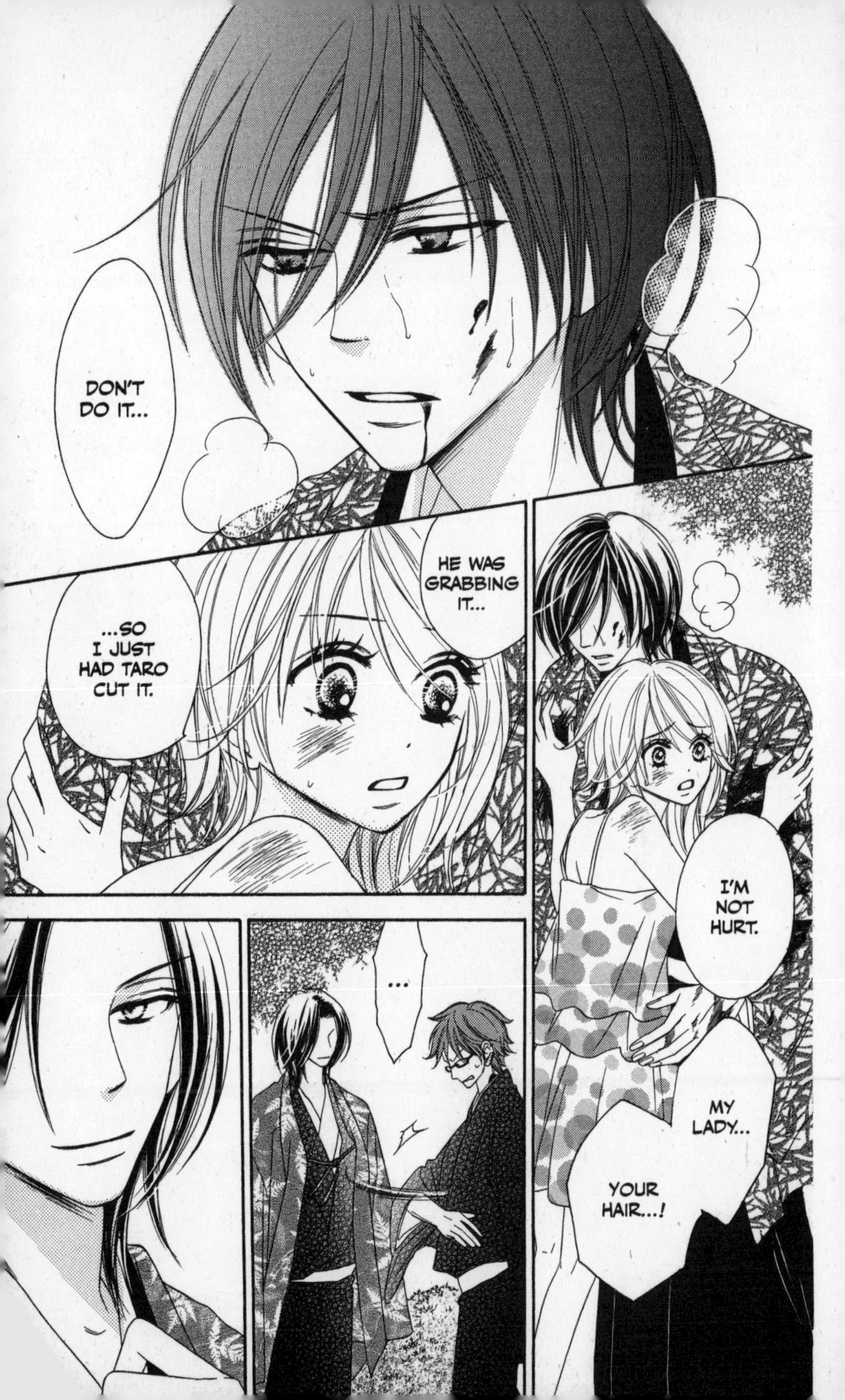
DON'T DO IT...
I'M NOT HURT.
MY LADY...
YOUR HAIR...!
HE WAS GRABBING IT...
...SO I JUST HAD TARO CUT IT.
...

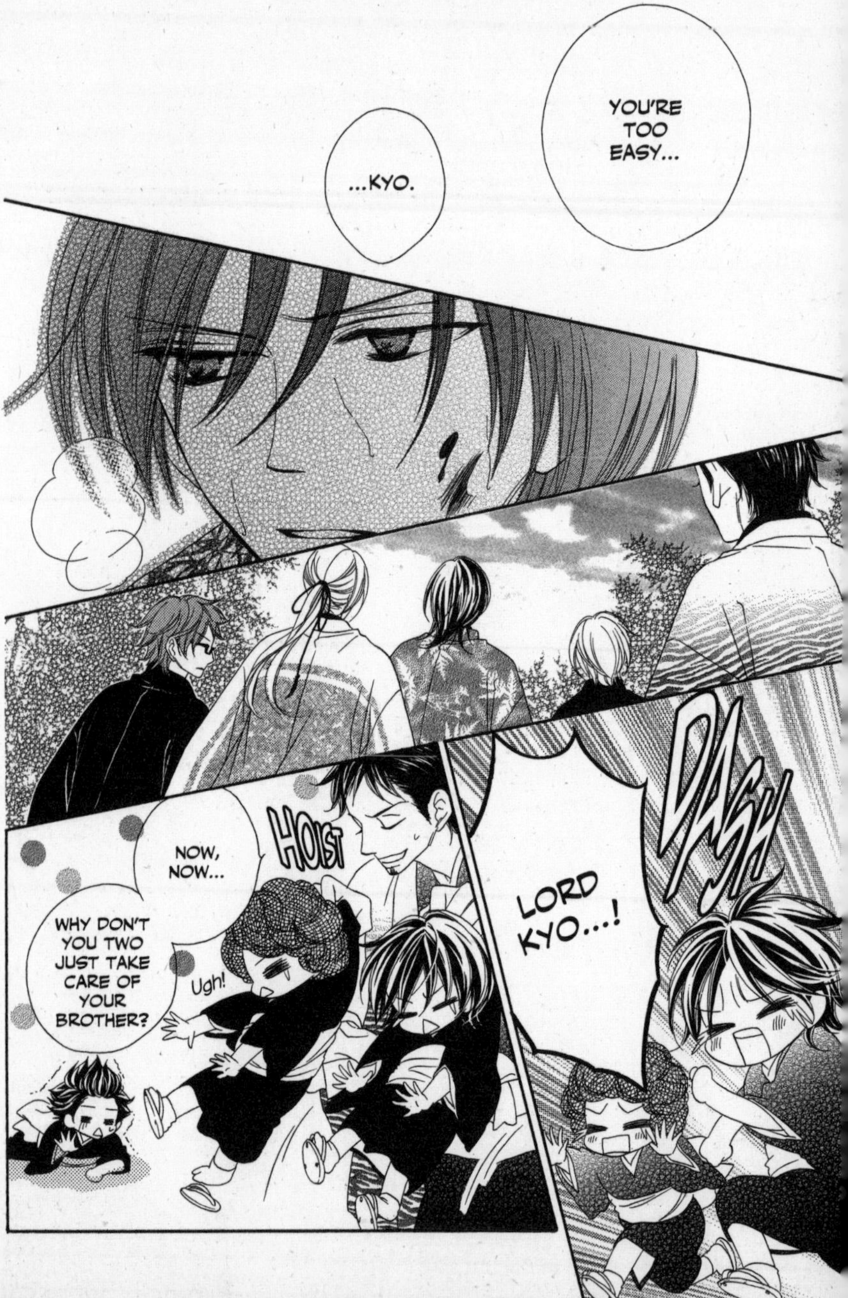
YOU'RE TOO EASY...
...KYO.
DASH
LORD KYO...!
HOIST
NOW, NOW...
WHY DON'T YOU TWO JUST TAKE CARE OF YOUR BROTHER?
Ugh!

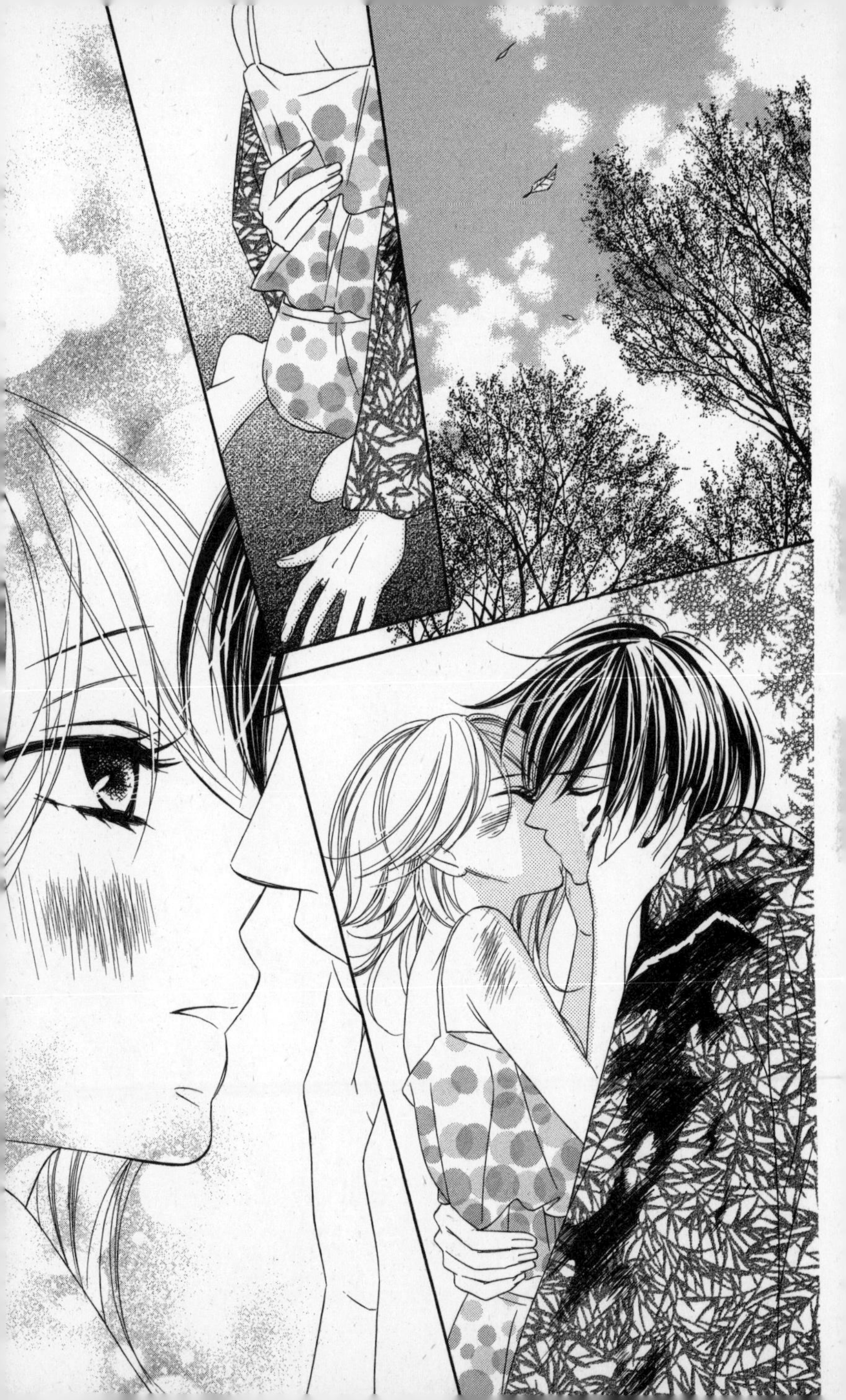

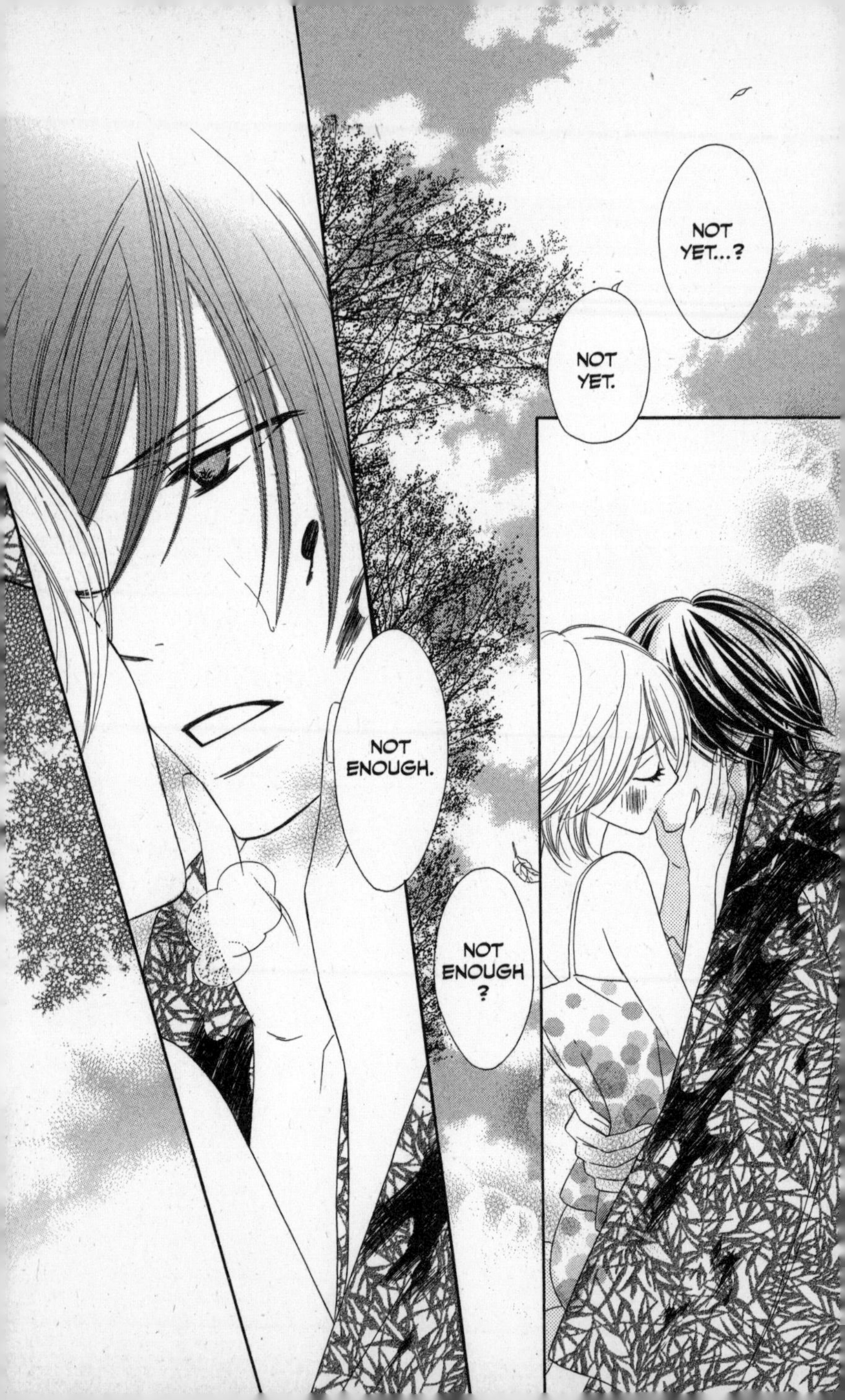
NOT YET...?
NOT YET.
NOT ENOUGH.
NOT ENOUGH
?

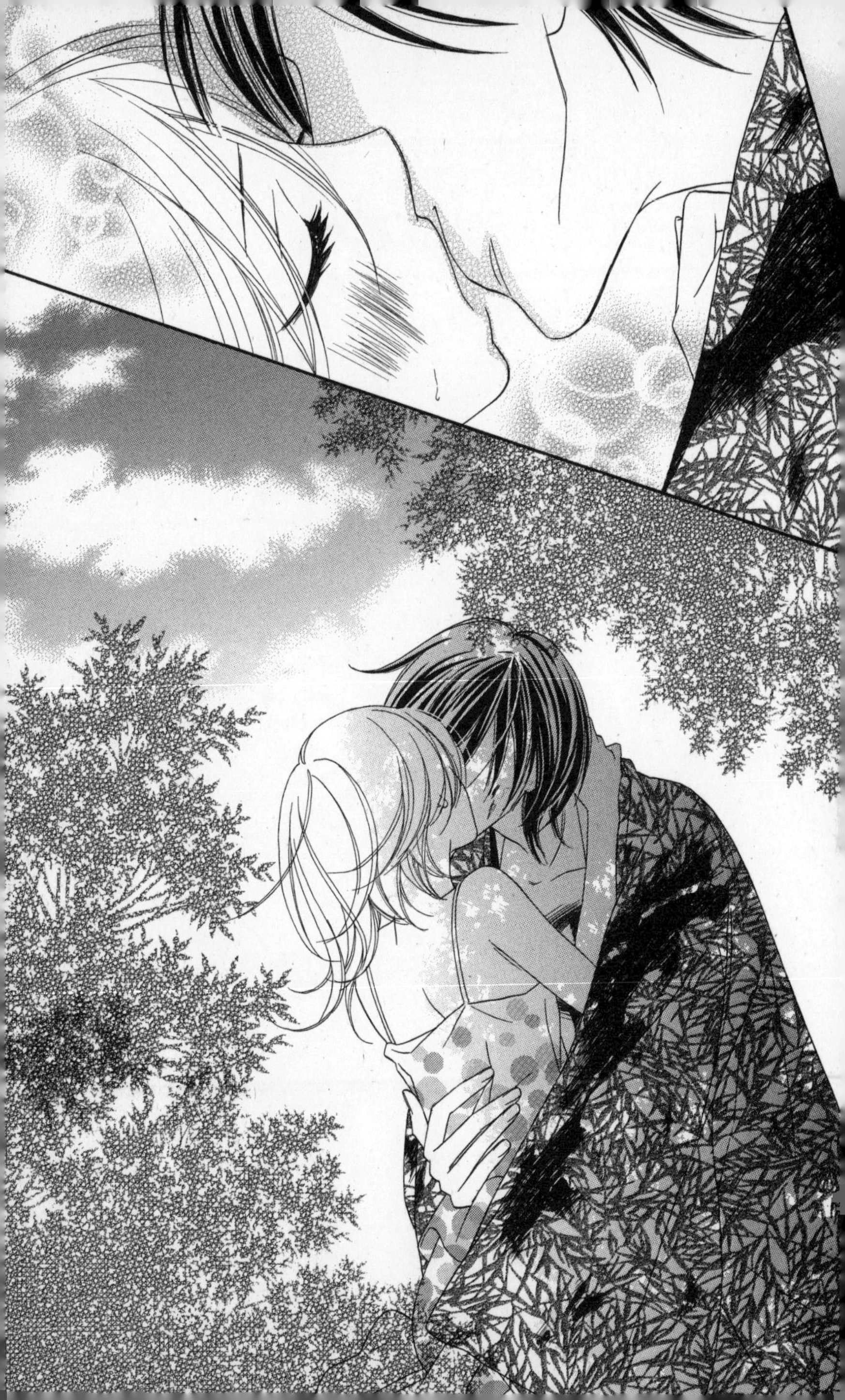

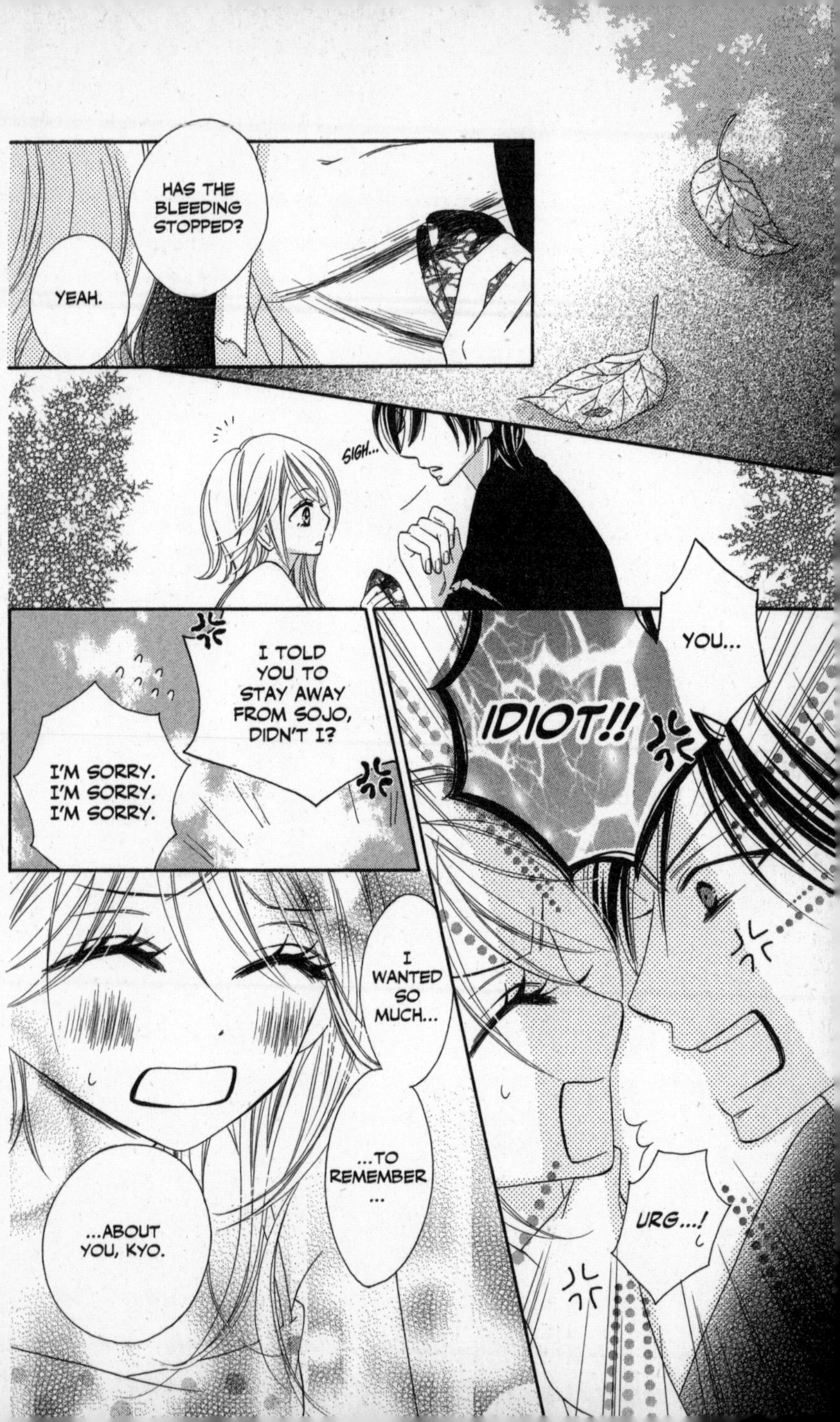
HAS THE BLEEDING STOPPED?
YEAH.
SIGH...
YOU...
IDIOT!!
URG...!
I TOLD YOU TO STAY AWAY FROM SOJO, DIDN'T I?
I'M SORRY. I'M SORRY. I'M SORRY.
I WANTED SO MUCH...
...TO REMEMBER...
...ABOUT YOU, KYO.

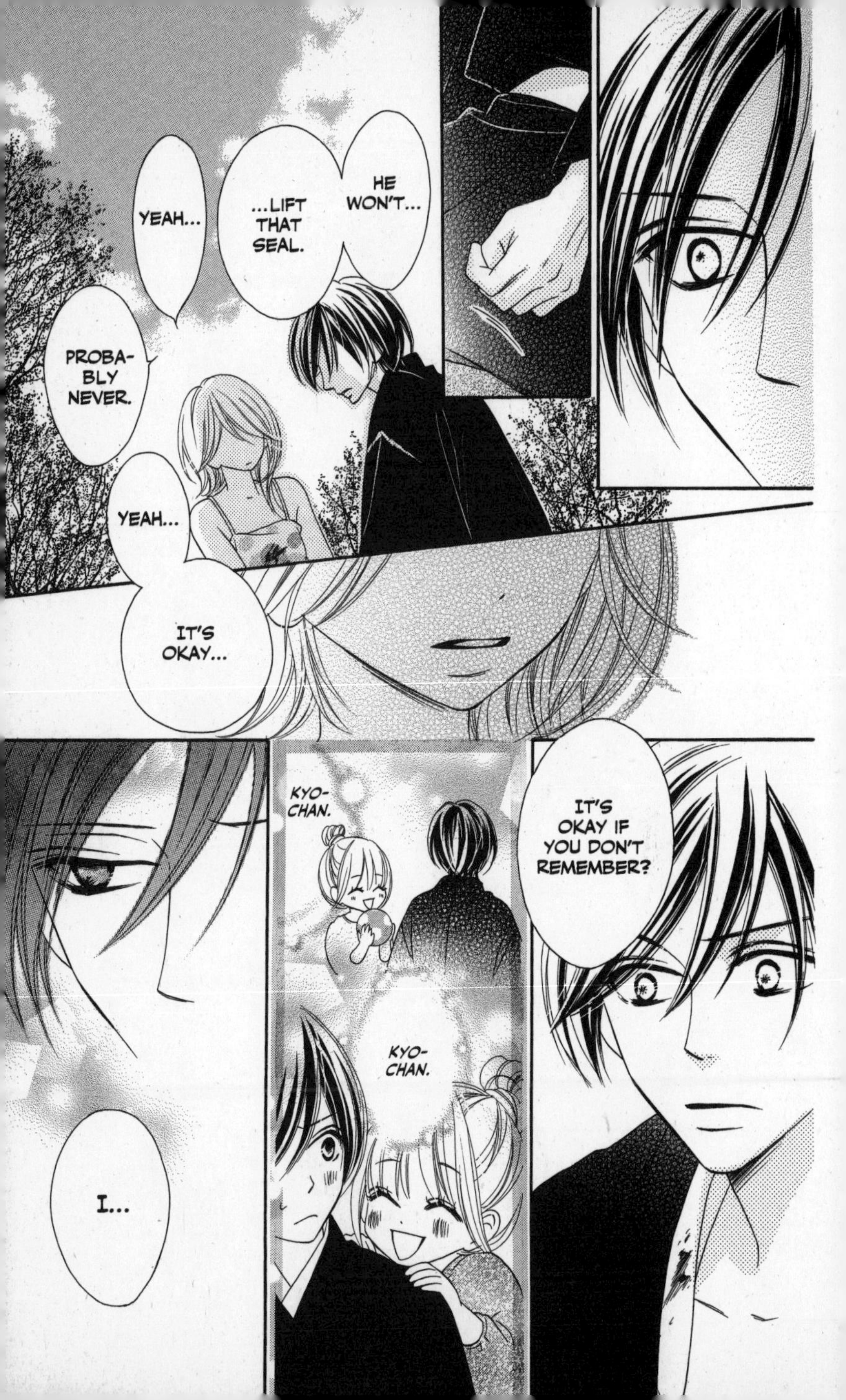
HE WON'T...
...LIFT THAT SEAL.
YEAH...
PROBA-BLY NEVER.
YEAH...
IT'S OKAY...
IT'S OKAY IF YOU DON'T REMEMBER?
KYO-CHAN.
KYO-CHAN.
I...

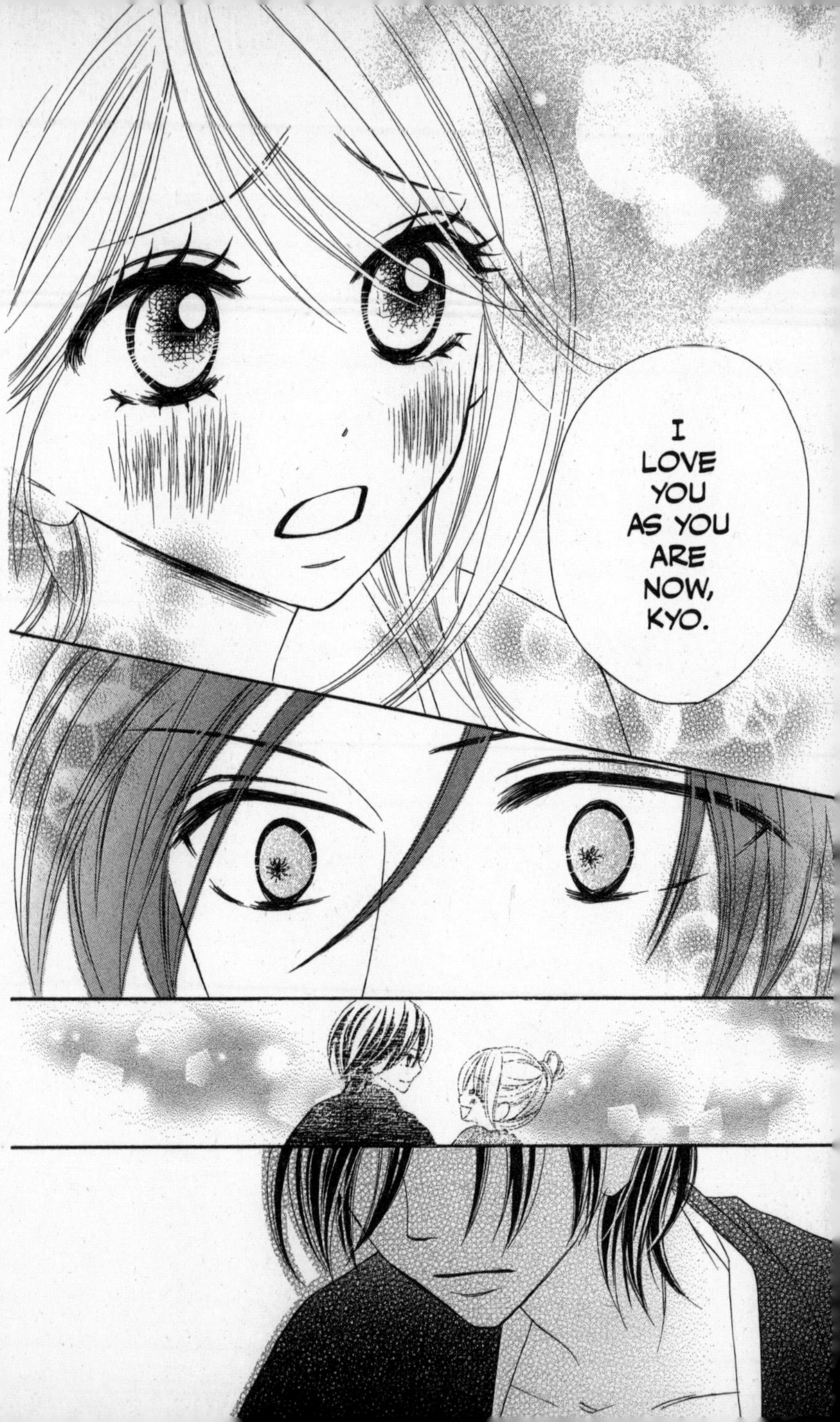
I LOVE YOU AS YOU ARE NOW, KYO.

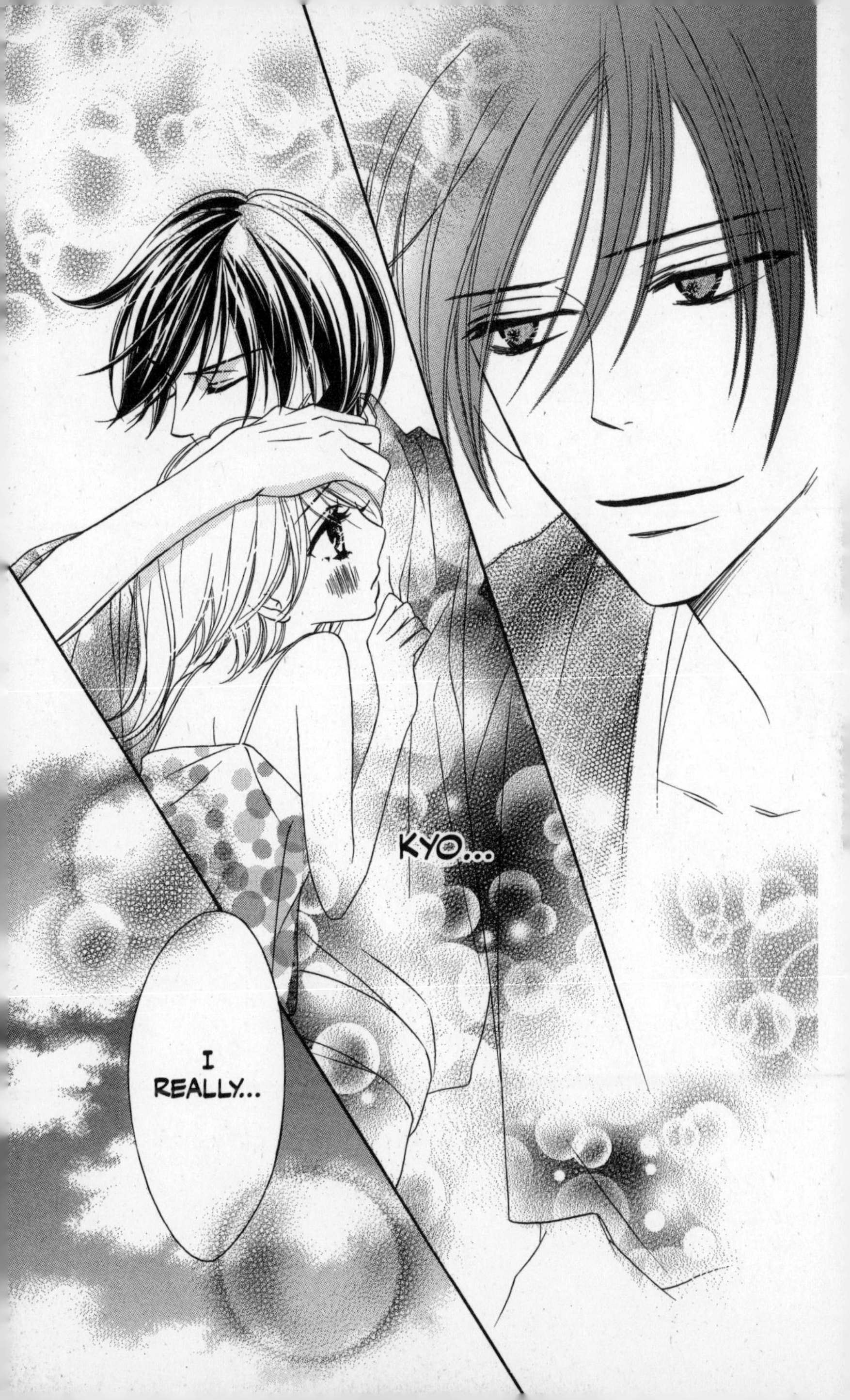
KYO...
I REALLY...

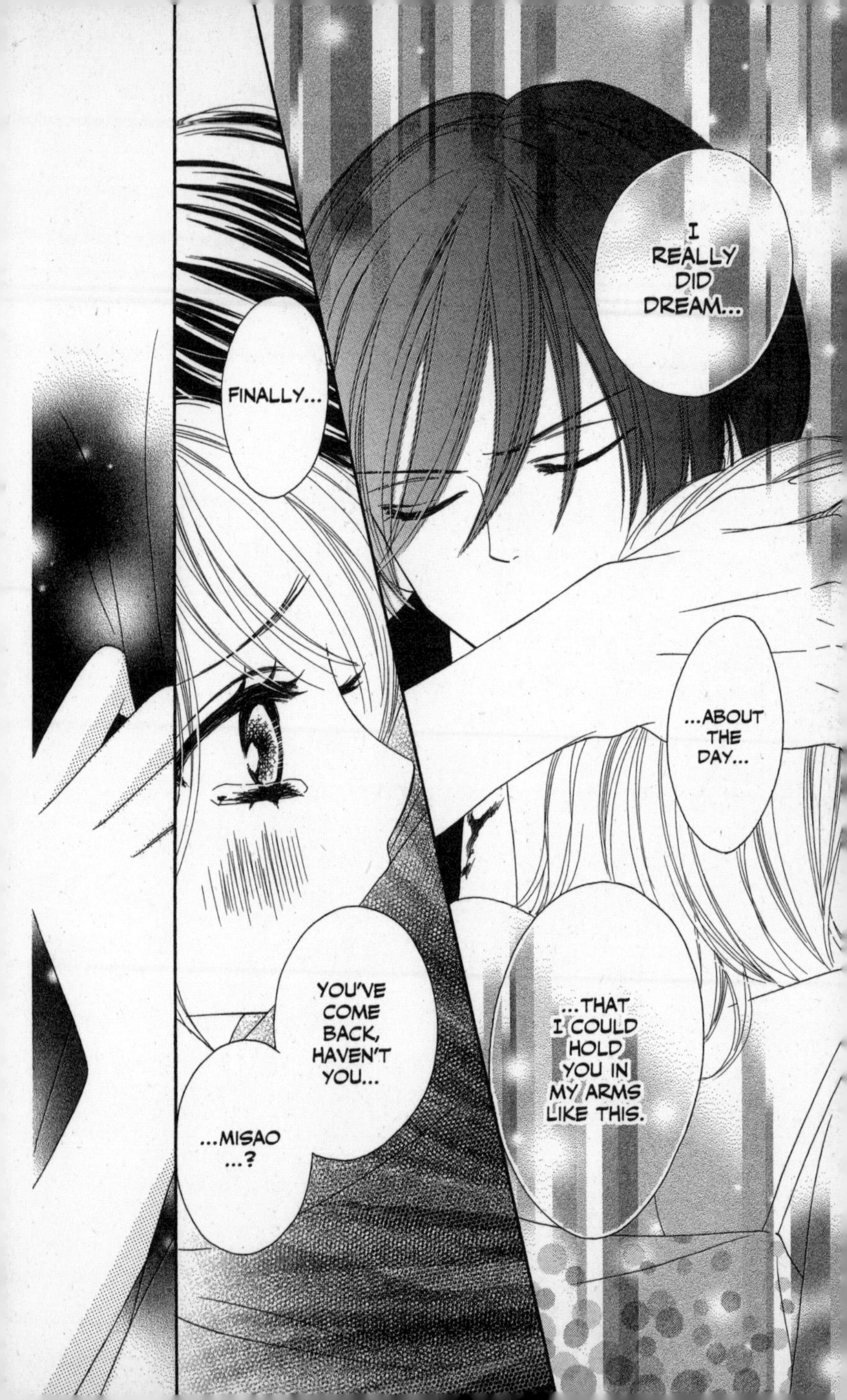
I REALLY DID DREAM...
...ABOUT THE DAY...
...THAT I COULD HOLD YOU IN MY ARMS LIKE THIS.
FINALLY...
YOU'VE COME BACK, HAVEN'T YOU...
...MISAO ...?

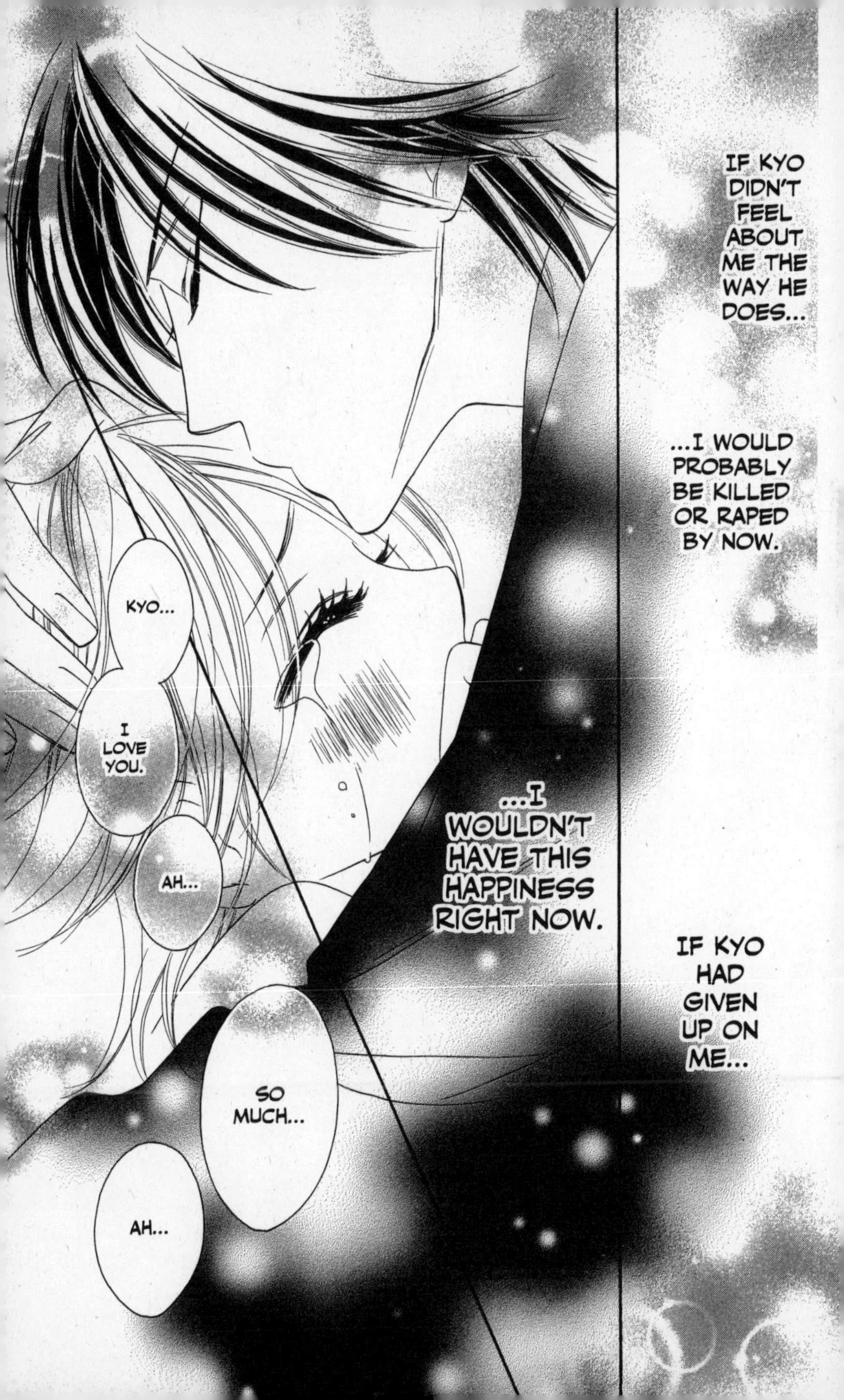
IF KYO DIDN'T FEEL ABOUT ME THE WAY HE DOES...
...I WOULD PROBABLY BE KILLED OR RAPED BY NOW.
IF KYO HAD GIVEN UP ON ME...
...I WOULDN'T HAVE THIS HAPPINESS RIGHT NOW.
KYO...
I LOVE YOU.
AH...
SO MUCH...
AH...

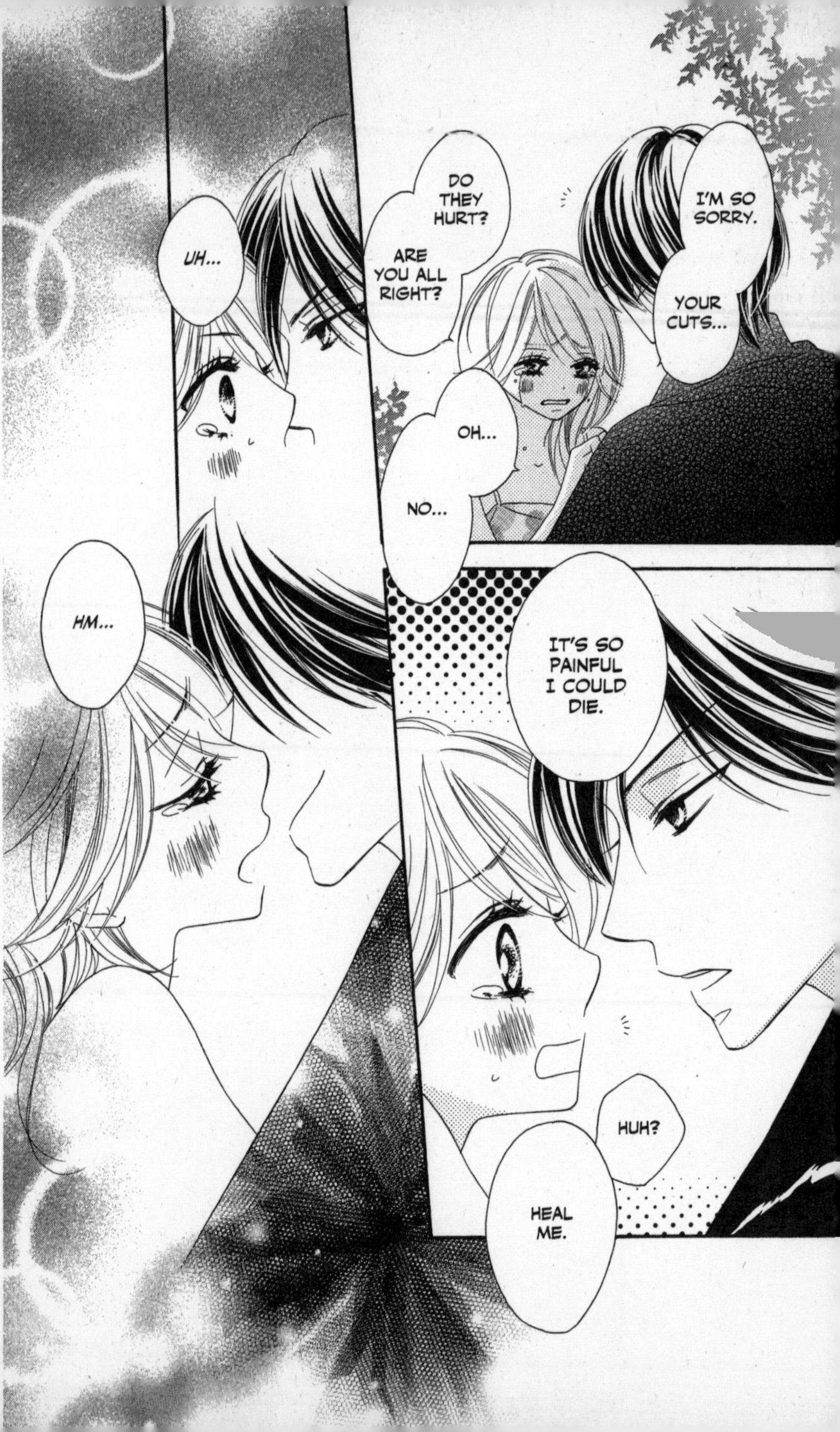
I'M SO SORRY.
YOUR CUTS...
DO THEY HURT?
ARE YOU ALL RIGHT?
OH...
NO...
UH...
IT'S SO PAINFUL I COULD DIE.
HUH?
HEAL ME.
HM...

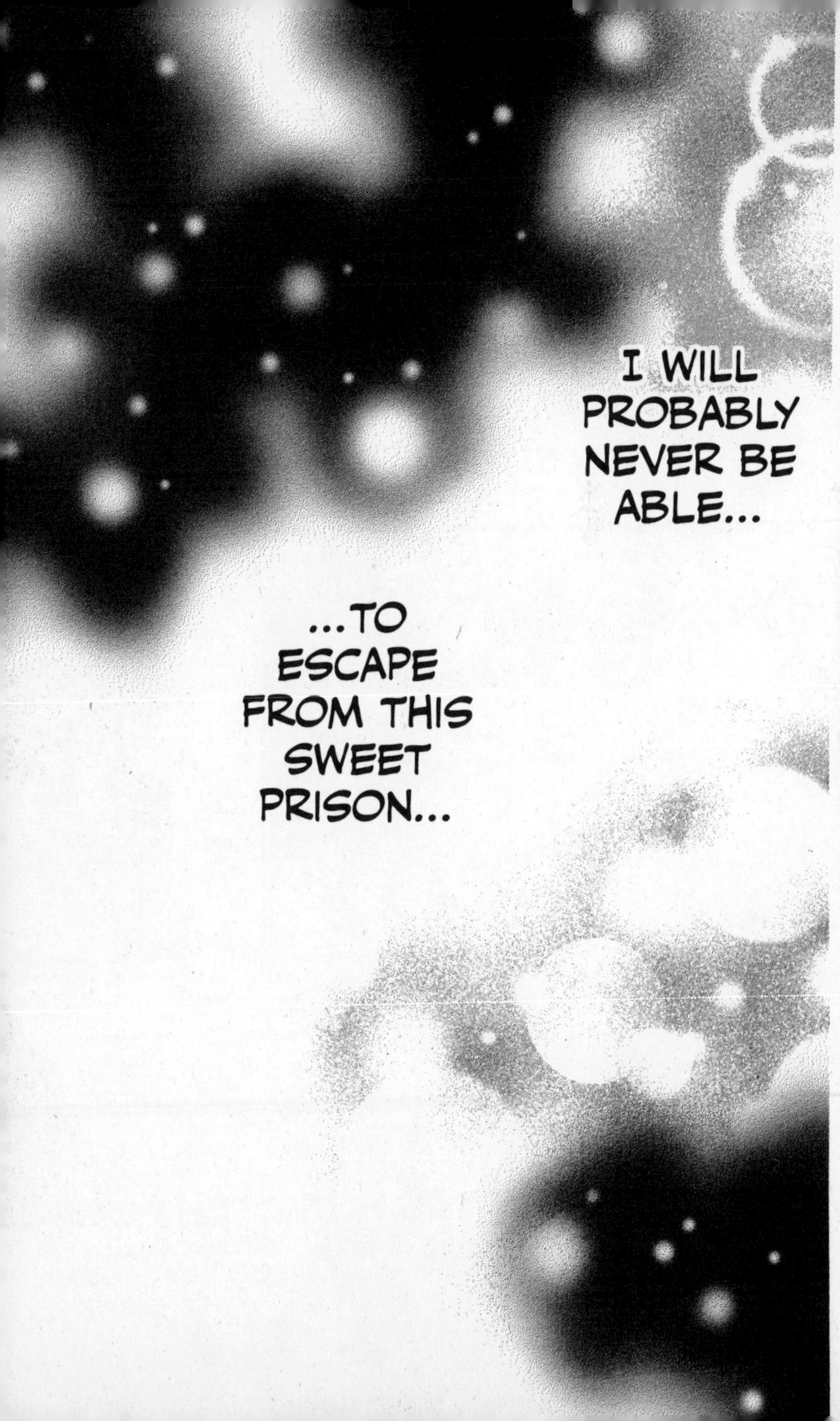
I WILL PROBABLY NEVER BE ABLE...
...TO ESCAPE FROM THIS SWEET PRISON...

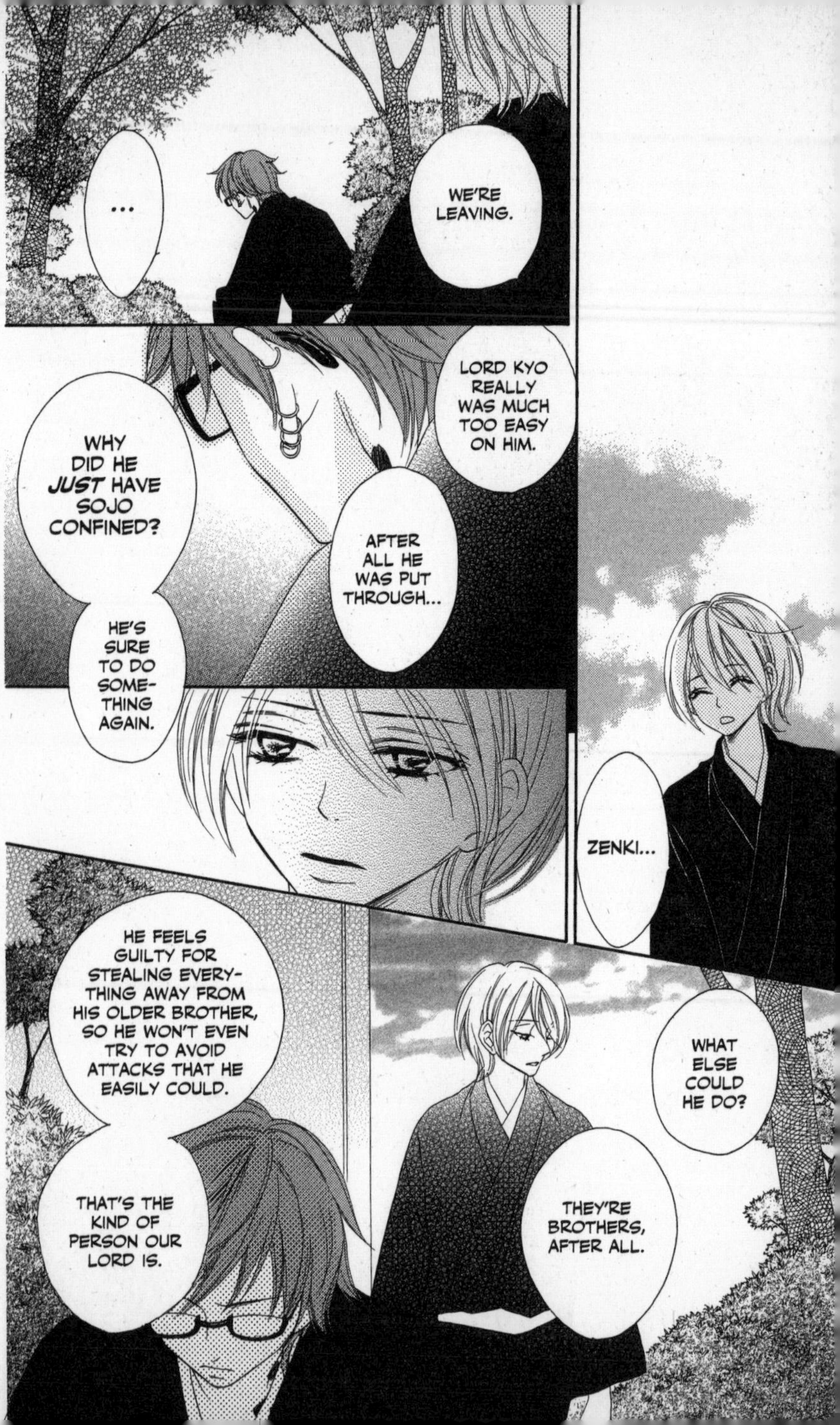
WE'RE LEAVING.
...
LORD KYO REALLY WAS MUCH TOO EASY ON HIM.
AFTER ALL HE WAS PUT THROUGH...
WHY DID HE *JUST* HAVE SOJO CONFINED?
HE'S SURE TO DO SOME-THING AGAIN.
ZENKI...
WHAT ELSE COULD HE DO?
THEY'RE BROTHERS, AFTER ALL.
HE FEELS GUILTY FOR STEALING EVERY-THING AWAY FROM HIS OLDER BROTHER, SO HE WON'T EVEN TRY TO AVOID ATTACKS THAT HE EASILY COULD.
THAT'S THE KIND OF PERSON OUR LORD IS.

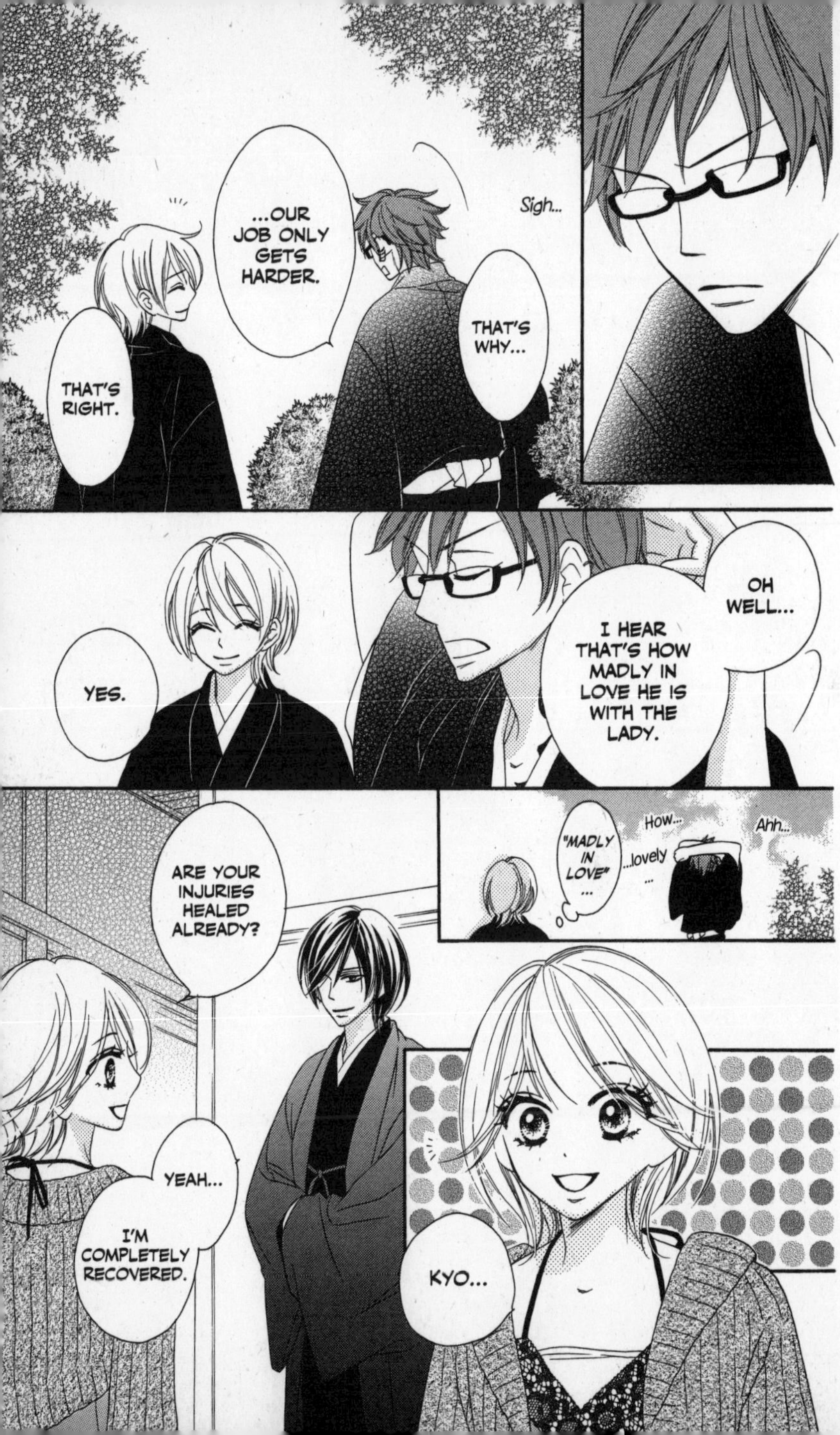
Sigh...
THAT'S WHY...
...OUR JOB ONLY GETS HARDER.
THAT'S RIGHT.
OH WELL...
I HEAR THAT'S HOW MADLY IN LOVE HE IS WITH THE LADY.
YES.
Ahh...
How...
...lovely
...
"MADLY IN LOVE" ...
KYO...
ARE YOUR INJURIES HEALED ALREADY?
YEAH...
I'M COMPLETELY RECOVERED.

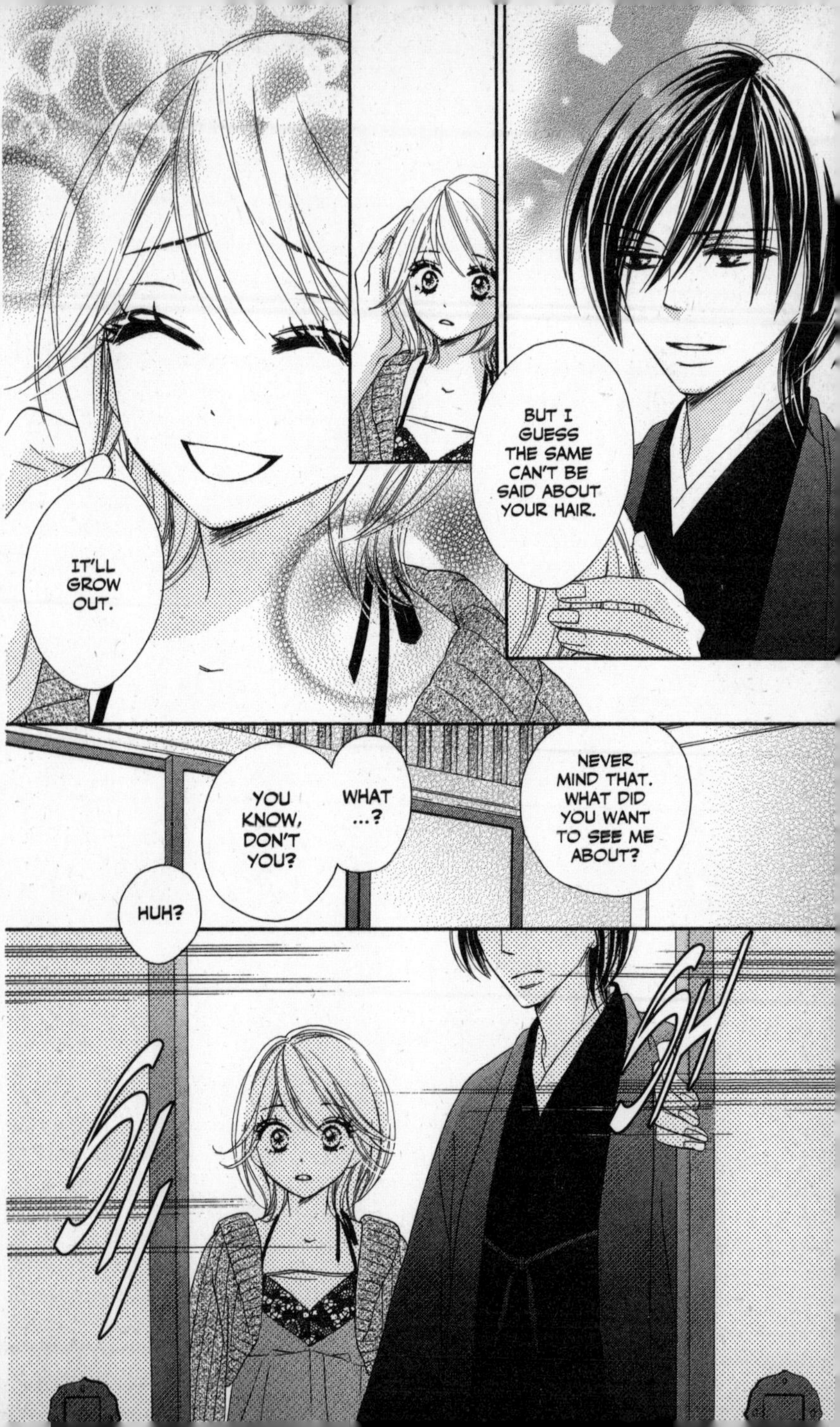
BUT I GUESS THE SAME CAN'T BE SAID ABOUT YOUR HAIR.
IT'LL GROW OUT.
NEVER MIND THAT. WHAT DID YOU WANT TO SEE ME ABOUT?
WHAT ...?
YOU KNOW, DON'T YOU?
HUH?

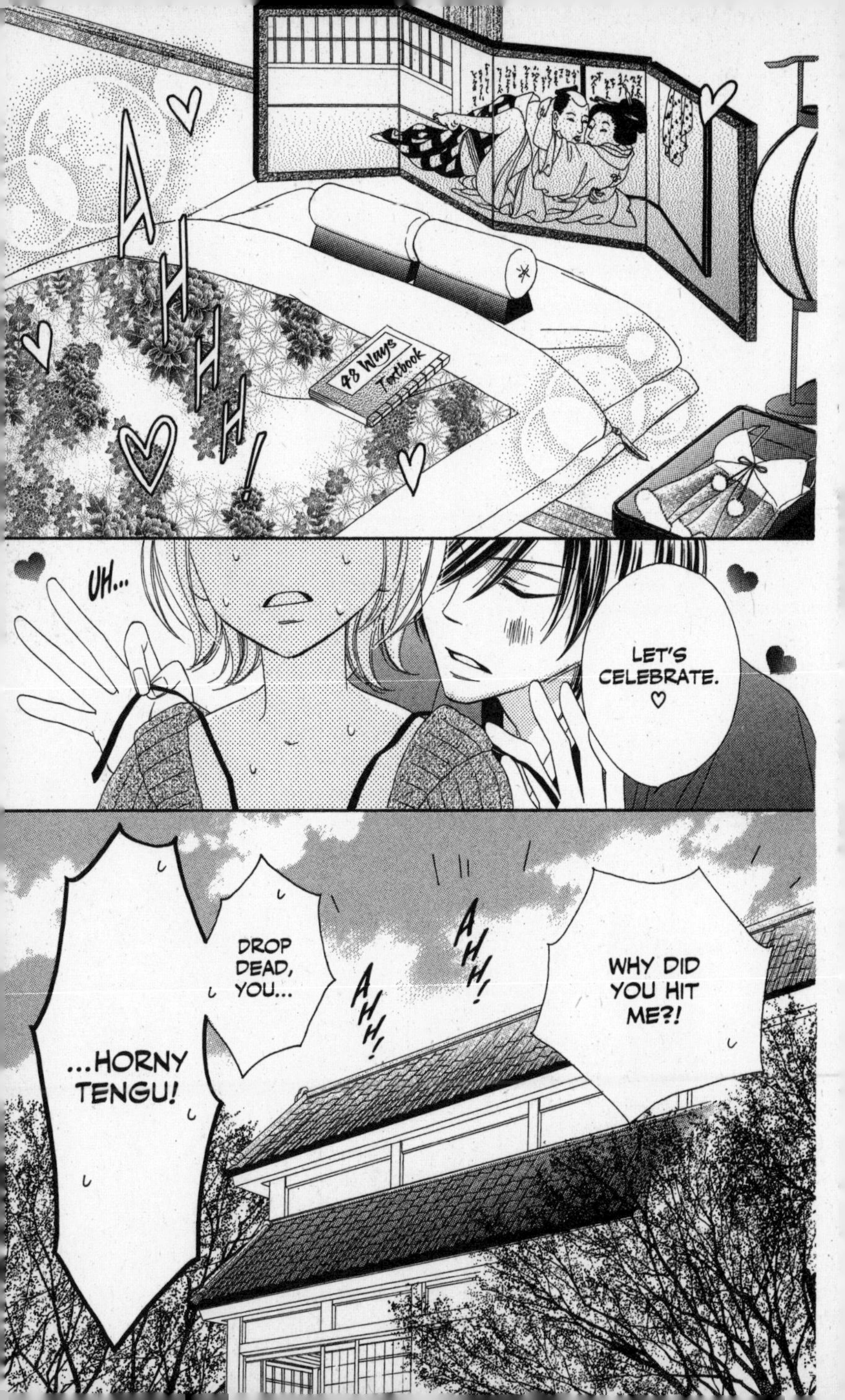
AHHHH!
48 Ways Textbook
LET'S CELEBRATE. ♡
UH...
WHY DID YOU HIT ME?!
AHH!
AHH!
DROP DEAD, YOU...
...HORNY TENGU!

On the Eight Daitengu

•Two•

I've tried to show below where the Eight Daitengu lived. Quite a few of them come from Western Japan. I guess early culture was centered in that area....

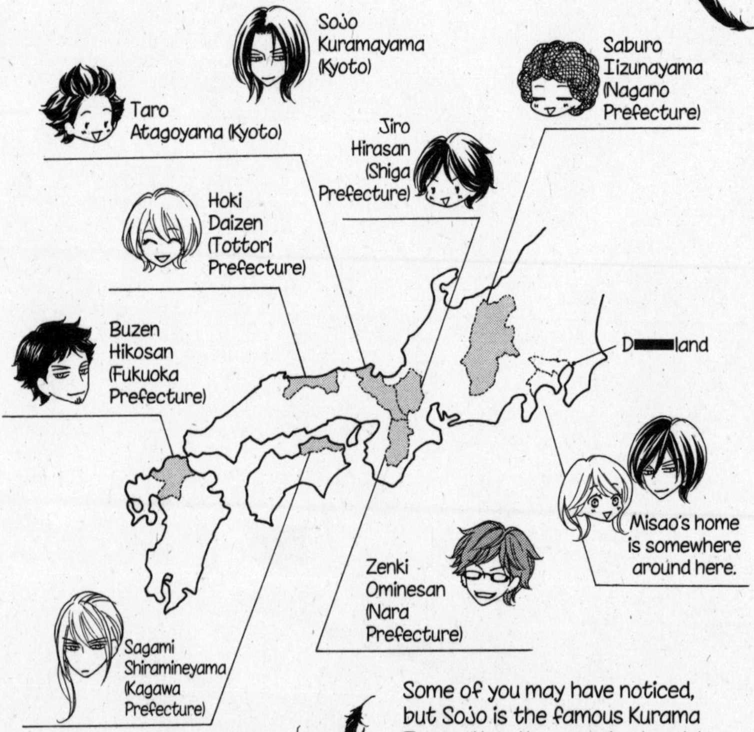

Sojo Kuramayama (Kyoto)
Saburo Izunayama (Nagano Prefecture)
Taro Atagoyama (Kyoto)
Jiro Hirasan (Shiga Prefecture)
Hoki Daizen (Tottori Prefecture)
Buzen Hikosan (Fukuoka Prefecture)
D[redacted]land
Misao's home is somewhere around here.
Zenki Ominesan (Nara Prefecture)
Sagami Shiramineyama (Kagawa Prefecture)

Some of you may have noticed, but Sojo is the famous Kurama Tengu. (He's the one who taught Ushiwakamaru to wield a sword.)
I'm sorry. I'm so sorry.

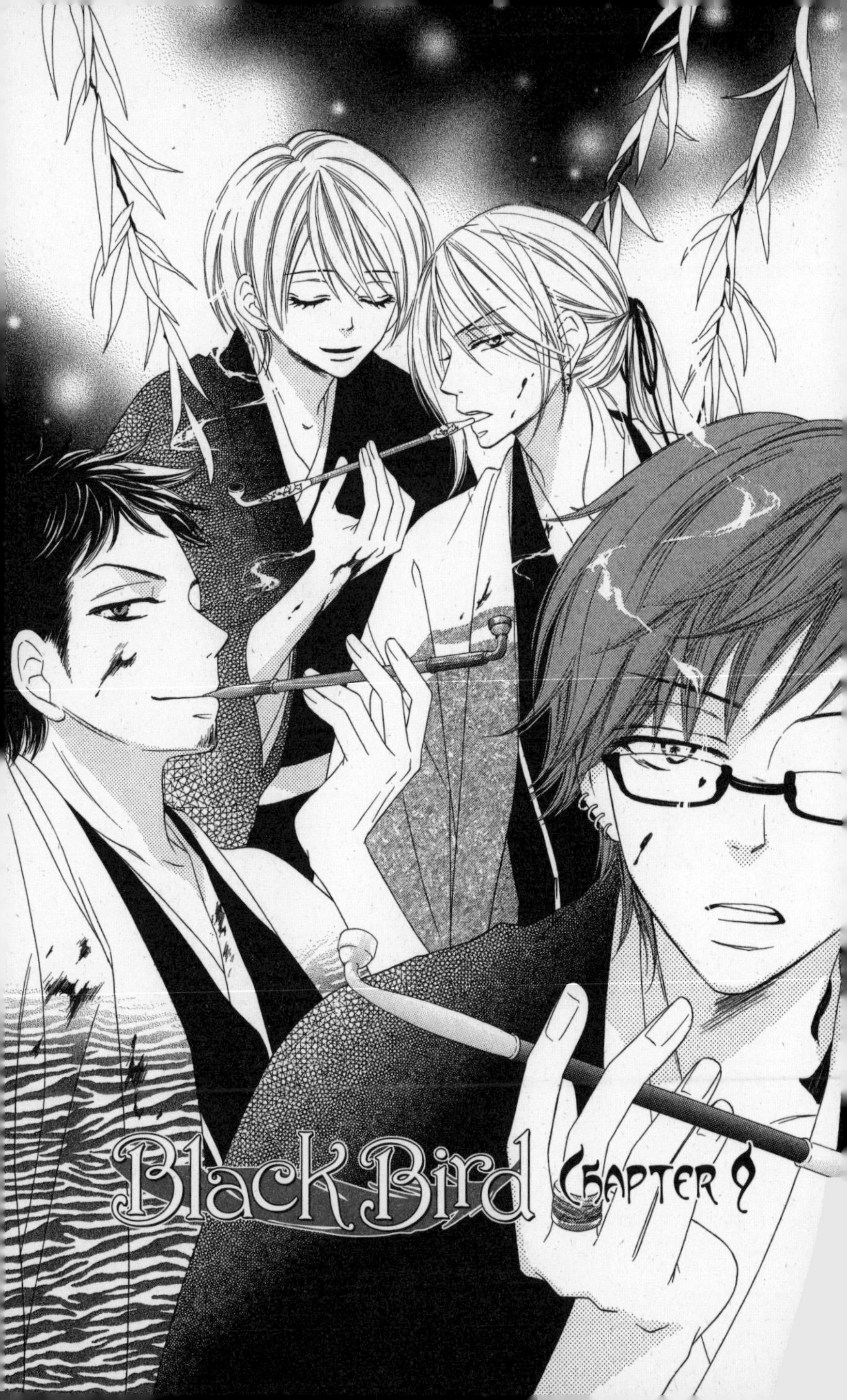
Black Bird
Chapter 9

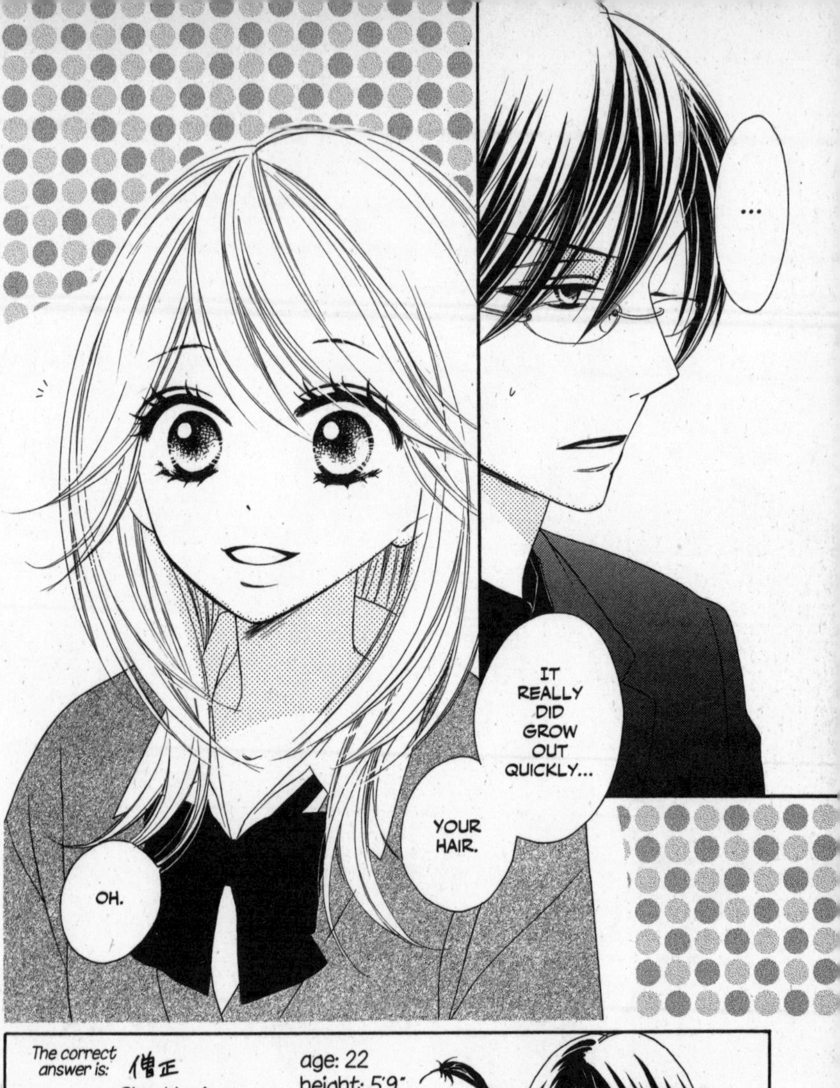
...
IT REALLY DID GROW OUT QUICKLY...
YOUR HAIR.
OH.

The correct answer is: 僧正 Sho Usui

age: 22
height: 5'9"

He has a personality problem, and he was supposed to have "the same face as Kyo but better looking," so I had trouble drawing him. I don't mind characters like his, but I kept wanting to turn him into a joke.

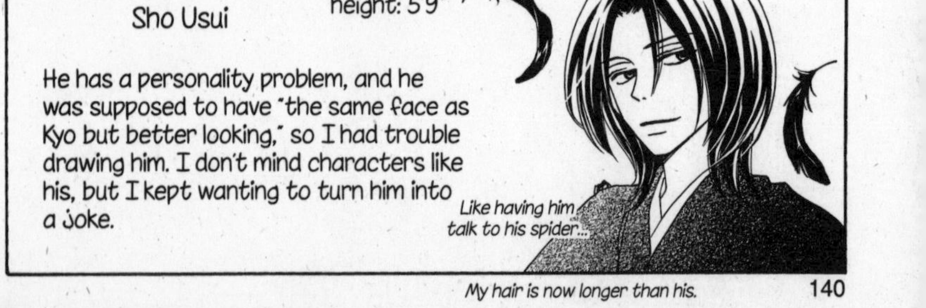

Like having him talk to his spider...

My hair is now longer than his.

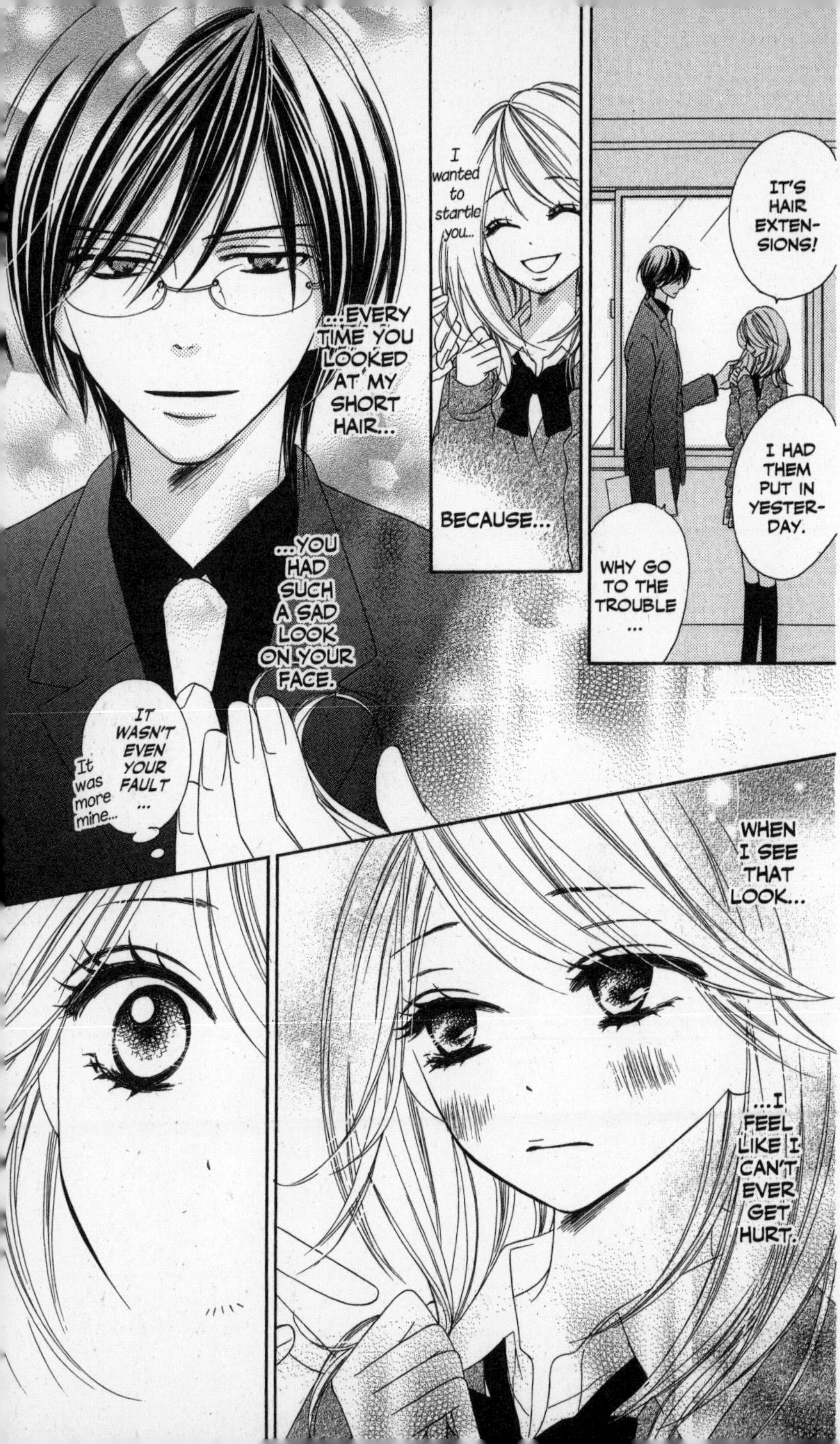
IT'S HAIR EXTEN-SIONS!
I HAD THEM PUT IN YESTER-DAY.
WHY GO TO THE TROUBLE ...
I wanted to startle you...
BECAUSE...
...EVERY TIME YOU LOOKED AT MY SHORT HAIR...
...YOU HAD SUCH A SAD LOOK ON YOUR FACE.
IT WASN'T EVEN YOUR FAULT ...
It was more mine...
WHEN I SEE THAT LOOK...
...I FEEL LIKE I CAN'T EVER GET HURT.

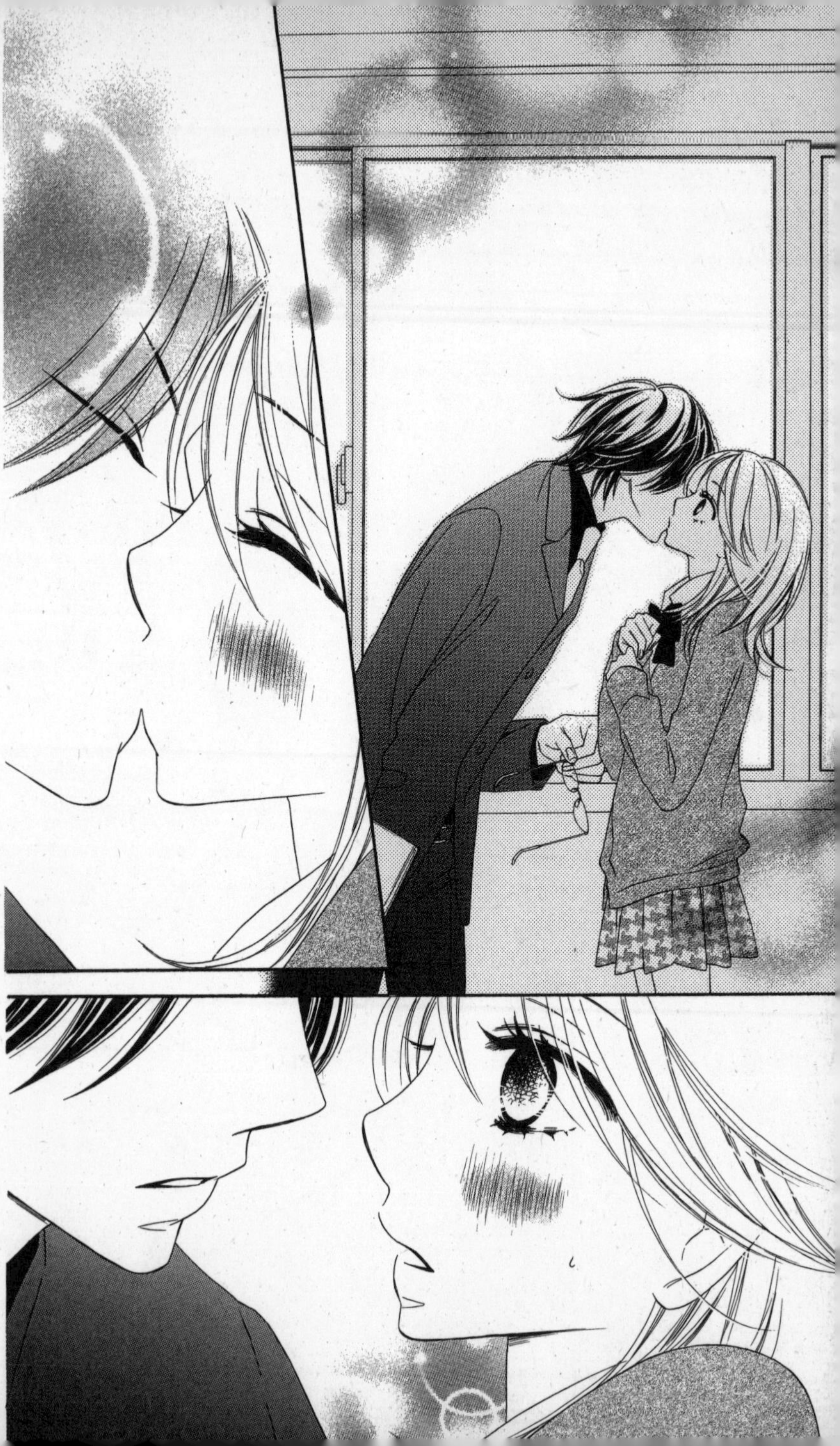

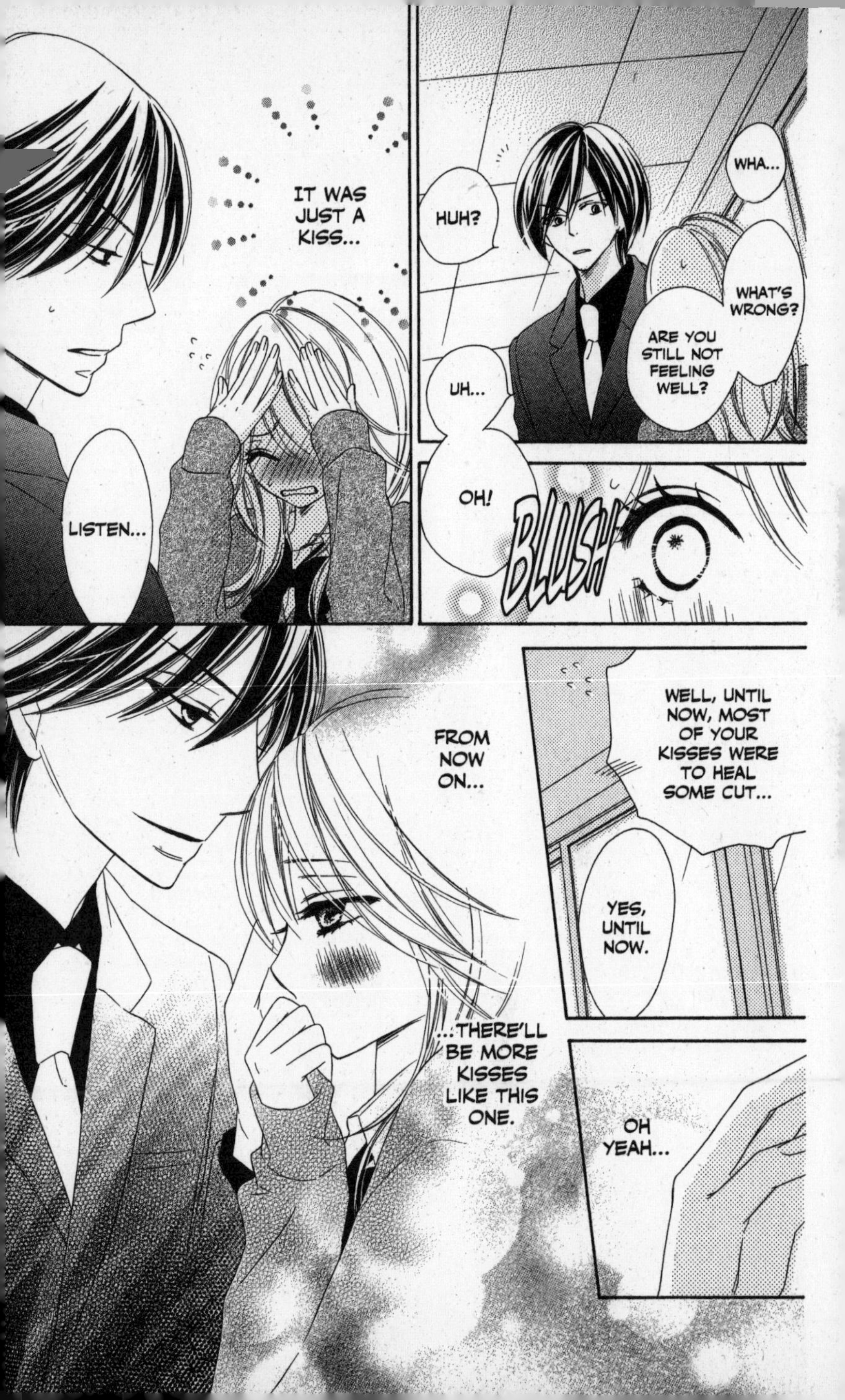
WHA...
WHAT'S WRONG?
ARE YOU STILL NOT FEELING WELL?
HUH?
UH...
OH!
BLUSH
IT WAS JUST A KISS...
LISTEN...
WELL, UNTIL NOW, MOST OF YOUR KISSES WERE TO HEAL SOME CUT...
YES, UNTIL NOW.
OH YEAH...
FROM NOW ON...
...THERE'LL BE MORE KISSES LIKE THIS ONE.

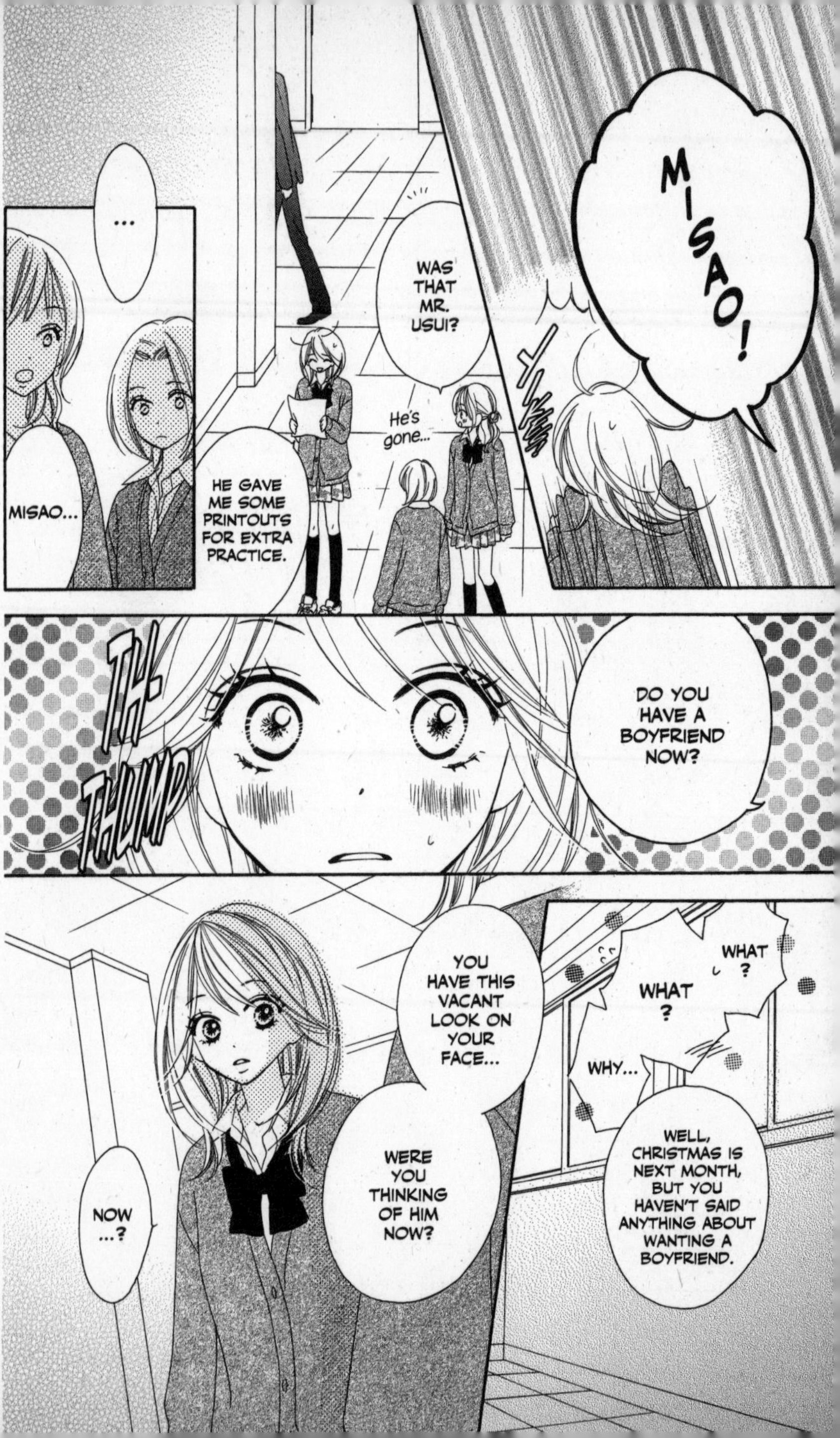
MISAO!
YANK
WAS THAT MR. USUI?
He's gone...
HE GAVE ME SOME PRINTOUTS FOR EXTRA PRACTICE.
...
MISAO...
DO YOU HAVE A BOYFRIEND NOW?
TH-THUMP
WHAT?
WHAT?
WHY...
WELL, CHRISTMAS IS NEXT MONTH, BUT YOU HAVEN'T SAID ANYTHING ABOUT WANTING A BOYFRIEND.
YOU HAVE THIS VACANT LOOK ON YOUR FACE...
WERE YOU THINKING OF HIM NOW?
NOW ...?

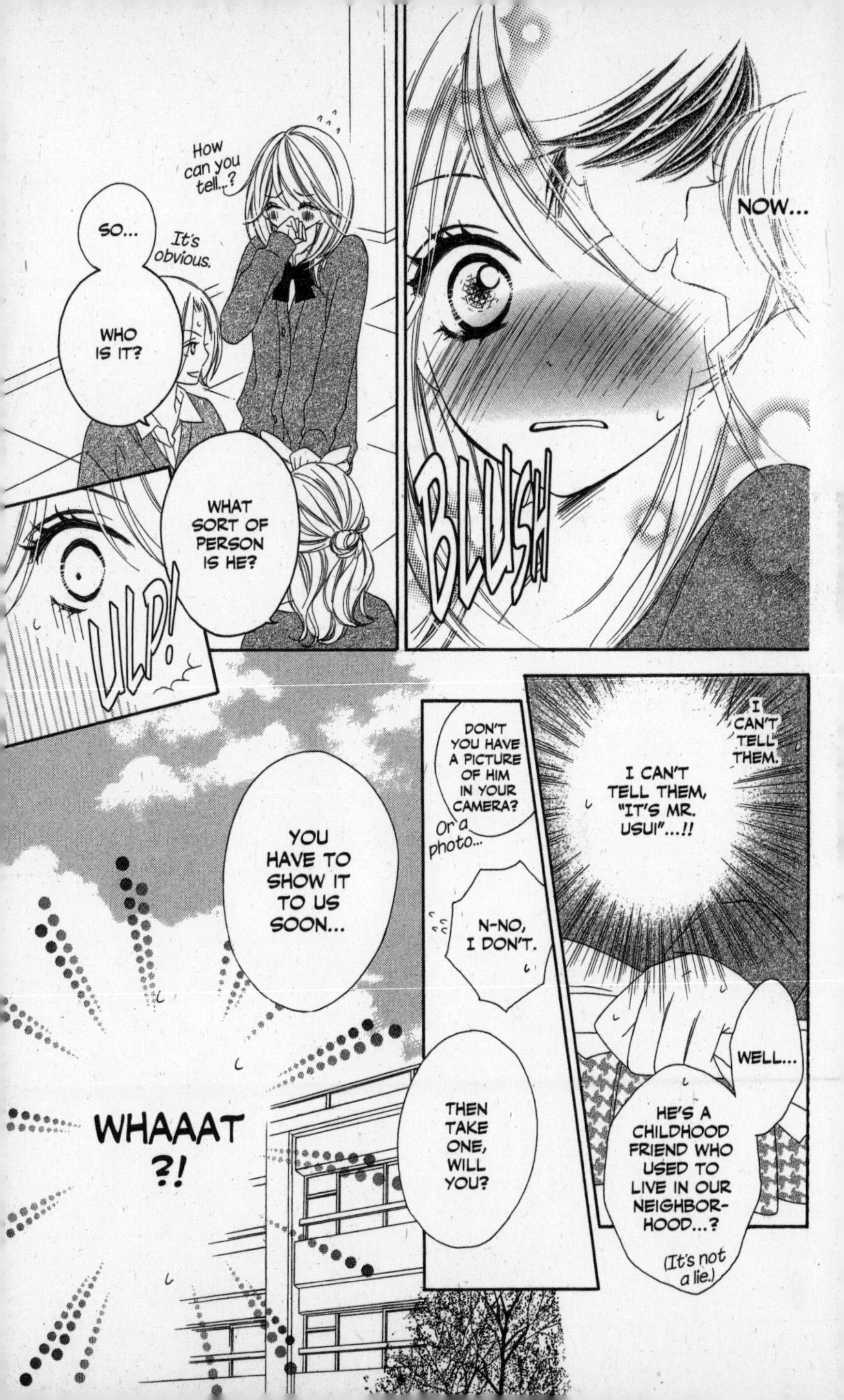
NOW...
BLUSH
How can you tell...?
SO... WHO IS IT?
It's obvious.
WHAT SORT OF PERSON IS HE?
ULP!
I CAN'T TELL THEM.
I CAN'T TELL THEM, "IT'S MR. USUI"...!!
WELL...
HE'S A CHILDHOOD FRIEND WHO USED TO LIVE IN OUR NEIGHBOR-HOOD...?
(It's not a lie.)
DON'T YOU HAVE A PICTURE OF HIM IN YOUR CAMERA?
Or a photo...
N-NO, I DON'T.
THEN TAKE ONE, WILL YOU?
YOU HAVE TO SHOW IT TO US SOON...
WHAAAT ?!

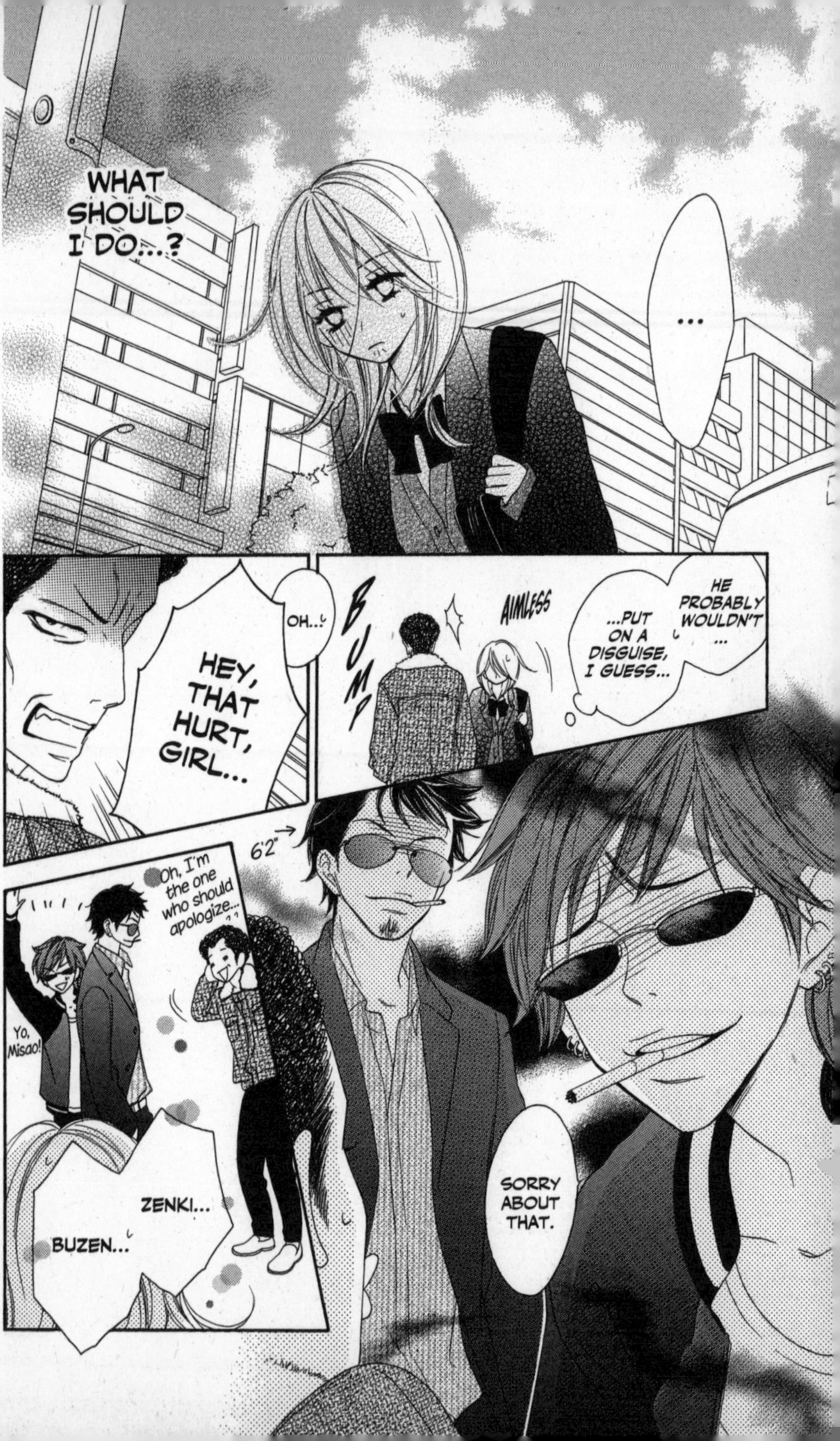
...
WHAT SHOULD I DO...?
HE PROBABLY WOULDN'T ...
...PUT ON A DISGUISE, I GUESS...
AIMLESS
BUMP
OH...
HEY, THAT HURT, GIRL...
6'2"
SORRY ABOUT THAT.
Oh, I'm the one who should apologize...
Yo, Misao!
ZENKI...
BUZEN...

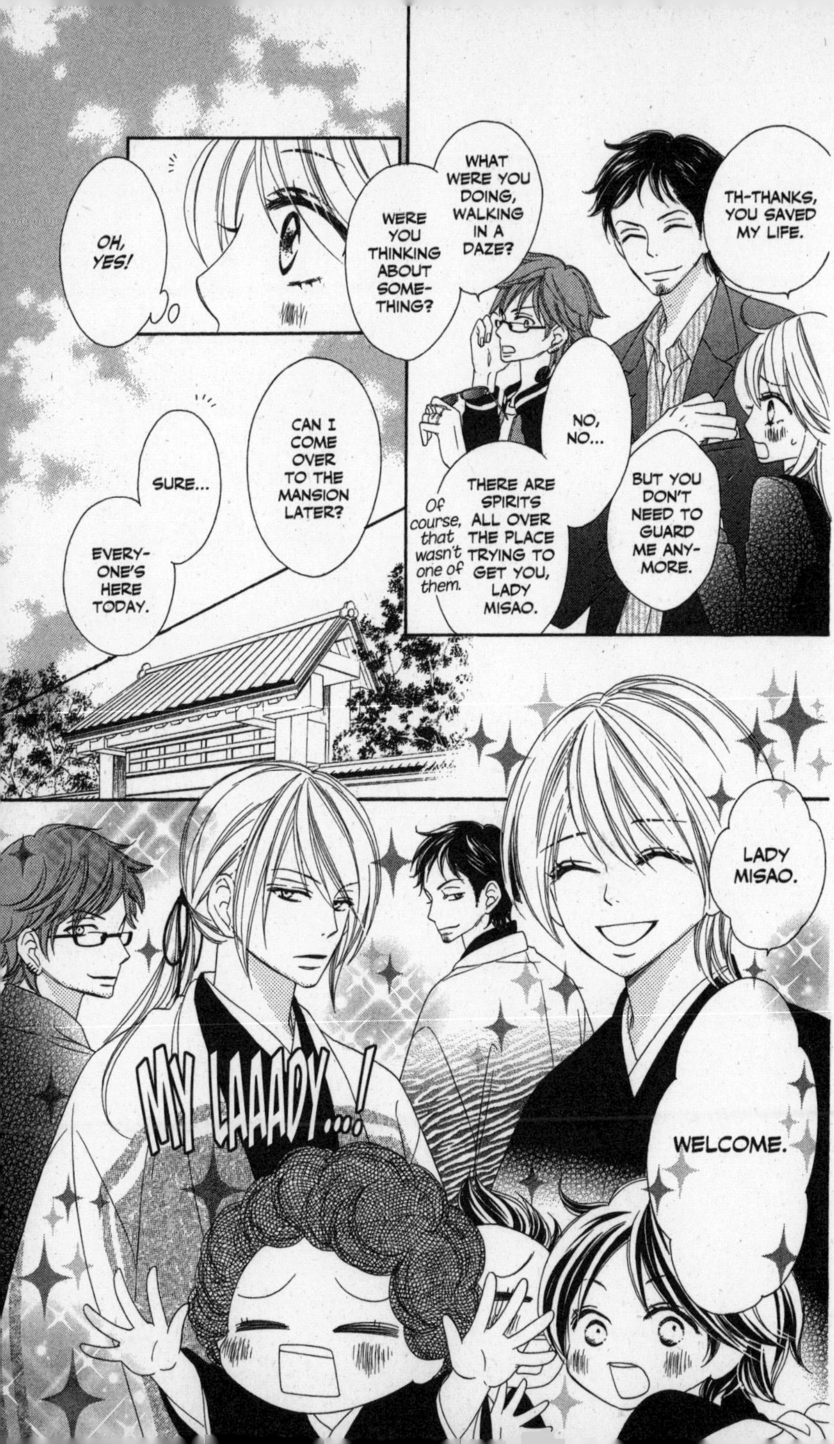
TH-THANKS, YOU SAVED MY LIFE.
WHAT WERE YOU DOING, WALKING IN A DAZE?
WERE YOU THINKING ABOUT SOME-THING?
NO, NO...
BUT YOU DON'T NEED TO GUARD ME ANY-MORE.
THERE ARE SPIRITS ALL OVER THE PLACE TRYING TO GET YOU, LADY MISAO.
Of course, that wasn't one of them.
OH, YES!
CAN I COME OVER TO THE MANSION LATER?
SURE...
EVERY-ONE'S HERE TODAY.
LADY MISAO.
WELCOME.
MY LAAADY...!

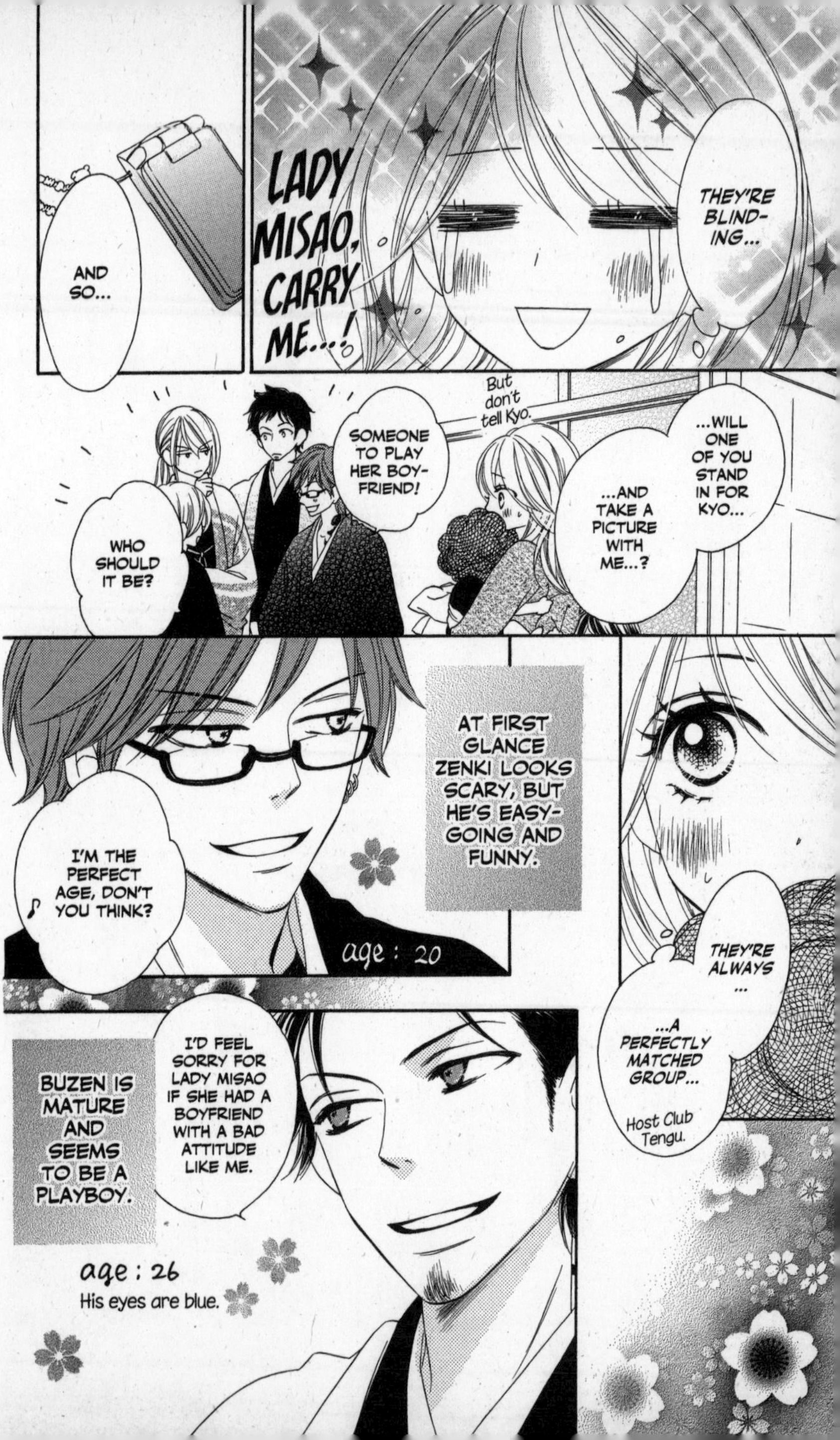
THEY'RE BLIND-ING...
LADY MISAO, CARRY ME...!
AND SO...
...WILL ONE OF YOU STAND IN FOR KYO...
...AND TAKE A PICTURE WITH ME...?
But don't tell Kyo.
SOMEONE TO PLAY HER BOY-FRIEND!
WHO SHOULD IT BE?
THEY'RE ALWAYS ...
...A PERFECTLY MATCHED GROUP...
Host Club Tengu.
AT FIRST GLANCE ZENKI LOOKS SCARY, BUT HE'S EASY-GOING AND FUNNY.
I'M THE PERFECT AGE, DON'T YOU THINK? ♪
age : 20
I'D FEEL SORRY FOR LADY MISAO IF SHE HAD A BOYFRIEND WITH A BAD ATTITUDE LIKE ME.
BUZEN IS MATURE AND SEEMS TO BE A PLAYBOY.
age : 26
His eyes are blue.

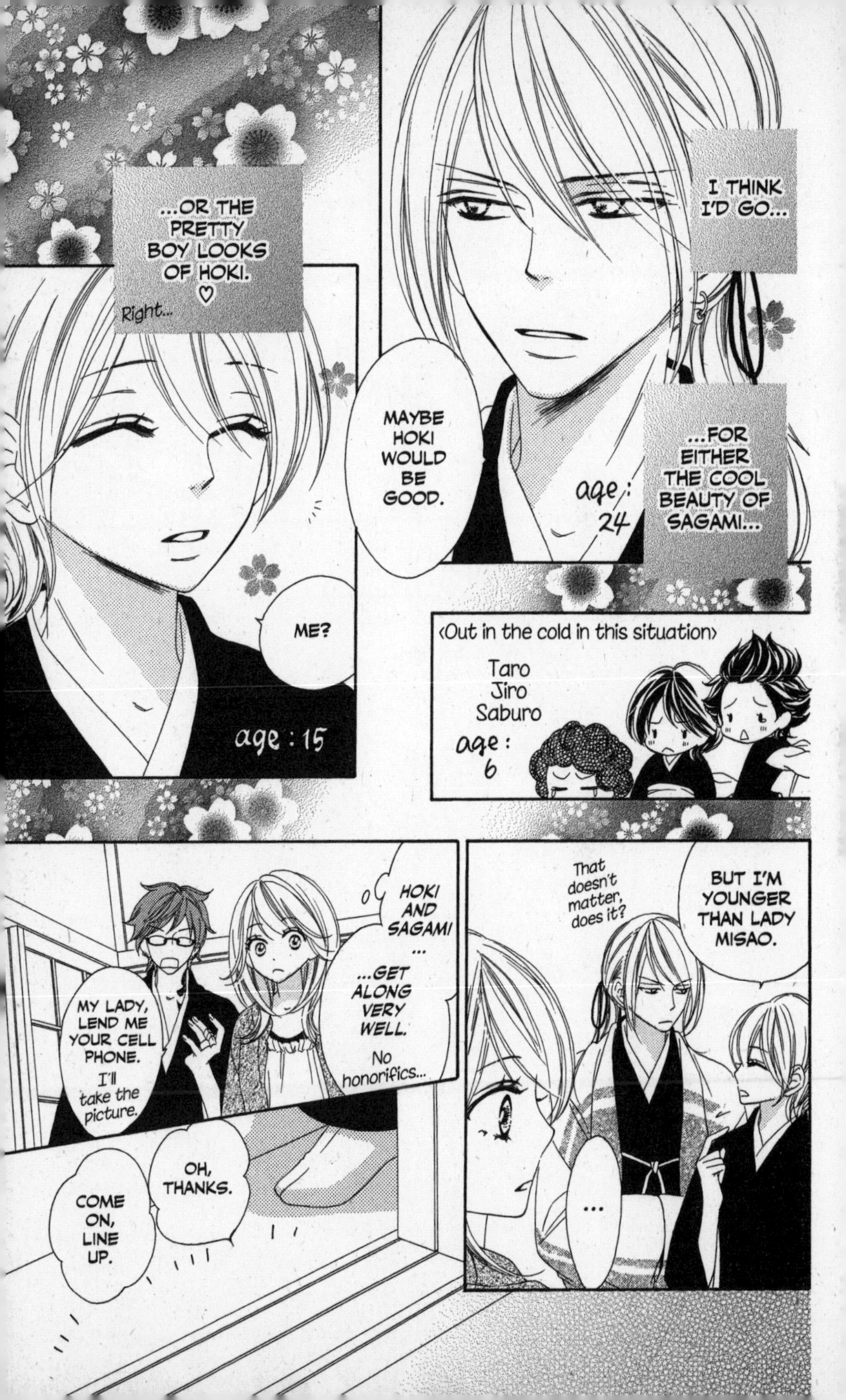
I THINK I'D GO...
...FOR EITHER THE COOL BEAUTY OF SAGAMI...
age: 24
...OR THE PRETTY BOY LOOKS OF HOKI. ♡
Right...
MAYBE HOKI WOULD BE GOOD.
ME?
age: 15
‹Out in the cold in this situation›
Taro
Jiro
Saburo
age: 6
BUT I'M YOUNGER THAN LADY MISAO.
That doesn't matter, does it?
...
HOKI AND SAGAMI ...
...GET ALONG VERY WELL.
No honorifics...
MY LADY, LEND ME YOUR CELL PHONE.
I'll take the picture.
OH, THANKS.
COME ON, LINE UP.

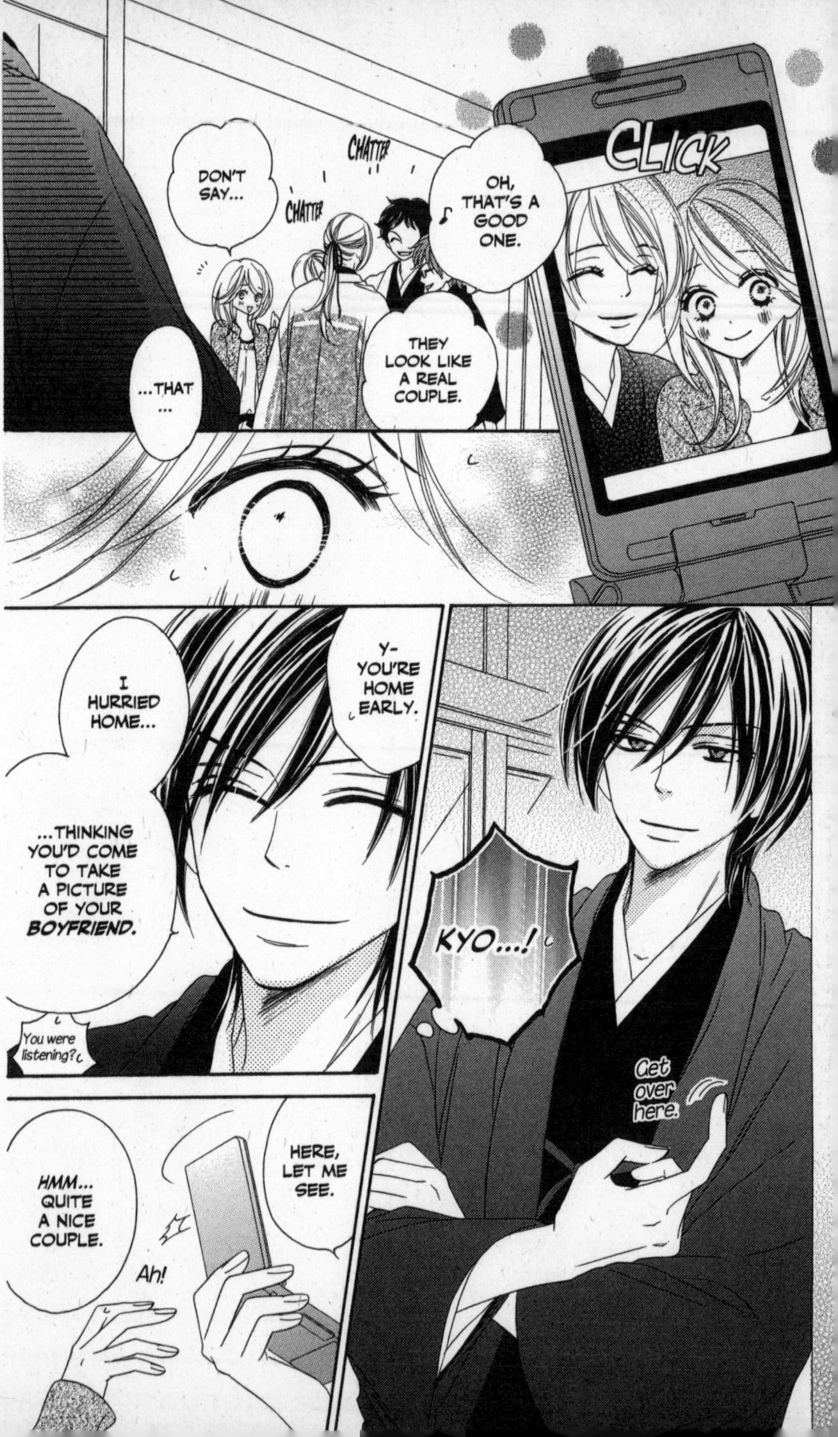
CLICK
OH, THAT'S A GOOD ONE.
CHATTER
CHATTER
DON'T SAY...
THEY LOOK LIKE A REAL COUPLE.
...THAT ...
KYO...!
Get over here.
Y- YOU'RE HOME EARLY.
I HURRIED HOME...
...THINKING YOU'D COME TO TAKE A PICTURE OF YOUR BOYFRIEND.
You were listening?
HERE, LET ME SEE.
Ah!
HMM... QUITE A NICE COUPLE.

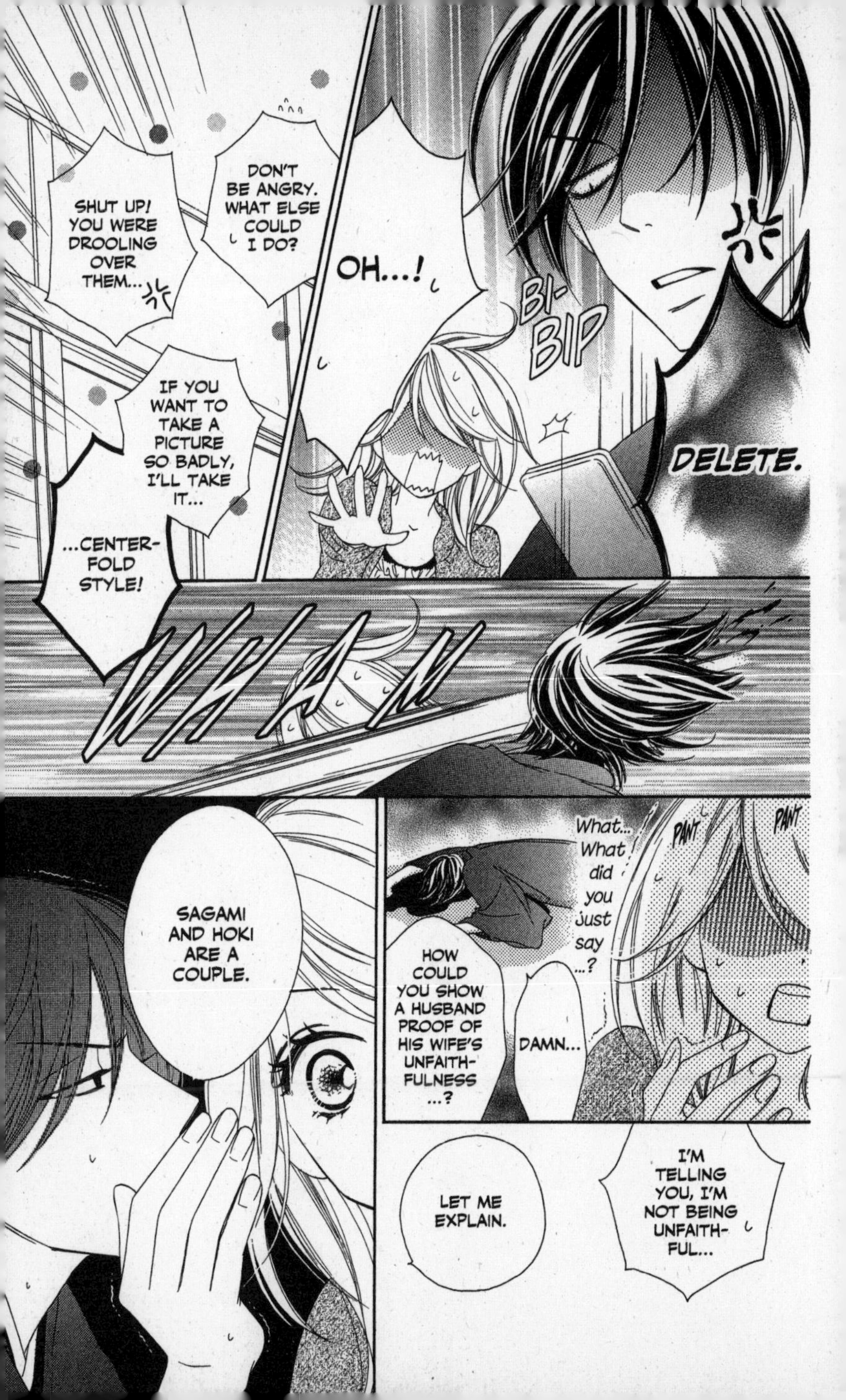
BI-BIP
DELETE.
OH...!
DON'T BE ANGRY. WHAT ELSE COULD I DO?
SHUT UP! YOU WERE DROOLING OVER THEM...
IF YOU WANT TO TAKE A PICTURE SO BADLY, I'LL TAKE IT...
...CENTERFOLD STYLE!
WHAM
PANT PANT
What... What did you just say ...?
DAMN...
HOW COULD YOU SHOW A HUSBAND PROOF OF HIS WIFE'S UNFAITHFULNESS ...?
I'M TELLING YOU, I'M NOT BEING UNFAITHFUL...
LET ME EXPLAIN.
SAGAMI AND HOKI ARE A COUPLE.

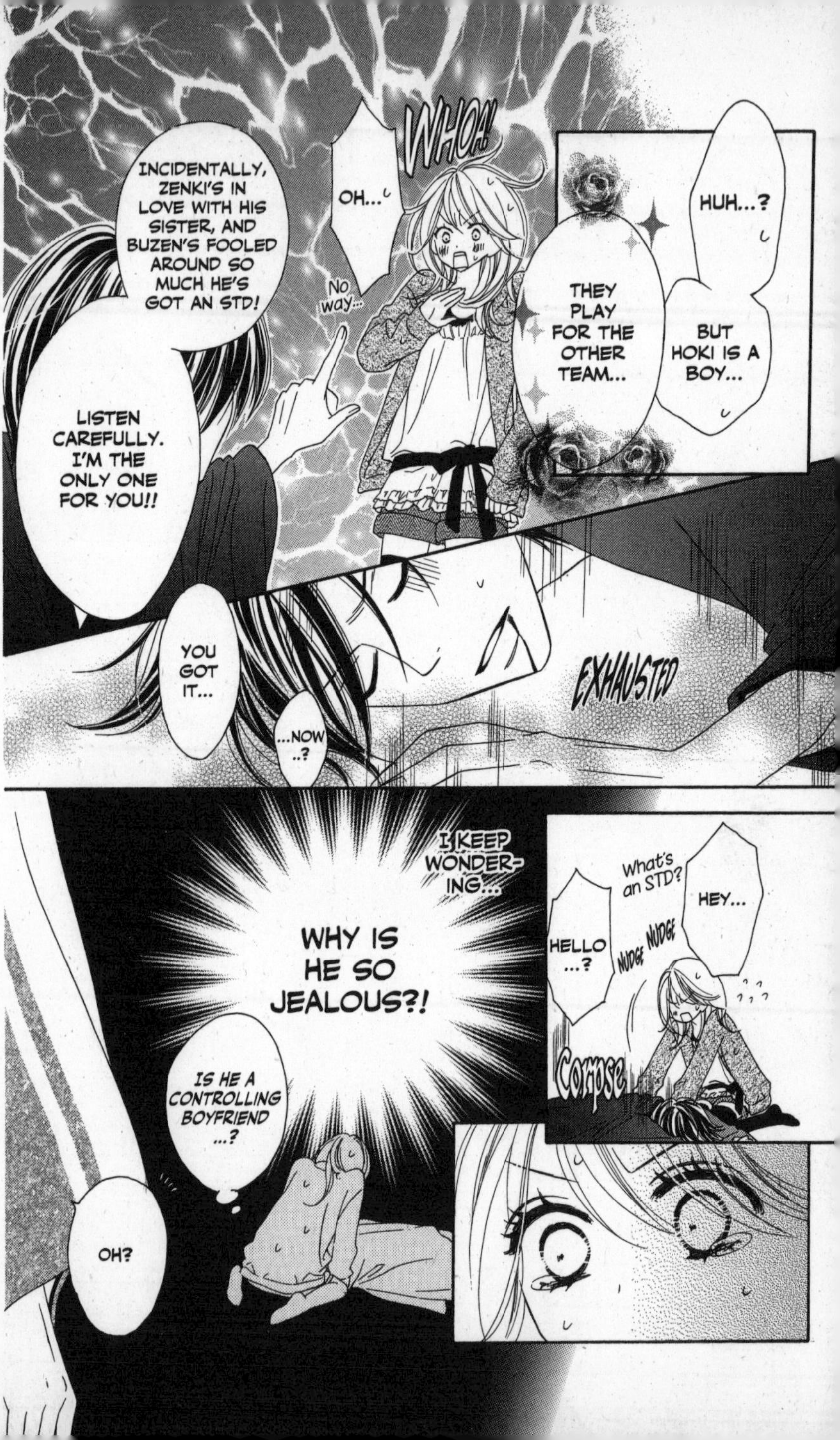
HUH...?
BUT HOKI IS A BOY...
THEY PLAY FOR THE OTHER TEAM...
WHOA!
OH...
No way...
INCIDENTALLY, ZENKI'S IN LOVE WITH HIS SISTER, AND BUZEN'S FOOLED AROUND SO MUCH HE'S GOT AN STD!
LISTEN CAREFULLY. I'M THE ONLY ONE FOR YOU!!
EXHAUSTED
YOU GOT IT...
...NOW ..?
HEY...
What's an STD?
NUDGE NUDGE
HELLO ...?
Corpse
I KEEP WONDERING...
WHY IS HE SO JEALOUS?!
IS HE A CONTROLLING BOYFRIEND ...?
OH?

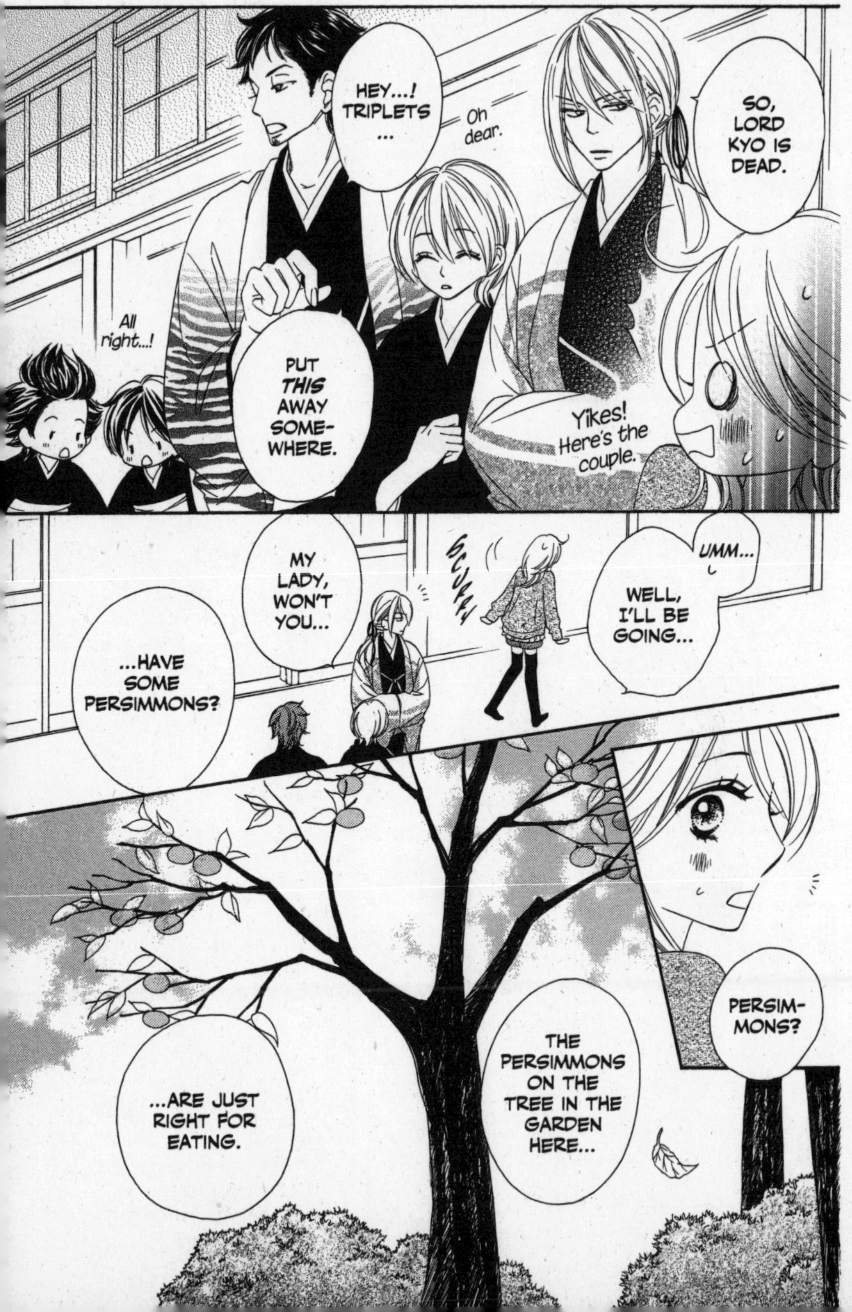
SO, LORD KYO IS DEAD.
Yikes! Here's the couple.
Oh dear.
HEY...! TRIPLETS ...
PUT THIS AWAY SOMEWHERE.
All right...!
UMM...
WELL, I'LL BE GOING...
SCURRY
MY LADY, WON'T YOU...
...HAVE SOME PERSIMMONS?
PERSIMMONS?
THE PERSIMMONS ON THE TREE IN THE GARDEN HERE...
...ARE JUST RIGHT FOR EATING.

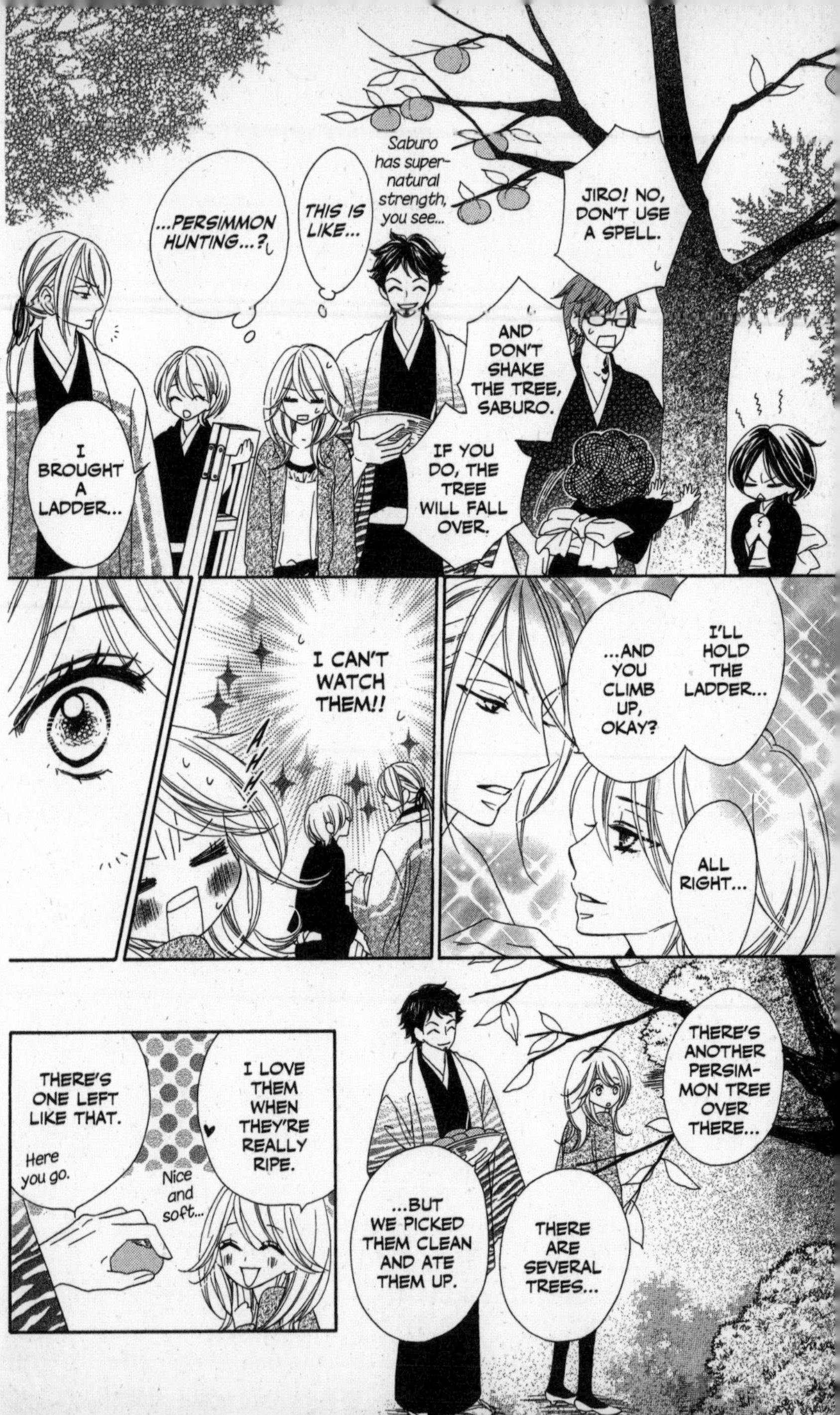
JIRO! NO, DON'T USE A SPELL.
Saburo has super-natural strength, you see...
THIS IS LIKE...
...PERSIMMON HUNTING...?
AND DON'T SHAKE THE TREE, SABURO.
IF YOU DO, THE TREE WILL FALL OVER.
I BROUGHT A LADDER...
I'LL HOLD THE LADDER...
...AND YOU CLIMB UP, OKAY?
ALL RIGHT...
I CAN'T WATCH THEM!!
AHH!!
THERE'S ANOTHER PERSIM-MON TREE OVER THERE...
THERE ARE SEVERAL TREES...
...BUT WE PICKED THEM CLEAN AND ATE THEM UP.
I LOVE THEM WHEN THEY'RE REALLY RIPE.
Nice and soft...
THERE'S ONE LEFT LIKE THAT.
Here you go.

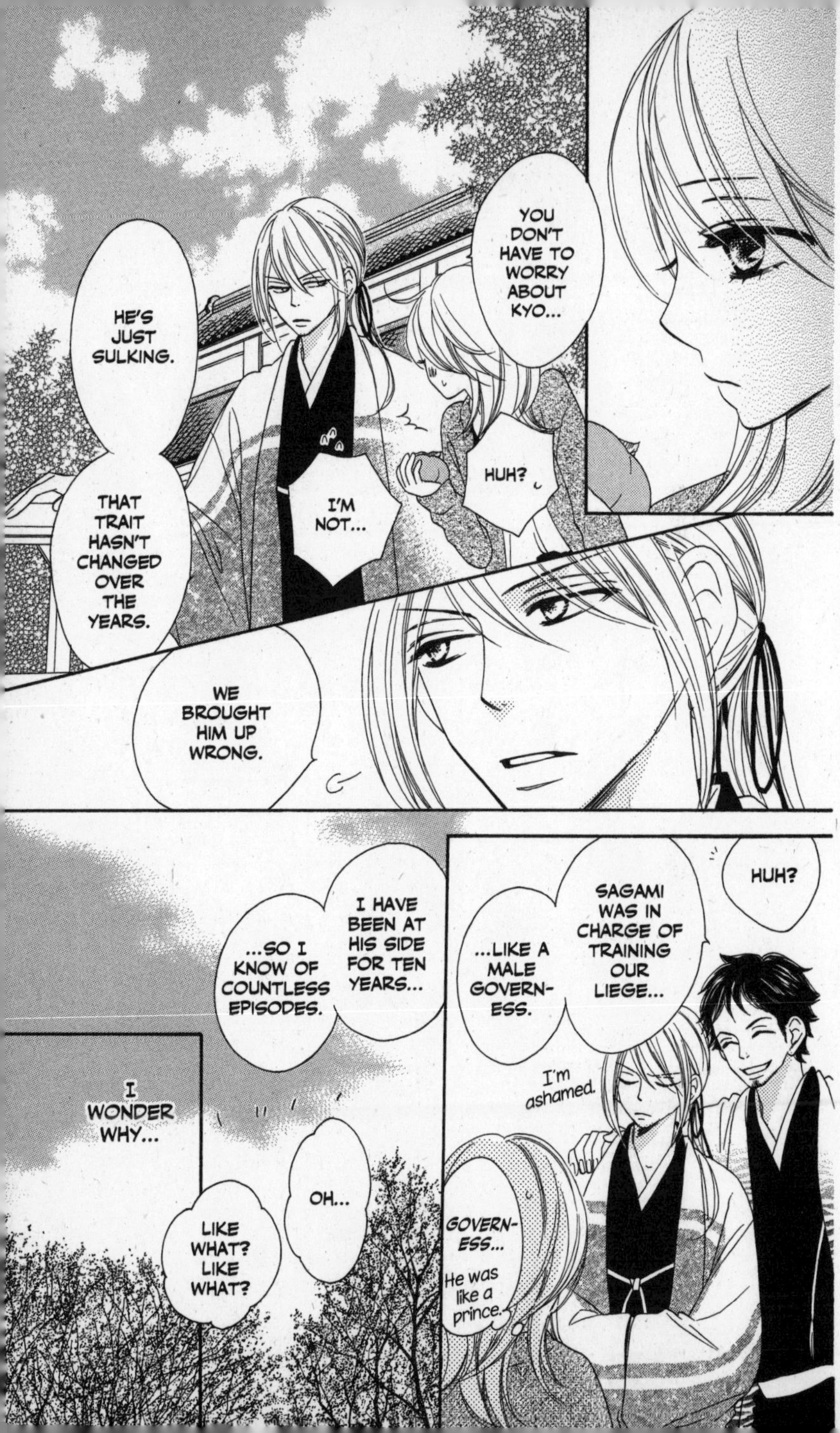
YOU DON'T HAVE TO WORRY ABOUT KYO...
HUH?
HE'S JUST SULKING.
I'M NOT...
THAT TRAIT HASN'T CHANGED OVER THE YEARS.
WE BROUGHT HIM UP WRONG.
HUH?
SAGAMI WAS IN CHARGE OF TRAINING OUR LIEGE...
...LIKE A MALE GOVERNESS.
I'm ashamed.
GOVERNESS...
He was like a prince.
I HAVE BEEN AT HIS SIDE FOR TEN YEARS...
...SO I KNOW OF COUNTLESS EPISODES.
OH...
LIKE WHAT? LIKE WHAT?
I WONDER WHY...

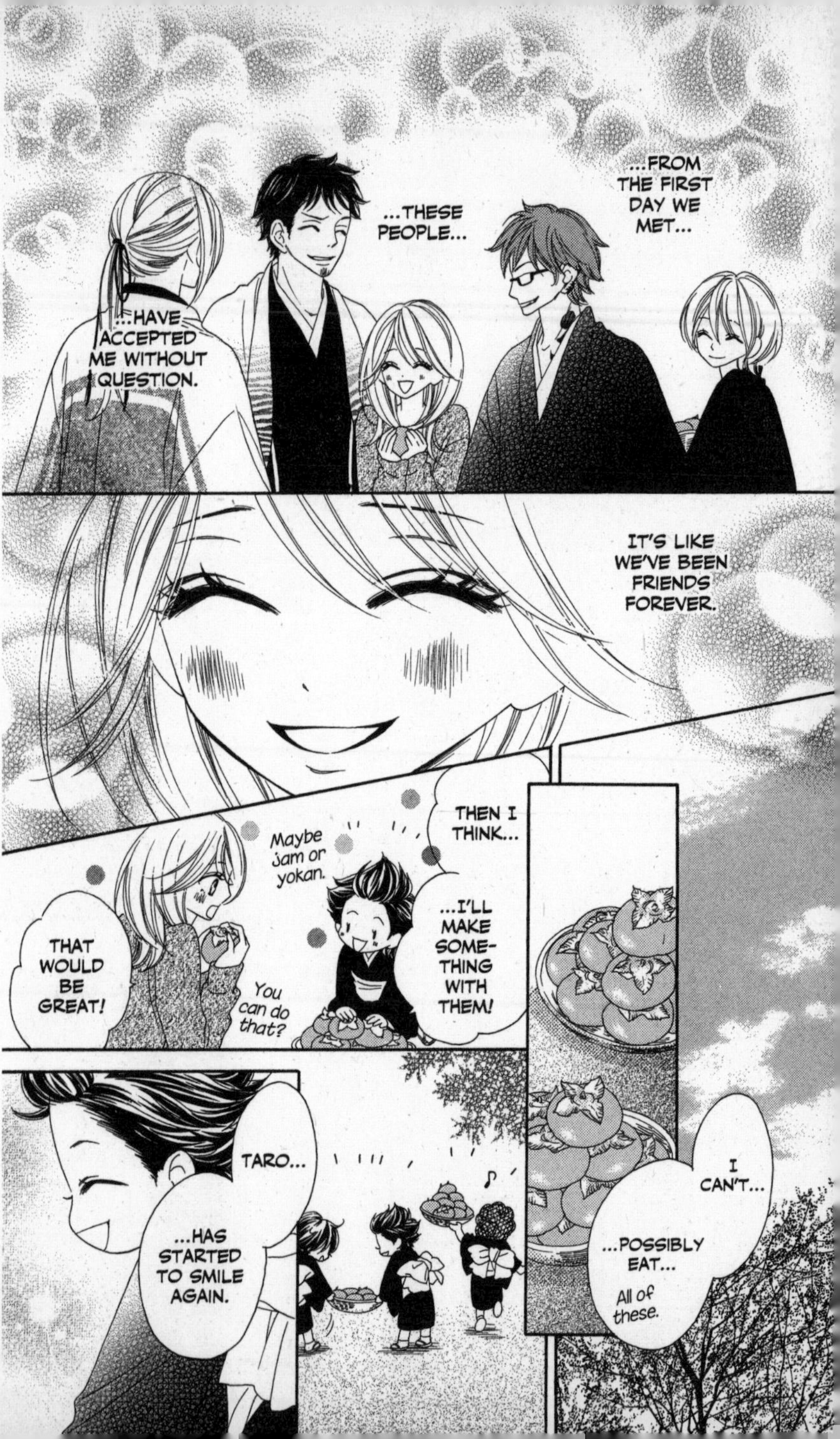
...FROM THE FIRST DAY WE MET...
...THESE PEOPLE...
...HAVE ACCEPTED ME WITHOUT QUESTION.
IT'S LIKE WE'VE BEEN FRIENDS FOREVER.
I CAN'T...
...POSSIBLY EAT...
All of these.
THEN I THINK...
...I'LL MAKE SOMETHING WITH THEM!
Maybe jam or yokan.
You can do that?
THAT WOULD BE GREAT!
TARO...
...HAS STARTED TO SMILE AGAIN.

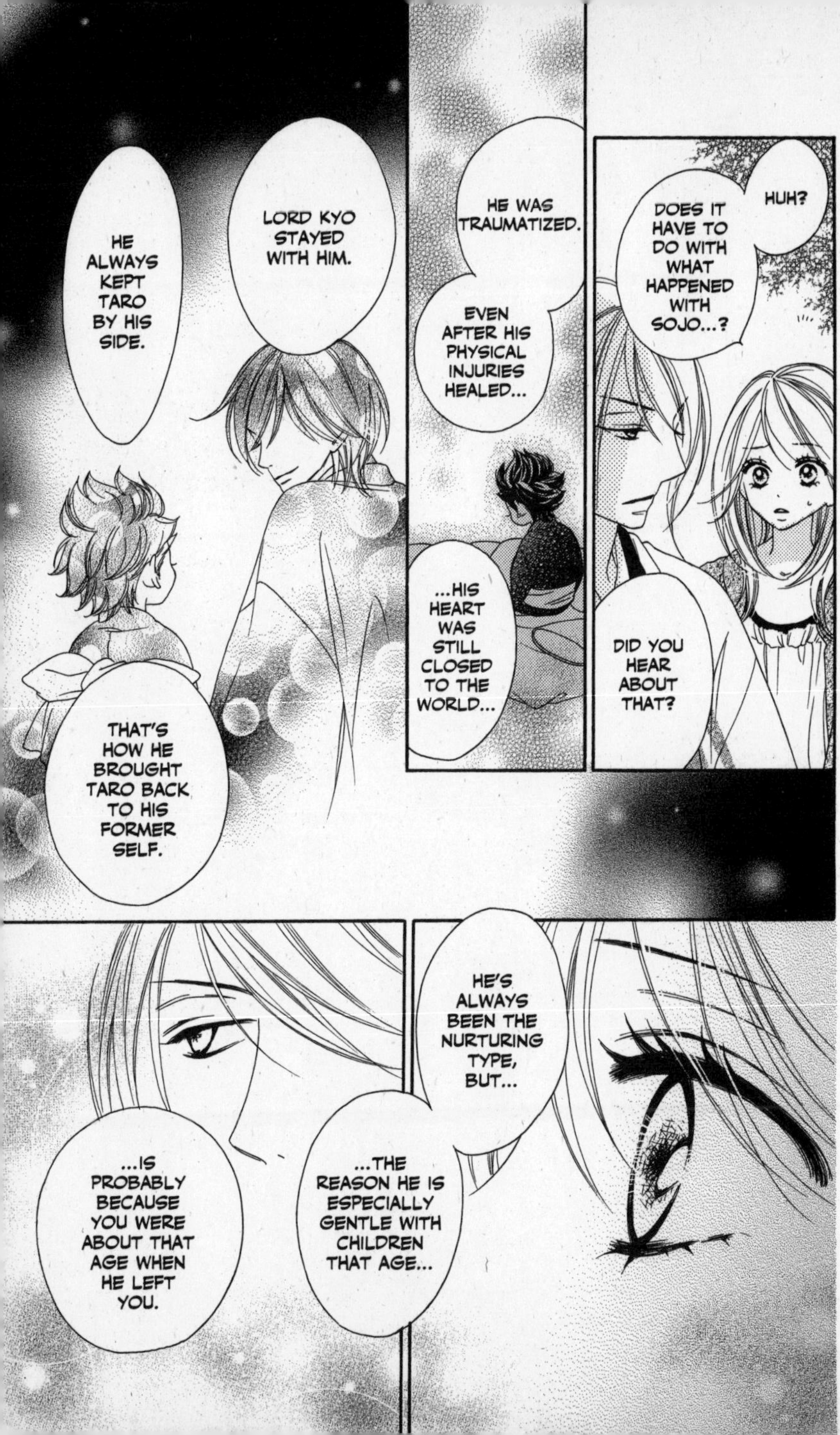
HUH?
DOES IT HAVE TO DO WITH WHAT HAPPENED WITH SOJO...?
DID YOU HEAR ABOUT THAT?
HE WAS TRAUMATIZED.
EVEN AFTER HIS PHYSICAL INJURIES HEALED...
...HIS HEART WAS STILL CLOSED TO THE WORLD...
LORD KYO STAYED WITH HIM.
HE ALWAYS KEPT TARO BY HIS SIDE.
THAT'S HOW HE BROUGHT TARO BACK TO HIS FORMER SELF.
HE'S ALWAYS BEEN THE NURTURING TYPE, BUT...
...THE REASON HE IS ESPECIALLY GENTLE WITH CHILDREN THAT AGE...
...IS PROBABLY BECAUSE YOU WERE ABOUT THAT AGE WHEN HE LEFT YOU.

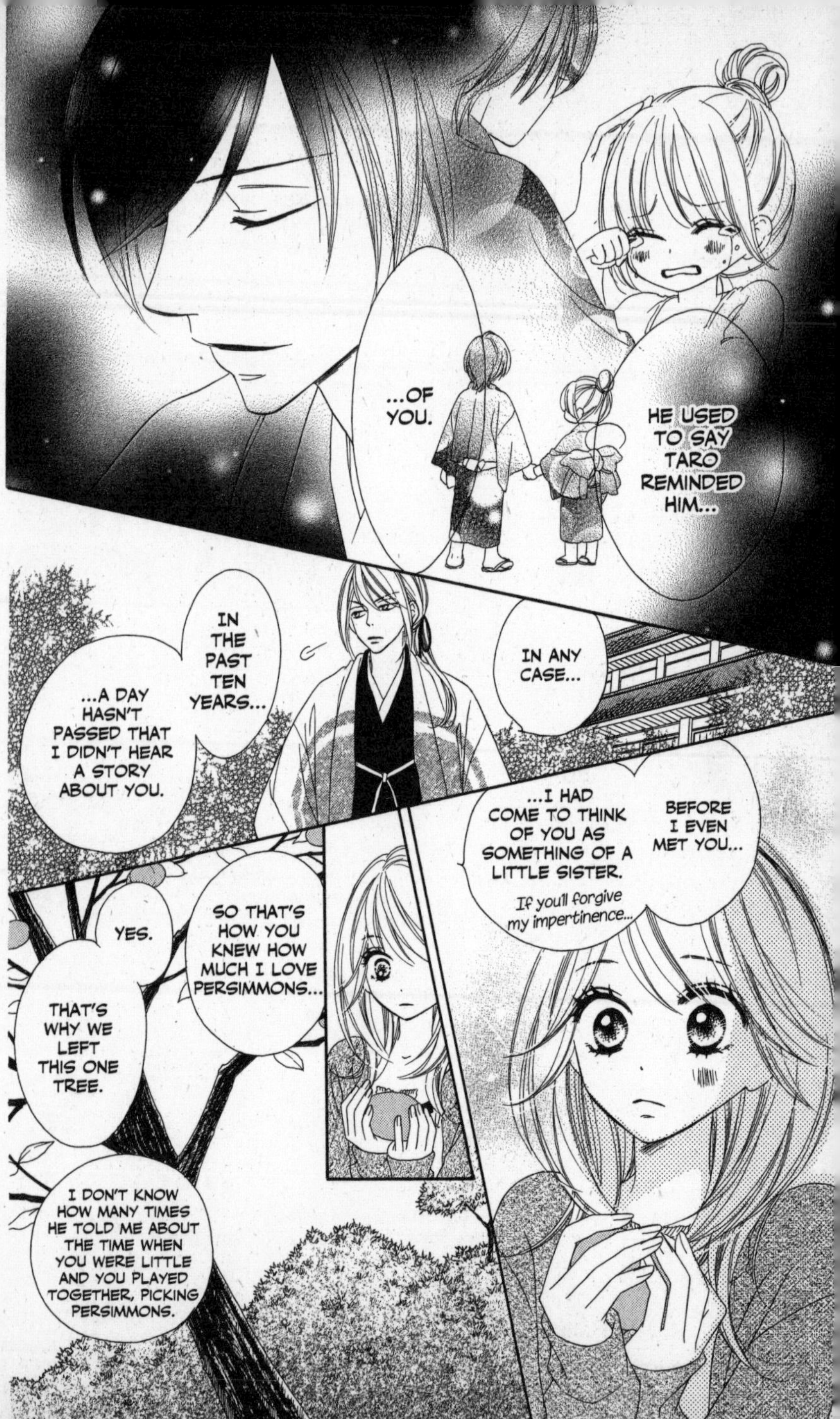
HE USED TO SAY TARO REMINDED HIM...
...OF YOU.
IN ANY CASE...
IN THE PAST TEN YEARS...
...A DAY HASN'T PASSED THAT I DIDN'T HEAR A STORY ABOUT YOU.
BEFORE I EVEN MET YOU...
...I HAD COME TO THINK OF YOU AS SOMETHING OF A LITTLE SISTER.
If you'll forgive my impertinence...
SO THAT'S HOW YOU KNEW HOW MUCH I LOVE PERSIMMONS...
YES.
THAT'S WHY WE LEFT THIS ONE TREE.
I DON'T KNOW HOW MANY TIMES HE TOLD ME ABOUT THE TIME WHEN YOU WERE LITTLE AND YOU PLAYED TOGETHER, PICKING PERSIMMONS.

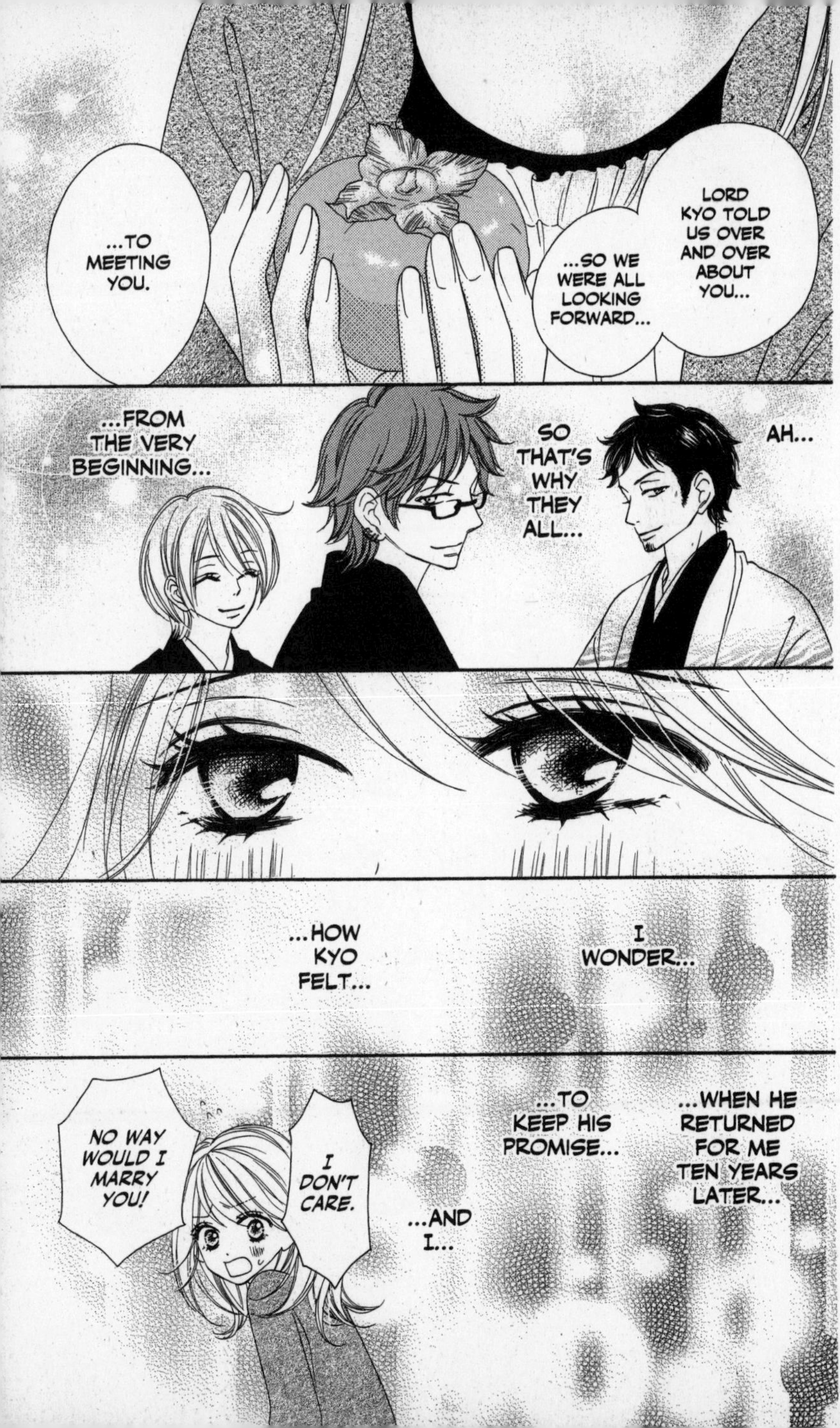
LORD KYO TOLD US OVER AND OVER ABOUT YOU...
...SO WE WERE ALL LOOKING FORWARD...
...TO MEETING YOU.
AH...
SO THAT'S WHY THEY ALL...
...FROM THE VERY BEGINNING...
I WONDER...
...HOW KYO FELT...
...WHEN HE RETURNED FOR ME TEN YEARS LATER...
...TO KEEP HIS PROMISE...
...AND I...
I DON'T CARE.
NO WAY WOULD I MARRY YOU!

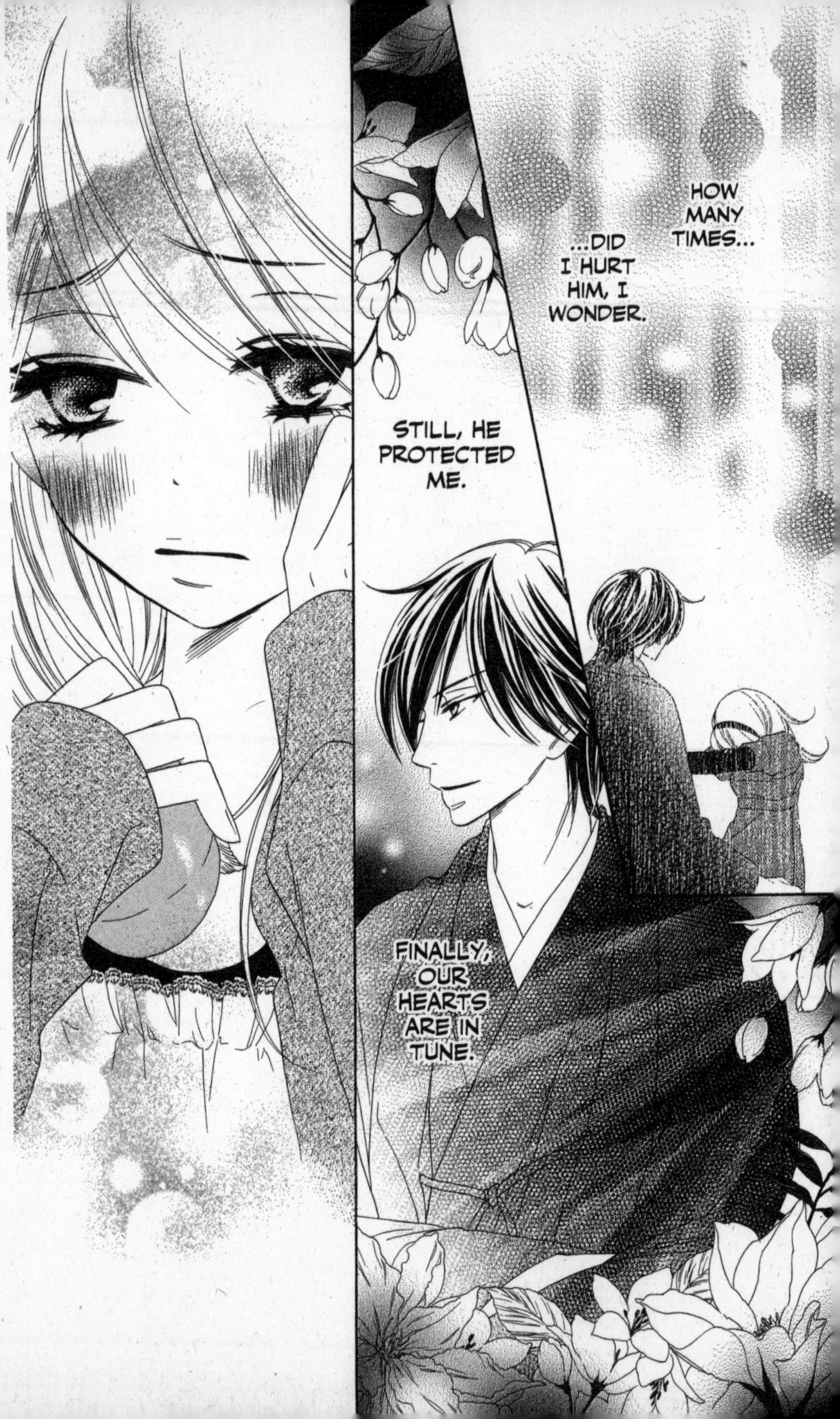
HOW MANY TIMES...
...DID I HURT HIM, I WONDER.
STILL, HE PROTECTED ME.
FINALLY, OUR HEARTS ARE IN TUNE.

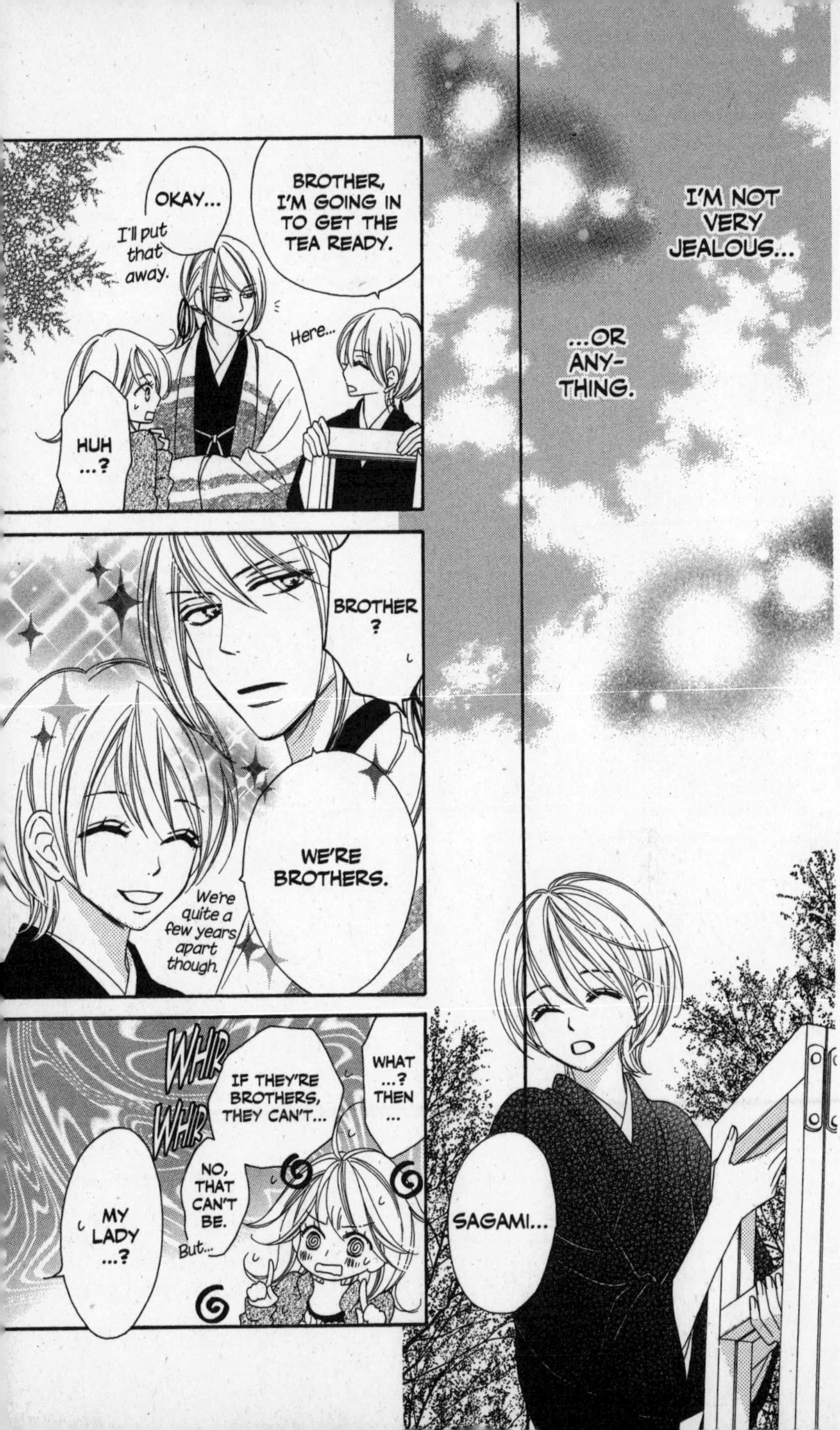
I'M NOT VERY JEALOUS...
...OR ANYTHING.
SAGAMI...
BROTHER, I'M GOING IN TO GET THE TEA READY.
Here...
OKAY...
I'll put that away.
HUH ...?
BROTHER ?
WE'RE BROTHERS.
We're quite a few years apart though.
WHAT ...? THEN ...
IF THEY'RE BROTHERS, THEY CAN'T...
WHIR WHIR
NO, THAT CAN'T BE.
But...
MY LADY ...?

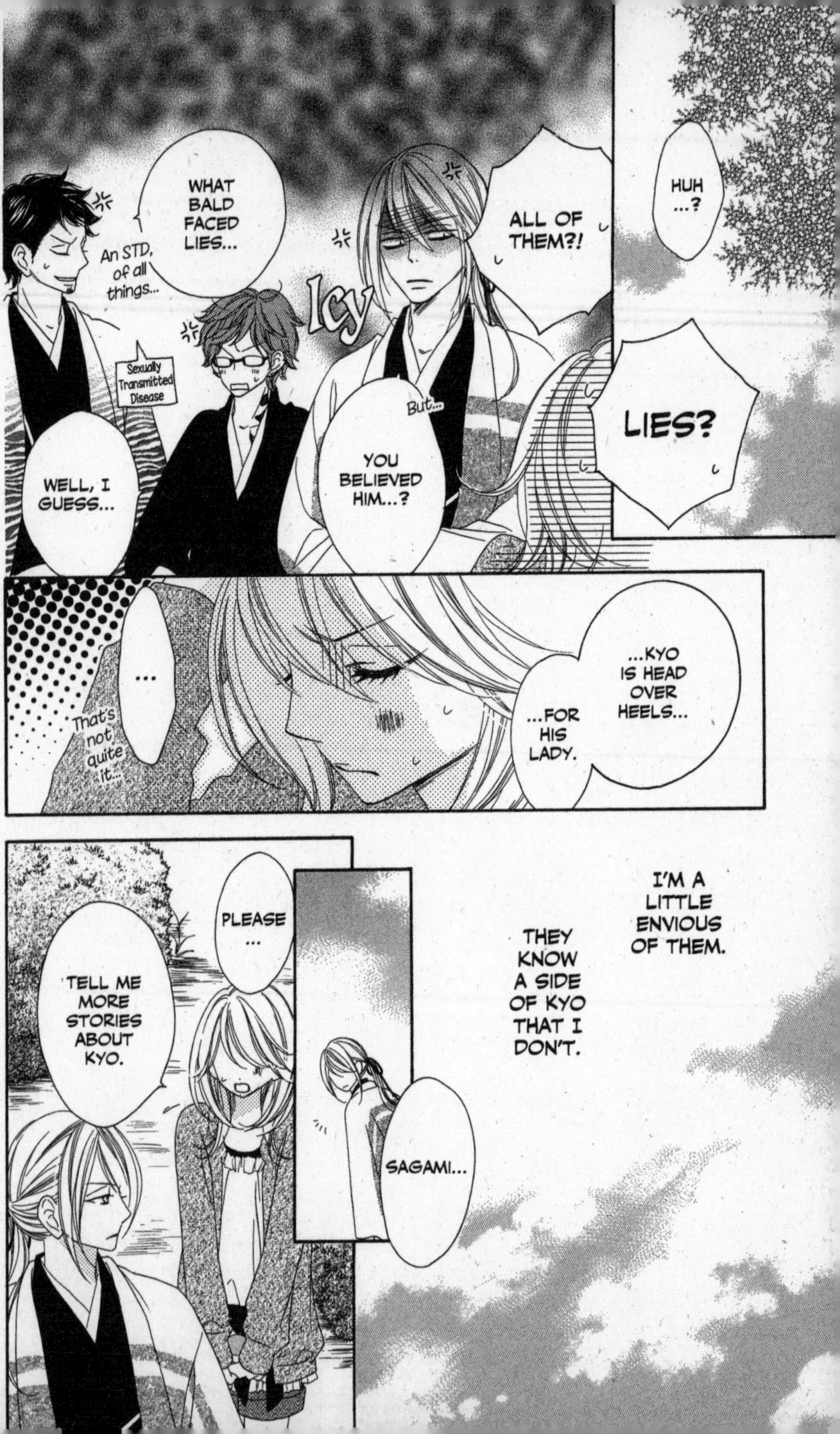
HUH ...?
LIES?
ALL OF THEM?!
WHAT BALD FACED LIES...
An STD, of all things...
Sexually Transmitted Disease
Icy
But...
YOU BELIEVED HIM...?
WELL, I GUESS...
...KYO IS HEAD OVER HEELS...
...FOR HIS LADY.
...
That's not quite it...
I'M A LITTLE ENVIOUS OF THEM.
THEY KNOW A SIDE OF KYO THAT I DON'T.
SAGAMI...
PLEASE ...
TELL ME MORE STORIES ABOUT KYO.

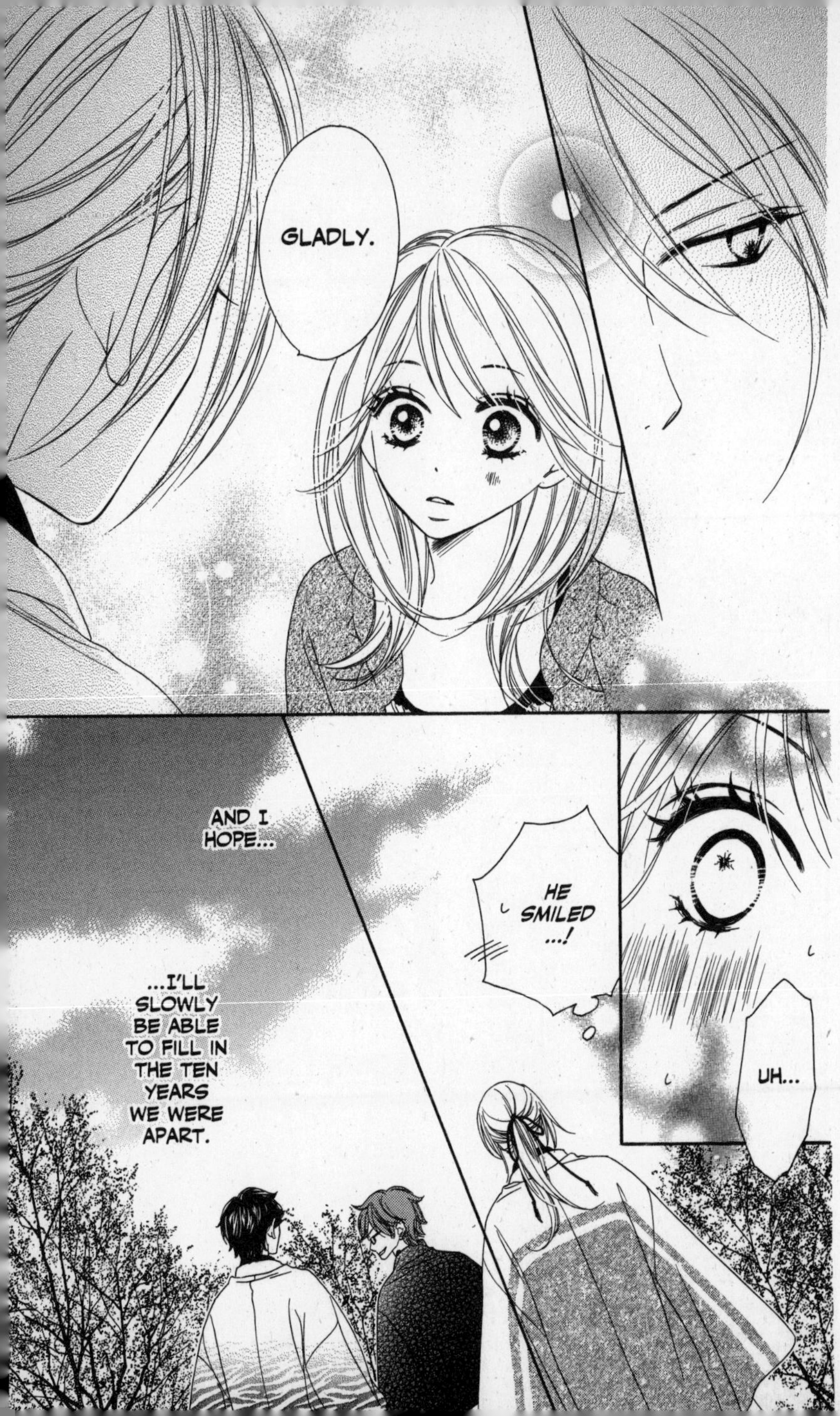
GLADLY.
UH...
HE SMILED ...!
AND I HOPE...
...I'LL SLOWLY BE ABLE TO FILL IN THE TEN YEARS WE WERE APART.

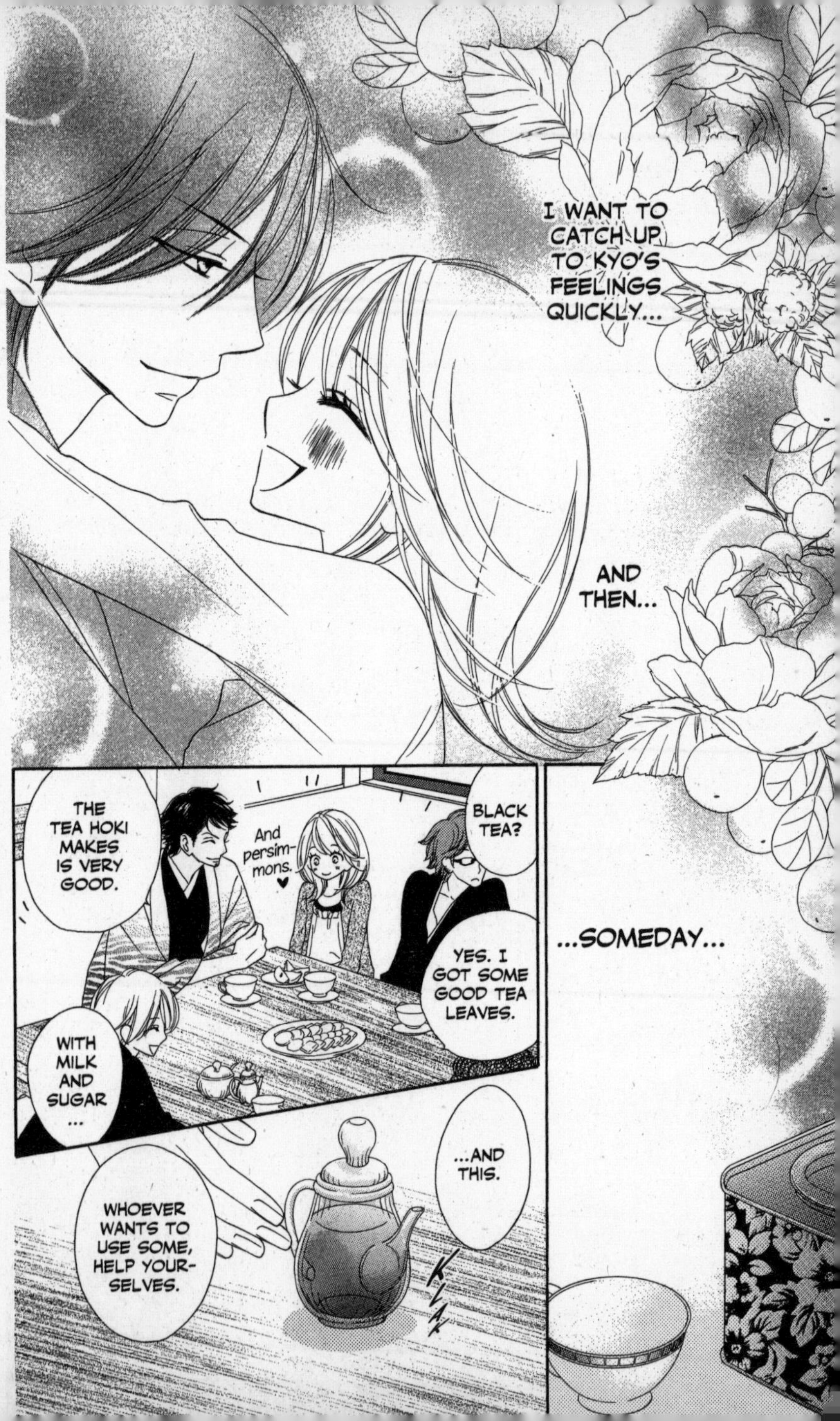
I WANT TO CATCH UP TO KYO'S FEELINGS QUICKLY...
AND THEN...
...SOMEDAY...
BLACK TEA?
YES. I GOT SOME GOOD TEA LEAVES.
And persimmons. ♥
THE TEA HOKI MAKES IS VERY GOOD.
WITH MILK AND SUGAR...
...AND THIS.
KLAK
WHOEVER WANTS TO USE SOME, HELP YOURSELVES.

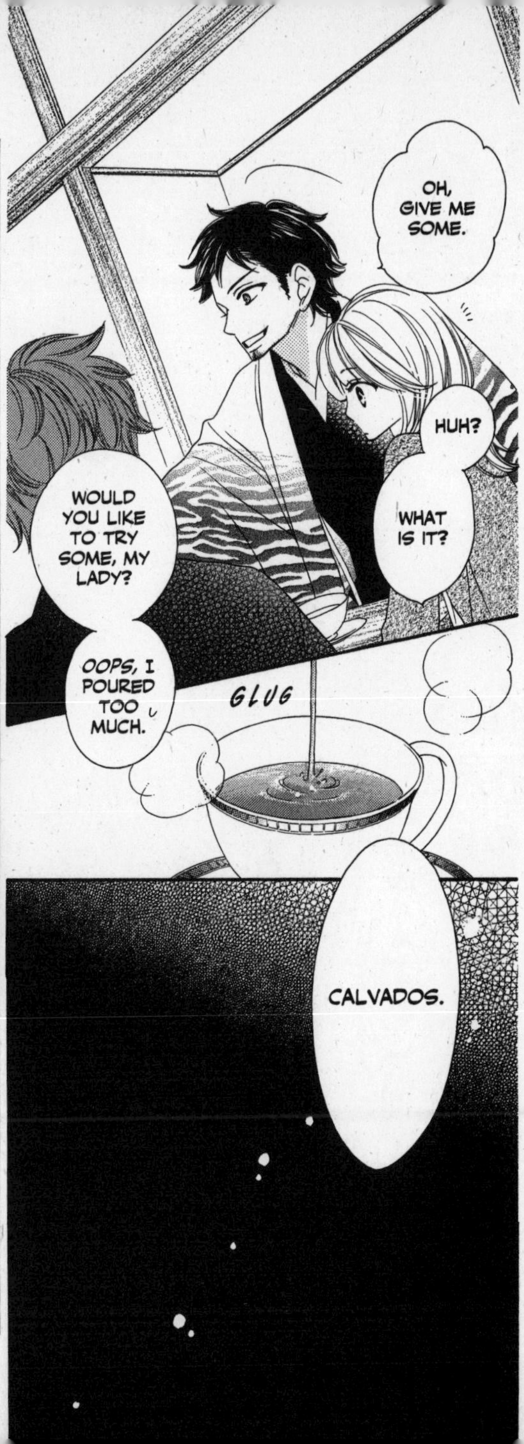
OH, GIVE ME SOME.
HUH?
WHAT IS IT?
WOULD YOU LIKE TO TRY SOME, MY LADY?
OOPS, I POURED TOO MUCH.
GLUG
CALVADOS.

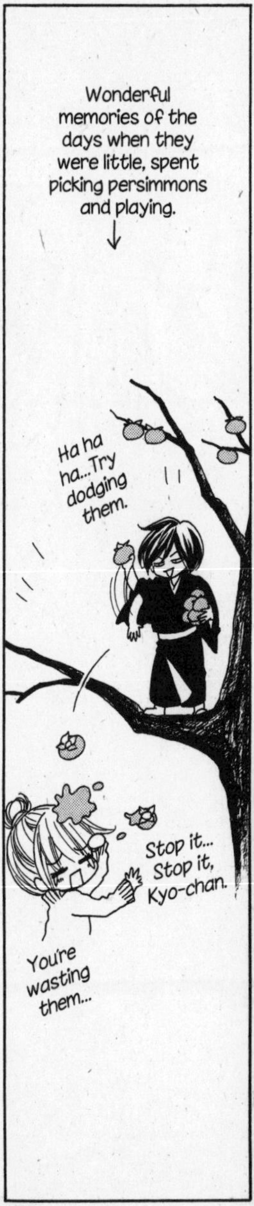
Wonderful memories of the days when they were little, spent picking persimmons and playing.
Ha ha ha...Try dodging them.
Stop it... Stop it, Kyo-chan.
You're wasting them...

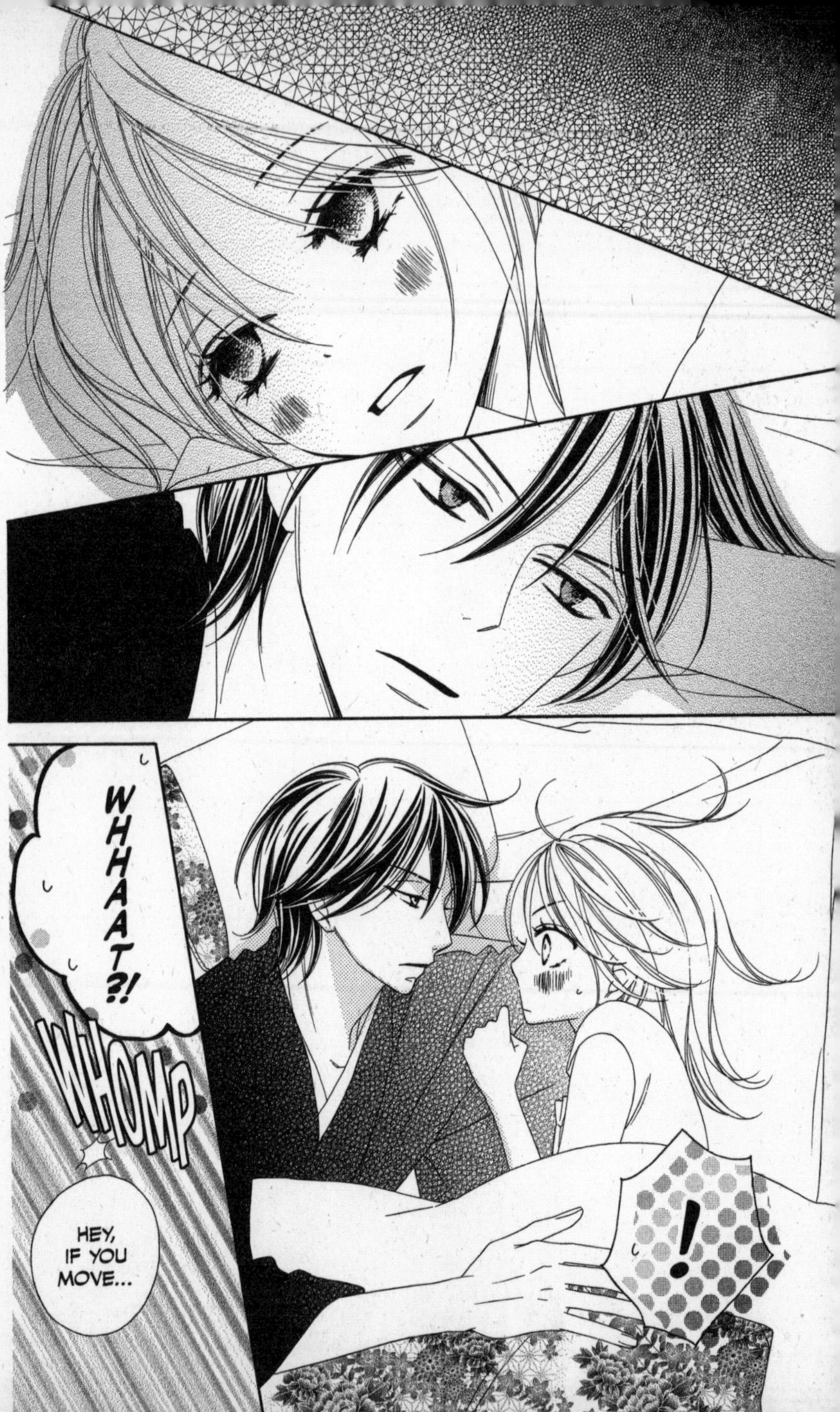
WHHAAAT?!
WHOMP
!
HEY, IF YOU MOVE...

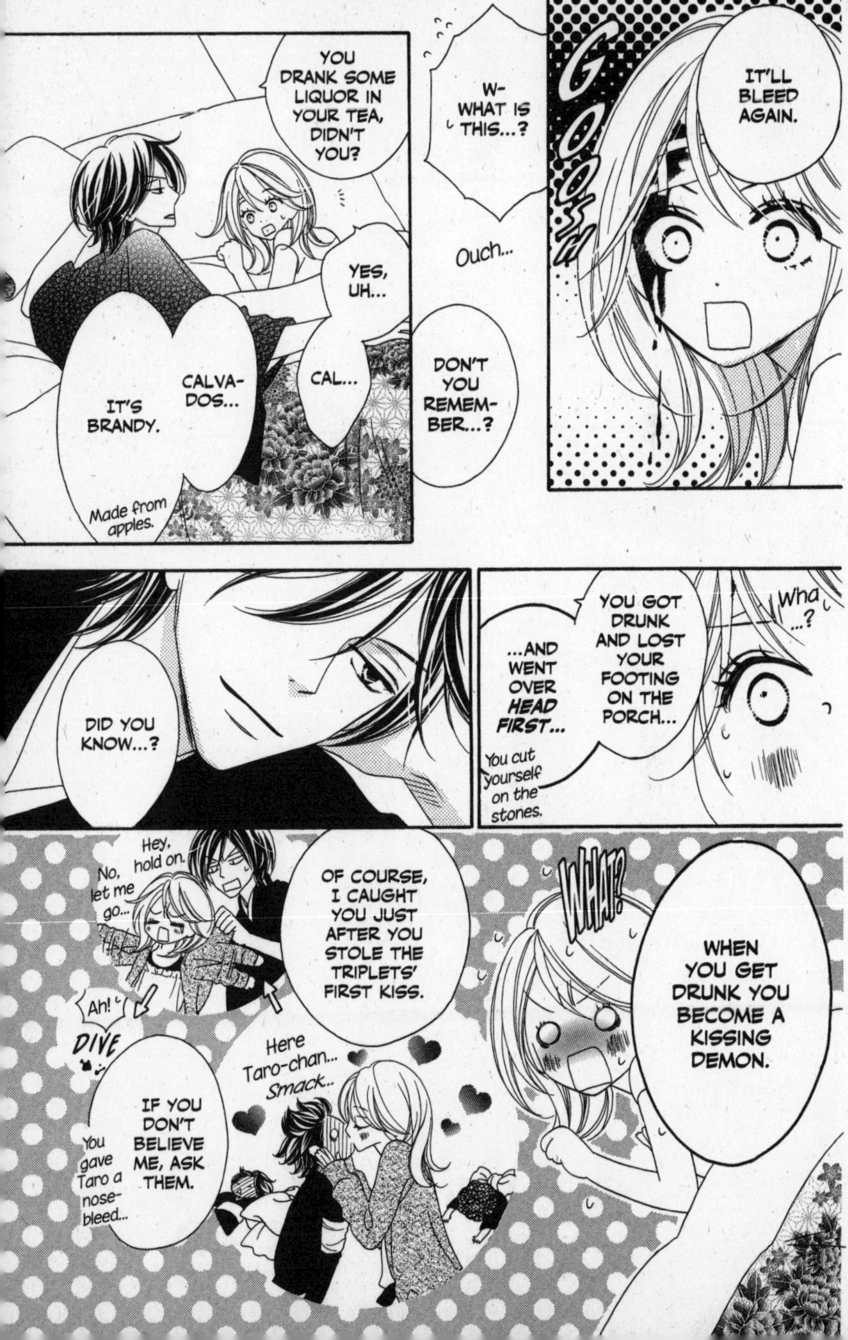
GOOOOH
IT'LL BLEED AGAIN.
W-WHAT IS THIS...?
Ouch...
DON'T YOU REMEMBER...?
YOU DRANK SOME LIQUOR IN YOUR TEA, DIDN'T YOU?
YES, UH...
CAL...
CALVADOS...
IT'S BRANDY.
Made from apples.
Wha ...?
YOU GOT DRUNK AND LOST YOUR FOOTING ON THE PORCH...
...AND WENT OVER HEAD FIRST...
You cut yourself on the stones.
DID YOU KNOW...?
WHAT!?
WHEN YOU GET DRUNK YOU BECOME A KISSING DEMON.
OF COURSE, I CAUGHT YOU JUST AFTER YOU STOLE THE TRIPLETS' FIRST KISS.
Hey, hold on.
No, let me go...
Ah!
DIVE
Here Taro-chan... Smack...
IF YOU DON'T BELIEVE ME, ASK THEM.
You gave Taro a nose-bleed...

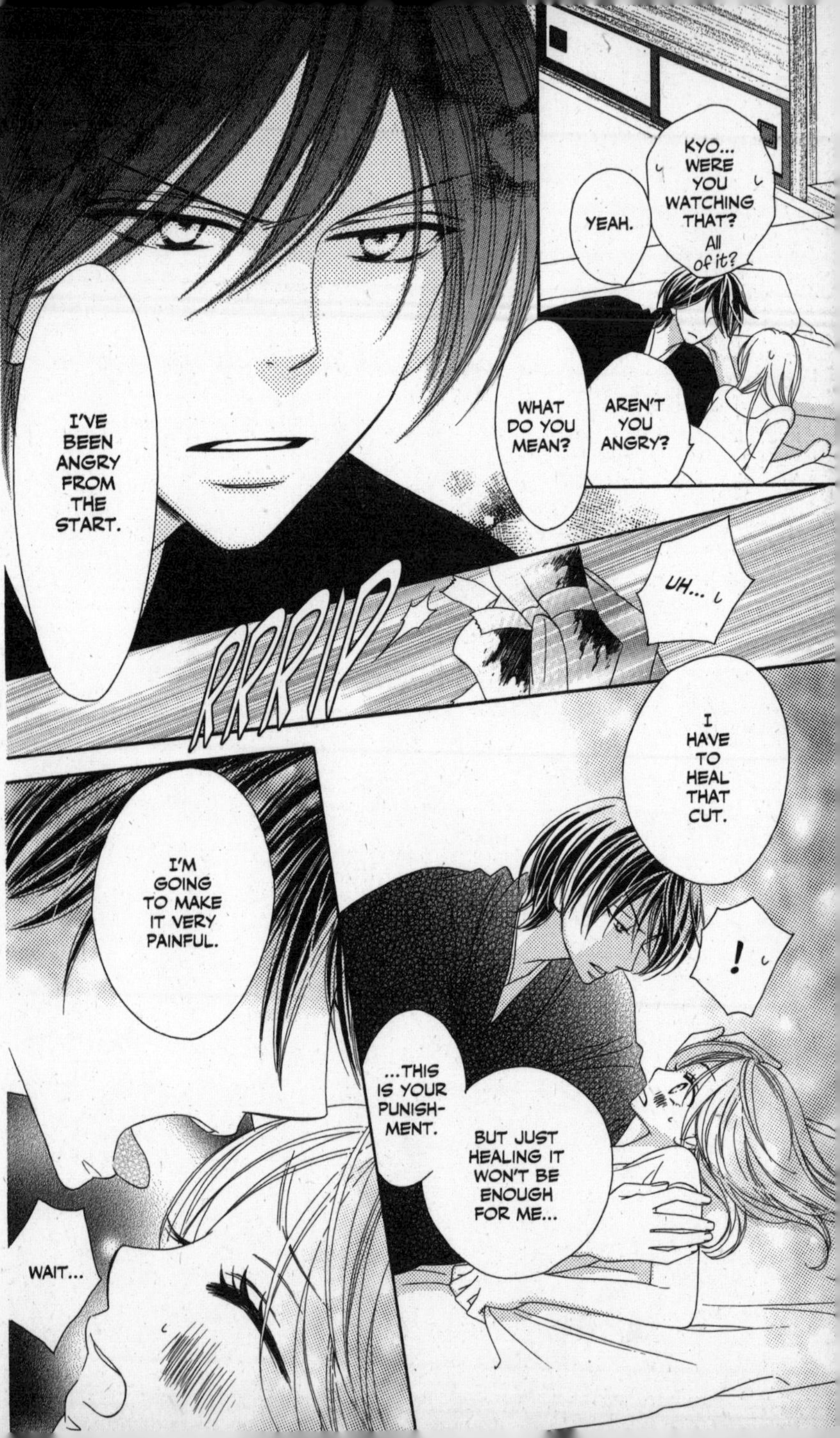
KYO... WERE YOU WATCHING THAT? All of it?
YEAH.
AREN'T YOU ANGRY?
WHAT DO YOU MEAN?
I'VE BEEN ANGRY FROM THE START.
UH...
RRRIP
I HAVE TO HEAL THAT CUT.
!
BUT JUST HEALING IT WON'T BE ENOUGH FOR ME...
...THIS IS YOUR PUNISH-MENT.
I'M GOING TO MAKE IT VERY PAINFUL.
WAIT...

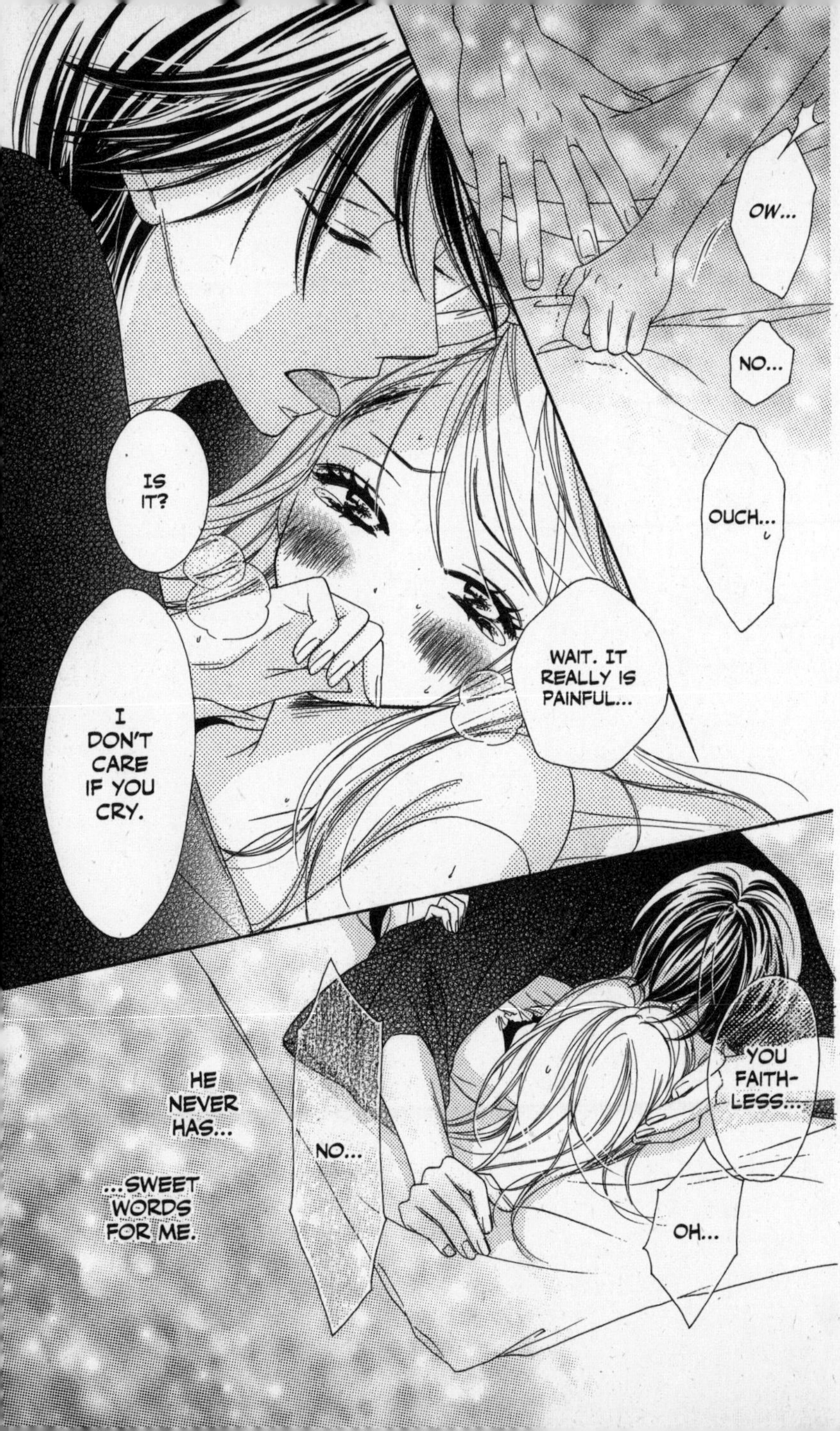
OW...
NO...
OUCH...
WAIT. IT REALLY IS PAINFUL...
IS IT?
I DON'T CARE IF YOU CRY.
YOU FAITHLESS...
OH...
NO...
HE NEVER HAS...
...SWEET WORDS FOR ME.

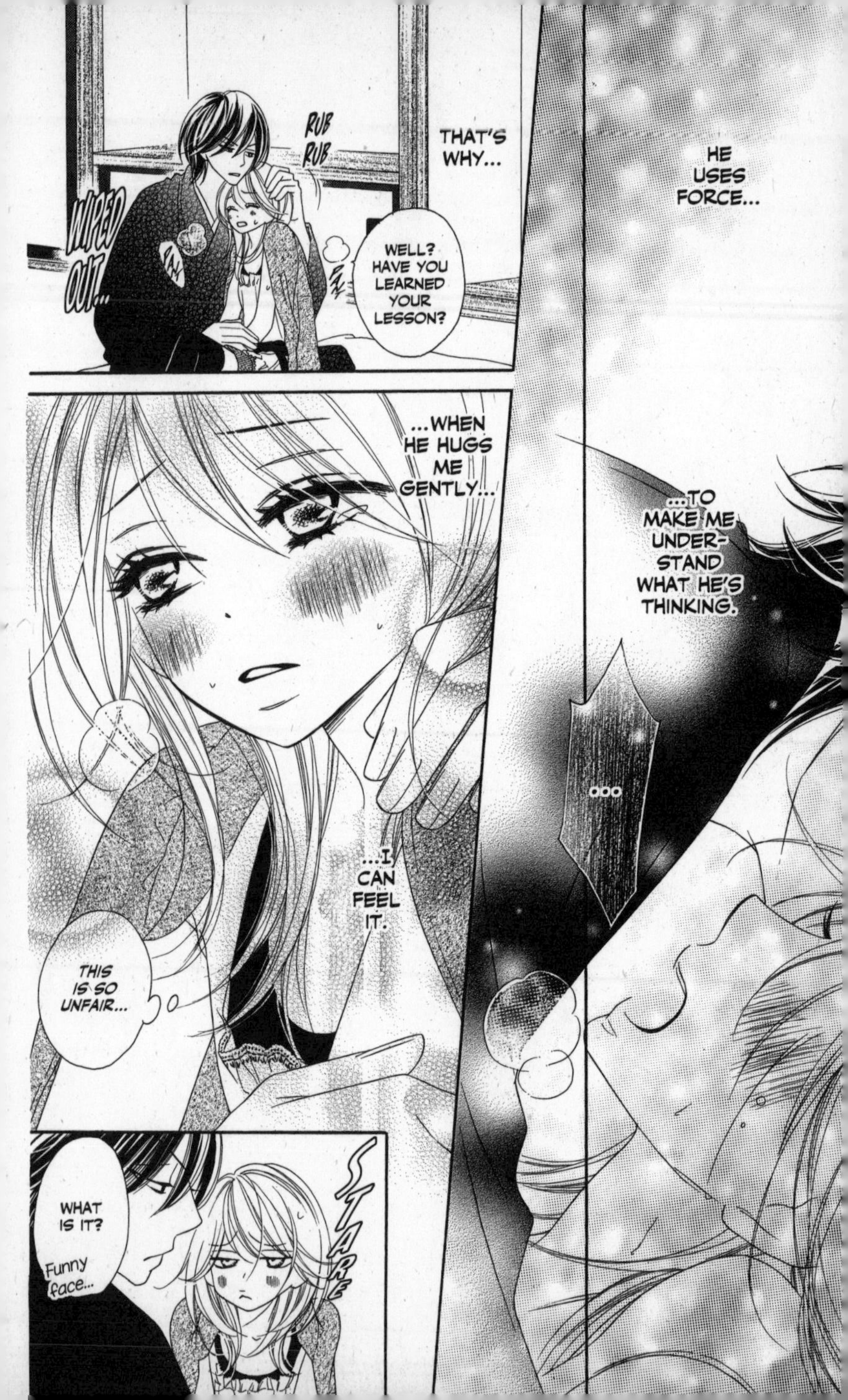
HE USES FORCE...
...TO MAKE ME UNDERSTAND WHAT HE'S THINKING.
...
THAT'S WHY...
RUB RUB
WELL? HAVE YOU LEARNED YOUR LESSON?
WIPED OUT...
...WHEN HE HUGS ME GENTLY...
...I CAN FEEL IT.
THIS IS SO UNFAIR...
STARE
WHAT IS IT?
Funny face...

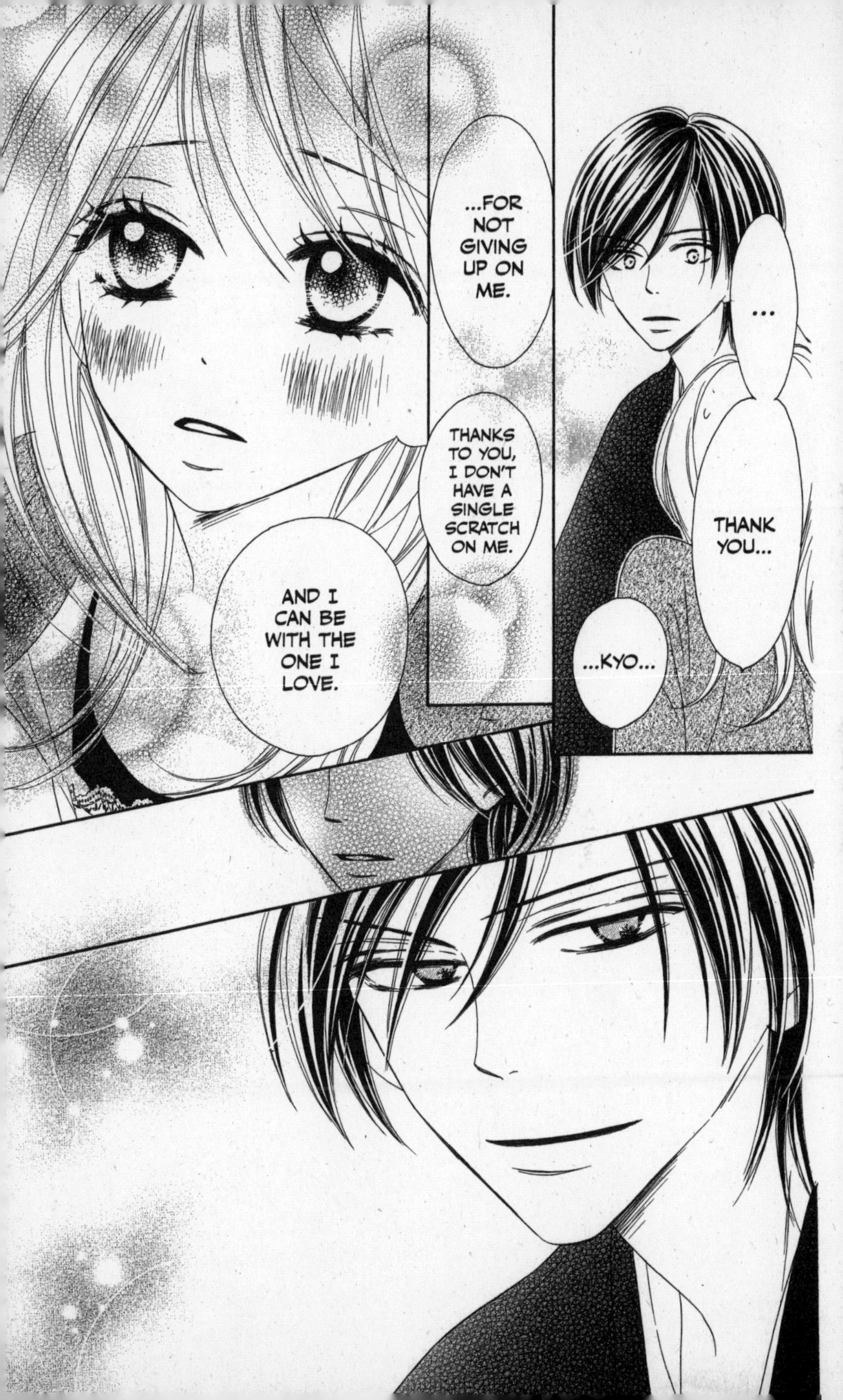
...
THANK YOU...
...KYO...
...FOR NOT GIVING UP ON ME.
THANKS TO YOU, I DON'T HAVE A SINGLE SCRATCH ON ME.
AND I CAN BE WITH THE ONE I LOVE.

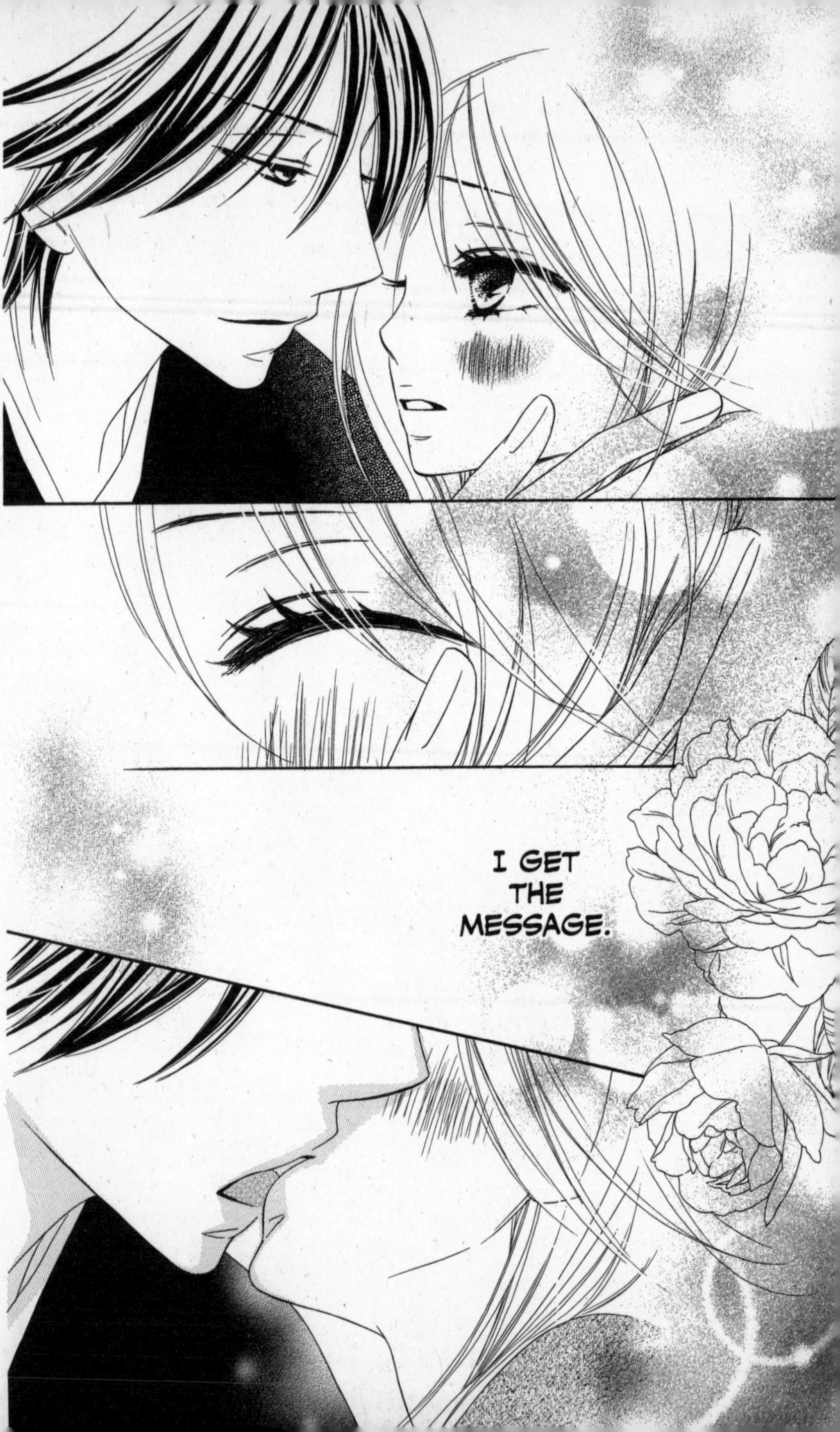
I GET THE MESSAGE.

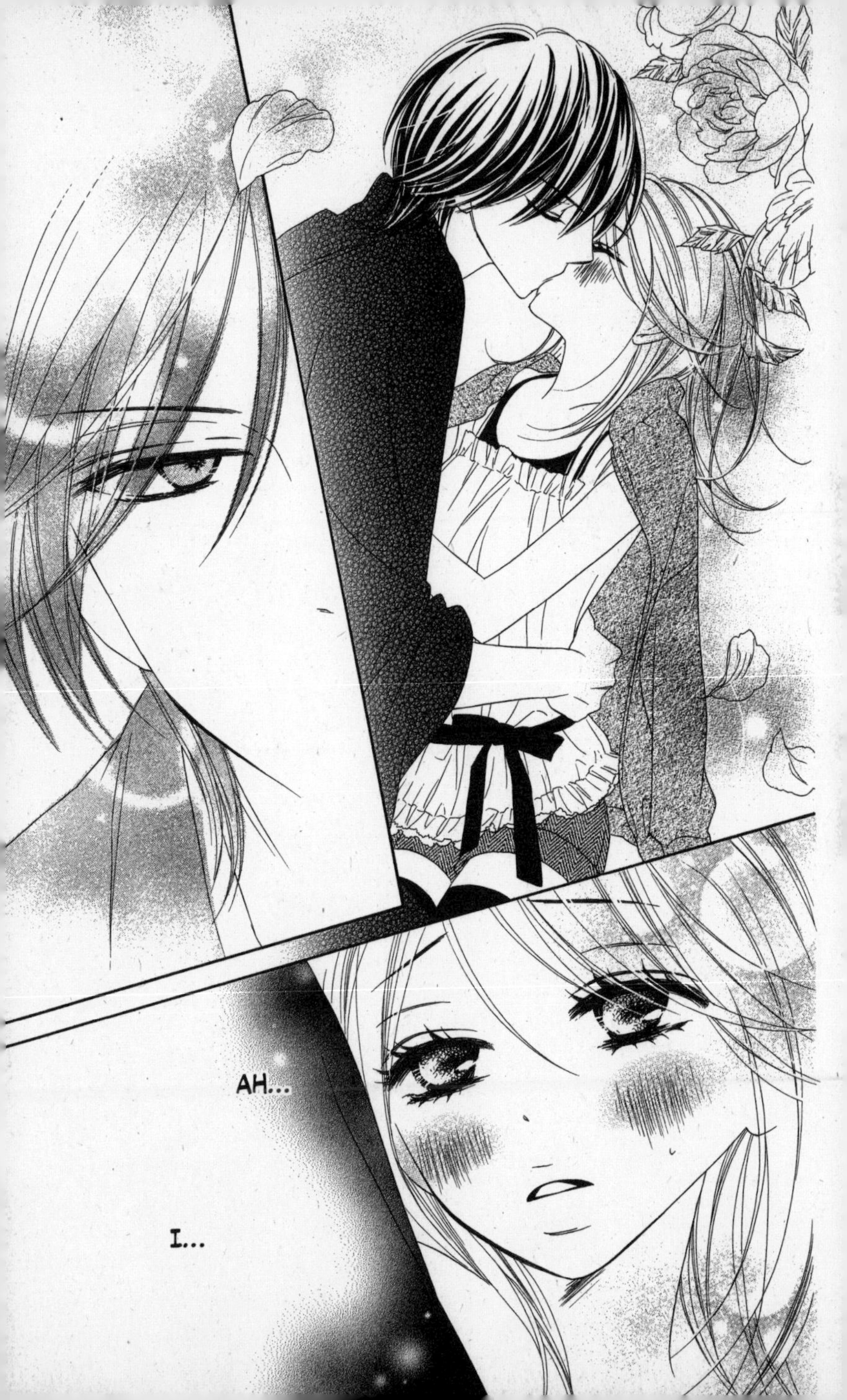
AH...
I...

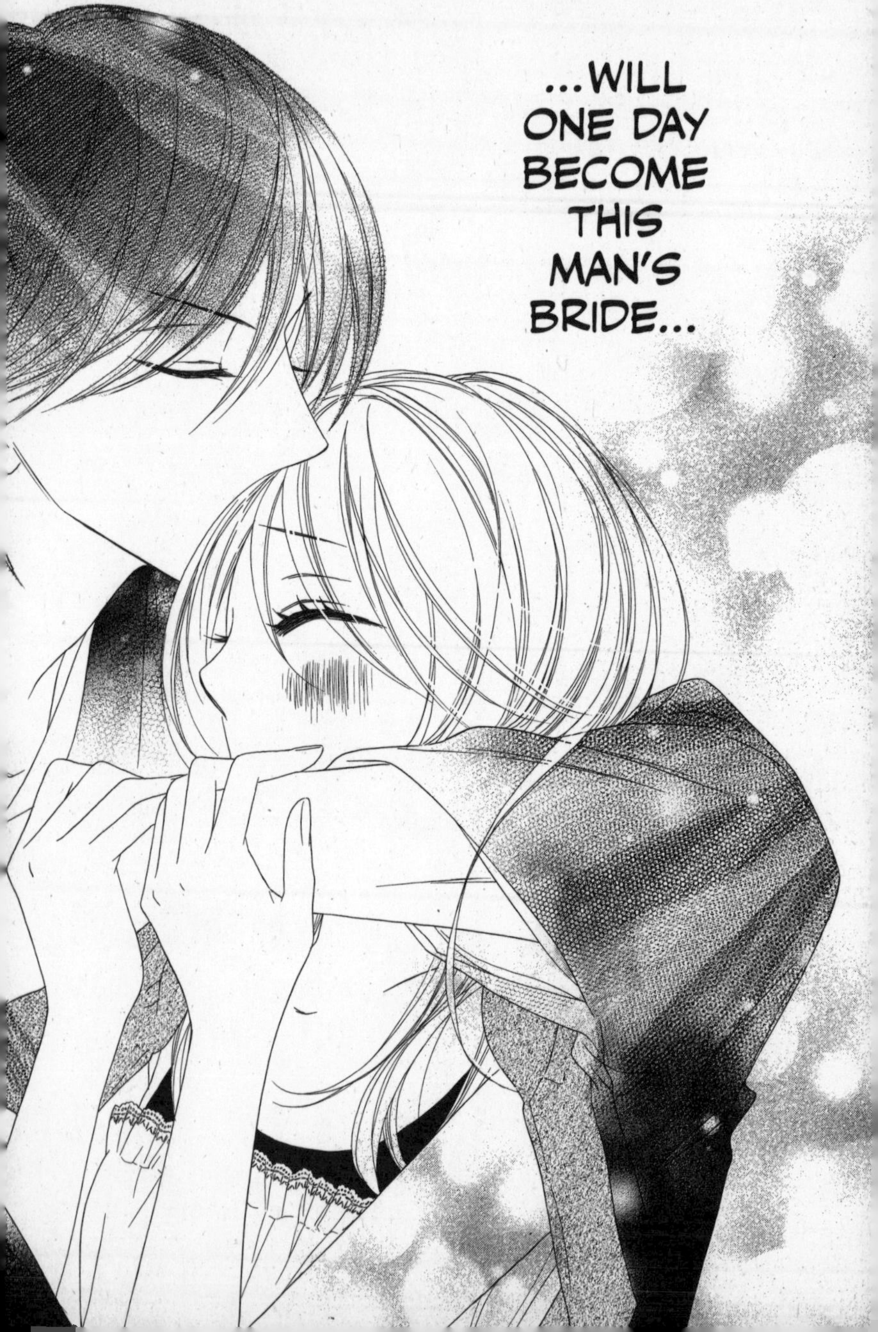
...WILL ONE DAY BECOME THIS MAN'S BRIDE...

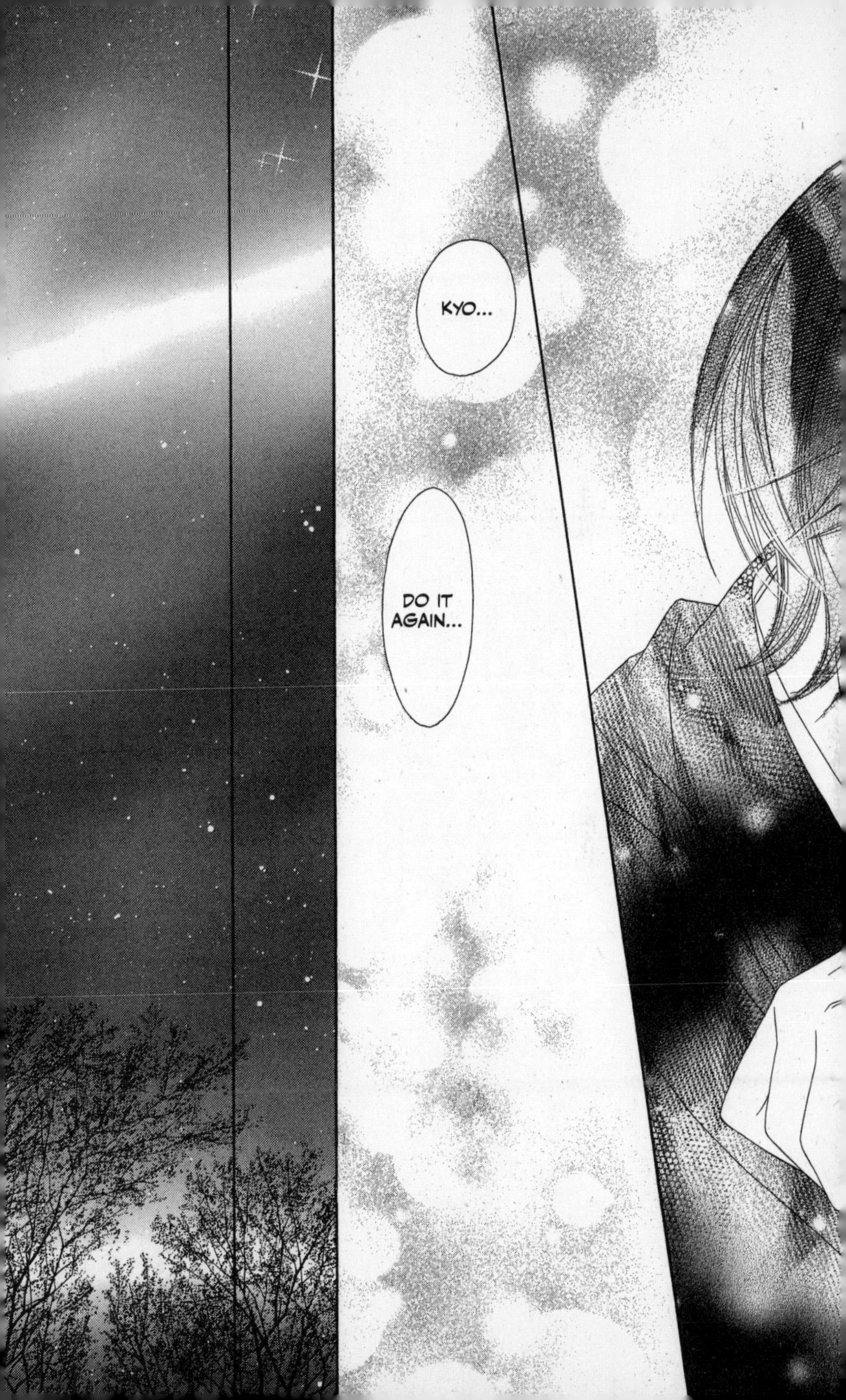
KYO...
DO IT AGAIN...

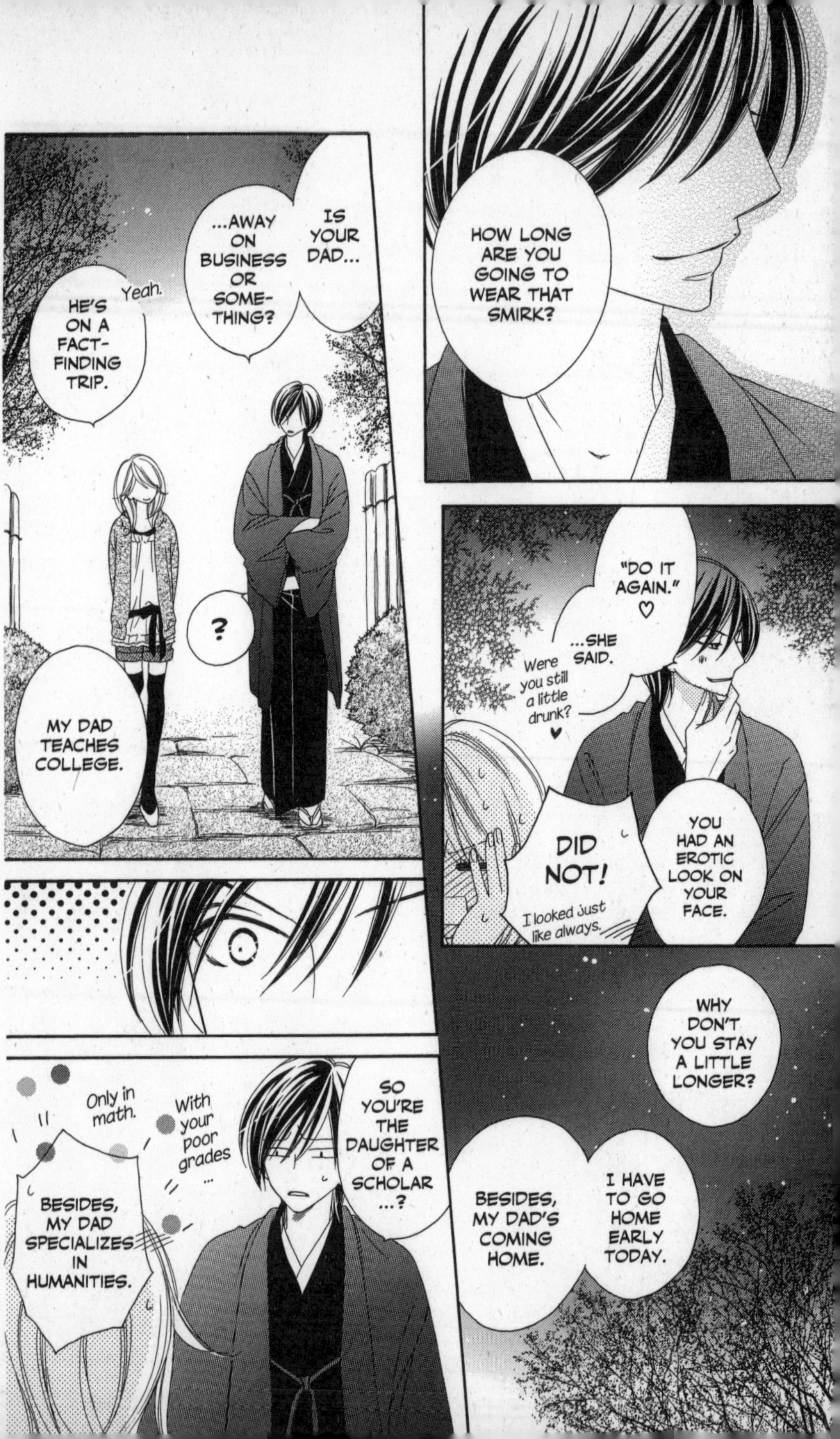
HOW LONG ARE YOU GOING TO WEAR THAT SMIRK?
"DO IT AGAIN." ♡
...SHE SAID.
Were you still a little drunk? ♥
YOU HAD AN EROTIC LOOK ON YOUR FACE.
DID NOT!
I looked just like always.
WHY DON'T YOU STAY A LITTLE LONGER?
I HAVE TO GO HOME EARLY TODAY.
BESIDES, MY DAD'S COMING HOME.
IS YOUR DAD...
...AWAY ON BUSINESS OR SOME-THING?
Yeah.
HE'S ON A FACT-FINDING TRIP.
?
MY DAD TEACHES COLLEGE.
SO YOU'RE THE DAUGHTER OF A SCHOLAR ...?
With your poor grades ...
Only in math.
BESIDES, MY DAD SPECIALIZES IN HUMANITIES.

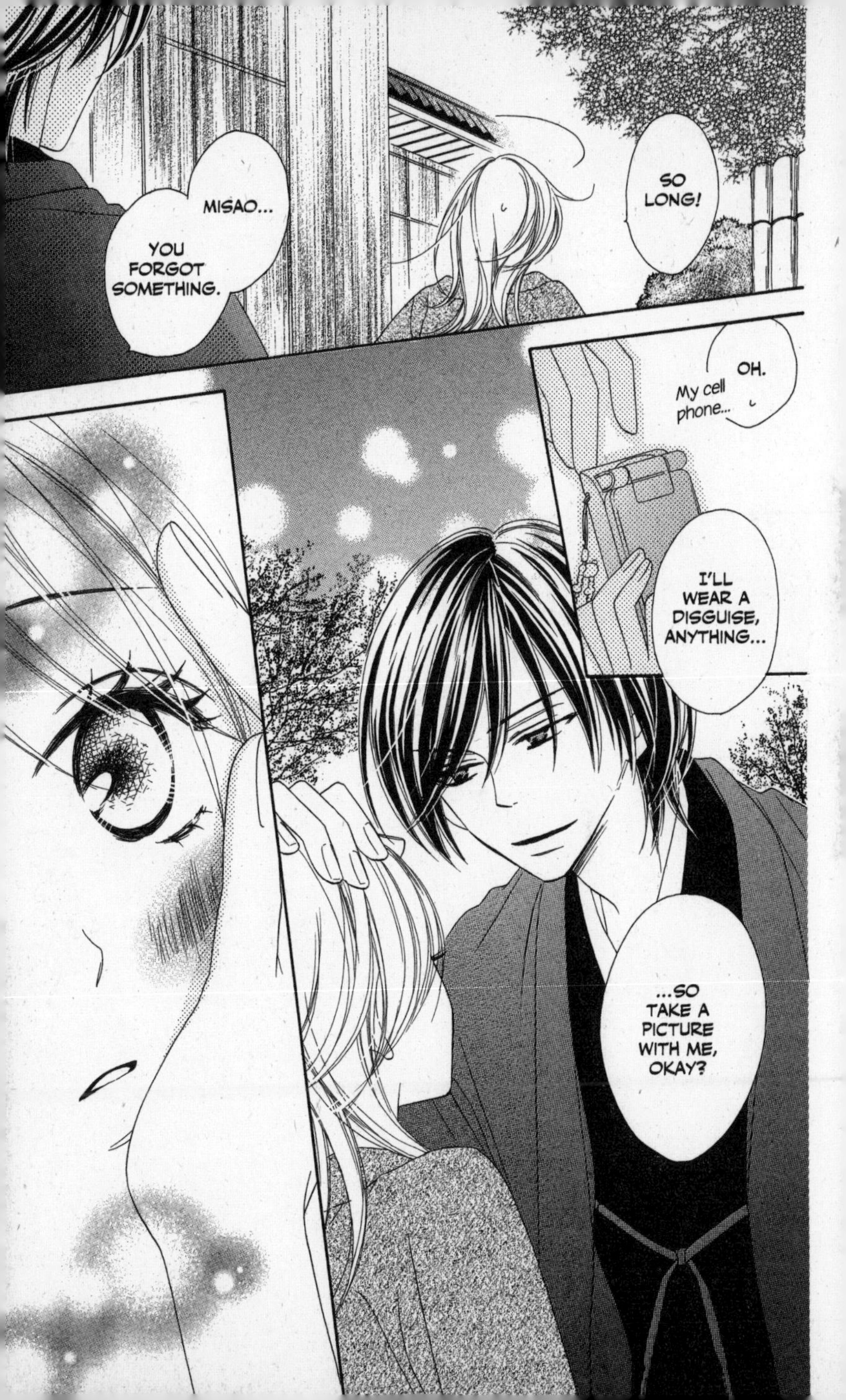
SO LONG!
MISAO...
YOU FORGOT SOMETHING.
OH.
My cell phone...
I'LL WEAR A DISGUISE, ANYTHING...
...SO TAKE A PICTURE WITH ME, OKAY?

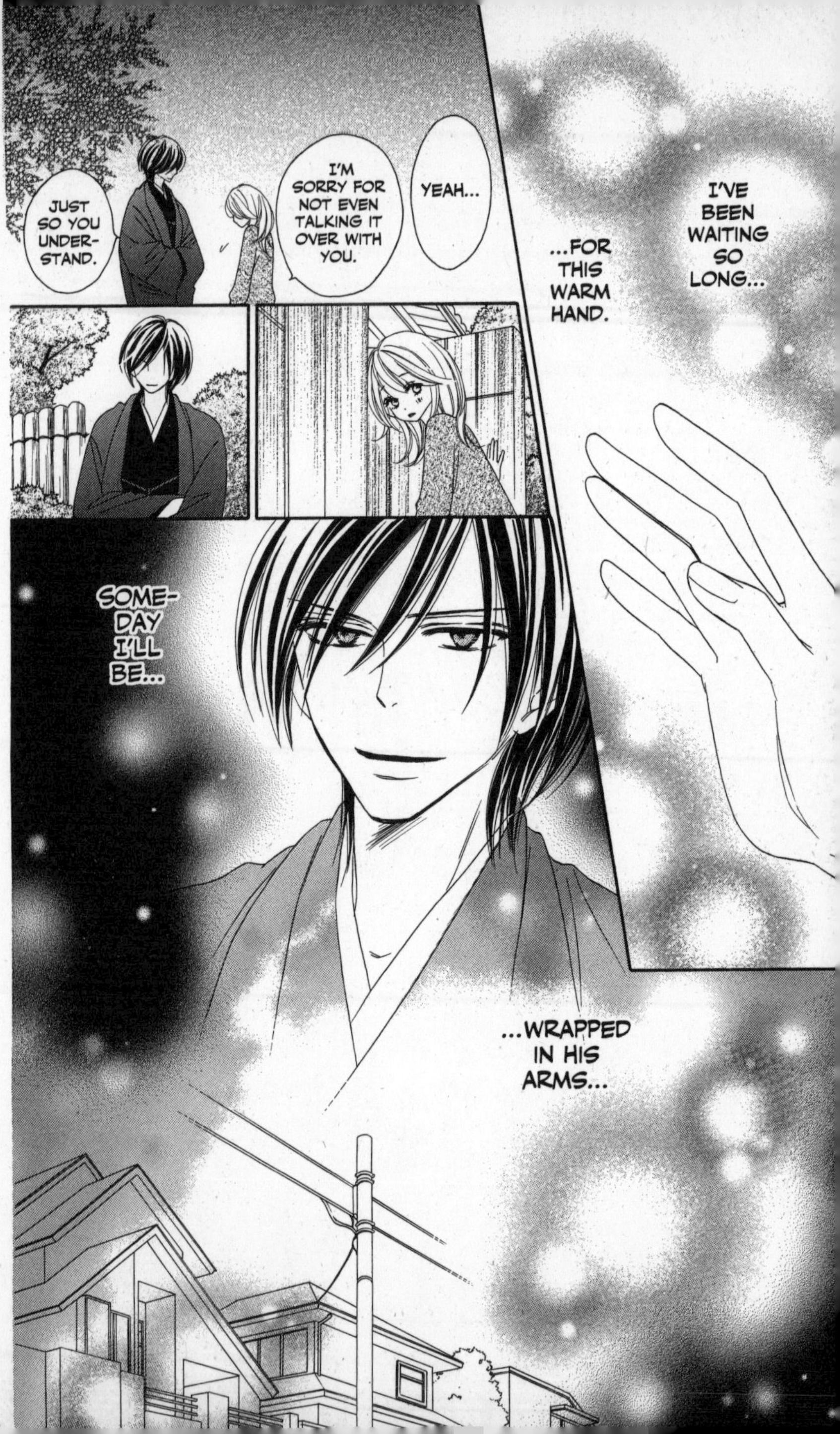

I'VE BEEN WAITING SO LONG...
...FOR THIS WARM HAND.
YEAH...
I'M SORRY FOR NOT EVEN TALKING IT OVER WITH YOU.
JUST SO YOU UNDER-STAND.
SOME-DAY I'LL BE...
...WRAPPED IN HIS ARMS...

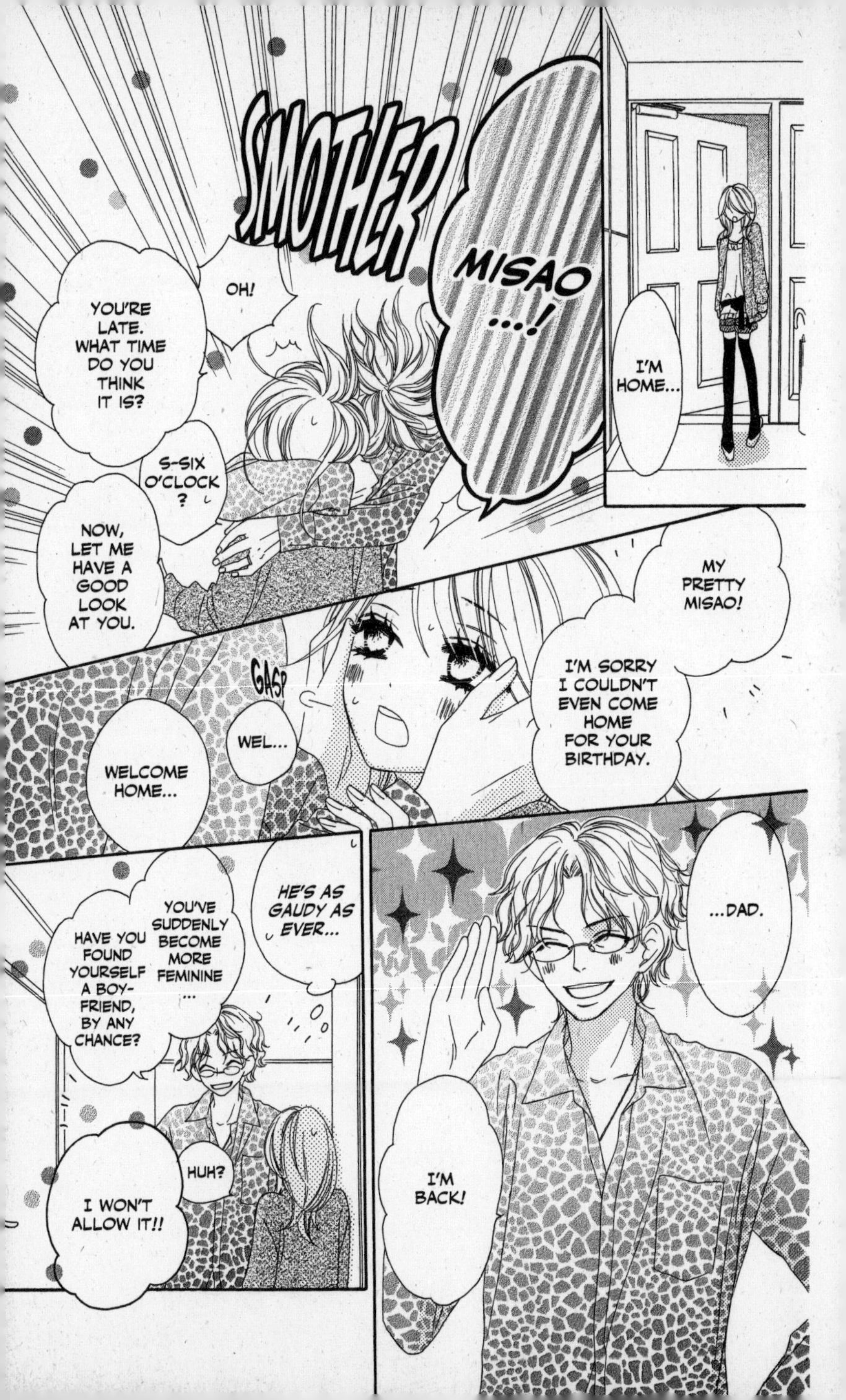
I'M HOME...
MISAO ...!
SMOTHER
OH!
YOU'RE LATE. WHAT TIME DO YOU THINK IT IS?
S-SIX O'CLOCK?
NOW, LET ME HAVE A GOOD LOOK AT YOU.
MY PRETTY MISAO!
I'M SORRY I COULDN'T EVEN COME HOME FOR YOUR BIRTHDAY.
GASP
WEL...
WELCOME HOME...
...DAD.
I'M BACK!
HE'S AS GAUDY AS EVER...
YOU'VE SUDDENLY BECOME MORE FEMININE...
HAVE YOU FOUND YOURSELF A BOY-FRIEND, BY ANY CHANCE?
HUH?
I WON'T ALLOW IT!!

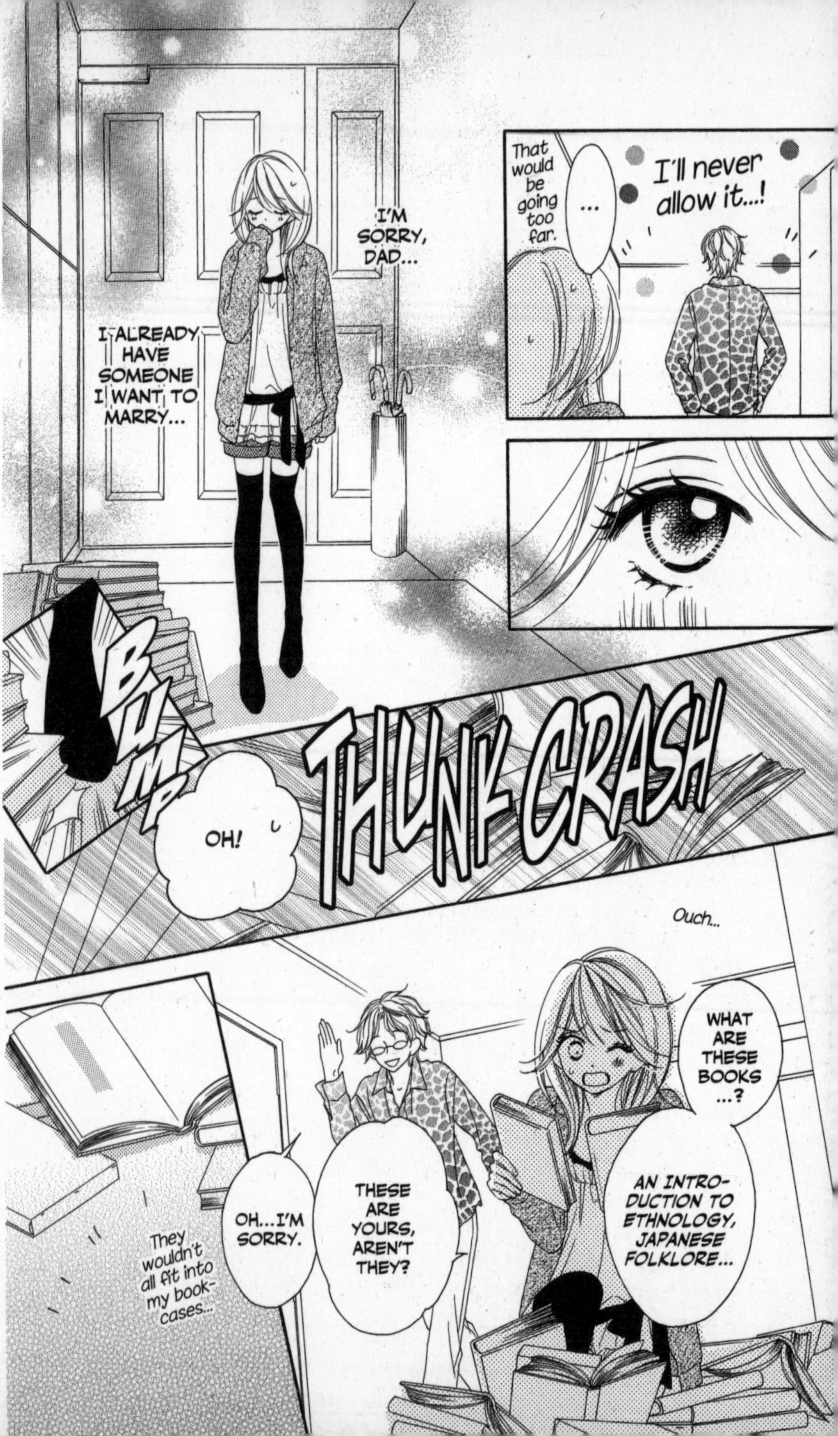
That would be going too far.
...
I'll never allow it...!
I'M SORRY, DAD...
I ALREADY HAVE SOMEONE I WANT TO MARRY...
THUNK CRASH
BUMP
OH!
Ouch...
WHAT ARE THESE BOOKS ...?
AN INTRODUCTION TO ETHNOLOGY, JAPANESE FOLKLORE...
THESE ARE YOURS, AREN'T THEY?
OH...I'M SORRY.
They wouldn't all fit into my book-cases...

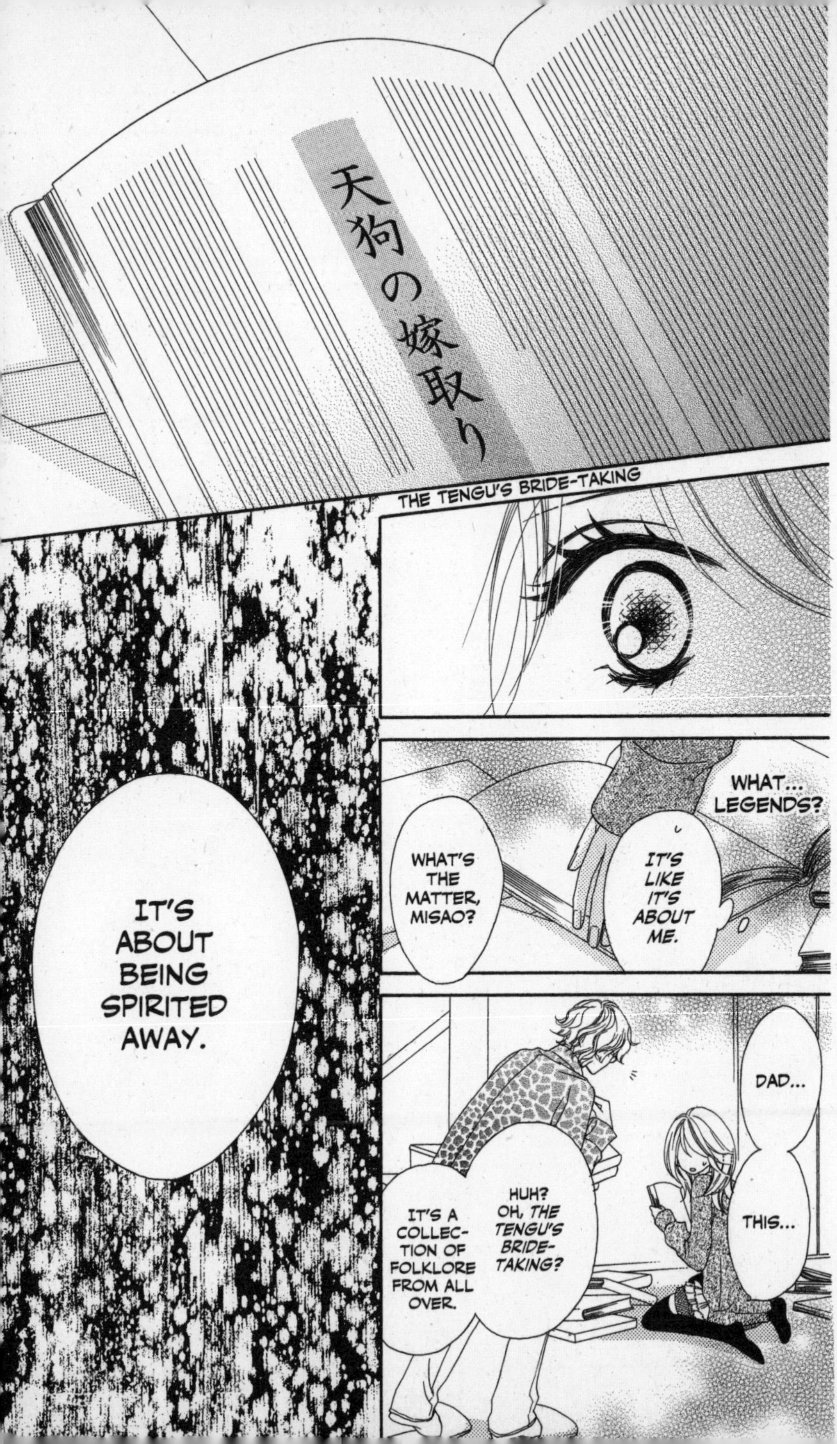

天狗の嫁取り
THE TENGU'S BRIDE-TAKING
WHAT... LEGENDS?
IT'S LIKE IT'S ABOUT ME.
WHAT'S THE MATTER, MISAO?
DAD...
THIS...
HUH? OH, THE TENGU'S BRIDE-TAKING?
IT'S A COLLECTION OF FOLKLORE FROM ALL OVER.
IT'S ABOUT BEING SPIRITED AWAY.

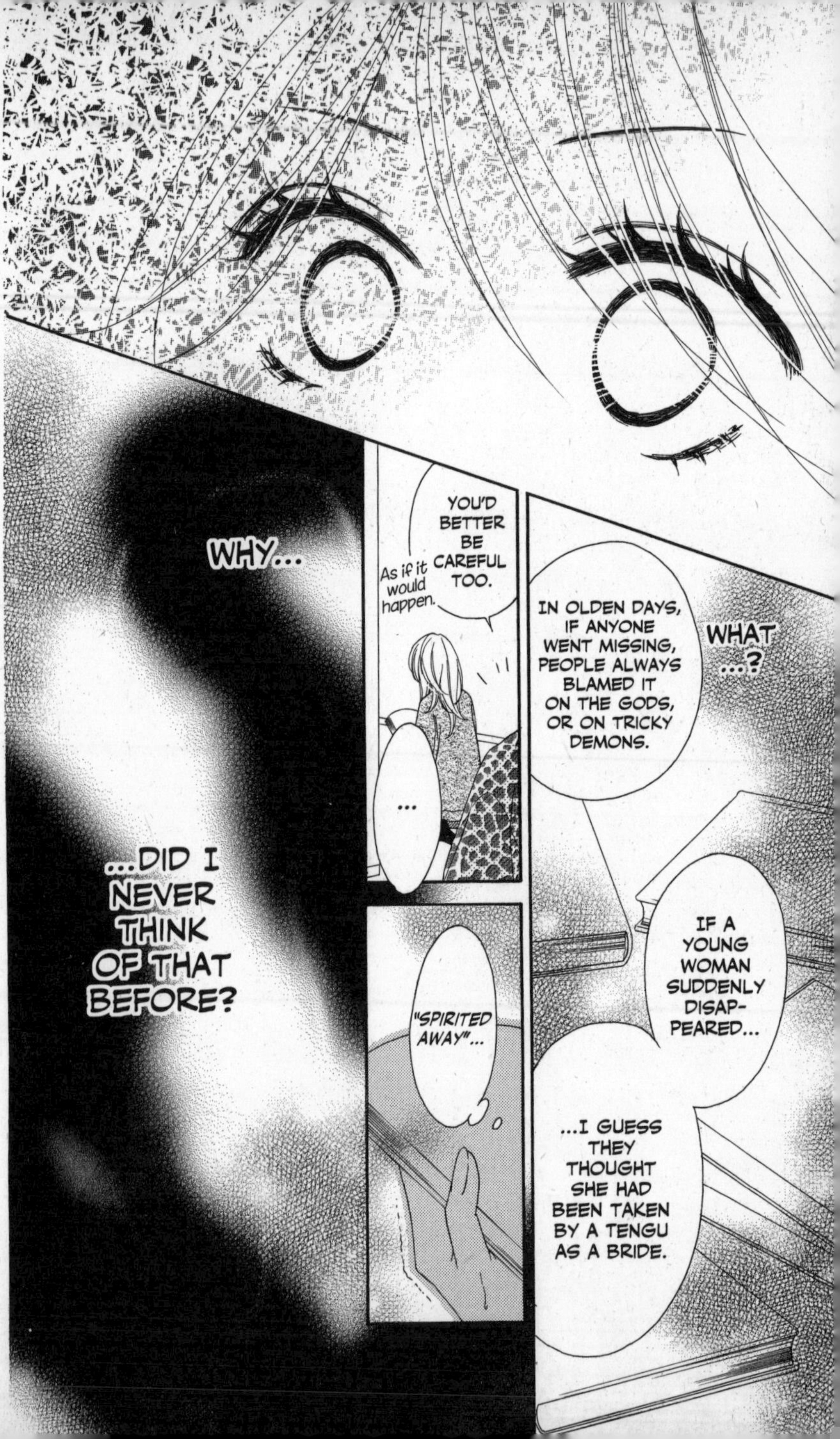
IN OLDEN DAYS, IF ANYONE WENT MISSING, PEOPLE ALWAYS BLAMED IT ON THE GODS, OR ON TRICKY DEMONS.
WHAT ...?
IF A YOUNG WOMAN SUDDENLY DISAP-PEARED...
...I GUESS THEY THOUGHT SHE HAD BEEN TAKEN BY A TENGU AS A BRIDE.
YOU'D BETTER BE CAREFUL TOO.
As if it would happen.
...
"SPIRITED AWAY"...
WHY...
...DID I NEVER THINK OF THAT BEFORE?

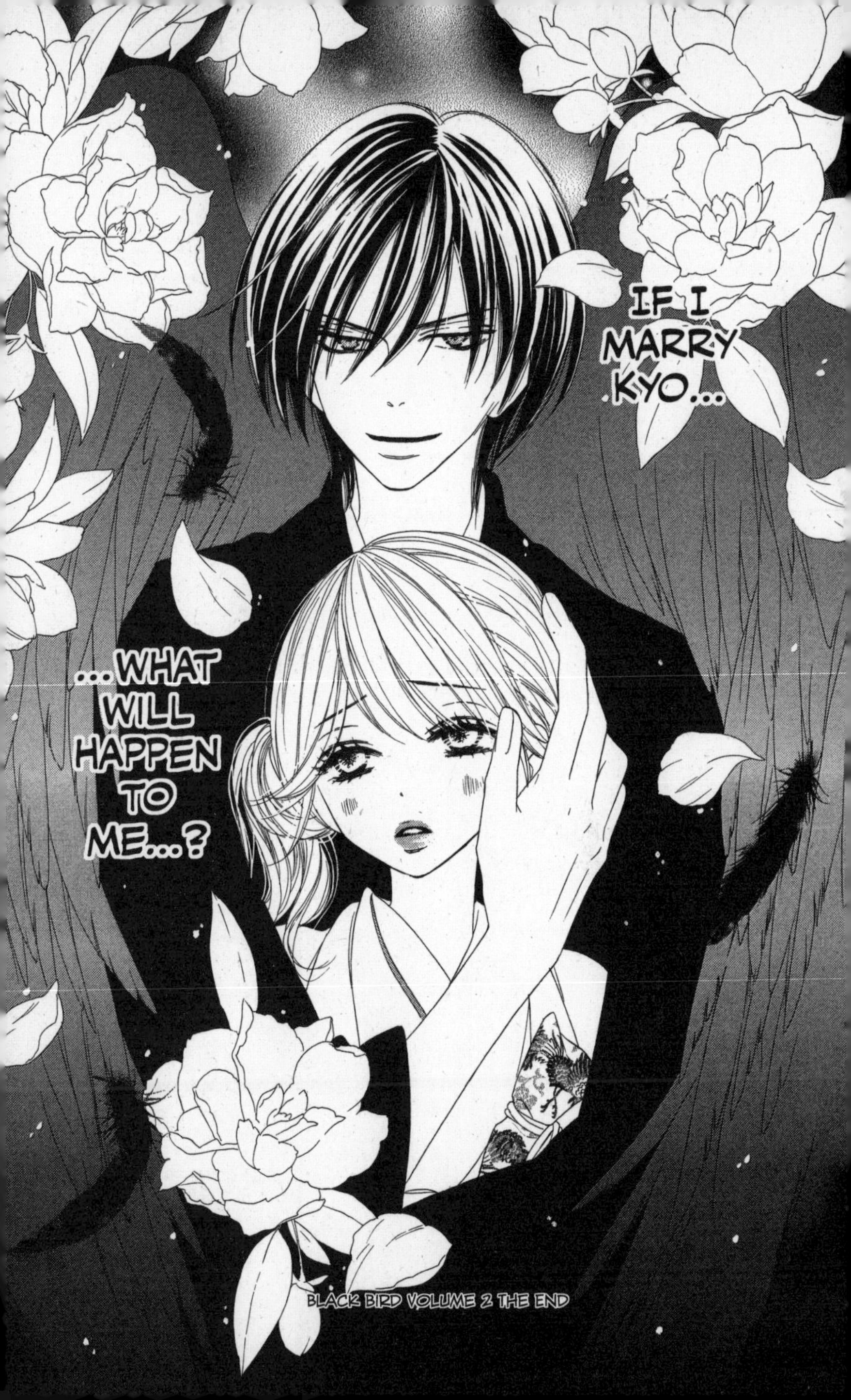
IF I MARRY KYO...
...WHAT WILL HAPPEN TO ME...?
BLACK BIRD VOLUME 2 THE END

←The Special Feature that follows was drawn sometime after chapter 4. (As far as the contents are concerned, this story comes before chapter 4.) The drawings are a little different... there's the soft glow of love.

Black Bird continues in volume 3 thanks to all of your support!

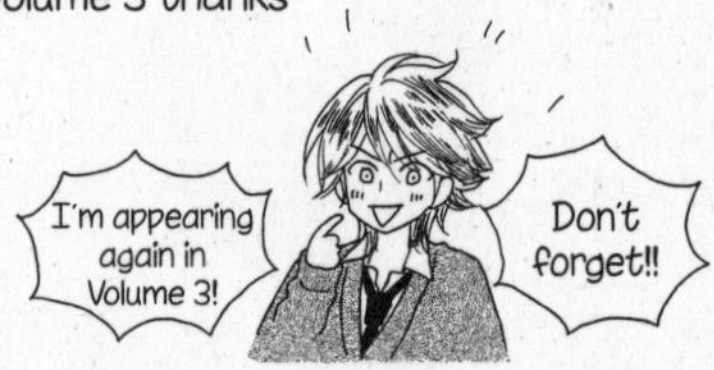
Don't forget!!
I'm appearing again in Volume 3!

I am always praying for the happiness of all of you who support me, and read my books.

May 2007 Kanoko Sakurakoji

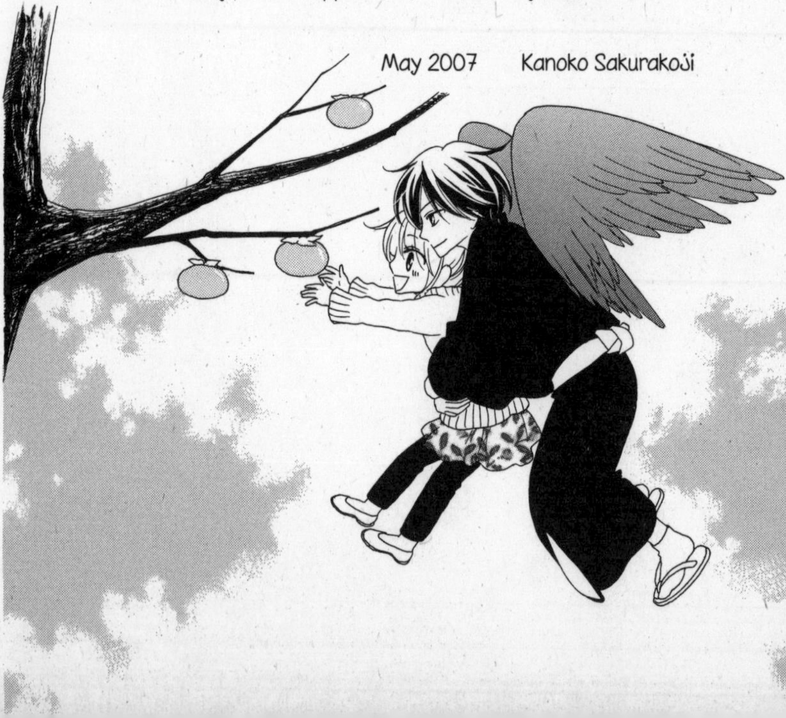

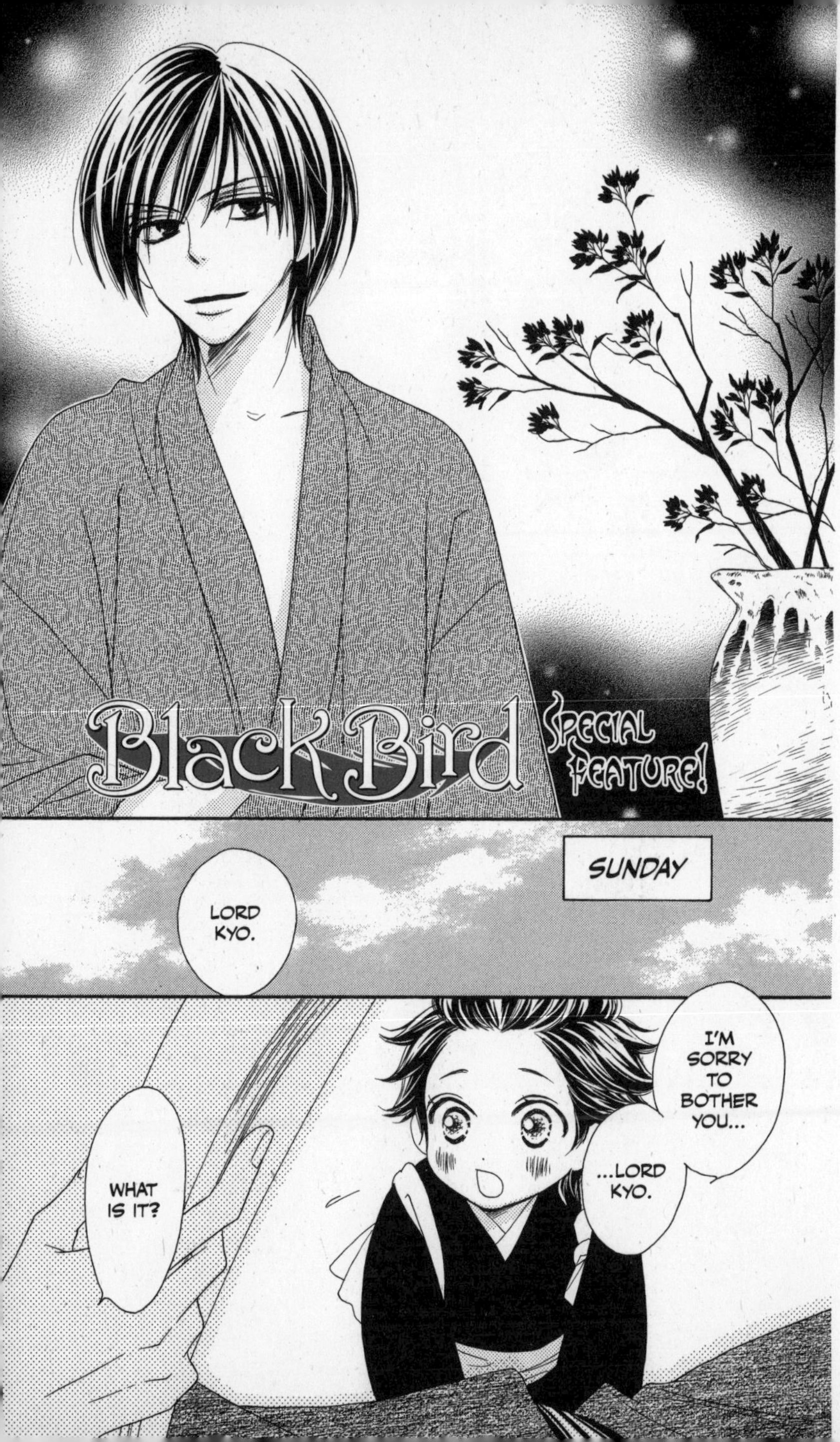
Black Bird
Special Feature!
SUNDAY
LORD KYO.
I'M SORRY TO BOTHER YOU...
...LORD KYO.
WHAT IS IT?

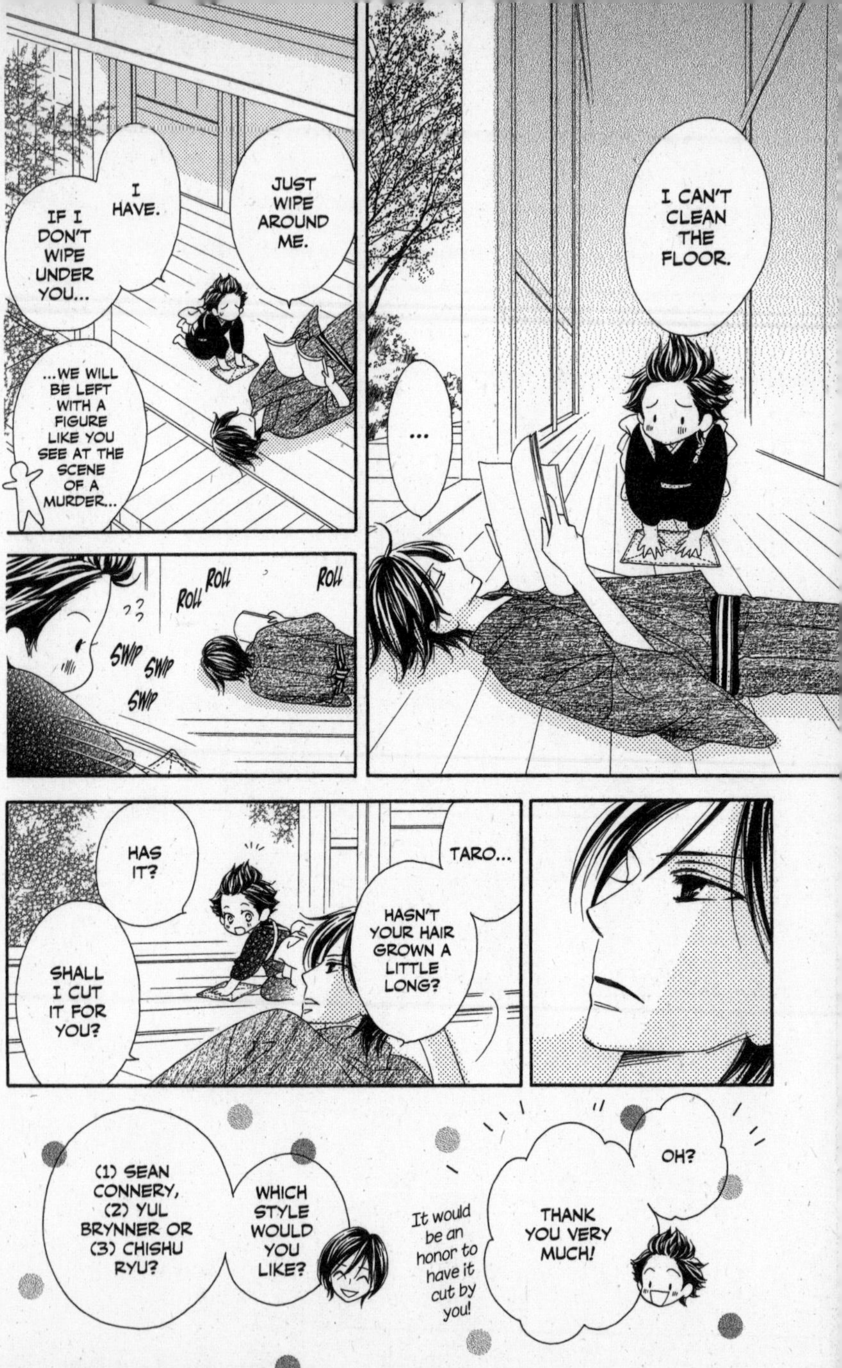
I CAN'T CLEAN THE FLOOR.
...
JUST WIPE AROUND ME.
I HAVE.
IF I DON'T WIPE UNDER YOU...
...WE WILL BE LEFT WITH A FIGURE LIKE YOU SEE AT THE SCENE OF A MURDER...
ROLL ROLL ROLL
SWIP SWIP SWIP
TARO...
HASN'T YOUR HAIR GROWN A LITTLE LONG?
HAS IT?
SHALL I CUT IT FOR YOU?
OH?
THANK YOU VERY MUCH!
It would be an honor to have it cut by you!
WHICH STYLE WOULD YOU LIKE?
(1) SEAN CONNERY, (2) YUL BRYNNER OR (3) CHISHU RYU?

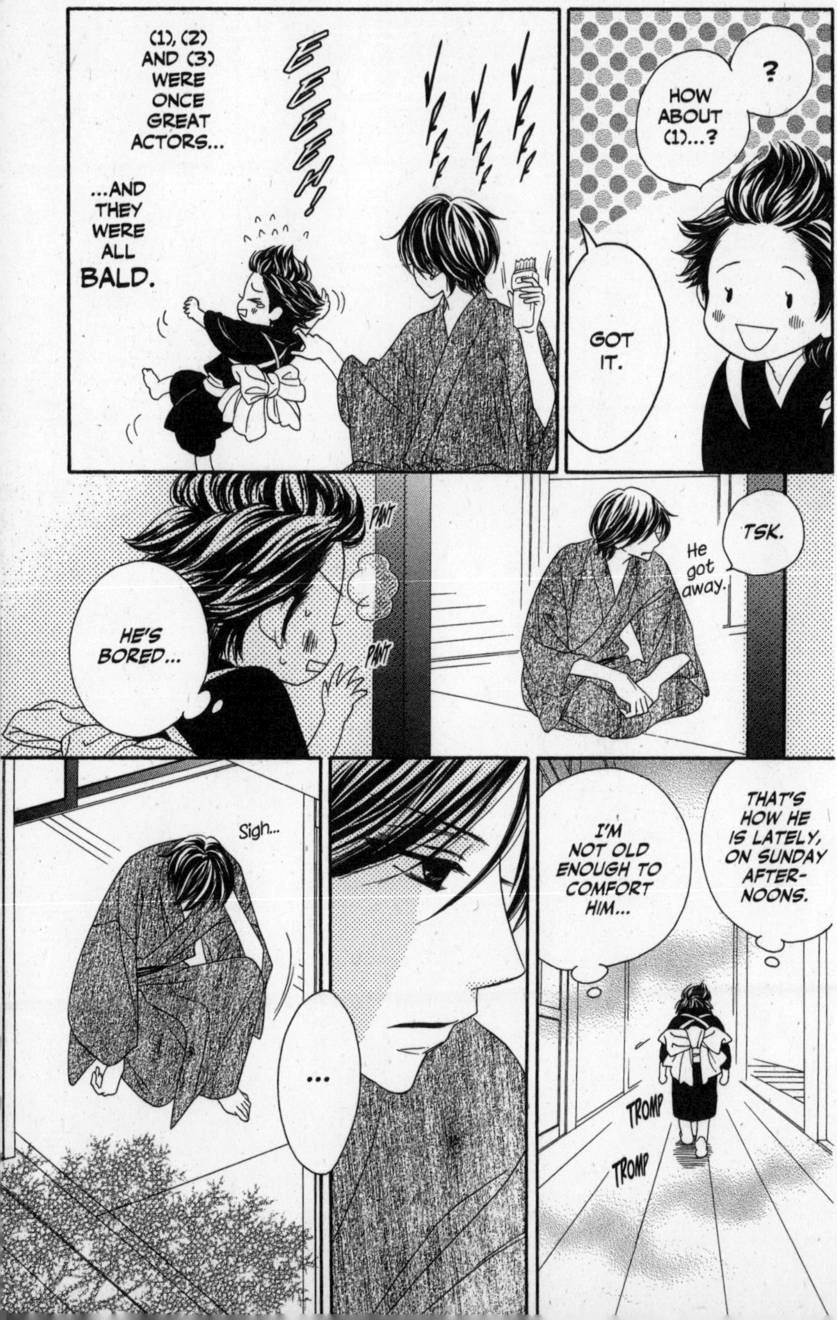
?
HOW ABOUT (1)...?
GOT IT.
(1), (2) AND (3) WERE ONCE GREAT ACTORS...
...AND THEY WERE ALL BALD.
EEEEEH!
TSK.
He got away.
PANT
PANT
HE'S BORED...
THAT'S HOW HE IS LATELY, ON SUNDAY AFTERNOONS.
I'M NOT OLD ENOUGH TO COMFORT HIM...
TROMP
TROMP
...
Sigh...

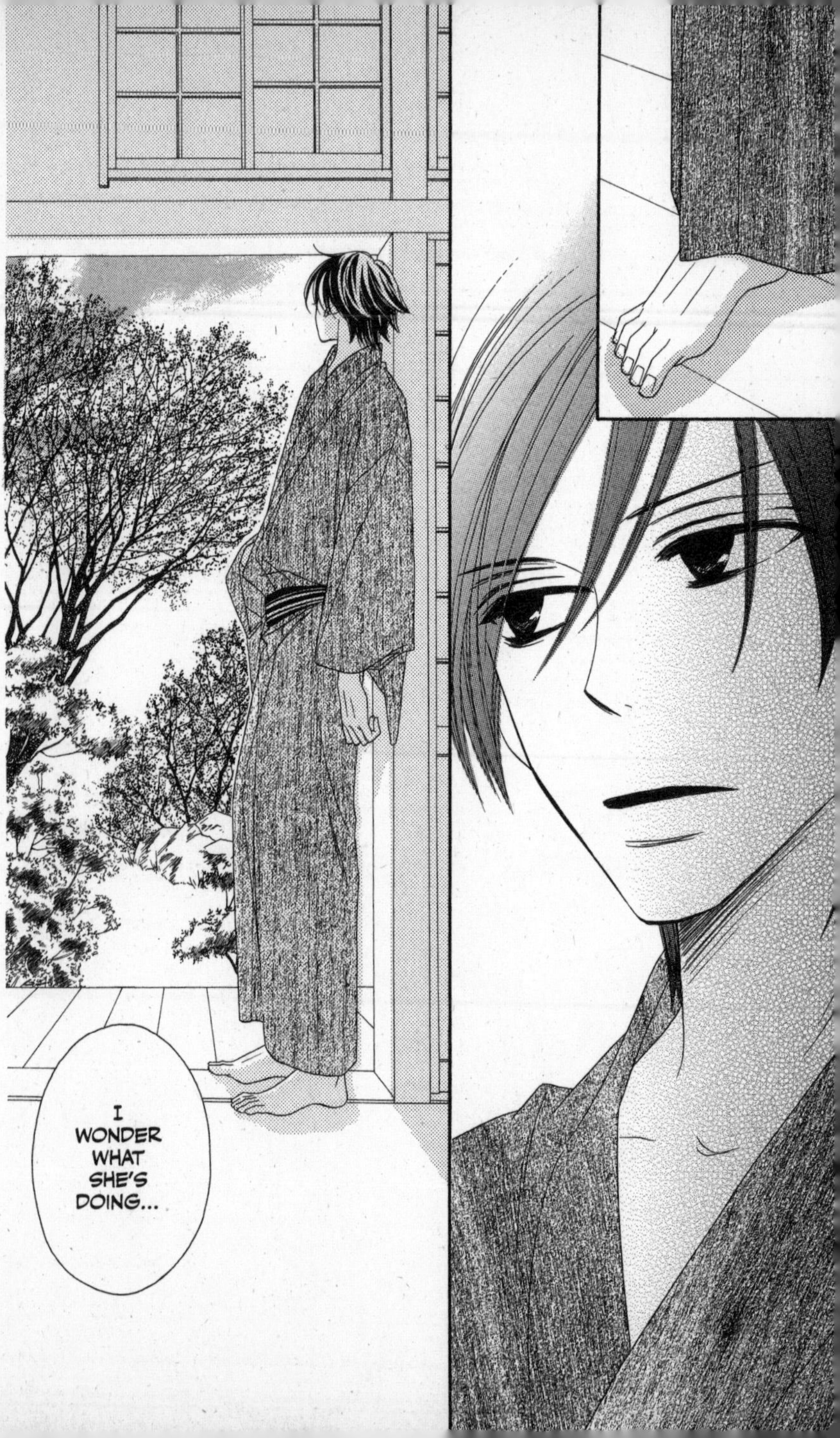
I WONDER WHAT SHE'S DOING...

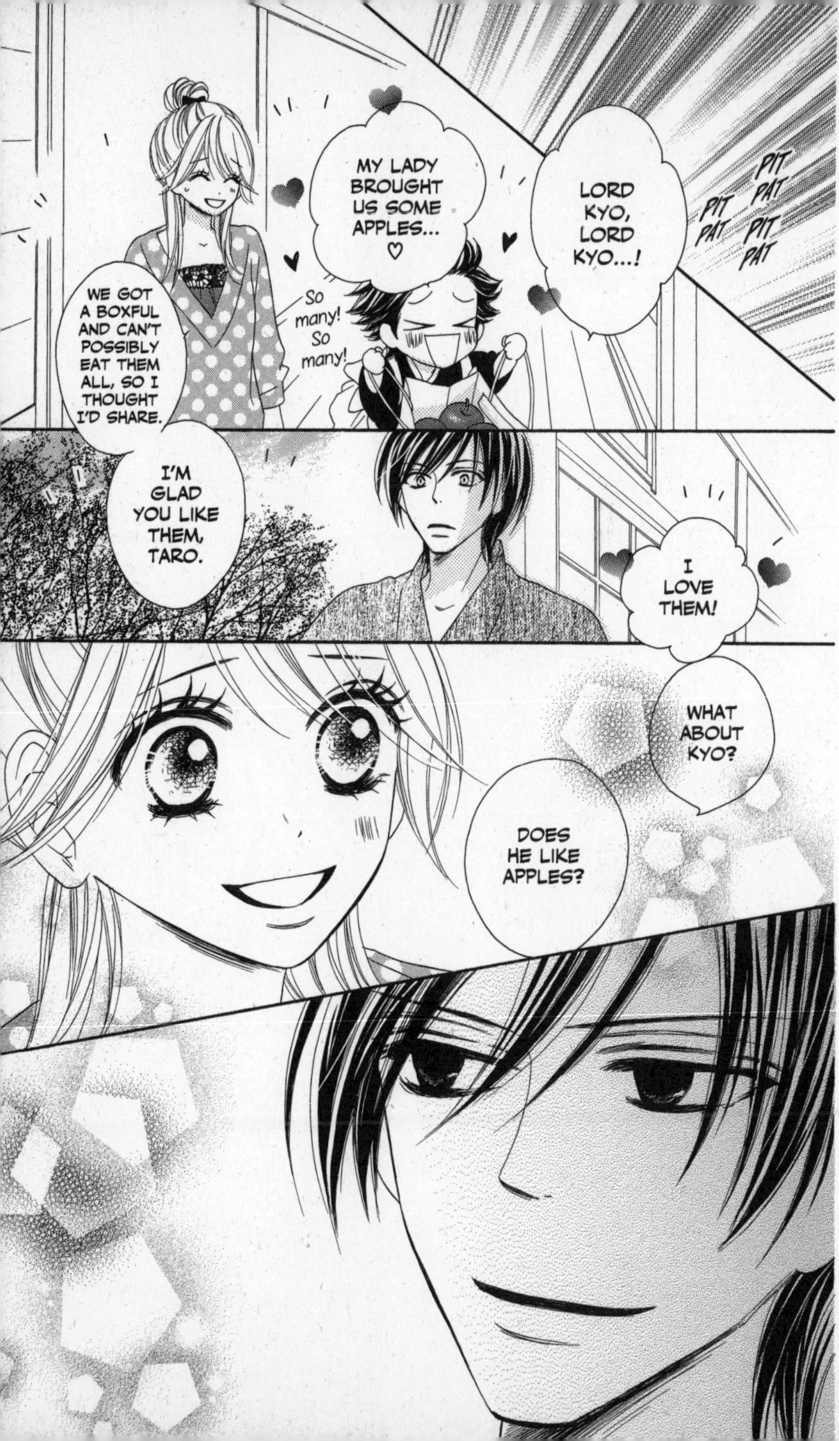
PIT PAT PIT PAT PIT PAT
LORD KYO, LORD KYO...!
MY LADY BROUGHT US SOME APPLES... ♡
So many! So many!
WE GOT A BOXFUL AND CAN'T POSSIBLY EAT THEM ALL, SO I THOUGHT I'D SHARE.
I LOVE THEM!
I'M GLAD YOU LIKE THEM, TARO.
WHAT ABOUT KYO?
DOES HE LIKE APPLES?

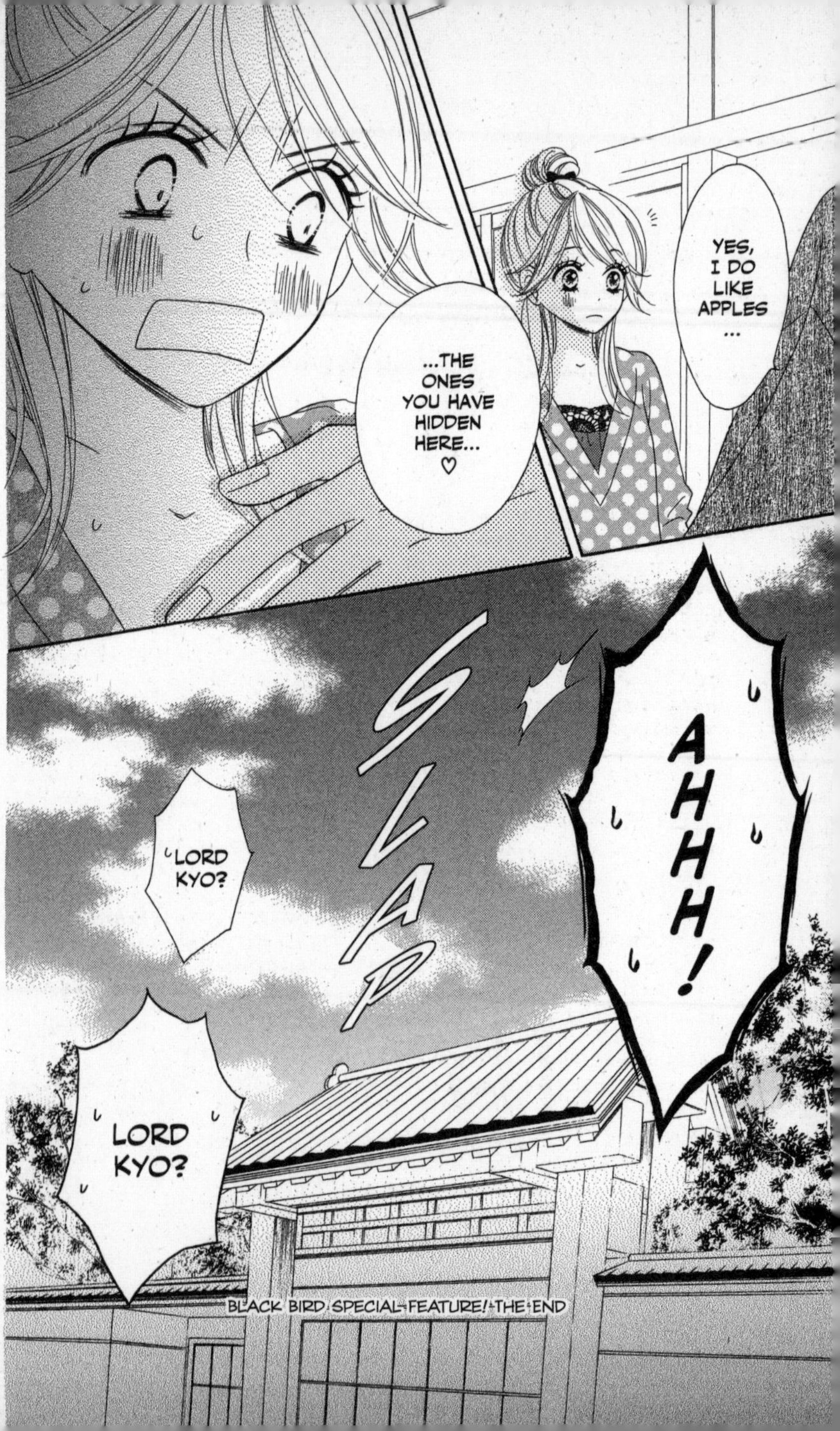

YES, I DO LIKE APPLES...
...THE ONES YOU HAVE HIDDEN HERE... ♡
AHHH!
SLAP
LORD KYO?
LORD KYO?
BLACK BIRD SPECIAL FEATURE! THE END

GLOSSARY

PAGE 15, PANEL 3: *Daitengu*
Literally means "great tengu." In Japanese folklore, tengu are sometimes divided into daitengu and kotengu (small tengu) based on intelligence or power.

PAGE 16, PANEL 1: *Host club*
Host clubs are a type of bar that caters to female patrons. Attractive men pour drinks, flirt and make conversation with the patrons.

PAGE 20, PANEL 3: *Spirits to rot*
In Japanese, "rot" implies an abundance of something, making the phrase somewhat similar to "money to burn."

PAGE 137, PANEL 2: *Let's celebrate*
In the original Japanese he says, "Let's cook sekihan tonight." Sekihan (red bean rice, 赤飯) is a dish that usually accompanies a celebration of something momentous such as a graduation from high school, a first paycheck, etc.

PAGE 138: *Kurama tengu, Ushiwakamaru*
The daitengu Sōjōbō, who lived on Mt. Kurama. Ushiwakamaru was the child-hood name of Minamoto no Yoshitsune, a famous 12th century Japanese warrior and younger brother of the founder of the Kamakura shogunate.

PAGE 149, PANEL 5: *No honorifics*
Sagami is much older than Hoki, so normally Hoki would show his respect by using honorifics and a more formal Japanese grammar. It's a sign of the closeness of their relationship that he uses more relaxed language.

PAGE 156, PANEL 5: *Yokan*
Yokan is a Japanese sweet usually made of red bean paste, sugar and agar. The agar gives it a firm, somewhat gelati-nous consistency.

PAGE 186, PANEL 6: *Chishu Ryu*
A famous Japanese actor who appeared in over 300 films. 1904–1993.

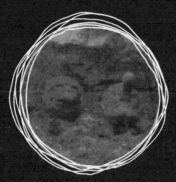

Kanoko Sakurakoji was born in downtown
Tokyo, and her hobbies include reading,
watching plays, traveling and shopping. Her
debut title, *Raibu ga Hanetara*, ran in *Bessatsu
Shojo Comic* (currently called *Bestucomi*) in
2000, and her 2004 *Bestucomi* title *Backstage
Prince* was serialized in VIZ Media's
Shojo Beat magazine. She won the 54th
Shogakukan Manga Award for *Black Bird*.

BLACK BIRD

VOL. 2
Shojo Beat Manga Edition

Story and Art by KANOKO SAKURAKOJI

TRANSLATION JN Productions
TOUCH-UP ART & LETTERING Gia Cam Luc
DESIGN Courtney Utt
EDITOR Pancha Diaz

VP, PRODUCTION Alvin Lu
VP, PUBLISHING LICENSING Rika Inouye
VP, SALES & PRODUCT MARKETING Gonzalo Ferreyra
VP, CREATIVE Linda Espinosa
PUBLISHER Hyoe Narita

BLACK BIRD 2 by Kanoko SAKURAKOUJI © 2007 Kanoko SAKURAKOUJI
All rights reserved. Original Japanese edition published in 2007
by Shogakukan Inc., Tokyo.

The rights of the author(s) of the work(s) in this publication
to be so identified have been asserted in accordance with
the Copyright, Designs and Patents Act 1988. A CIP catalogue
record for this book is available from the British Library.

Published by VIZ Media, LLC
P.O. Box 77010
San Francisco, CA 94107

10 9 8 7 6 5 4 3 2 1
First printing, November 2009

www.shojobeat.com   www.viz.com

A Past Shrouded in Mystery

BLANK SLATE

by Aya Kanno

Zen's memory has been wiped, and he can't remember if he's a killer or a hero. How far will he go—and how hard will he have to fight—to uncover the secrets of his identity?

Find out in *Blank Slate*—manga on sale now!

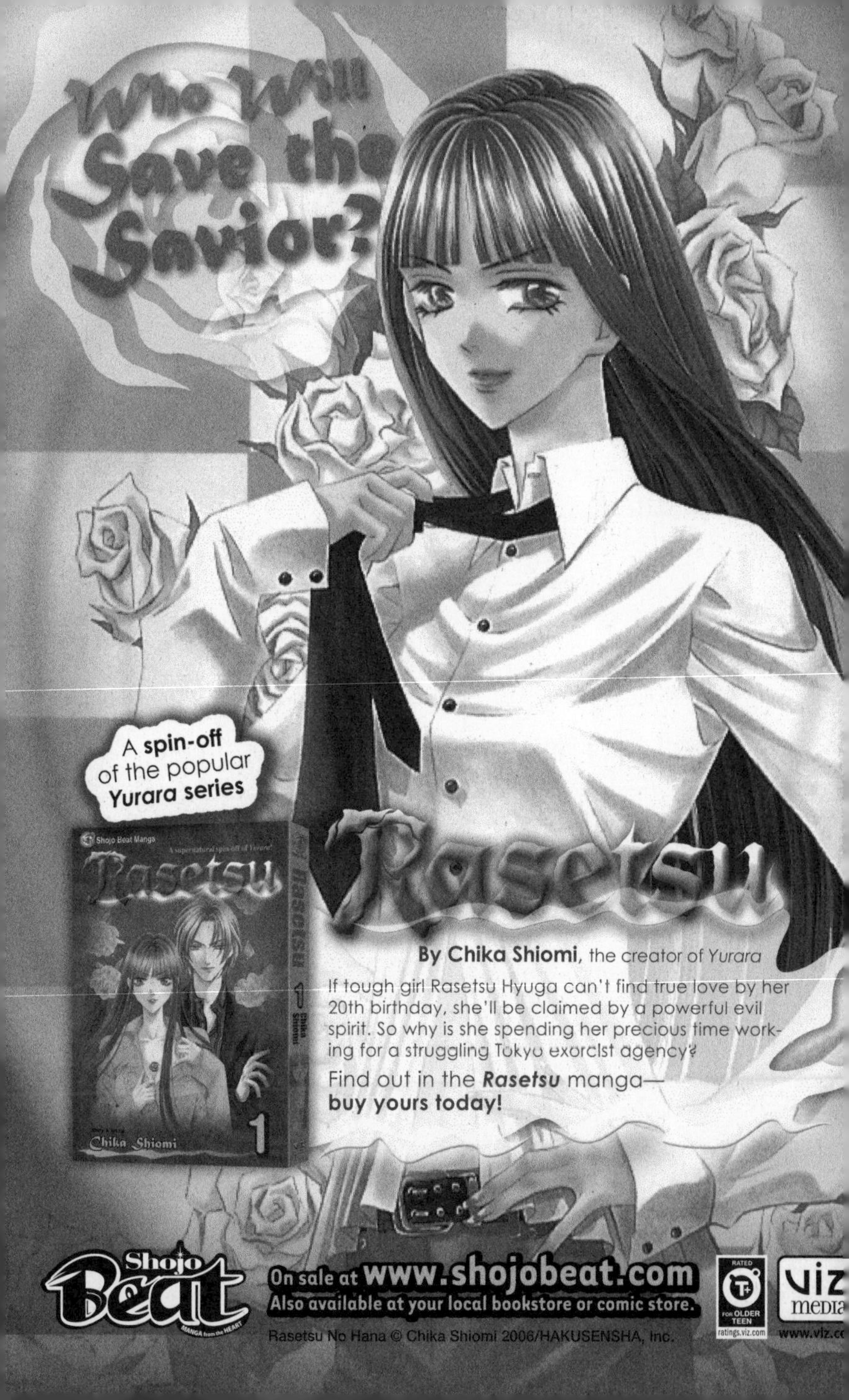
Who Will
Save th
Savior?
A spin-off of the popular Yurara series
Shojo Beat Manga
A supernatural spin-off of Yurara
Rasetsu
1
Chika Shiomi
Rasetsu
By Chika Shiomi, the creator of Yurara
If tough girl Rasetsu Hyuga can't find true love by her 20th birthday, she'll be claimed by a powerful evil spirit. So why is she spending her precious time working for a struggling Tokyo exorcist agency?
Find out in the Rasetsu manga—buy yours today!
Shojo Beat
MANGA from the HEART
On sale at www.shojobeat.com
Also available at your local bookstore or comic store.
RATED T+ FOR OLDER TEEN
ratings.viz.com
VIZ media
Rasetsu No Hana © Chika Shiomi 2006/HAKUSENSHA, Inc.

Hot Gimmick™

Will our hapless heroine ever figure out the game of love? Find out in *Hot Gimmick*—get the complete collection today!

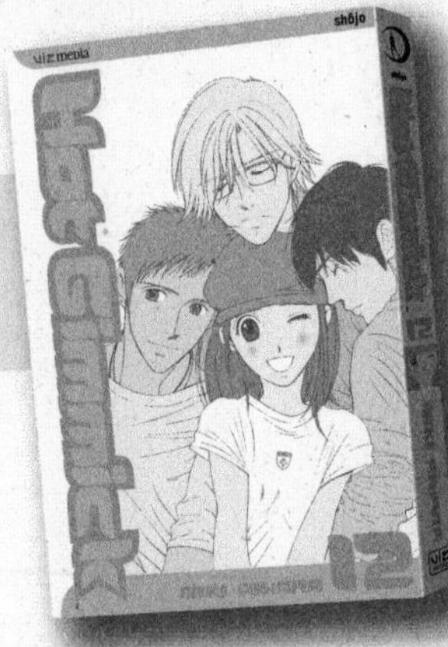

shōjo
viz media
Hot Gimmick
12

Read the original manga—all 12 volumes available now

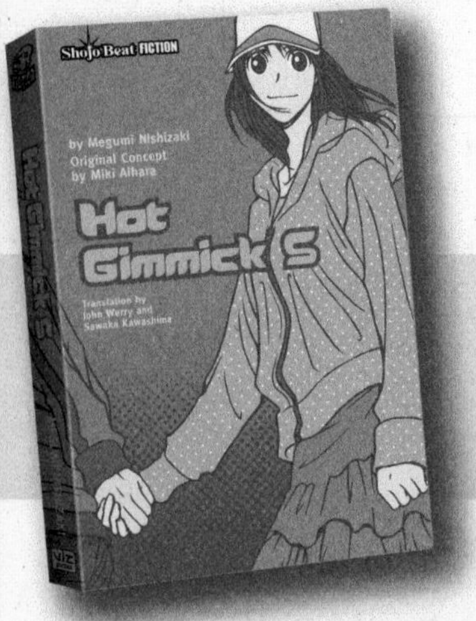

Shojo Beat FICTION
by Megumi Nishizaki
Original Concept by Miki Aihara
Hot Gimmick S
Translation by John Werry and Sawaka Kawashima

SB FICTION

A novelization of the popular manga, with alternate ending and a bonus manga episode!

From the creator of *Tokyo Boys & Girls*—available from our Shojo Beat Manga line

viz media™

www.viz.com

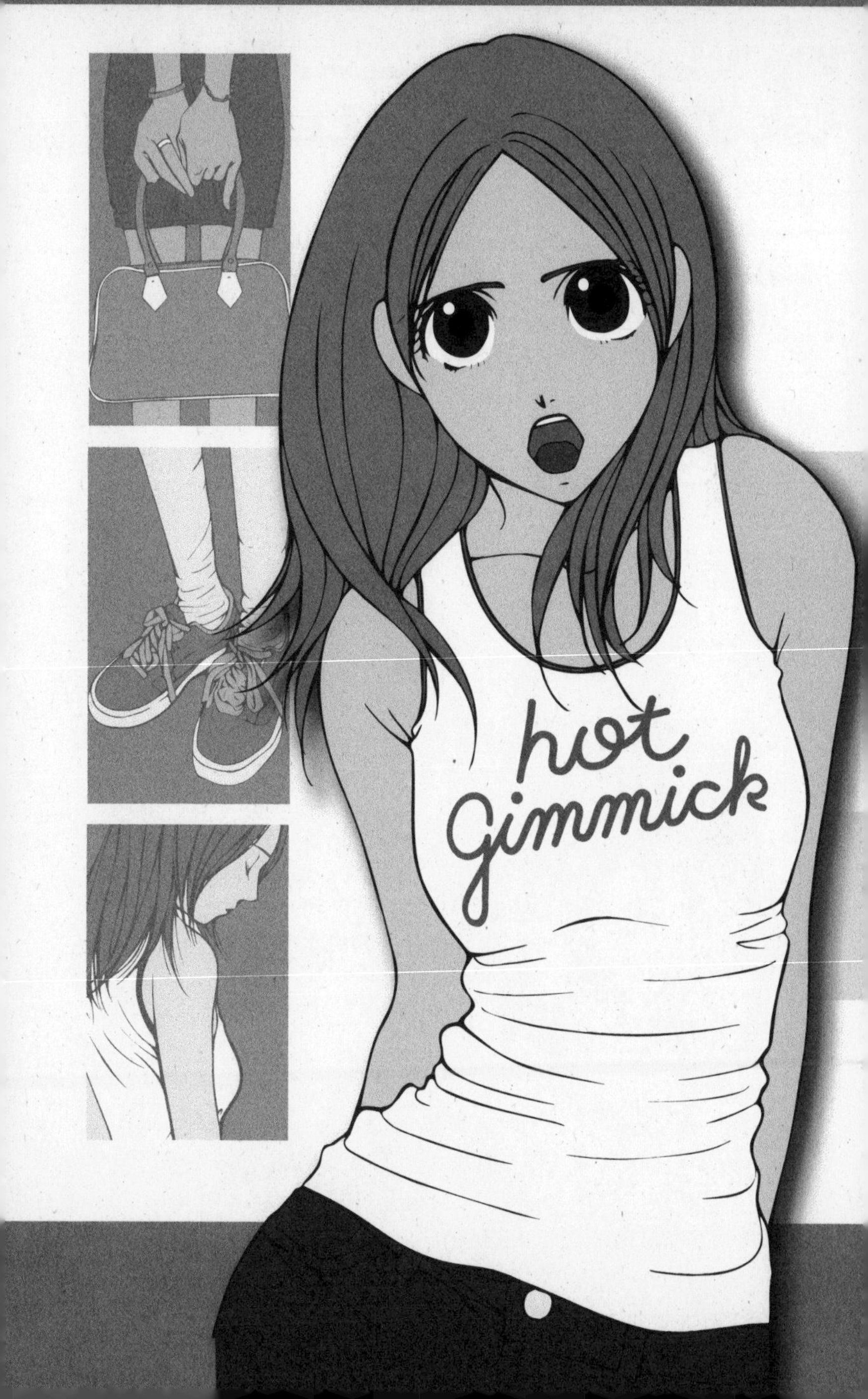
hot Gimmick